afterlife

a modern guide to the unseen realms

ian lawton

Rational Spirituality Press RSP

First published in 2019 by Rational Spirituality Press.

All enquiries to be directed to www.rspress.org.

A CIP catalogue record for this title is available from the British Library.

ISBN 978-0-9572573-7-5

Cover design by Ian Lawton.
Cover photograph by skypixel, licensed by dreamstime.com.
Author photograph by Simon Howson-Green.

Use every argument and all the forcefulness you can to show what a little thing, a tiny span, the earth life is. Real life begins when the heavy, material body is left behind, and the soul springs upward into the unlimited regions of thought-life. There all grows, learns, expands into perfect fullness of being until one becomes a perfectly developed spirit, able to blend with other spirits similarly developed and perfected. There is no beginning and no end, then, to the heights he can ascend; no joy that is unknown or untested; no wonder of the universe of which he does not become a part.

Anonymous spirit communication received by Emily French

If this journal has a specific message it is an attempt to convey something of the quality of our living, its joy and beauty and fullness of life beyond any human comprehension. It is also a warning that whatever one sows on earth will be fully reaped here.

Spirit communication from TE Lawrence (of Arabia)

CONTENTS

TABLES OF SOURCES

CHANNELLED SOURCES

Name of Medium	*Name of Spirit*	*Period of Experiences*	*Introduced on page*
William Stead	Julia Ames	1892-7	243
A Farnese	Franchezzo	1896	95
Emily French	Various	1910s/1920s	24
John (JSM) Ward	Henry Lanchester (uncle), 'WA', 'The Officer', 'JBP'	1914	109
Elsa Barker	David Patterson Hatch	1912-18	150
George Vale Owen	Emma (mother), Kathleen, Astriel, Zabdiel (guide), Arnel	1913-1919	142
Anthony Borgia	Robert Benson	1920s/30s	86
Geraldine Cummins	Frederic Myers	1924-31	122
Jane Sherwood	TE Lawrence (of Arabia), 'EK', Andrew (husband)	1930s-50s	100
Alice Gilbert	Philip (son)	1945-9	87
Cynthia Sandys	Arthur (husband), Joe (brother), Pat (daughter) and others	1950s-1970s	123
Helen Greaves	Frances Banks	1965-7	124
Ruth Montgomery	Arthur Ford	1971	88
Anonymous	'John'	1970s	96
Jamie Butler	Erik Medhus	2013	251
Annie Kagan	Billy Cohen	2014	253

NEAR-DEATH EXPERIENCE SOURCES

Name of Subject	*Date of Experience*	*Introduced on page*
Maurice Rawlings (researcher)	n/a	155
Bruce Greyson (researcher)	n/a	157
George Ritchie	1943	89
Bettie Eadie	1973	257
Dannion Brinkley	1975	256
Mellen-Thomas Benedict	1982	125
Howard Storm	1985	153
Eben Alexander	2008	33

OUT-OF-BODY EXPERIENCE SOURCES

Name of Subject	*Date of Publication*	*Introduced on page*
Emanuel Swedenborg	1758	35
Charles Leadbeater	1890s-1920s	90
Annie Besant	1898	90
Vincent Turvey	1909	37
Swami Panchadasi a.k.a. William Walker Atkinson	1915	161
Oliver Fox a.k.a. Hugh Callaway	1920	46
Yram a.k.a. Marcel Forhan	1925	162
Caroline Larsen	1927	90
Gladys Leonard	1931	19
Peter Richelieu	1953	204
Frederick Sculthorp	1961	46
Robert Monroe	1971-1994	48
Vee Van Dam	1989	435
Stylianos Atteshlis	1992	418
William Buhlman	1996-2013	240
Bruce Moen	1997-2001	54
Rosalind McKnight	1999-2005	126
Graham Dack	1999	60
Albert Taylor	2000	258
Gordon Phinn	2004-08	93
Waldo Vieira	2007	53
Jurgen Ziewe	2008-2016	72
Robert Bruce	2009	189
Frederick Aardema	2012	61

PREFACE

As the prophets of old spake, so speak these messengers now, and if they speak with clearer voice, with less veiled metaphor, it is because man is no longer in his infancy and needs now that he should be shown the reason and the science upon which his beliefs and hopes must be founded.

Spirit communication from Franchezzo

The afterlife. It has fascinated us ever since our primitive ancestors started to ponder their mortality. We are all going to experience it at some point, whatever it might or might not be. Moreover, despite the fashionable trend towards scientifically-inspired materialism in intellectual circles in the West, which rejects anything beyond the apparently 'physical', a huge majority of the world's population do still believe that some part of them will survive their supposed 'death'.

Since writing was invented this fascination has spawned myriad attempts to fathom and describe the mysteries of 'what lies beyond', and in recent decades these haven't been limited to purely religious or esoteric texts. The simplest search will reveal hundreds of books with the word *afterlife* in the title. So what has motivated me to produce yet another? There are two main reasons.

It is widely accepted in spiritual circles that sometimes someone departing our earthly world can become 'trapped' in what we might call the 'near-earth' plane. They might die so suddenly they don't even realise they're dead, or they might continue to identify strongly with their former life due to a sense of unfinished business, or they might simply be unable to conceive of any other form of existence. As a result they might be perceived by some human sensitives as 'ghosts'.[1]

Prior to 2012 I'd always tended to assume – as I suspect do many spiritual people – that this only affects a small minority of the human population, and that in any case there's plenty of help on hand for such unfortunates. That was before I started to read about the experiences of a variety of brave pioneers who've learned to deliberately take themselves 'out of body' (OOB) as part of my research for volume one of this series, *Supersoul*. These indicated that far, far more people departing our earth are trapped in this way than I'd previously appreciated, and that some are so emotionally deranged they find themselves in genuinely hellish-type realms of the type I'd previously dismissed as the fabrications of those who wished to exert religious control over their followers. I also learned that many OOB explorers are engaged in regular rescue missions to clear the huge backlog of spirits that have built up over millennia, working with spirit helpers from other realms. There was even a suggestion that this is particularly important now in order that their confused energies don't disrupt the 'shift in consciousness' that many people believe has been progressing on and around our planet for some time.

The OOB reports referred to above also revealed that our expectations of what will happen to us after death have a significant bearing on what we experience, and that as a result huge numbers of departed spirits find themselves in an almost infinite variety of 'heavens'. For some this might be an almost exact recreation of the environment they enjoyed on earth, even if it's just a small flat in a city or a semi-detached in suburbia; for others it might be a church or temple in which they can continue to worship their religious icons; for others still it might be a beautiful earth-like vista involving seas, mountains, forests, meadows or any combination thereof. It all sounds wonderful, doesn't it – each to their own, enjoying themselves for eternity with no pressures or worries, especially after all the trials and tribulations of earthly life? Until we recognise that these are all just another form of illusion, and that their inhabitants are also effectively trapped because they remain blissfully unaware of the far broader possibilities for progression that exist beyond their sphere of attention.

Of course for centuries various religious, spiritual and esoteric texts have tried to prepare their followers for what happens after death – such as the well-known *Tibetan Book of the Dead*, with its warnings about the 'realms of hungry ghosts' and so on. However they tend to use arcane language, and to rely heavily on complex and obscure symbolism, rendering them somewhat impenetrable except to more committed seekers. So my first clear objective for this book is to put together a state-of-the-art framework that provides a realistic view of the pitfalls that can potentially prevent people from progressing in a healthy way in the afterlife – this time in modern, simple language, and based on the latest available research.

Admittedly while I was planning it several colleagues expressed doubts about this enterprise, mainly because they felt I would be scaring people unnecessarily. I thought about this long and hard but came to the conclusion that, while this is a possibility, it's outweighed by the benefits. After all, if you're sensible you wouldn't travel to a potentially dangerous country on earth without trying to arm yourself with maps and advice about the do's and don'ts in advance. The same is perhaps even more true of the afterlife realms. So for those who don't want to leave it to chance my aim is to provide the best routemap our current knowledge can provide.

Although in the last century we've managed to split the atom, put a man on the moon and even decode the human DNA sequence, in many ways we've gone backwards spiritually. I am not for one moment suggesting there haven't been great leaps forward in our spiritual understanding, and an increasing move away from the binding dogma of orthodox religion, in certain circles. But partly because of the rise in supposedly scientific materialism, and partly because of an increasing obsession with possessions, celebrity and so on, the vast majority of the population of the Western world in particular is probably now more ignorant about death than at any time in the past. For most people it's the great taboo, swept under the carpet, not thought about or discussed – even though we know it's something we'll all have to face sooner or later.

We have already seen that this ignorance can leave many departed spirits trapped and confused. But there's another aspect that's equally concerning. In the modern world we encourage those left behind to fully express their grief – and it would be completely inhumane not to sympathise with the yawning void left by the death of a loved one, especially if they pass suddenly or before their time. Yet in due course we'll find departed spirits themselves telling us that prolonged, intense grief exerts a huge energetic pull, holding them back and preventing them from moving on properly away from this plane. This is a basic fact about death that modern Western society seems comprehensively unable to appreciate.

More than this, though, there seems to be a general underestimation of what awaits us after death. Many people tend towards a vague idea that the afterlife will be a place where they can meet up with their loved ones again, hopefully in a reasonably pleasant environment. But the evidence suggests that this falls way short of what truly awaits us, and of the potential for progression to planes of existence against whose wondrous experiences the pleasures of our earthly world pale by comparison.

By contrast, but with similar effect, while many modern converts to the idea of reincarnation do accept that the afterlife experience involves learning and growth, they still regard the *human* experience itself as the ultimate proving ground – the corollary being that we need to return to earth again and again to truly progress. But what if this highly popular view reverses the true picture? What if the challenges of the human experience only scratch the surface of the almost limitless opportunities for progression and growth in other, less restricted planes?

So the second objective of this book is to stress that in no way should we be scared of death, at least not if we're properly prepared. Instead we should celebrate the potential it brings, and even look forward to it with relish as a new beginning. As for sadness about those we're leaving behind, all the evidence suggests that genuinely close relationships of whatever nature do survive the ultimate test of time.

We have already mentioned the work of pioneering OOB researchers, and a significant portion of this book is based on evidence gleaned from their journeys. Near-death experiences (NDEs) are similar, and we will use some material derived from these too, but because they typically involve a single experience they tend to include a fair degree of subjectivity. By contrast OOB pioneers train themselves to *repeatedly* visit the very realms we'll all move into after we pass on, making every effort to analyse and compare their experiences and to learn from any initial misinterpretations. That surely puts them in prime position to find out what's really going on. What is more they tend to use relatively modern language and idioms far more suited to our culture and understanding than religious and esoteric texts written centuries ago. Indeed I'd suggest that the proliferation of OOB pioneers in the last half century has put them at the absolute forefront of consciousness exploration – and I can but agree with one of the leading practitioners, William Buhlman:[2]

> I contend that the discoveries of out-of-body explorers are far more important than we can even begin to imagine. In fact, they represent a true quantum leap in the evolution of our species. These explorers may be so advanced that our current physically immersed states of consciousness cannot acknowledge, much less comprehend, the sheer magnitude of their discoveries... All existing human discoveries pale in light of this new knowledge. I find it amusing that every day we swim in a magnificent ocean of multidimensional energy while our sciences are still examining the grains of sand on the beach.

Some people have suggested to me that these pioneers can hardly have proper experience of the *after*life realms precisely because they're not really dead, and their access thereto must therefore be restricted. I discuss exactly why this represents a comprehensive misunderstanding of the OOB experience, and why much of the time the term 'out-of-*body*' is itself a misnomer, in chapter 10.

In fact the evidence suggests that we all go OOB every night when asleep, as we'll see in chapter 26. Although some people will remain effectively unconscious during these periods, others will be up to all sorts of activities in the afterlife planes. What is more many of us regularly remember vivid dreams that are clearly realistic and not just the brain processing information from the day just completed, and these are almost certainly reflections of our OOB journeying, even if distorted and incomplete. Sometimes we also wake up with important ideas impressed upon us – particularly if we're involved in some sort of research or creative endeavour – which we might take as evidence of the background work that other parts of our consciousness are engaged in.

Nevertheless, in general this book deliberately *isn't* based on any personal OOB travels of my own. What most interests me, indeed where my skill sets most lie, is in comparing the experiences and research of many others, then extracting the consistent elements and analysing them. To a significant extent this is what I did with the 'interlife' experience in *The Big Book of the Soul*, it's what I did with various reports of OOB experiences when researching *Supersoul*, and I'm doing the same again here except from a different perspective. In fact I'd suggest that it's only by extracting these consistent elements from pioneers' reports that one can hope to reach any even vaguely objective conclusions, and to provide descriptions that are hopefully less clouded by the more personal, subjective aspects of their experience.

However there is another key source of information and evidence for this book. For some decades now spiritualist mediums seem to have concentrated primarily on connecting with the departed in order that those left behind can gain comfort. The contrasting aim of most modern 'channellers' is to communicate the wisdom of 'wise' entities who purport to tell us much about the true nature of reality, about the human condition, and so on. Indeed I have used the wisdom of sources such as Seth, Abraham, Neale Donald Walsch's 'god' and others extensively in my other books, most notably in *The Power of You*.

Yet there was a time when mediums and channellers regularly attracted ordinary discarnate humans who, although not claiming to possess any special wisdom, had enough experience of the afterlife realms to pass on a reasonable idea of the lay of the land. Indeed many were fervent in their desire to educate a woefully ignorant human race, and in the first half of the twentieth century a plethora of absolutely invaluable reports were obtained – many of them rarely if ever mentioned in more modern books. The situation has changed little, and we remain woefully ignorant. Especially given the widespread consistencies between this older channelled material and more contemporary OOB reports, and indeed with a smaller number of more modern channelled sources, I take the view that it's high time to bring it back centre stage and to build on it.

If we are to continue to describe ourselves as civilised and educated people, we might think it high time that we temper our contemporary focus on the material world with a desire to learn more about our ultimate fate when we shuffle of this mortal coil. Nor does the excuse that 'we can't possibly know what will happen so it's best not to worry about it' retain any validity. But we won't move forward if all we do is return to religious dogma, or to the supposed esoteric wisdom of the past. Instead it surely behoves us to open our hearts and minds to the wondrous possibilities that await us after death, by embracing the state-of-the-art material on the afterlife realms provided from both sides of the divide in the last century or so.

It is only right that I point out that collating all this material has represented a serious personal challenge. Thousands of the most difficult hours of my entire researching life have gone into this book. Nor has it merely been an exercise in collation so that readers don't have to individually refer to the countless books I've used as source material. A massive amount of sifting and sorting has been involved, because every single source's map of the afterlife planes is at least slightly different – and sometimes markedly so – necessitating a significant amount of difficult interpretation on my part. Indeed the challenge of trying to incorporate the consistent elements of all this material into a universal framework has been so huge that it sometimes felt insurmountable. So, in fairness to myself, it would be quite wrong to perceive me – as some have in the past – as merely a reproducer and collator of other people's work. What is more, without the quite unique and original framework of Supersoul Spirituality that I've developed over recent years, much of this afterlife material would have no proper context.

All that having been said I can merely lay this book in front of potential readers, and trust that my extensive efforts to present the most comprehensive, evidence-based map of the afterlife currently available have not been entirely in vain.

Ian Lawton
June 2019

AUTHOR'S NOTE Channelled material is presented here in the approximate order of the earliest year of transmission. Similarly NDE reports are presented in the order of the year of the experience. By contrast, because OOB pioneers don't always reveal exactly when their experiences occurred, their reports are presented in order of earliest publication. Comments in square brackets in quotes are mine, for clarification, while ellipses are used to indicate the omission of intervening words, sentences or paragraphs that are repetitive or irrelevant.

PLEASE NOTE: If you already firmly believe in an afterlife, and take the view you're balanced enough that you won't be going anywhere near the lowest planes when you pass on, feel free to skip Part 1 and all except the final chapter of Part 3.

PART ONE

CAN WE PROVE THE AFTERLIFE EXISTS?

A rational view of life's continuity, and a clear statement of what awaits them in the beyond, are among the greatest and most truly answerable demands of the twentieth century.

Anonymous spirit communication received by Emily French

PLEASE NOTE: If you already firmly believe in an afterlife, feel free to skip this part.

1

THE SCIENTIFIC VIEW

Many people instinctively believe in the idea of an afterlife. Even if they're not especially religious, as a bare minimum they may have a strong feeling that they'll be reunited with departed loved ones when they too 'shuffle off this mortal coil'. But is this just wishful thinking, as hard-headed materialists would have us believe?

To answer this question, and to find out whether so many people's instincts are indeed correct, the underlying question we need to tackle is whether consciousness continues to exist beyond the confines of the physical brain. Although it might seem counterintuitive to many of us, there are plenty of materialists involved in various branches of modern science who insist that all consciousness is a random product of evolution – indeed that it's merely a *by-product* of brain activity. In other words, when we die everything stops.

By contrast other scientists in various fields have come to the conclusion that this cannot be the case. They liken consciousness to a television or radio transmitter and the brain to an aerial that picks up the signal, so even if the aerial is destroyed the transmitter continues to broadcast. More than this, they insist that consciousness underlies everything, and is the primal constituent of the entire universe. Nor is this merely a modern development. Max Planck, the theoretical physicist who originated the idea of quantum theory in 1900, made the following bold and unequivocal statement:[1]

> I regard consciousness as fundamental. I regard matter as derivative from consciousness.

This worldview was shared by many of his most brilliant contemporaries in the first half of the twentieth century. Although they don't all go quite as far as Planck in print, here's a selection of celebrated quotes from celebrated scientists that provides strong reinforcement for this view:

> If quantum physics hasn't profoundly shocked you, you haven't understood it yet. *Niels Bohr*

> The pursuit of science leads to a religious feeling of a special sort. *Albert Einstein*

> Not only is the universe stranger than we think, it is stranger than we can think. *Werner Heisenberg*

> It would be most satisfactory of all if physis and psyche (i.e., matter and mind) could be seen as complementary aspects of the same reality. *Wolfgang Pauli*

> Consciousness cannot be accounted for in physical terms. For consciousness is absolutely fundamental. It cannot be accounted for in terms of anything else. *Erwin Schrodinger*

> The day science begins to study nonphysical phenomena, it will make more progress in one decade than in all the previous centuries of its existence... If you want to find the secrets of the universe, think in terms of energy, frequency and vibration. *Nikola Tesla*

> It was not possible to formulate the laws of quantum mechanics in a fully consistent way without reference to consciousness. *Eugene Wigner*

What is more this view has formed the basis of the most profound spiritual and esoteric traditions since time immemorial. But in recent decades much scientific thinking seems to have regressed to a more purely materialist stance, caricatured by the comedian and author Rob Newman in his 2017 book *Neuropolis* as 'magical scientism'. His imputation is that the maintenance of a simplistic, restricted worldview that flies in the face of much of the available evidence can be encountered in scientific just as much as in religious circles.

At this point it's worth taking a moment to make a clear distinction between atheism and materialism. In the strict sense of the term *atheists* don't believe in some sort of omnipotent god or gods that exist outside of us and exercise some form of control over our lives – this view typified by many of the world's *religions*, but not, for example, Buddhism. In that sense I too am an atheist. But it's only hard-nosed *materialists* who reject any form of *spiritual* but not necessarily religious worldview at all, and insist that the material, apparently physical world is all there is – thereby rejecting anything regarded as *para*normal. It may be that scientists of the latter persuasion predominate at the current time, but in fact there are at least some who are atheist yet not against spirituality generally. What is more, some of them are high profile.

Although as in the quote above he uses the word *religious* instead of spiritual, the latter being a less used term then, Einstein himself was undoubtedly an atheist yet absolutely wedded to a spiritual worldview – as the following lengthier quote indicates:[2]

> A knowledge of the existence of something we cannot penetrate, of the manifestations of the profoundest reason and the most radiant beauty, which are only accessible to our reason in their most elementary forms – it is this knowledge and this emotion that constitute the truly religious attitude; in this sense, and in this alone, I am a deeply religious man.

Similarly the neuroscientist and philosopher Sam Harris was described in 2007 as one of the 'four horsemen of atheism', along with fellow high-profile intellectuals Richard Dawkins, Daniel Dennett and Christopher Hitchens. These latter can almost certainly be characterised as materialists, yet Harris expresses very similar views to Einstein in his 2014 book *Waking Up: A Guide to*

Spirituality Without Religion. This just shows to what extent we need to be careful in choosing the terms we use to describe different people's worldviews.

But, to return to main topic at hand, this book isn't intended as a detailed treatise on the science of consciousness, and on the various *theoretical* arguments on either side of the debate, although we'll at least summarise these in this chapter. What will be particularly useful after that, though, is to collate a variety of paranormal and sometimes little-known *evidence* that suggests consciousness does indeed exist separate from the physical brain and body. Because, *if* we decide this evidence is persuasive, then we *know* there must be some sort of afterlife in which our consciousness will continue to exist – and that it's worth examining what that afterlife might be like.

So let's begin with the theory. Perhaps one of the finest contributions we can consider is that of Peter Russell.[3] Like so many people of a scientific bent, when he was first studying mathematics and physics at Cambridge University he was a confirmed atheist. But, having spent time studying Eastern philosophy and meditation in India, he switched to experimental psychology at Bristol and is now one of the leading champions of the primacy of consciousness. Indeed he insists that, because materialism still underlies almost all currently accepted frameworks of scientific understanding, this prevailing 'metaparadigm' is simply unable to explain the so-called 'hard problem' of the existence of consciousness.[4] As Russell asserts in his seminal 2002 book *From Science to God*:[5]

> Nothing in Western science predicts that any living creature should be conscious. It is easier to explain how hydrogen evolved into other elements, how they combined to form molecules and then simple living cells, and how these evolved into complex beings such as ourselves than it is to explain why we should ever have a single inner experience.

He further argues that we therefore need a shift to a whole new metaparadigm, with consciousness at its heart.

A corollary worldview is that of panpsychism, which holds that *everything* has some form of consciousness or at least *experience*. This is allied to the many primarily Eastern philosophies that are based on the idea there's no single, *external* 'God', but rather a 'universal consciousness' that exists *within* everything. As Russell points out plants, for example, are sensitive to daylight, temperature, humidity and so on, and are likely to be having some from of experience, even if it's nothing like as rich as our human one. Some materialists simplistically misinterpret this to mean that plants have thoughts and feelings, in order that they can then ridicule the idea, but this isn't what's being suggested at all. Russell carries on:[6]

> If a bacterium's experience is a billionth of the richness and intensity of a human being's, the degree of experience in the crystals of a rock might be a billion times dimmer still. They would possess none of the qualities of human consciousness – just the faintest possible glimmer of experience.

There are further fundamental problems with the current metaparadigm's view that consciousness is merely a by-product of the material world. For millennia various esoteric traditions have understood that as humans we only form a *perception* of what appears to be 'out there' in the apparently material world, based on our five senses. Our brains process this sensory date to give us an image of the world around us, but we can never have *direct* experience of the underlying reality. Eastern traditions refer to our false perceptions of this reality as *maya* or illusion. Indeed every species has a different way of perceiving the underlying reality in which we're all operating. Moreover it's now commonly understood that atoms are almost entirely made up of empty space, while quantum theory has shown that even the constituents of these atoms – electrons and so on – behave more like probability waves than physical particles. So our understanding of the nature of underlying reality itself is surely moving us away from a materialist stance too.[7]

In fact there are strong reasons to suppose that, rather than the material world creating consciousness, everything works precisely the other way around – it's actually our consciousness itself that *creates* or *manifests* the reality we experience. We are going to find in chapter 23 that this process is absolutely transparent in various of the other realms we're drawn to after we die, but there are reasons why it's less obvious in our 'earth reality'. First the constraints of space-time that we operate under introduce a delay between what we project with our consciousness and what we subsequently experience. Second ours is very much a shared or 'consensus' reality in which we're interacting with the desires, beliefs and intentions of others, which makes the underlying dynamics of the manifestation process much more complex and difficult to trace. Third our *sub*conscious plays a huge part in what we're projecting and, because we're programmed with 'limiting beliefs' from childhood onwards, is often at serious odds with our conscious, surface desires.[8]

Indeed the main objective of volume two of this series, *The Power of You*, is to summarise the main consistent message of eight of the most celebrated sources of channelled wisdom of the last half-century: that we each use the 'law of attraction' to create *every* aspect of our experience of this reality, which only acts as a mirror to reflect back our beliefs, thoughts and intentions. This level of responsibility will be a step too far for some, but for others the realisation that each of us is a true 'creator god' helps us to remember just what incredibly powerful and divine beings we really are.

2

MEDIUMSHIP EVIDENCE

When we now turn to *evidence* for the ability of consciousness to exist separate from the physical body, an obvious place to start is with mediums who purport to channel messages from the deceased to their loved ones left behind. We must preface this chapter by accepting that the use of 'cold reading' is widespread – that is, using leading questions to extrapolate from gullible sitters' responses so that in fact nothing paranormal is occurring at all. Particularly where money is changing hands or reputations are at stake there's an obvious motive for fraud. Yet the picture is unlikely to be as clear-cut as any given medium is either genuine or a fraud. A genuine medium who's under pressure to perform may be tempted to fake it sometimes.

That proviso aside, there are a great many anecdotal stories of gifted practitioners achieving incredible 'hits', by coming up with obscure evidential information about their sitters' deceased friends or relatives that they couldn't possibly have achieved by cold reading. There are alternative *paranormal* explanations that need to be considered, albeit that these clearly aren't compatible with a materialist worldview either. For example, the possibility of telepathy between sitter and medium, although one way of creating a 'blind' against this is to employ 'proxy sitters'. Another paranormal explanation is that somehow the medium is merely tapping into some sort of universal databank containing the memories of the deceased – sometimes referred to as the 'akashic records'. This means it's only if communication is *proactively led by* the deceased that it can be used as evidence for the survival of their consciousness.

THE MYERS CROSS CORRESPONDENCE MESSAGES

One intriguing set of evidence that is commonly held to fall into the latter category is what have come to be called the 'cross correspondence' messages transmitted by Frederic Myers, Henry Sidgwick and Edmund Gurney in the early years of the twentieth century. All three had been founders of the British Society for Psychical Research (SPR), and not long after Myers' death in 1901 they purportedly began to transmit messages to various mediums around the world, most unknown to each other. Indeed it was only after some years had passed that investigators from the SPR realised what was being attempted from the other side, and ensured that the messages from each medium were kept entirely secret from the others involved.

The method used to communicate was primarily 'automatic writing', and the transcripts extend to some 6400 pages. The SPR investigators claimed that, while these messages made little sense to the mediums themselves, they *did* make sense when assembled – particularly by people with a good knowledge of classical Greek and Latin texts, in which Myers specialised.[1]

These transcripts are held only in the SPR's private records, and few people have had the time to research all of them thoroughly. But one man who devoted some thirty years to their study, the astronomer and later president of the SPR, Archie Roy, went into great detail in his 2008 book *The Eager Dead* – prompting former sceptic Colin Wilson to write in the foreword that they represented 'the most convincing proof of the reality of life after death ever set down on paper'.

It will be no surprise that sceptics have argued against this evidence, although whether any of them have taken the same trouble to read the huge volume of source material is extremely doubtful.[2]

GLADYS LEONARD, OLIVER LODGE AND RAYMOND

Another example of proactively led communication is provided by the renowned physicist Sir Oliver Lodge, who was also president of the SPR in the early years of the twentieth century. His son Raymond was killed early in World War I and so he and his wife attended a number of séances conducted mainly by the medium Gladys Leonard. The results of these were recorded in his best-known book, *Raymond or Life and Death*, in 1916. Unsurprisingly given his scientific reputation this received some degree of criticism at the time, but one piece of evidence in particular seems well worth noting.[3]

During one sitting Lodge's wife attended with a medium referred to as 'Peters' less than two weeks after Raymond's death, the information was volunteered, unprompted, that two photographs had been taken of him on his own in his military uniform, and another in which he was in a group of fellow officers. In particular the medium emphasised that in the latter he was carrying his walking stick. Lodge's wife knew about the first two but had never seen the third. However several months later she received a letter from one of Raymond's fellow officers mentioning exactly such a photo and asking if she would like a copy.

She responded in the affirmative, but it took some time for the photo to arrive. In the meantime Lodge had a sitting with Leonard – who knew nothing about the photographs – and specifically asked about this group one. From her he elicited that in it there were more than a dozen officers, some were seated, including himself, and behind them others were standing. Further details were forthcoming about the initials of the surnames of several of the men – albeit that Raymond didn't know all of them; that one of them – 'B' – was particularly prominent; that there were vertical lines in the background; and, most important of all, that the officer behind Raymond had been leaning on his shoulder.

When the photo finally arrived, all these details were confirmed. There are three rows of some twenty-one officers in total, with the first – including Raymond – seated on the ground, the second on chairs and the third standing at the back. The hut behind them has very clear vertical lines on its sloping roof. But, best of all, he alone seems to be rather squashed and is attempting to shift away from the officer behind whose arm and leg are clearly jammed hard against him – the only example of this in the photo.

Quite apart from her work with Lodge, Leonard was actively engaged in all sorts of mediumistic activities, including direct voice and other more physical forms of mediumship, of which more later. All of this is described in her 1931 book *My Life in Two Worlds*, with a foreword by Lodge, which abounds with highly evidential examples of the survival of consciousness.

The following example involves a South African woman who had occasionally attended her séances during the war because her son had, like Raymond, been killed in action. Before returning to her home country she asked Leonard to write to her occasionally. Although it doesn't involve proactively led communication, this is a fine example of automatic writing, the method used for much of the channelled material we'll rely on in future parts of this book. What is more the following description is particularly instructive as Leonard was not normally a great letter writer:[4]

> I suddenly found that I could not think of a word to say to her. I really knew very little of her personally, and tried hard to think of some item of news that might interest her. As I sat there quietly, my mind being in a passive yet receptive condition owing to my waiting for what I thought would be a 'normal' inspiration, I felt that my hand wanted to move though I was not conscious of what it would write. I had begun my letter, 'Dear Mrs. L…' but now my hand began to write the word 'Mother'. I let it do so, and felt it wanted to go on, in a rather curious cramped style. Some more words were written with a certain amount of difficulty. My hand and arm felt stiff and moved jerkily.
>
> After a few moments the speed increased, and two or three pages of note-paper were covered with a small handwriting. Part of the time I had no idea what was coming next, but now and again I knew what the next sentence was going to be, while

my hand was actually writing the previous sentence. The communicator ended just as an ordinary letter from a very affectionate son to a mother would do, and I found my hand signing a man's name – a pet name – which was not the one that his mother had used when speaking to me about her son.

When the writing ceased, I read over the last two or three sentences, but saw that they were of an obviously intimate and private nature referring to family matters, so I did not like to look through all the messages; in fact, I had a strong feeling that it was not intended that I should do so, so I simply added a postscript, telling the lady briefly what had happened and begging her not to think me quite mad in sending her the whole thing as it was, as, for all I knew, it might have been a farrago of nonsense; I had so little personal experience of automatic writing.

Later, I had a reply from her, telling me that she had perfectly understood all the messages, and that they were most evidential and asking me to send her any others that might come. I saw that the communication had been a great comfort to her, and as soon as I could spare the time, I sat down and waited expectantly for her son to come and write again, but nothing happened, though I waited for nearly an hour. I tried again, with no result.

Then a few months afterwards, while writing to another friend, I suddenly felt I must write to Mrs. L. in South Africa again. I got out some larger sheets of paper, and as soon as I had written a few words to her on my own account, I felt the same stiff jerkiness come into my writing that I had noticed on the previous occasion. Again the son wrote a letter to his mother, and she wrote later and told me that he had referred to a series of spiritual meetings she had arranged, and about which no one in England knew, but she had mentally asked her son to help her with them.

GERALDINE CUMMINS AND THE SCRIPTS OF CLEOPHAS

Geraldine Cummins was a gifted British medium who we'll encounter in a variety of capacities, but the publication of her *Scripts of Cleophas* in 1928 caused a sensation.[5] The three 'parchments' that stretch to nearly 300 pages were again produced via automatic writing in many sessions spanning several years from 1923, all witnessed by her friend Beatrice Gibbs. Neither had any interest in or detailed knowledge of Christian theology or the early Church.

Cummins had written novels and plays but for these she struggled to produce more than 600–700 words every couple of days, with multiple corrections. By contrast four witnesses saw her produce 1750 words of automatic script that required no corrections at all in just over an hour. A number of eminent theologians and other experts witnessed various sessions, and overall the extensive and detailed scripts show a knowledge of the early Christian Church that not only equates perfectly with known texts but also, according to the Rev. John Lammond in his prefatory note, 'shed fresh light on the labours of Paul and the other Apostles, and give a new meaning to several passages in the Acts of the Apostles which otherwise would be obscure'.

GARY SCHWARTZ AND ALLISON DUBOIS

Gary Schwartz, a professor of psychology at the University of Arizona, has been conducting research into paranormal phenomena for many years. His VERITAS project, which concluded in 2008, was specifically targeted at testing whether consciousness survives death and involved working with celebrated mediums such as John Edward and Allison DuBois – the latter being the inspiration for the television series *Medium*. In his 2005 book *The Truth About Medium* he records the results of working with Dubois and three other mediums in 'triple blind' tests, which were carefully designed to preclude the possibility of fraud, cold reading, telepathy and sitter misinterpretation and subjectivity.[6]

These worked as follows. A research assistant selected eight sitters from a group of undergraduate volunteers, and asked them for basic information about the deceased loved one they would like to contact. These were paired into 'discarnates' who were relatively dissimilar in their characteristics, so as to provide some proper differentiation, and the first names only of each pair were given to the proxy sitter, Schwartz's colleague Julie Beischel. With the sitters having been informed of the timing of the experiments and asked to concentrate on their loved ones at that point, she then conducted a session with each medium, giving them only the two first names to work from and asking for both general and specific information – the latter in four categories: physical description, personality, hobbies or activities and cause of death. The information obtained was recorded and transcribed, and each pair of transcripts was sent to the two real sitters involved, with no identification of which one related to their deceased relative. They were asked to rate each reading using a score or 0 for no correct information through to 6 for excellent information with no inaccuracies.

The results were pretty astounding. The eight sitters gave the 'control' or second reading an average score of only 2.1, broadly signifying that there was some correct information but not enough to go beyond mere chance. By contrast they gave their own readings an average score of 4.6, which broadly signified a good reading with only some or even relatively few inaccuracies. DuBois' scores in particular showed a wider disparity at 1.5 and 5 respectively. It is worth noting that the information she gave wasn't so vague that it could apply to anyone, but included plenty of specifics such as height, age at death, names of relatives and so on.

Nevertheless, as noted earlier, to preclude the possibility of information being obtained from some sort of universal databank we require some sort of proactive involvement by the discarnate personality. In this context Schwartz records the details of some intriguing apparent interactions between DuBois and the deceased British paranormal researcher Montague Keen.[7] Although Schwartz had known Keen quite well, Dubois apparently didn't know him at all and in the first instance was only given his wife's nickname and told to contact her husband. Most important for our current purposes is that in later single-blind sessions Keen appeared to *proactively* provide certain information through DuBois, particularly relating to the manner of his death, which even Schwartz himself didn't know until it was subsequently verified.

Meanwhile researchers at the Institute of Noetic Sciences in California have performed similar controlled tests on the accuracy of mediums' readings, and in particular have noted differences in their EEG/brain activity when conducting genuine readings compared to merely using their imagination.[8]

EMILY FRENCH AND EDWARD RANDALL

We conclude this chapter with some material that I only came across relatively late on in this investigation. It is also the earliest evidential mediumship material presented here, but I've decided to follow the maxim 'leave the best till last'. We have seen that real-time interaction with discarnates who proactively direct the information communicated is the best evidence of personality survival. By far the most convincing form of mediumship from this perspective is 'independent direct voice', whereby the medium's own vocal chords aren't used at all. Instead the participating discarnates supposedly use the medium's and any sitters' own energy fields to create a nonphysical voice box through which their thoughts are filtered – and which even reproduces the exact sound their human voice once made.

This form of mediumship seems to have all but disappeared, but the best-known exponent in Britain was Leslie Flint, who rose to prominence in the mid-twentieth century.[9] His work attracted some degree of criticism, but it appears he was independently tested on a number of occasions, and despite appearing in front of vast audiences he never charged a penny for his services. This was also the case with his much less well-known American predecessor Emily French, who was frail, ill and seriously deaf by the time she was doing her best work in her sixties and seventies.[10] The story begins properly in 1890, when the prominent lawyer and businessman Edward Randall agreed to investigate her work, confident that he'd be able to prove it a hoax. Instead she passed every test he could think of, and he went on to work closely with her for twenty-two years right up to her death, publishing five books of transcripts from 1905 to 1922. These are now extremely hard to find, but fortunately for us the most important extracts have been collated by N Riley Heagerty into one volume entitled *The French Connection*.

Contact was made with a huge variety of discarnates over this period, some known to Randall, others not. The most impressive phenomenon noted by all who witnessed the sittings was that, while French was frail and quietly spoken, some of the voices were male, deep and loud. Not one person who investigated the pair ever suggested even the remotest possibility of deliberate fraud, especially given Randall's continuing role as a prominent businessman, and their sessions passed every test.[11]

We will see in later chapters just how valuable was the information they obtained about other planes, but for now we must focus on the evidential. One of the investigators urged to check out the French-Randall sessions was the renowned psychic researcher Isaac Funk, who requested that French come to New York to hold sittings in various places of his choosing – thus precluding the most obvious fraud of human voices being projected from some adjacent room or cellar.[12] This she agreed to do, despite the fact that by this time she was extremely frail and, of course, wasn't going to benefit in any pecuniary way. She was accompanied not by Randall but by a single female companion. In all twelve sittings were held over a fortnight in mid-1905, and various tests were carried out – including Funk holding each of French's hands and getting her to talk to him *at the same time* as one of the communicants was speaking.

Most intriguing of all, however, was that Funk himself passed on not long after having written up his investigation in his 1907 book *The Psychic Riddle*, in which he showed himself impressed but, perhaps unsurprisingly, left various loopholes in case fraud was ever identified. During one of the French-Randall sessions held not long afterwards, a male voice claiming to be Funk came through.[13] Turning the tables nicely, and using the same protocols on which they'd always insisted to ensure that mischievous communicants couldn't derail their important work, Randall indicated he'd only talk to this person if they could prove their identity. At this point Funk revealed the exact method he'd suggested Randall should use to test French, which was to put his hand on the table, get her to put her mouth upon that, then put his other hand on the back of her head. Most important Randall knew that only he and Funk, and no one else, had been privy to that conversation in the latter's office.

3

REMOTE VIEWING EVIDENCE

This area of paranormal research involves getting people to focus their minds on distant sites to obtain information about them, sometimes using merely geographic coordinates. From the 1970s the Stanford Research Institute (SRI) in California conducted tests lasting several decades, involving practitioners who would go on to become celebrated figures such as Ingo Swann, Pat Price and Joe McMoneagle. This research was funded by the US Defence Intelligence Agency and the CIA to the tune of at least $20m, the aim being to obtain information about enemy bases. In the end the conclusions of official investigations were that the results were weak at best, and funding was terminated.[1] Moreover, of course, fraud or exaggeration based on the desire for continued funding cannot be ruled out.

Yet, again, some of the apparent results are intriguing to say the least. While researching her book *Extraordinary Knowing*, psychologist Elizabeth Mayer conducted extensive interviews with Hal Puthoff, the founder of the SRI programme, in which he singled out two cases as worthy of particular note. The first occurred in 1974 and was part of an initial group of experiments conducted using CIA-provided latitude and longitude coordinates alone.[2] The target was several thousand miles away in West Virginia. Price was asked to view it and provided a five-page report that began by merely describing a couple of log cabins by a road. But he continued that over a ridge was the site they must really be interested in, a high security military installation, and provided many details of this. The CIA's response was that the latter description was way off, even though the coordinates provided had indeed been for a staff member's vacation cabin. Yet separately, and with no collusion, Swann provided a report with some similar details. The CIA were sufficiently intrigued to send an officer out to investigate, whereupon he found not only his colleague's cabin but also a secret military base that even the CIA didn't know about. Some details were found to be wrong, but many were right. Most stunning of all, Price had written down security codes based on the game of pool, such as 'cue ball', 'cue stick' and so on – which turned out to be exactly those used to label the secret files in a locked drawer in the underground facility. He even reported the code name of the site itself, 'Haystack'.

The second case involved McMoneagle and occurred in 1979.[3] The National Security Council (NSC) had a photo of a large, industrial building somewhere in remote northern Russia, but they knew nothing more about it. Armed only with the geographical coordinates he described a large industrial building in an icy wasteland, not far from an ice-covered sea. The NSC confirmed this matched the location, Sverodvinsk on the White Sea, so next McMoneagle was given the photo and asked to view its interior. In a building he described as being 'as large as two or three shopping centres' he saw 'two huge cylinders being welded side to side', and realised it was a massive, twin-hull submarine, 'about twice the length of an American football field and nearly seventy feet in width'. Afterwards he provided detailed drawings of the craft, in particular noting the eighteen to twenty slanted missile tubes. Initially this was met with disbelief, because no submarine of this size and design had been attempted before, let alone in a building with no obvious access to the sea.

However McMoneagle was asked to make a repeat visit to estimate the date of completion, which from the progress made he judged to be about four months away. He also reported that bulldozers were cutting a channel through the ice from the facility to the sea. To everyone's surprise all the major details he provided were confirmed when, four months later, reconnaissance photos showed the first of the new Typhoon class of massive, twin-hull submarines being towed down the canal – along with its twenty slanted missile tubes.

If cases such as this can be even partially relied upon, they do suggest that the consciousness of the remote viewers is doing something abnormal – and most likely is 'bilocating' so that it's partly operating outside the normal confines of their physical bodies.

4

NEAR-DEATH EXPERIENCE EVIDENCE

A number of interesting evidential cases have been reported by people undergoing an NDE. They have returned with memories of their physical surroundings and of events that, on the face of it at least, they couldn't possibly have witnessed with their normal physical senses – which were in any case inoperative at the time.

I discuss four of the most interesting at length in *The Big Book of the Soul*, so we'll begin by summarising them here.[1] The first involves a thirty-five-year-old American musician called Pam Reynolds. After she had been operated on for a brain aneurysm she described how, during the procedure, she'd floated outside of her body and 'seen' the 'toothbrush-like' saw with 'interchangeable blades' in 'what looked like a socket wrench case' that had been used to cut open her skull. She also 'heard' a conversation about the size of her arteries, as well as identifying the music that was being played in the operating theatre as she re-entered her body.

The second was reported by Dutch Cardiologist Pim van Lommel, who performed an extensive thirteen-year study of NDEs in ten Dutch hospitals and published his results in the prestigious medical journal *The Lancet* in 2001. The most striking case, reported and verified by a nurse, involves a man who had had a cardiac arrest subsequently recognising the nurse who removed his false teeth when he was first brought in, comatose, and reminding her she'd placed them in a drawer at the bottom of a medical trolley.

The third, and perhaps most impressive of all, involves a gifted Russian neuroscientist and confirmed atheist called George Rodonaia. To avoid him taking his talents to the US the KGB ran him over while he waited for a taxi to the airport. He was pronounced dead but resuscitated after three days in a morgue. Eventually he was well enough to not only relate a wonderfully transcendental experience that would see him become a Christian minister, but also to explain how, while OOB, he'd seen a sick baby in the main hospital who wouldn't stop crying because doctors couldn't diagnose what was wrong. George told them that with his OOB perception he'd been able to 'see' she had a greenstick fracture of the hip, evidently suffered during birth, which was subsequently confirmed.

The fourth saw a US migrant worker called Maria being taken to a Seattle hospital after a cardiac arrest. She described how, while OOB, she'd seen a tennis shoe abandoned on a third-floor window sill. This wasn't visible from outside or inside the building without already knowing it was there, but eventually and with some difficulty the nurse was able to locate it.

In terms of other cases I've come across since I wrote that book, several are provided by Maurice Rawlings, a cardiologist at the University of Tennessee, in his 1978 book *Beyond Death's Door*. One of his patients, who was adopted, reported meeting his birth mother during his NDE. He subsequently identified her from amongst a number of family photos provided by her sister, even though she died when he was only fifteen months old, his father remarried shortly afterwards and he'd never previously been shown any sort of picture of her.[2] Others accurately remembered details of what was going on in the hospital room where they temporarily died.[3]

Another excellent case that's new to me arose from a 2011 YouTube video in which the late US cardiac surgeon Lloyd William

Rudy was interviewed about a patient he'd operated on in the late 1990s or early 2000s, the details of which were subsequently verified when his assistant surgeon that day, Roberto Amado-Cattaneo, posted a response and was contacted by researchers for a full confirmatory statement.[4] After the patient had had heart valve surgery they couldn't stabilise his blood pressure despite repeated attempts, and eventually were forced to switch off the heart-lung machine that was artificially keeping him alive. Disappointed they retired to an anteroom to disrobe, while an assistant stitched him up ready for autopsy.

In the meantime nobody had thought to turn off the various pieces of monitoring equipment, which continued to give read-outs showing a complete absence of heart beat and blood pressure. They were therefore dumbfounded when, after an interval of 20 to 25 minutes, the monitors started showing a weak heartbeat again, and blood pressure that gradually increased and stabilised without mechanical assistance. But now for the pièce de résistance. The man remained completely unconscious throughout the whole operation and for at least a day or two afterwards, but when he did come round not only was he mentally unaffected but he also explained to the surgeons that he'd been floating outside of his body and seen them standing talking in the doorway, arms folded, and also seen the anaesthetist rushing back in when called.

Best of all though, he described how he saw a row of Post-it notes stuck on one of the monitoring screens near the foot of the operating table, which were telephone messages placed there by a nurse during the operation that Rudy would need to respond to afterwards. This is surely an obscure practice that wouldn't be common knowledge or an educated guess? What is more, as Rudy himself points out, even if the patient had been conscious on entering the theatre, at that stage there wouldn't have been any messages. While during the operation his physical eyes would have been taped shut, even if he had been conscious and alive – which he wasn't. Unfortunately neither surgeon could remember the patient's name, so hospital records couldn't be checked, but this should not detract from what is a stunning veridical case.

On a more general note, British medical doctor Sam Parnia has also attempted experiments in the cardiac wings of various hospitals in Europe and North America. These involve, for example, placing random numbers on cards on the top of cupboards and so on where they could only be seen by someone floating OOB, in the hope of achieving repeatable results. But as yet these haven't proved conclusive.[5]

Many sceptics simplistically write off NDEs as explainable by various physiological phenomena, seemingly oblivious to the fact that in the cases summarised here the key element is the veridical evidence involved. What is more, while those few who *do* take the trouble to examine them properly don't suggest that deliberate fraud is involved, they do tend to tie themselves in knots trying to show how the subjects *just might* have been able to obtain the information via normal means. Yet almost certainly the *simplest* explanation for the evidence is, again, that their consciousness was operating outside of their physical bodies.

EBEN ALEXANDER

To bear this out, our final NDE case isn't included because of impressive veridical evidence but because of who it involves. As an eminent neurosurgeon, just like so many of his colleagues in the medical community, Eben Alexander thought he had it all figured out. This is how he describes his worldview before the experience that would change his life, in his book *Proof of Heaven*:[6] 'Modern neuroscience dictates that the brain gives rise to consciousness... and I had little doubt that it was correct.' But the incredible week-long OOB journey he went on in 2008, while in coma suffering from a rare form of bacterial meningitis, turned his thinking on its head. The following powerful statements come from various chapters of his book:[7]

> Spiritual wasn't a word that I would have employed during a scientific conversation. Now I believe it's a word that we cannot afford to leave out.

> While I was in coma my brain hadn't been working improperly. It hadn't been working at all. The part of my brain that years of medical school had taught me was responsible for creating the world I lived and moved in and for taking the raw data that came in through my senses and fashioning it into a meaningful universe: that part of my brain was down, and out. And yet despite all of this, I had been alive, and aware, truly aware.
>
> The more I read of the 'scientific' explanations of what NDEs are, the more I was shocked by their transparent flimsiness. And yet I also knew with chagrin that they were exactly the ones that the old 'me' would have pointed to vaguely if someone had asked me to 'explain' what an NDE is.
>
> Far from being an unimportant by-product of physical processes (as I had thought before my experience), consciousness is not only very real – it's actually more real than the rest of physical existence, and most likely the basis of it all. But neither of these insights has yet been truly incorporated into science's picture of reality.
>
> Like many other scientific sceptics, I refused to even review the data relevant to the questions concerning these phenomena. I prejudged the data, and those providing it, because my limited perspective failed to provide the foggiest notion of how such things might actually happen. Those who assert that there is no evidence for phenomena indicative of extended consciousness, in spite of overwhelming evidence to the contrary, are wilfully ignorant. They believe they know the truth without needing to look at the facts.
>
> With me, two events occurred in unison and concurrence, and together they break the back of the last efforts of reductive science to tell the world that the material realm is all that exists... I'm living proof.

Alexander's book, which bravely pulls no punches, truly should be required reading for all medics – indeed all scientists generally. We will return to various elements of his experience in later chapters.

5

OUT-OF-BODY EXPERIENCE EVIDENCE

As impressive as all the foregoing might be, in my opinion by far the most compelling evidence for consciousness operating outside of the body, and indeed underlying everything, comes from our final area of research – and this time it's extensive.

EMANUEL SWEDENBORG

Some researchers assert that deliberate OOB journeying has formed part of spiritual exploration for millennia, and was the main modus operandi used by the Egyptian and Greek mystery schools, by Hindu, Sikh and Sufi mystics, by Tibetan lamas, and by leading religious figures such as Zoroaster, St Paul and Muhammad.[1] Others have added to this list the ancient Chinese and Japanese, the Romans, and various indigenous tribal cultures around the globe.[2]

Nevertheless the first set of comprehensive, written reports of other realms that clearly derive from deliberate OOB journeying come from the eighteenth-century Swedish scientist, inventor, philosopher and mystic Emanuel Swedenborg.[3] It wasn't until he was 53 that he had his 'spiritual awakening', but from then on he was apparently free to travel in the afterlife planes and report back on them. He is widely admired by many dedicated followers around the world, but there's a problem with his work in that it has a hugely Christian bias. In fact he maintained that he was instructed by 'the Lord' to reveal the true spiritual meaning of the Bible, the result being his monumental, eight-volume *Arcana Caelestia* or 'Heavenly Mysteries', which initially was published anonymously from 1749 to 1756. This is an incredibly difficult book to penetrate.

However his next major work, *Heaven and Hell*, was published two years later and is rather easier to digest. He still retains his Christian bias – claiming, for example, that non-Christians have to be converted to the 'true faith' in the afterlife, and that Moslems have to reject Muhammad in favour of Christ.[4] So we should be clear that, for all his superb contribution, his OOB travels weren't without their distortions. Nevertheless there are a number of elements of his journeys that are very much in line with more modern reports. As such we'll examine them in more detail in later chapters.

For the moment, though, we're interested in some fascinating evidential experiences of his that have been widely reported.[5] Some seem to have involved talking to departed spirits and returning with information known to nobody else but them and perhaps one other person – one of these even involved the Swedish Queen herself, and was witnessed and attested by the former Prime Minister Carl Tessin. But others were more in the form of prophecies and visions. By far the best-known and best-attested of these was his insistence, while having dinner in Gothenburg, that a huge fire had started in Stockholm some 300 miles away. He was agitated for several hours and kept excusing himself to go outside, before announcing with some relief that the fire had stopped three doors from his home. Word spread and he was even summoned to the provincial governor's house the following day, where he gave a full account of how it had started, how long it had lasted, and how it had been put out. The evening after that messengers began to arrive with confirmation that his visions had been accurate. It isn't clear exactly how Swedenborg received them, nor was this necessarily an OOB experience per se, but from the published accounts it does at least seem to involve some sort of bilocation or dual consciousness.

VINCENT TURVEY

There was then a lengthy delay until, in the late nineteenth century, a widespread interest in all things psychic and paranormal began to emerge. Mediumship, telepathy and the appearance of 'doubles' or *doppelgängers* were all being investigated with varying degrees of rigour in attempts to prove the separate existence of the soul and its survival of bodily death. This was led as much as anyone else by Frederic Myers, who we met in chapter 2, and whose writings refer to both the bilocation of consciousness and to 'travelling clairvoyance' – although as we've seen these phenomena may be more akin to what we now call remote viewing. By contrast in typical OOB experiences, as with NDEs, the subject's entire consciousness and focus shifts elsewhere, while their body remains in a form of suspended animation, or even asleep.

Turning more specifically to these, by the time *Tess of the D'Urbervilles* was first published in 1892 Thomas Hardy's heroine was clearly familiar with the subject:[6]

> I don't know about ghosts... but I do know that our souls can be made to go outside our bodies when we are alive... A very easy way to feel 'em go... is to lie on the grass at night and look straight up at some big bright star; and, by fixing your mind upon it, you will soon find that you are hundreds and hundreds o' miles away from your body, which you don't seem to want at all.

Fiction aside, as far as I can tell one of the very first people of relatively recent times to write openly and simply about his OOB experiences was a British researcher called Vincent Turvey, whose name is almost never mentioned in any reviews of the early literature on the subject. His book *The Beginnings of Seership* came out in 1909, way before all other offerings, apart from those of Swedenborg and the rather more obscure late-nineteenth century material of early theosophists Charles Leadbeater and Annie Besant – albeit that I do discuss their important contribution to the field at some length in *Supersoul*, and we'll meet them again in later chapters.[7] In any case Turvey was apparently a very fit, keen cyclist before a series of debilitating illnesses laid him low from the age of only twenty-nine.[8] Indeed it seems he should have died repeatedly but always made miraculous recoveries, only to be struck down again. The silver lining to this was that he spent thousands of hours recuperating in a tent in his garden in Bournemouth, during which time he meditated extensively, as well as reading all the Yogic, Vedic and Gnostic teachings he could lay his hands on. This apparently allowed him to rediscover and develop a range of extraordinary gifts that he'd been born with but had for a time suppressed.

This man was a true pioneer in his attempts to document and verify his paranormal talents in the fields of clairvoyance, prophecy and, most interestingly for our current purposes, the *deliberate* use of his 'energy bodies' to travel to other locations. What is more, as often as possible he would get the people involved and any independent witnesses to write affidavits of their experiences, which form a significant portion of his book. This was a time when sceptics actually took the trouble to engage in debate about evidence, even if their arguments were often as simplistic and reductionist as those of their modern counterparts – few of whom even bother to acknowledge that such evidence exists. So Turvey's amazing gifts, and his efforts to do everything reasonably in his power to forestall sceptics' objections – even to prove that his powers involved far more than mere telepathy – surely deserve considerably more credit than they've received.

Somewhat contrary to my earlier comments, and unlike virtually any other OOB explorer I'm aware of, he was nearly always completely conscious in his physical body at the same time as he was projecting. In fact his description of this dual consciousness, and of the variable interplay in terms of faculties and dominance between his physical 'me' at his home and his projected 'I', is absolutely fascinating.[9] Moreover his projected consciousness often retained other senses such as hearing and even smell, and on at least one occasion was apparently able to lift a bed with two people in it – something that as a semi-invalid in his normal body he'd never have been able to achieve.[10] It is factors such as these, amongst others, that nevertheless lead me to categorise his bilocation of consciousness as OOB projection rather than remote viewing, because in the latter the projected portion of consciousness appears to be relatively passive – although that view could be open to debate.

Turvey documents a series of evidential experiments that were subsequently verified in one way or another.[11] The simplest but most evidentially useful involved him projecting part of his consciousness into other people's houses that he'd never visited before, and accurately describing their layout and what they were doing or wearing. For example, here's one letter of confirmation:

> I have great pleasure in testifying to the correct description you gave me at your house last Tuesday evening, 4th June 1907, viz. that very late, about eight days and nights previous, you in spirit came in through my window and saw me sitting on the edge of my bed, partly undressed (trousers and vest), pillow end, facing the window, thinking deeply. You also gave me a true description of the size of the bed (four feet long; brass knobs), furniture, etc., of which I give a plan. You also gave me the description of a spirit form of a small old lady who came into the room whilst I was in the position described, whom you thought had passed on some seventeen or twenty-seven years ago. This spirit really passed on seven years ago and was a great-aunt of mine who was over eighty years of age.

Another confirmation even came from a sceptic who was trying to put him to the test and catch him out, but about whose house in Ireland Turvey brought back eight or nine pieces of accurate information that the sceptic was forced to attest in writing.

All in all I cannot praise Turvey's pioneering work highly enough, particularly because of his scrupulous documentation of independent corroboration of his experiences. Unfortunately in the cases that follow such corroboration hasn't been obtained, so they're more anecdotal. But in evidential cases that involve verifiable information, there are really only three possible explanations. First, the subject somehow knew the information already but had consciously forgotten it. However in the following cases, which have been scrupulously selected by me, the information tends to be so personal, or obscure, or otherwise unobtainable by the person in any normal physical manner, that this explanation is usually the *least* likely. This leaves only two. Either they're making the whole thing up, or they're accurately recording an experience they had while OOB. Ask yourselves which is the most likely in each case that follows, given the nature of the people involved and the context.

ED MORRELL

The next case is fascinating in the light of the belief that the spirit or soul can choose to leave the body at times of great stress, especially just before a highly traumatic death. Ed Morrell was the inspiration for US author Jack London's 1915 novel *The Star Rover* – as in 'someone who can rove about among the stars' – and his story is a riveting one.

Sentenced to life in Folsom State Prison in California in 1894 for aiding the escape of a notorious train robber, Morrell suffered barbaric torture both before and after his transfer to San Quentin around five years later. He was placed in solitary confinement *for life* because he was suspected of knowing where some firearms were hidden in the prison – although in truth there were none, so he was simply unable to divulge where they were. As he records in his autobiography *The Twenty-Fifth Man*, published much later in 1924, one of his worst tortures was to be placed in a straitjacket laced almost impossibly tight:[12] 'For nearly half an hour my heart pounded incessantly. The cords in my neck were bulging out ready to burst. My breath left my body, forced grudgingly through my throat in sharp, hot gasps.' This heinous operation was inflicted on him again and again, the longest session lasting *four days*. No wonder the guards couldn't believe that Morrell didn't die or at least 'break', when every time he was released from the straitjacket he was covered in faeces and in burns from his own urine.

This turned out to be because of a quite unexpected side effect: he repeatedly found himself leaving his body when this horrendous torture was inflicted. Let us allow him to speak for himself at some length:[13]

> From the brutal jacket and the dungeon hell I learned to project myself into the living, breathing, outside world of today, witnessing events... I was present during a shipwreck, just outside the Golden Gate, heard the cries of women and children, saw them swallowed by the sea... This wreck was an actual occurrence as I afterwards found out. It happened on the very day that I had left my body encased in the straitjacket in San Quentin's dungeon.
>
> At other times, unbelievable as it may seem, my mind was projected outside of the dungeon, playing a part in the lives of people I was later destined to meet, some of whom were to aid materially in my rehabilitation and freedom. I had become a master of self-hypnosis, suspended animation, call it what you will, and I believe I am one of few mortals who ever expressed the claim that intelligence endured, or that there was any continuity of thought or knowledge of time and events while in this state... I was indeed the 'Star Rover' of the ages, and Jack London's book but mildly touches upon that prison life of mine, leaving the most amazing phenomena unwritten, the most wonderful of my travels and doings untouched. He called those experiences 'the little death'. I prefer to call them 'my new life in tune with a power divine'...
>
> A force over which I had no control invariably led me out and away beyond the walls of the prison to travel through space with the speed of lightning, perhaps to some strange distant land where the people dressed in odd clothes and spoke in guttural languages. Again, I might view seas, desert islands, rivers, with here and there flashes of the tropics... only

> to return in the space of a moment to scenes more homelike, and to people whom I knew in my world of living realities...
>
> I have spent whole days in San Francisco, wandering about until night-fall. To me these were the most glorious times, because of the myriad lights of the big city... One time I entered a large and beautifully lighted church. I was drawn there by the sounds of the organ. The congregation were standing, singing a hymn; and fearful of disturbing them in their devotion I stole along through the main aisle looking for an empty seat. I found one beside an elderly woman. She was singing in a rich, well-trained voice. All through the service I was conscious of her presence, and registered how happy she made me feel. Still, I did not lose a word of the pastor's sermon or any of the wonderful singing of the choir, and I felt that I wanted to stay there forever. To me, that church was a shrine of peace and love...
>
> I could not explain to my mind why people never answered when I addressed them. Their indifference nonplussed me, because I believed they heard. There were many discrepancies, incongruous, incompatible with logic and reason. For instance, I could look through people as if I were an x-ray. Opacity meant nothing to me. I could flit through doors without opening them. Solid walls were as tissue paper, intangible, non-existent, when I wished to pass beyond. A moving train going at the highest speed was just an ordinary escalator for me to step off and on at will. And yet all this never appeared to be other than real...
>
> I had no chance to check up my experiences away from the dungeon, and it was not until I had finally left solitary that the means presented and I verified many of them, such as the occurrence of the wreck of the big steamship outside of the Golden Gate.

While OOB he also visited a fellow convict in solitary confinement and noted him pulling at a loose tooth, something he was again able to subsequently verify.[14] One interesting series of excursions were to a young schoolgirl, who he'd visit in her classroom and who would later become his wife, co-author and lecture partner. He also occasionally found himself shadowing a man who lived in nearby Alameda. Morrell would later recognise him as John C Edgar, who went on to become the new warden of San Quentin and who, after researching the case, became responsible for advocating his pardon – which was forthcoming in 1909. In fact based on information given to him while OOB Morrell had predicted his release to the previous warden who was having him tortured – which, coming on top of his refusal to break, only added to the latter's fury. It is interesting to note that his OOB travels ended with the conclusion of his torture, and were never subsequently replicated.

Intriguingly he was also given an OOB preview of an entirely new sort of penal system based on proper justice and rehabilitation – and it's almost impossible to give him enough credit for the fact that, on his release, he devoted himself to penal reform. What courage he showed in refusing to give in to bitterness. Admittedly some time later, because of London's book, his experiences received considerable exposure. But given the nature of the man and the context it seems highly unlikely he made them up. More specifically for our current purposes, the very fact he survived such terrible torture for so long might in its own right be argued to be highly evidential of his consciousness operating outside of his physical body during such episodes. In that case his witnessing of the shipwreck, and of his fellow prisoner's loose tooth, only add to the evidential nature of his experiences. Meanwhile his OOB shadowing of unknown people who would later play so influential a role in his life gives us pause to marvel at the intricate workings of this wonderful universe in which we live.

OLIVER FOX (A.K.A. HUGH CALLAWAY)

The OOB pioneer most studies commence with is Sylvan Muldoon, an American who had his first spontaneous experience aged twelve. In 1929 he teamed up with paranormal researcher Hereward Carrington to write *Projection of the Astral Body*, which contained details of Muldoon's own experiences and the techniques he developed to trigger them. After a considerable gap they followed this up with *The Phenomena of Astral Projection* in 1951, which was the first major survey of other people's largely spontaneous experiences and attempted to classify them in terms of triggers.

In the introduction to their first book Carrington – presumably unaware of the contributions of the theosophists and of Turvey – talks about the OOB literature of that time being restricted to just three sources.[15] The first two both involved French research into using hypnosis to attempt to persuade subjects' astral bodies to part company with their physical counterparts.[16] The third comprised two articles in the *Occult Review* of 1920 by another British pioneer, Hugh Callaway – who wrote under the pseudonym Oliver Fox and is only occasionally mentioned in contemporary works. His articles were expanded into a book called *Astral Projection* that was published much later in 1938, when he was fifty-two.[17] It reads rather like a charming autobiography although, coming from a scientific background, he does attempt to examine his experiences with some degree of rigour.[18]

Most important from an evidential perspective is Fox's account of a fascinating episode with a sweetheart to whom he gives the pseudonym Elsie, which occurred many years before when they were both quite young.[19] As a devout Christian she felt that his deliberate OOB experiments were 'wicked', but when he taunted her she revealed she too could go OOB in her dreams, and set the intention that she'd visit him that night. Not only did he become aware of her presence in his room, but when they discussed the experience the next day she accurately recalled all the main details of his bedroom layout – which, remembering this was at the turn of the twentieth century, she'd never seen – in terms of the positions of his door, bed, window, fireplace, washstand, chest of drawers and dressing table. Not only that but several further details she provided were seriously obscure and couldn't have been simply guessed at: his position lying on the left side of his double bed; an old fashioned pin cushion; a black Japanese box covered with red, raised figures; and a leather-covered desk lined with gilt. Best of all he'd seen her standing next to the desk running her fingers along it, and she confirmed this and said it had a pronounced ridge. He was generally impressed but said she was mistaken on that one tiny detail: there was no ridge on the desk, and she must have felt the gilt inlay. Yet she was adamant, and when he returned home and checked he found that a lengthy hinge normally obscured from his view formed just such a ridge.

Once more we have no independent confirmation of this evidence. But, again, is it likely that Fox made the whole thing up?

GLADYS LEONARD

In chapter 2 we briefly met Gladys Leonard, who was the primary channel for Sir Oliver Lodge's communication with his son Raymond. But, although best known as a medium, in *My Life in Two Worlds* she also describes several OOB experiences that have excellent evidential value.[20]

In the first she was lying down one afternoon in her bedroom in the flat she shared with her husband, preparing for the arrival of two regular sitters who had lost their son. Unexpectedly she found herself OOB and next to her husband at the door of their flat, where he was talking to the gasman – who she recognised from his uniform. At the same time a maid from an upstairs flat came down the stairs, and her husband slipped her a coin without comment. All this information subsequently proved correct – apparently the maid had undertaken some small service for him at a time when he didn't have any change.

But the experience didn't end there. She next found herself in an unknown sitting room, where the couple she was expecting later that afternoon were talking to a striking looking man whose appearance she noted well – because, unexpectedly, they were inviting him to accompany them to the sitting with her, when this was normally an intensely private affair. Nor was even *that* the end, because next she found herself on some stairs at the top of which she recognised their deceased son Philip – from having clairvoyantly gained an impression of his appearance in a previous sitting – and he recognised her too. The sound of a piano was coming from the drawing room next to him, and she entered to see a young woman playing, who Philip reported was Gertrude – who had played for him every week when he was alive, and continued now he'd passed. Again she made a careful note of the girl's appearance.

Back in her body Leonard made a point of describing the gentleman she had seen in some detail to her husband, although both were doubtful anyone would accompany the couple. But when they arrived the Leonards were amazed to find that they'd brought the lady's brother with them – he'd been visiting and had expressed an interest in joining them – and his appearance was exactly as described. What is more, they then confirmed that Gertrude was a cousin of Philip's who had played the piano for them once a week but had passed on some six years before – and the description of her was accurate too.9k4

These details are too obscure to be mere coincidence and misinterpretation. So did Leonard just make all this up? Or is this further proof that our consciousness can genuinely leave our body and continue operating without our physical brain?

FREDERICK SCULTHORP

Another poorly remembered OOB pioneer is Frederick Sculthorp, an English shopkeeper who only became interested in spiritual matters after his wife's death in 1934.[21] He visited a medium and gained what to him was highly evidential confirmation of his departed wife's presence – given that he made absolutely sure not to provide leading information, and some of what she told him was highly obscure and yet absolutely correct. But she then advised him to try mediumship for himself, and in practising at home he found himself in the presence of a guide who then, better still, helped him to go OOB. As we'll see in later chapters his travels took him to a broad spectrum of afterlife planes, and by the time he published *Excursions to the Spirit World* in 1961 they spanned two decades – albeit that his humility meant he took some persuasion to publish his experiences. For our current purposes the most evidential one involved his two incarnate daughters:

> In 1939 my two daughters were on holiday in the Isle of Wight, some ninety miles distant from my home. After lunch one day I felt very lonely over their absence and sat in the armchair and asked to be taken to them... Presently I was projected and found myself walking behind my two daughters. I could not see the general landscape but the girls were walking a few yards apart and tossing some object from one to the other. Then a lady approached from behind... then between my two girls. The elder girl, without looking, threw the object and hit the lady in the back. I was annoyed at such carelessness and this thought immediately drew me back to the physical body... I made a note of the time and the day.
>
> Later, when my daughters were telling me all about their holiday, I suddenly asked the elder one if she had thrown something and hit a lady. She reddened, and the younger one giggled and said: 'Mabel hit a lady in the back with a ball!' The elder one explained that after lunch on the day I had noted, while walking on either side of a path to the beach, they were throwing a ball back and forth to each other, and she did not notice the lady overtake and walk between them.

CHARLES TART AND MISS Z

Another interesting evidential case is recorded by renowned American parapsychologist Charles Tart, whose specialism was investigating different states of consciousness. In an article published in the *Journal of the American Society for Psychical Research* in 1968 he documented his experiments with a young woman, Miss Z, who'd had spontaneous but conscious OOB experiences once or twice a night all her life – although involving little more than the classic scenario of floating near the ceiling and observing her body beneath her.[22] Having said that, on one occasion around the age of fourteen she found herself 'inside' the body of a girl walking down a street in a deserted part of her home town, wearing clothes she didn't recognise, terrified because she was being followed. The person caught up with her, raped her then stabbed her to death. Miss Z was extremely traumatised by the realism of this 'nightmare', no less so when the following morning's newspapers reported the rape and murder of a girl wearing the same clothes in the same part of town.

Tart started by getting her to place a piece of paper with a number from 1 to 10 on it by her bedside table, having selected it blind from a box. The table was sufficiently high she couldn't see it from her bed. Seven nights in a row she went OOB and memorised the number correctly. He then brought her into his lab on four separate occasions and hooked her up to monitoring equipment on a bed, just before she went to sleep. The wires were long enough to allow her to turn over but not to sit up in bed, and any attempt to disconnect them would immediately show on the equipment. After she was asleep he used random number tables to select a five-digit number, which he wrote on a piece of card before quietly slipping into the lab and placing it on a shelf some six feet above the bed. There was also a clock just above the shelf.

On the first night nothing unusual happened. On the second she called out 'write down three thirteen' at around 03.15, suggesting she had woken up and floated high enough to be on a level with the clock but not to be able to see the numbers on the shelf – as she confirmed the next morning. On the third night, somewhat against her will she found herself projecting into her own home some miles away, where she apparently found her sister also OOB, but Tart was unable to obtain independent verification of this from the latter before the two had talked about it themselves. Then, finally, on the fourth night they hit the jackpot. Although Tart was relaxed, Miss Z herself was somewhat frustrated at her inability to memorise the number so far. But at 06.04 she called out 25132 – exactly the right number. The odds of her guessing this randomly were 1 in 100,000.

ROBERT MONROE

Undoubtedly the most influential OOB researcher of modern times is Robert Monroe. A highly successful broadcaster who ended up with his own radio and TV network, he had his first spontaneous experience in 1958 while in his forties, and when it happened several more times he increasingly devoted himself to exploring the phenomenon. Although he could apparently be somewhat challenging to deal with, his books back up his reputation as a highly intelligent man with widespread interests who was fastidious in his approach to his research – and in particular to the documentation and analysis of his huge number of OOB experiences.

He had nearly six hundred in the twelve years leading up to the publication of his seminal *Journeys Out of the Body* in 1971, this being followed by *Far Journeys* and *Ultimate Journey* in 1985 and 1994 respectively.[23] By the time he passed into the realms he knew so well in 1995 he'd made huge strides in advancing our knowledge of the phenomenon and, perhaps even more important, given thousands of ordinary people the comfort that they weren't going crazy. Indeed in the early days Monroe himself was keen to prove that he wasn't just imagining his experiences and, like Turvey, took considerable trouble to document his attempts at evidential experiments. These tended to involve friends who had at least some knowledge of his exploits, and are described in his first book.[24]

The first saw him deliberately setting the intention to visit a doctor friend who lived nearby but was ill in bed, since Monroe knew his house but had never seen his bedroom, and hoped to obtain an accurate description that could later be verified. When he approached the house from the air he was confused to find the doctor leaving it with his wife, but pulled himself together enough to make a note of what they were wearing. That evening he phoned the doctor's wife and simply asked what they'd been doing between 4 and 5 o'clock that afternoon. She confirmed she had needed to go to the post office and her husband had decided to accompany her to see if the fresh air would do him good. When questioned further she described how she was wearing a black coat and trousers, her husband a light-coloured hat and overcoat – just as Monroe had noted in his diary.

In another, while staying away from home, he found himself OOB with no fixed intentions. First he was aware of a boy walking along tossing a ball in the air. Then he saw a man attempting to manoeuvre an awkward device into the back seat of a large sedan, noting that it seemed to have wheels and an electric motor. Finally he witnessed people sitting around a table while one of them appeared to be dealing large white playing cards to the others, even though the table was covered with dishes – which confused him somewhat. That evening he visited some friends in the area and immediately intuited that the scenes he had witnessed involved them. First he enquired what their son had been doing between 8.30 and 9 o'clock that morning, and the boy said he'd been walking to school – and on closer questioning revealed he'd been throwing a baseball in the air and catching it. Then the boy's father revealed that with some difficulty he'd been loading a Van DeGraff generator into the back of his car, which was mounted on wheels and had an electric motor. Finally his wife described how for the first time in two years, because they were all running late, she'd brought the morning mail to the breakfast table and been handing it out – meaning the large white playing cards Monroe had seen were in fact envelopes.

A third experience involved him again deliberately setting his intention, this time to visit a business friend who was taking a holiday in New Jersey, although Monroe had no idea where. In no time he found himself in a kitchen setting where his friend was sitting to his right, while on her left sat two teenage girls, one blonde the other brunette, all three with glasses in their hands. Although she was still talking to the girls he had a subconscious conversation with his friend in which she told him she was aware of his presence and would remember his visit. He nevertheless said he wanted to be sure, so he made an effort to gently pinch her on her left side, just above her hips. He wasn't even convinced he'd be able to achieve this while OOB, so was surprised when she let out a loud 'Ow!' On her return she confirmed that between 3 and 4 o'clock on the previous Saturday afternoon was one of the few times their beach cottage hadn't been full of people, and she'd been sitting in the kitchen with her dark-haired teenage niece and a blonde friend. He then repeatedly pressed her if she remembered anything else, but drew a blank. Finally in desperation he asked if she remembered being pinched. Completely astonished she lifted her sweater to reveal bruising at exactly the point he'd pinched her, and told him it had really hurt. She was somewhat less sceptical about his activities after that.

Again these experiences are purely anecdotal, but is it likely Monroe just made them up – especially when he more than anyone needed to know that he wasn't going mad and just imagining everything?

TOM CAMPBELL

One man has perhaps done more than anyone else so far to put together a complete, scientific view of how our apparently physical universe represents a tiny subset of a multi-layered virtual reality – an idea that's pretty fundamental to Supersoul Spirituality, which we'll talk about more in chapter 8. This view takes us way beyond where even the most radical and open-minded physicists and cosmologists would normally dare to tread – but Tom Campbell arguably has the perfect combination of experience to form an educated view of this 'big picture', being by training a nuclear physicist who has the added advantage of having projected himself OOB for decades.

He also has the remarkable distinction of having assisted in the setting up the Monroe Institute in 1972, along with close friend Dennis Mennerich who had a masters in electrical engineering. Indeed it was they who introduced the binaural beat audio technology that would lead to Monroe's 'Hemi-Sync' system.[25] It was also during this time at the Institute that Campbell's memories of having had extensive OOB experiences from the age of five were triggered. In fact he recalled that they were closely guided and involved a variety of learning and tests similar to those Monroe himself had been through. They were brought to an abrupt halt by his guides at the age of eight, and over time forgotten, only for his extensive natural abilities to be rekindled some twenty years later – initially while learning transcendental meditation as a postgraduate lecturer and researcher, and then in vivid and highly evidential experiences shared with Mennerich and others under Monroe's supervision. After these three went their separate ways in the late 1970s, Campbell embarked on a program of solo research over two decades that would culminate in the publication of his astonishing three-volume work *My Big T.O.E.* – or 'theory of everything' – in 2003.

The evidential research that convinced them their experiences had a high degree of independent reality isn't described in great detail therein.[26] However multiple joint projections were apparently attempted in Monroe's laboratory under control conditions, during which both projectors provided a real-time commentary on their experiences that was recorded and subsequently compared. This is Campbell's reaction to the debrief after his first joint session with Mennerich:

> 'Listen to this!' Bob said... The correlation was astonishing. For almost two hours we sat there with our mouths open, hooting and exclaiming, filling in the details for each other... I was dumbfounded. There was only one good explanation: this stuff was real!.. We repeated that experiment with similar results. It wasn't a phenomenon that depended on the two of us. Nancy Lea [Monroe's stepdaughter] and I shared equally astonishing joint experiences. We tried other things as well. We read three and four digit numbers written on a blackboard next to the control room. Somebody would write a random number and we would read it while our bodies lay asleep. Then they would erase it and write another one, and so on and on.

In a repetition of Monroe's own experiments described previously they then turned to projecting to friends' and colleagues' homes to see what they were doing, then called them the next day to check the results. They also diagnosed illnesses in people they'd never met but who colleagues or friends knew well. Apparently their later experiences tended to be even more dramatic than the initial ones, leading Campbell to conclude: 'Dennis and I were the same demanding and sceptical scientists that had started this adventure, but we had stopped asking if it was real. We now knew the answer.'

Anecdotal evidence again perhaps, but arguably this time even more compelling. Are serious physicists and engineers with a full scientific background, training and approach likely to have made all this up, or to have totally misinterpreted their joint experiences?

WALDO VIEIRA

Arguably even more prolific than Monroe, although less well known in the West, is the Brazilian consciousness explorer Waldo Vieira. A medical doctor by profession, he started deliberately projecting in 1941 at the age of nine, and by the time he wrote *Projections of the Consciousness* in 1981 his experiences numbered in the many hundreds. Indeed this book describes more than sixty varied projections from the second half of 1979 alone. He originated the study of 'conscientiology' and its subset 'projectiology', and the massively detailed treatises published both by Vieira and his successors in the International Academy of Consciousness (IAC) are somewhat intimidating, being replete with sometimes difficult and obscure terminology.

Nevertheless he does describe at least one interesting evidential experience in which he intentionally projected early one evening during a storm.[27] He floated into his living room and was surprised not to find his wife there. He examined a shelf containing ornamental dishes and vases, before closely observing the numbers 376-500 in a location he wasn't subsequently able to remember. He then proceeded outside and was surprised that the raging thunderstorm had no effect on him while OOB. On his return to the body he got up and discussed his experience with his wife. Initially neither of them was able to think of where the figures he'd seen might be, until she recalled they were the serial numbers of a set of magazines bound together on a shelf some nine feet from the ground – with the label clearly displaying 376-500.

LUIS MINERO AND SILVANA MEIRA

Afterlife researcher Alan Hugenot's 2015 film *The Nature of Consciousness* contains an interesting interview with OOB explorer and IAC director Luis Minero. He describes how as a teenager he deliberately projected a few blocks away from his apartment and memorised the sequence of colours of several cars and one licence plate, then came back into his body and went out to verify them.[28] Unfortunately he doesn't mention this in his own book, *Demystifying the Out-of-Body Experience*, published in 2012. But he does describe a similarly evidential experience of IAC colleague Silvana Meira.[29] She set the intention to visit a particular friend she hadn't seen for some five years and found him in his house, sitting at a table opposite a woman she didn't recognise who was facing away from her. She noted that he was wearing a light blue shirt and no longer had a beard. She returned to her body, made notes and the following day contacted him, at which point he confirmed all these details.

BRUCE MOEN

Although they don't involve our earth plane, we might note in passing the experiences of Bruce Moen, an engineering consultant who attended a number of courses at the Monroe Institute – as a result of which he produced the four-volume *Exploring the Afterlife* series between 1997 and 2001. In the last of these he describes a number of 'partnered' explorations similar to the pioneering ones of Campbell and Mennerich, in which he and a fellow student called Rebecca set the intention to achieve certain goals while OOB together in other planes. They independently recorded their experiences in writing then compared them and, according to Moen, achieved some impressive 'hits'.[30]

6

CONCLUSION

The idea that the materialist metaparadigm cannot account for the existence of consciousness, not just in humans but in anything, may not be shared by all scientists and philosophers as yet. But most of the really brilliant minds of the last few centuries do seem to have recognised that materialism can only take us so far.

Much of the remaining evidence presented here in Part 1 could easily be dismissed as purely anecdotal and uncorroborated. Moreover there are obvious challenges when attempting to perform replicable consciousness experiments under controlled conditions. Yet surely, given that the likelihood of widespread fraud is virtually zero, the body of evidence collated here is at least strongly suggestive of the fact that consciousness is *not* located in or dependant upon the physical brain, and can – indeed does – exist entirely separate from it. And as we said at the outset, if we can say *that*, then we can directly infer that there must be other realms in which consciousness operates in different forms – in other words that, from a human perspective, there must be an *afterlife* worth investigating.

The use of such a word for denoting what happens after we pass on will have different connotations for different people. It may even be commonly associated with traditional religious notions of there being only a small selection of experiences or realms awaiting us when we pass on – for example, either a heaven filled with angels playing harps on fluffy white clouds, or a hell where demons stick red-hot pokers in unmentionable places. But in fact we'll find that all the evidence points towards the existence of an almost infinite variety of realms or planes with hugely disparate inhabitants and characteristics.

Before we can explore them properly, though, and find out exactly what sorts of heavens and even hells might await us, we need to set up a few ground rules.

PART TWO

A NEW TAKE ON THE SEVEN PLANES

The only religion that will save the world from its sin, and raise it from its degradation, must find its way to the hearts of men through the filtering process of human reason. Science and philosophy will be its handmaids, and eternal laws and immortal truths its gospels.

Anonymous spirit communication received by Emily French

7

THE BIG PICTURE

The idea that there are seven planes through which our soul or spirit progresses is pretty much universal to all religious and esoteric worldviews down the ages, as is the notion that each one involves an increasingly refined level of energy, frequency or vibration. So when we refer to 'higher' planes this has no spatial connotation. In the afterlife, it appears that what first attracts us to a given plane, and then allows us to progress from one to another, is a combination of our degree of emotional balance and our spiritual awareness, which in turn dictates the energetic frequency at which our consciousness is operating. This is why cultivating such awareness while we're still alive is potentially so important.

One major problem we face in writing about these planes is that the various classifications found in different traditions are inconsistent in their labelling and even their basic descriptions, especially when we're dealing with the higher planes. To then attempt to relate these to the hugely varied experiences recorded by our many channelled sources and OOB pioneers, and to use them to propose a differently weighted – and arguably more intelligible and relevant – framework, appears at first sight close to impossible. Yet that is what we're at least going to attempt here in Part 2.

But before we can even start to discuss these planes we need to consider the far broader context. I indicated in chapter 5 that one of the finest explanations of the big picture that I've come across is provided by physicist and OOB explorer Tom Campbell. He proposes that the existence of an almost infinitely varied collection of universes or realities can be explained using only two propositions.[1] Although on first exposure it's an uncomfortable idea for most people, the first is that the 'primal cause' underlying everything wasn't some sort of perfected and ultimately divine 'Source' energy as most spiritual approaches assume, but an entirely primitive and undifferentiated consciousness. The second is that all consciousness ever wants to do is 'lower its entropy' – or, in simple terms, organise itself better. This idea at least partly mirrors those esoteric teachings that refer to the primal source 'creating order out of chaos'.[2]

How does consciousness do this? By diversifying into differentiated units, each one capable of creating new and ever more sophisticated realities, and each one in turn projecting individualised aspects of itself into those realities. The purpose being? To *experience*. Nothing more, nothing less. So consciousness lowers its entropy by experiencing – or, as an alternative way of looking at it, by *expanding* its database of experiences.

Not everyone will resonate with such challenging ideas, especially concerning the concept of the ultimate Source, but fortunately they're not fundamental to the arguments in this book. What *is* important is that theories like this are based on the idea that, underneath the many illusions, all levels of reality are essentially information-based and digital. So it can be useful to think of these various realities as endless computer-style simulation games being played out by different levels or aggregations of consciousness. As long, that is, as this doesn't conjure up images of humanity being slaves to whoever's in control of the game, because that's absolutely *not* what's being described here. Instead every level of consciousness in these various simulations is operating with complete free will.

The point is that whatever follows about different planes of existence is only relevant to *our version* of the 'game', 'system', 'hologram', 'universe' or whatever we want to call it. Other systems will have entirely different ways of organising themselves, although almost certainly any system will have multiple planes, and underlying all of them will be the hugely powerful consciousnesses that created them. Of course this book can only concentrate on our system because we have little if any knowledge of any others.

In addition there's a high statistical likelihood that there are many other planets playing host to a huge variety of lifeforms scattered throughout a universe of which our earth forms such a tiny part – although whether any of these are also human or even humanoid is one of the million-dollar questions. As with the entirely different systems just discussed, we can make few assumptions about any other nonhuman but intelligent lifeforms that share our universe – because we know precious little, even about those who might already be in contact with us, that's reliable or relevant to this discussion. So, precisely because they could have vastly different levels of consciousness, and of energetic frequency and therefore physicality or ethereality, it would seem entirely presumptuous to assume they have the same experiences as humans when they go through their equivalent of our earthly death – if they do at all. But one thing we can say is that only a handful of OOB pioneers mention making contact with nonhuman consciousnesses, and this only tends to occur in the higher planes. So, further, we will be forced to concentrate on only the *human* aspects of our system.

Meanwhile some OOB explorers regularly experience 'earth-like' but slightly different environments, populated by what appear to be living human beings. For example, in his 1998 book *The Out-of-Body Experience* British explorer Graham Dack describes multiple earth-like projections, many of which start outside his house, in his own street, but with slight differences.[3] In one of these he finds himself at a house party where a woman comes up and takes him outside, whereupon they walk to an area in the centre of the town, with her telling him this is where she was actually due to meet him. He intuits that she must think he's her husband and, understandably fascinated but concerned lest he should meet his counterpart in this other plane, he makes an excuse to leave and hides out of sight – only to see an exact replica of himself, apart from different clothes and wearing glasses, coming to meet her. Similarly Frederick Aardema, a clinical psychologist at the University of Montreal who is also an experienced OOB pioneer, describes various experiences in what he refers to as 'parallel fields of consciousness' in his 2012 book *Explorations in Consciousness.*[4] In one he finds himself in a completely different house, much simpler and cheaper furnished than his own, in what he feels is Eastern Europe – although his wife Monique is still very much part of this other life.

Certainly both of these experiences seem to involve some form of earth-equivalent world that could well represent another closely related version of the 'human game'. Especially given that the other versions of Dack and of Aardema's wife looked identical, this *could* mean there are multiple identical versions of each of us operating in different versions of a similar human game. This is a pretty mind-boggling suggestion. But unless each version of us was to operate in a completely separate set of afterlife planes too – which isn't completely impossible, but somehow feels less likely – it's not something born out in afterlife reports, which never contain the idea of encountering close to identical other versions of ourselves.

So the alternative explanation for these experiences is that the OOB explorer is temporarily tuning into what Campbell too describes as 'parallel' worlds – yet what he means is that these are only different *theoretical* versions of the game that exist only as potentialities until or unless they're triggered by different free-will choices.[5] To draw the full analogy, a computer game has to be programmed with a full scenario that plays out based on every possible choice made or action taken by the player or players. But at least in simplistic terms any one actual player will only plot one actual course through the game. Such experiences wouldn't therefore involve a fully independent version of the OOB explorer, and wouldn't have the same ontology as the everyday life on which they're normally focussed – but they might *appear* just as real during a temporary visit.

By contrast Robert Monroe has a series of somewhat more divergent but still earth-like experiences in what he refers to as 'Locale III':[6]

> The scientific development is inconsistent. There are no electrical devices whatsoever... No electric lights, telephones, radios, television or electric power. No internal combustion, gasoline, or oil were found as power sources. Yet mechanical power is used. Careful examination of one of the locomotives that pulled a string of old-fashioned looking passenger cars showed it to be driven by a steam engine... The actions of the technicians all seemed to indicate [radiation as the power source]...
>
> Their version of our automobile is much larger. Even the smallest has a single bench seat that will hold five to six people abreast... Wheels are used, but without inflated tyres. Steering is done by a single horizontal bar. Motive power is contained somewhere in the rear. Their movement is not very fast, at something like 15 to 20 miles per hour. Traffic is not heavy.

Even more fascinating is that Monroe found his consciousness temporarily 'merging' with the body of one of the inhabitants of this realm – a rather lonely and introverted architect. During these mergers Monroe had no awareness of the mind or memories of this man, so it's anyone's guess what was happening to the man's own consciousness. But in later journeys Monroe repeatedly found himself in the company of the man's new wife, suddenly parachuted into his body with no idea how to respond to her questions – at which point he usually returned to his own body to avoid further embarrassment. In one encounter he was suddenly driving their car up a hill and, with no idea how it worked, drove it off the road.

With the other man not being an exact physical counterpart, and with the other world generally having a clearly different technological development path, Monroe's excursions into Locale III suggest strongly that more divergent versions of the human game exist too, and are running alongside ours. Moreover, whatever the connection was that drew him into the body of the other man, this time the latter was a different individual and not another version of Monroe. It is impossible to say how many of these more divergent versions of the game there might be, but this time it does seem fair to assume that humans operating in these other versions will have similar experiences to ourselves in the afterlife, and that therefore they probably form part of the same overall system.

For all these reasons this book will primarily concentrate on what we might refer to as the 'human system' and its afterlife planes, which may not be representative of those experienced by other lifeforms – particularly in respect of the lower and even middle planes. But having established that, we now need to understand the context of how different levels of consciousness operate in our human system, because it's against this backdrop that its various planes of existence must be placed.

8

SUPERSOUL SPIRITUALITY

'Supersoul Spirituality' is a framework of understanding I began to develop in late 2012, which has taken me away from the traditional reincarnational focus that had dominated my research and writing for more than a decade under a schema I called 'Rational Spirituality'. The first edition of *Supersoul*, published in November 2013, presented the relevant OOB and channelled evidence and also a variety of theoretical models of how consciousness might operate in our system. It took much intense thought over the next eighteen months before I was able to come down in favour of just one of these in the second edition.

As a result I felt that, perhaps for the first time, I had a model that coherently merges three well-known concepts to which we often pay lip service, but whose full implications have usually been avoided:

- EVERYTHING IS HAPPENING IN THE NOW: Time is only a form of illusion that allows humans to make sense of our experience of this plane. But fundamentally, as so many wise spiritual traditions have indicated down the ages, the apparent past and future don't exist as a continuum – instead there's only *now*. Another way of putting this is that time is 'a discrete series of now-moments'. The implication is that our various lives cannot be *consecutive*, as traditional reincarnation models suggest, but instead must be *simultaneous*. In other words, irrespective of what human era they appear to involve, all our 'life personalities' are operating *alongside each other*, rather than one after the other. This idea is extremely difficult to understand in any fully logical way with mere human brains, but it's the clear implication of the idea that only now exists. The further implication, of course, is that it no longer makes sense to talk about *past-life* karma or *next-life* plans. Nevertheless it remains clear that each of us has a set of what I call 'birth givens', and that these vary widely – in terms not just of our sex, but also of our main psychological and physical traits and propensities, and of the socio-economic position and geographical location of our parents. So who chooses these?

- EACH OF US IS A GOD IN OUR OWN RIGHT: The choice of our birth givens must fall to a level of our consciousness operating outside of space-time, its aim being only to expand itself through different experiences in different worlds and realities via different forms. I call this the *supersoul* to distinguish it from the *higher self* or *oversoul*, both of which terms are used in different and conflicting contexts. This is a level of individuated consciousness repeatedly described by pioneering OOB explorers, whose encounters with such creative and wise entities lead them to think they're in the presence of a true divinity – until they come to realise this is just another aspect of *themselves*, and it's actually *who they really are*. Supersouls are the very entities who create whole new universes to play in – or new simulations in the vast digital game. Yet we should be clear that there are myriad supersouls projecting aspects of themselves just into this version of the game called the earth plane, so we're talking about something quite different from any concept of 'Source' or 'universal consciousness'. The implication of this is that if only we understood just how powerful we really are, and that we've only temporarily taken on the form of human actors in a grand play called 'earth reality', we might finally recognise that we're *not* limited and puny beings constantly buffeted by and dependent on God's will, outrageous fortune and so on – but instead we're magnificent 'creator gods' in our own right.

- THE LAW OF ATTRACTION REIGNS SUPREME: As we'll see in chapter 23, our sources universally report that in the higher planes their thoughts and emotions instantly translate into what they experience. The same principle underlies our earth reality. However here the constraints of space-time mean there's usually a time delay between thought and manifested result. Meanwhile the fact the ours is a 'consensus' or shared reality – in which our own thoughts and intentions are mingling and sometimes competing with those of our fellows around us – means the link between thought and manifested result is even more difficult to trace. Couple this with the fact that our subconscious thoughts and beliefs are hugely powerful and often in conflict with our conscious desires, and you have the recipe for a hugely persuasive illusion where it *seems* that things are happening *to* us. But they're not. Instead everything each one of us experiences is, one way or another, created or attracted *by* us. The implication of this is that, as all of the wisest channelled sources have been telling us for the last fifty years, the reality we're experiencing only acts as a mirror that projects our own thoughts and beliefs back to us. Of course this doesn't apply until we become adults and take on responsibility for ourselves, and it's also subject to any insurmountable limitations imposed by our birth givens.

As a result the formal definition of the supersoul that I've put together is as follows:

> A supersoul is a grouping of hundreds, maybe thousands, of souls. Myriads of supersouls are projecting individual soul aspects of themselves into this and myriad other realities, meaning they are very far from the ultimate consciousness. Yet

> to be fully connected to your supersoul is to have boundless wisdom and creative power, and as a full holographic representation of it you are already more divine than you can hope to conceive – divine enough, even, to nullify further speculation about what lies beyond.

The key theoretical distinction between this new supersoul model and a more traditional reincarnation-based model is that the latter tends to identify, working from the bottom up, the 'life personality' that incarnates, then a 'higher self' that starts off as a complete beginner but is enhanced or grows as a result of its repeated incarnations. By contrast the supersoul model contends that each life personality is one of a myriad of essentially separate projections from a supersoul that was already supremely wise and divine when it and its fellows created the earth game and various variants thereof. Moreover that each life personality carries exactly the same awareness into the afterlife planes that it had in the earth plane, but then is able to grow and expand in these planes as it desires. Finally it starts to become aware of the supersoul consciousness of which it's just one projection, and of the other projections from that supersoul that have been operating alongside it.

There is a substantial difference between the two models. First, under the new model we're no longer merely paying lip service to the concept of time being essentially an illusion and of the 'eternal now' – instead we're fully examining its logical and practical implications, even if they're hard to fully comprehend. Second, there's no longer a potential dichotomy between the idea of having a life plan substantially agreed in advance, but also apparent free will to use the law of attraction to manifest whatever experiences we desire – because the concept of a life plan no longer makes sense under the new model. Third, and perhaps most important of all, under the traditional model it was easy to divert attention away from our responsibility for creating everything about *this* life we're experiencing *now*, by making excuses related to supposed past-life karma or life plans – whereas under the supersoul model this is no longer feasible, so all possibility of victimhood is eradicated. Not everyone is ready for this level of responsibility – but for those who are the sense of control over our *own* destiny is hugely liberating.

For completeness the 'ten principles' of Supersoul Spirituality are summarised in the Appendix.

9

WHAT DO WE MEAN BY 'PHYSICAL'?

This is a key question we must tackle before we can start to develop our new take on the seven planes. When discussing the scientific view in chapter 1 we saw that what appears to us to be physical matter is in fact, at least in one sense, only energy vibrating with a particular frequency that resonates with our human senses – and allows us to form an apparently physical picture of the world around us. From this perspective it's clear that, as long as our consciousness is operating in a plane that involves some degree of 'form', then if we're totally resonant with the frequency of that realm it will still appear physical to us.

It is true that when departed spirits and OOB explorers are operating in the near-earth plane they find they can pass through apparently solid doors, windows, walls and so on. This is almost certainly because – even though they're not yet operating in the astral planes proper – they're nevertheless occupying their astral rather than their earthly body, and the former has a higher vibratory level. But certainly when departed spirits move into the astral realms they tend to find that their surroundings appear just as physical as those on earth, and that the usual constraints of doors, walls and so on apply, because they're attracted to the plane or even sub-plane with which their energy is most resonant. We will garner multiple endorsements of this view from our sources in chapter 23. It is for this reason that from now on we'll attempt as much as possible to avoid the word *physical* to describe our earth plane, because this clearly isn't its most distinctive feature. So what *is*?

This is a question that never seems to be considered by OOB explorers or esoteric philosophers, despite them all being aware of the aforementioned basic facts. So, perhaps for the first time, I'm going to propose that the most obvious distinguishing factor of any earth-equivalent experience is surely that it's primarily inhabited by fully *incarnate* human beings. In other words we're immersed in a full human journey in a relatively low-vibration, space-time dominated plane in which our bodies tend to age as we move from birth through to apparent death. By contrast the afterlife planes are inhabited by discarnates who no longer age and have usually fixed their appearance and personality at a particular point from their earthly lifetime – for example, what they looked like when 'in their prime'. For this reason the terms *incarnatory* or *earth* plane, rather than physical plane, are used in our new model.

10

WHAT DO WE MEAN BY 'OUT-OF-BODY'?

This is another important question for contextual reasons, and because we'll be relying so heavily on the testimony of OOB explorers. The phrase *out-of-body* itself implies that they're *going* somewhere. But is that really the case?

As we saw in the last chapter, just as with many NDEs, the subjects of conventional and especially spontaneous OOB experiences usually find themselves operating in the near-earth plane in their astral body – although some modern pioneers use the term 'first energy body'. However the distance they can travel in this body appears to be limited, not least by the so-called 'silver cord' that they can often perceive still connecting them to their earthly body. This is why some people assume that OOB evidence can't be particularly useful when trying to gain a broader perspective of the higher planes. However that's a somewhat outdated view, because many modern OOB explorers describe projecting in their 'mental' or 'second energy body' too, in which their range of travel is massively increased – not so much in terms of apparent distance as of access to higher planes.

More important still, the majority of our sources report that the other planes aren't 'out there' in some different place, but rather they all occupy the same 'space' as our earth plane. In other words the different planes are effectively superimposed on each other.

What is more, the higher the plane the further *inward* the OOB pioneer has to focus their consciousness. So, at least as far as projections to the higher planes are concerned, they're not really *moving* anywhere but instead focussing on what they often refer to as *inner* realms.[1]

To take this a step further let's bring in Jurgen Ziewe, a UK-based artist who condensed more than four decades of OOB journeying into his books *Multidimensional Man* and *Vistas of Infinity*, published in 2008 and 2016 respectively. He reports that he now exclusively uses classical meditation to take himself into the same inner worlds he experienced during more conventional second-body projections.[2] In this he and others are only following the example of the early theosophists, whose accessing of what they too called the inner planes via 'astral clairvoyance' almost certainly involved various forms of meditation – although they didn't explicitly reveal their methods. What is more, it's likely that even they were only following guidelines laid down centuries or even millennia before in more obscure esoteric teachings. We will return to them in the next chapter.

All this perhaps casts doubt on the appropriateness of the phrase *out-of-body* itself, at least as far as deliberate projections of consciousness into higher planes are concerned. Because the fundamental issue is that these involve the disconnection of the consciousness from the constraints of the human brain, perhaps *out-of-brain* journeying would be a better description of what these pioneers are doing – something to be born in mind from now on when the abbreviation OOB is used.

11

A STATE OF THE ART APPROACH

The theosophical movement was founded in London by Helena Blavatsky in 1875, and two of its best-known proponents were Charles Leadbeater and Annie Besant, who we mentioned briefly in chapter 5. Without wishing to be disparaging to any other approaches, it seems to me that its model of the seven planes is probably our best starting point when attempting to put together a contemporary, more intelligible and relevant, state-of-the-art version. First of all it's based on the same 'ancient wisdom' as esoteric Hinduism, often referred to as Vedanta, which gives it a strong foundation. Second it's framed in the English language so, as obscure as the descriptions and even naming conventions may appear to the uninitiated, it's significantly easier for us in the West to grasp than the Sanskrit-based frameworks from which it derives. By contrast the Jewish Qabalah, for example, still uses many Hebrew words, and therefore remains somewhat impenetrable except to its most devoted students.

One of the major problems with the theosophical approach, however, is that it's arguably a somewhat top-heavy model aimed at true devotees of its path. In other words it arguably places the emphasis more on the higher planes than on the lower. Yet it's the multiple potential delusions and illusions of the lower and intermediate planes that most of us will want to understand and avoid after we pass on. Moreover experiential rather than theoretical reports of the highest and most rarefied planes are far less common – and also more subjective and unreliable, because by their very nature they're far harder for mere human intelligence to both understand and describe. So I've chosen to switch the emphasis and to present what I refer to as an '*Astral* Routemap' model that's more heavily weighted towards the lower and intermediate planes.

Indeed I suspect that the leading theosophist Alfred Sinnett would endorse this approach, since he admitted that he and his colleagues were perhaps somewhat elitist:[1]

> One might laboriously trace the way mistakes were made in the beginning, but as regards authentic teaching from the Masters, on the strength of which the theosophical movement was launched, the subject of astral life immediately following the death of the physical body was simply neglected. Somehow we were drifted in the beginning into concerning ourselves with the gigantic principles governing human evolution on a large scale, and disregarded opportunities of understanding our immediate future better than before, in a way which painfully reminds one of the old story about the star gazer who fell into the ditch.

So what amendments have I made? If we refer to the table, I've renamed the highest plane the 'metaconscious', and condensed three of the higher planes of theosophy into one, the 'superconscious'. I have then separated the astral into 'upper', 'mid' and 'lower' because each of these seems to involve very different *qualities* of experience. The 'near-earth' is also separately designated to allow distinctions to be made between how incarnates and discarnates interact with the earth environment.[2] These distinctions are more fully explained in the next chapter.

Finally, when we come to the vivid descriptions of the various planes we'll discover that the energies of the lower astral are far denser than those of the mid and upper astral – indeed so dense that some would argue it operates at a lower frequency even than that of the earth and near-earth planes, and that departed spirits can *sink down* into it from the latter.[3] I have followed this convention in the Astral Routemap model, even though in terms of the order of the chapters I deal with the near-earth *before* the lower astral, because that seems to reflect the order in which they'll actually be experienced by some unfortunate discarnates.

A COMPARISON OF THE PLANES	
Theosophy [4]	*Astral Routemap*
7 Divine/Logoic	Metaconscious
6 Monadic 5 Spiritual/Nirvanic 4 Buddhic/Intuitional	Superconscious
3B Causal/Devachanic 3A Mental	Mental
2 Astral/Emotional	Upper Astral Mid Astral
1B Etheric 1A Physical	Near-Earth Incarnatory or Earth Lower Astral

12

THE ASTRAL ROUTEMAP MODEL

To give us some initial context let's take a brief introductory look at each of the planes, and at what their inhabitants get up to, before we explore them in more detail in the remaining chapters.

THE INCARNATORY OR EARTH PLANE

Of course we're all familiar with this plane since it's the one we're currently focussed in, but remember it potentially encompasses experiences of other human, earth-like realities too.

THE NEAR-EARTH PLANE

The evidence suggests that, without prior warning of what to expect, most departed spirits will initially find themselves in the equivalent of the earth plane, except they'll discover they can't influence it as they used to – and this may be extremely confusing, at least at first. In other words they can't move objects and other people don't take any notice of them, indeed they might even walk right through them. They may feel hugely drawn to trying to comfort their loved ones, often in vain, and may be 'held' close to the earth plane by the intense energetic pull of their friends' and families' grief. Yet soon enough most will find themselves able to move on to the mid astral, sometimes with assistance from both incarnate and discarnate helpers and guides.

But, as we saw in the Preface, the near-earth also plays host to trapped spirits who continue to be ignorant of their passing, or are attracted by unfinished business, or simply can't conceive of anything other than earthly life. These may find it harder to move on and, although helpers are always on hand to rescue them, not all are open to this assistance.

THE LOWER ASTRAL PLANES

The lower astral is where departed spirits with more serious issues tend to find themselves. They will usually start off in the near-earth and then find themselves drawn, indeed sinking down, into lower astral environments. The key distinction between the two, apart from their energetic frequency, is that the lower astral planes are no longer shared with incarnate humans. As to their inhabitants, they tend to be so emotionally disturbed that they create their own tormented environment, or join others of like mind in one that already exists. Here they remain until they grow tired or more inquisitive, and open up to the help that again is always on hand.

The lower astral encompasses a wide variety of planes, with the most deluded and emotionally warped personalities sinking into the lowest – from which most truly horrific and hellish descriptions of the afterlife derive.

THE MID ASTRAL PLANES

Those who've spent time in the lower planes should sooner or later be attracted or retrieved into the relative 'light' of the mid astral. Meanwhile those departed spirits who expect to have some form of afterlife and have had time to prepare themselves for it will tend to transition straight into these planes, although again sometimes with assistance. As always there are multiple layers or sub-planes within the mid astral, each corresponding to a level of vibration, and departed spirits will be attracted to that which most resonates with their energy and level of awareness. All we can probably say is that the greater the healing and acclimatisation required, the lower the entry level will be.

Any direct progression to these somewhat higher levels of

vibration is often accompanied by initially overwhelming feelings of freedom, of euphoria and even of love – as in most NDEs, for example. But we shouldn't let this mask the fact that, as 'heavenly' as some of these environments may appear, they still involve greater or lesser degrees of illusion, and their inhabitants' awareness may even be in stasis and not progressing at all. Perhaps the most obvious examples of this are religious congregations of all sizes and denominations who continue to play out the rituals of their faith with devout earnestness, unaware of the more expansive states of awareness available to them.

THE UPPER ASTRAL PLANES

The distinction between the mid and upper astral seems in practice to be somewhat blurred, but the main difference I want to emphasise is that in the latter the illusions are starting to fall away and real progression is beginning to occur in terms of expansion of consciousness. Initially this may only take the form of sporadic visits to 'halls of learning' and other library or university-type environments, but the stasis is ended – and that's why I include the upper astral with the other higher planes in the main chapter layout. Some departed spirits may engage in this kind of progressive activity relatively swiftly, while others might take considerably longer to break free from the charms of the various illusory heavens.

THE MENTAL PLANES

Entrance to these planes requires the shedding of the astral body, or the 'second death' as it's sometimes called. This means that while there may still be some sense of form and of space, the environment is generally less concrete and more fluid, and the level of energy vibration is significantly higher. While the astral planes are primarily characterised by emotion, the mental are primarily characterised by pure thought.

The inhabitants of these planes may also start to have some level of awareness of the other personalities projected by the supersoul of which they form part.

THE SUPERCONSCIOUS PLANES

This is where planes start to lose any sense of form and everything is becoming timeless. The inhabitants have almost certainly achieved a state of superconsciousness whereby they not only have an awareness of all the other personalities projected by their supersoul, but are also in the process of remerging or reblending with this higher level of consciousness and are therefore sharing its hugely expanded awareness. Nevertheless they retain a strong sense of individuality, even if not of separateness, and may well still be engaged in various high-level guidance and coordination activities relating to the earth plane.

THE METACONSCIOUS PLANES

There undoubtedly exist planes even beyond the superconscious which would exist at least partly outside of our system, so we can have little concept of their nature. But we can speculate that at least some of the inhabitants of these planes would be fully reintegrated supersouls who are ready to involve themselves in new creative ventures in other systems.

13

PRELUDE TO REMAINING PARTS

The Astral Routemap model we've established here in Part 2 can only be an approximation at best, but compared to more traditional or esoteric models it should be more easily accessible to ordinary people – and more relevant in helping us to prepare to navigate the various planes our consciousness is most likely to be attracted to after death. So, now that we've established our basic framework, we can endeavour to find out what's really going on in these planes, using the vivid descriptions painted by OOB explorers as well as by departed spirits channelling their experiences back to us. Remember it's because these reports come from those who've experienced them *first-hand* that what we'll be presented with is some of the most reliable, contemporary and wide-ranging evidence ever collated.

Having said that we need to consider a couple of important, final preliminaries before we begin our journey through the afterlife.

THE CONTINUATION OF THE PERSONALITY

The first point that needs to be emphasised is that there can be no doubt that our individual human personality survives its passing on from the earth plane entirely intact. Hopefully our consciousness will alter and indeed expand in time, but all the evidence suggests that our thoughts, feelings, memories and psychological makeup remain exactly as before when we first transition to the other side. This is what various channelled sources have to say on the matter:

> When the soul leaves the body it remains exactly the same as when it was in the body... It retains the mind, knowledge, experience, the habits of thought, the inclinations; they remain exactly as they were.[1]

> You who think a spirit has changed all his thoughts and desires at the moment of dissolution, how little you understand conditions beyond the grave.[2]

> One of the great facts of spirit life is that souls are exactly the same the instant after passing into spirit life as they were the instant before.[3]

> We are born into the next world with all our limitations, with all our narrowness of outlook, with all our affections and dislikes. We are, in short, thoroughly human.[4]

To reinforce the point a variety of OOB pioneers express exactly the same view:

> Almost all the people who arrive from this world are as astonished as they can be to find that they are alive and that they are just as human as ever... and that nothing at all has changed... We take with us everything that pertains to our character except our earthly body... We want, wish, crave, think, ponder, are moved, love and intend the way we used to.[5]

> Death makes no sort of difference in a man's moral and mental nature, and the change of state caused by passing from one world to another takes away his physical body, but leaves the man as he was.[6]

> As man is prior to death, so he will be after death... his virtues and vices remain the same.[7]

> I have found that we retain a great many of the characteristics of who we are in this life, both the positive and the negative.[8]

> Our desires, our thoughts, our interests, all these will continue after the dissolution of our material body.[9]

All this of course runs directly contrary to two relatively widespread sets of beliefs. First those of the traditional reincarnation model, which expects the departed spirit to remerge with its higher self in pretty short order, thereby having instant access to the higher wisdom of all its past lives. Second those of people who insist that, because any sense of individuality is only an illusion, the soul remerges with the universal Source on the instant of death. In fact several of our channelled sources rather scoff at such an idea:

> Individuality is not eliminated, but rather accentuated... There is no breach or break in the continuity of individual existence.[10]

> It is folly to think that because we swapped in our physical bodies for spiritual ones we automatically have achieved oneness with God.[11]

The plain fact is that neither of these sets of beliefs is supported by the evidence, even for people who develop a spiritual enlightenment of the highest order while incarnate.

THE INDIVIDUALITY OF THE EXPERIENCE

Although we can take the many common elements from our many and varied sources and group them together to form a coherent picture of what awaits, that should never detract from the way in which no two individuals will have exactly the same experience of the afterlife in every detail. Everyone's human experience is unique, so why wouldn't their afterlife experience be also? As the first great OOB pioneer Emanuel Swedenborg points out:[12] 'Hell is never the same for any two people, nor is heaven.' Some degree of subjectivity is bound to come into play, therefore.

Indeed how could this not be the case when we consider our experience on earth? If the family members who share a house were asked to describe what it's like to live there, there would be a great deal of consistency about the basic layout and so on. But as soon as they started to describe their feelings and personal life experiences while therein, the uniqueness of these would become apparent. The same would be true to an increasingly greater extent if multiple people were to describe living in the same street, town or country.

Imagine, then, that they start to describe visiting other countries on holiday – that is, places where they don't live most of the time. The variation in their descriptions of these locations will increase still further, and that's before we factor in the ever-varying emotional conditions and so on of their visit. But even in these cases there will be similarities. For example, Europeans travelling to various central African countries would still be likely to describe – as a very broad generalisation – the heat, the terrible poverty in many rural areas, the stark contrast between poverty and affluence in some cities, the cheerfulness and hospitality of the people despite the foregoing, and the fact that most of them have very dark skin.

There will always remain some core consistencies. So it is with the afterlife realms.

PART THREE

PLANES OF CONFUSION DELUSION & OBSESSION

At death, another quantum leap occurs that is shocking as they discover themselves to be popped back into another vibrational state that often triggers great fear. Very few beings upon your human plane have entered death consciously.

Jeshua, 'The Way of Mastery'

PLEASE NOTE: If you take the view you're balanced enough that you won't be going anywhere near the lowest planes when you pass on, feel free to skip to the final chapter of this part.

14

THE NEAR-EARTH PLANE

We saw in chapter 12 that the near-earth plane is typically inhabited by those to whom death comes unexpectedly, in an accident or via sudden illness, and who as a result and for a time may not even realise they're dead. Similarly those who haven't ever believed in an afterlife and have expected their consciousness to be extinguished on the death of their physical body tend, on finding themselves still conscious and in an astral body that still feels physical, to refuse to believe they've passed on. Such spirits naturally experience a degree of confusion, especially when incarnate humans ignore them and so on.

As we noted in the Preface, particularly in the modern Western world we're generally very poor at preparing for the afterlife, as a result of which a significant proportion of departed spirits will find themselves in this plane after passing, even if only for a short time. Those in higher realms try to reach out and help those who don't automatically pass through the near-earth planes, but if they're very confused and somewhat self-absorbed they may close themselves off to the presence of the helpers and guides who are always around but often go unseen. Moreover they may remain effectively trapped for months or even years of earth time although, as we'll find in chapter 23, elapsed time is experienced very differently in other planes. So the longer-term inhabitants of this plane we're primarily concerned with here won't necessarily be hugely emotionally disturbed – but they nevertheless tend to be confused, or very much wrapped up in their former earthly life and finding it hard to leave behind, or both.

Let us now turn, then, to our three types of evidence to see what our sources have to say about this plane. We will always commence with channelled material, before turning to NDE and, last but by no means least, OOB reports.

CHANNELLED MATERIAL

ANONYMOUS (VIA EMILY FRENCH AND EDWARD RANDALL)

In chapter 2 we met Emily French and Edward Randall, and one of the communicants in their séances provides this view of continued religious devotion in the near-earth plane:[1]

> While the majority there know they have left the body, others have such an imperfect appreciation of the change, or have led such immoral lives, that they are not conscious of the fact... One would think that an individual, having passed through the portal called death and finding nothing as he had been taught, or as he had believed, would give up the old notions... but, strange as it may seem, many even then cling to the old beliefs as if in fear, as if to doubt were sacrilege, and in many ways excuse their failure to find what they expected. They go into your churches and mingle with other people, a great invisible host, hear the same old teachings, say the same creeds and continue in the same mental attitude until some condition is brought about that guides them into the avenue of knowledge.

ROBERT BENSON (VIA ANTHONY BORGIA)

One fascinating source of channelled information is *Life in the World Unseen* by the medium Anthony Borgia.[2] This book was transmitted via automatic writing by a former friend he met as a young teenager, Robert Benson. The son of a former Archbishop of Canterbury and a priest himself, Benson passed on in 1914 having written a number of religious works. He had also been a natural psychic while incarnate, but under pressure from the Church had attempted to restrict his gifts to only those few which fitted in with orthodox doctrine, which in turn massively restricted what he transmitted to others via his books. For these reasons he was now highly desirous of correcting the inaccuracies of the Christian theology he'd been advocating. It is unclear exactly when the transmissions for Borgia's book occurred, but unusually it was some years after Benson's passing – indeed he describes how dedicated he had to be in learning how to properly communicate with someone still on the earth plane.[3] The book's two parts were originally published separately in the 1940s then combined into one volume in 1954. He dictated two follow-ups to Borgia, but the first is by far the most useful source for our purposes.

Here then is Benson describing the problem of attempting to help those who don't realise they've passed on:[4]

> There are a surprising number of people who do not realise they have passed from the earth at the death of the physical body. Resolutely they will not believe that they are what the earth calls 'dead'. They are dimly aware that some sort of change has taken place, but what that change is they are not prepared to say. Some, after a little explanation – and even demonstration – can grasp what has actually happened; others are stubborn, and will be convinced only after prolonged reasoning. In the latter case we are ofttimes obliged to leave such a soul for a while to allow a little quiet contemplation to work its way. We know we shall be sought out the instant that soul feels the power of our reasoning.

PHILIP GILBERT (VIA HIS MOTHER ALICE)

Alice Gilbert was a British medium who'd developed a strong telepathic link with her son Philip while he was away at sea. So much so that when he died in a road accident it was only a matter of days before he came through to her from the afterlife, and together they worked out a method of daily telepathic communication. The messages in *Philip in Two Worlds* cover the first three months after his death in 1945, while *Philip in the Spheres* covers those received in the following three years.

Here he summarises why departed spirits find themselves in

the near-earth or even lower planes:[5]

> Many people die prematurely of illnesses which are short and sudden, or in accidents like mine, and their physical link is strong. Others, even when old, have not learned much and are so obsessed by earthly predilections that they continue to live in them afterwards, in a complete illusion, created by their own strongly woven thought images. Really unpleasant types – and you'd be surprised: there are not so many as you would think... – stay in their illusions, but in compulsory company with others like them, or with those they have wronged if the latter are full of resentful hate.

ARTHUR FORD (VIA RUTH MONTGOMERY)

A rather more recent channelled source is Ruth Montgomery's *A World Beyond* in which her former friend, the famous US medium and psychic Arthur Ford, comes through to her just after his death in 1971 – using automatic writing on her typewriter and a 'control spirit' called Lily. Ford tends to provide general commentary about what happens on the other side, rather than citing his own or other specific cases, so to some extent his material is more conjectural than most.[6] Nevertheless some of it is worth quoting. Here he provides comfort for those who might have lost loved ones to sudden accidents, war and similar who, given our opening comments, might be concerned about them becoming trapped:[7]

> They are at first astonished to find that they are here and that those on your plane no longer recognise their presence, but if they were not antagonistic to the idea of a hereafter they will begin to adjust without too much delay. They sometimes sleep a little longer than those who, after long illness, know that death is at hand, but when they have committed no great wrong, there are so many of us here willing to help them through the adjustment that they rapidly begin to understand and are sometimes more eager than others to plunge zestfully into the new work which awaits them.

We will repeatedly encounter this concept of a degree of 'sleep' being required by those making the transition as we go along.

NDE REPORTS

GEORGE RITCHIE

In 1943 twenty-year-old medical student George Ritchie was recruited by the US army, which was desperately short of doctors for its coming war effort. Soon afterwards he contracted pneumonia and suddenly found himself having an NDE, as narrated many years later in his 1978 book *Return from Tomorrow*.[8] Although he's escorted around the afterlife realms by a being he resolutely identifies as Jesus, and as a result many of his descriptions have a somewhat Christian bias, he nevertheless provides some fascinating eye-witness reports.

Initially he experiences the panoramic 'life review' reported so often as an element of NDEs, which we'll concentrate on fully in chapter 22:[9] 'Everything that had ever happened to me was simply there, in full view, contemporary and current, all seemingly taking place at that moment. On all sides of us was what I could only think of as an enormous mural – except that the figures on it were three-dimensional, moving and speaking.'

More important for our current purposes, though, is that he then finds himself being flown over the streets of various towns and cities, where he sees various departed spirits desperately trying to contact incarnate people.[10] Each is engaged in a repetitive cycle of patterned behaviour concerning something that was hugely important to them in their earthly life and from which they simply can't release themselves. Each, too, experiences constant unfulfilment of their desire because the people they're trying to talk to simply can't hear them.

He describes, for example, a discarnate businessman yelling instructions at a former colleague as he goes about his business oblivious; a long-deceased mother still nagging her son about his wife and so on, even though they now appear to be of a similar age to her; and others following former loved ones, begging for a forgiveness that never comes.

OOB REPORTS

CHARLES LEADBEATER AND ANNIE BESANT

Charles Leadbeater, the OOB-projecting theosophist who we met briefly in earlier chapters, emphasises the role that poor education about death plays:[11]

> We have so mismanaged our teaching in these Western countries on the subject of immortality that usually a dead man finds it difficult to believe that he is dead, simply because he still sees and hears, thinks and feels. 'I am not dead', he will often say, 'I am alive as much as ever, and better than I ever was before.' Of course, he is; but that is exactly what he ought to have expected, if he had been properly taught.

This idea of being 'better than before' – in other words being free of all disease, feeling lighter and sharper and so on – is regularly reported and a fundamental aspect of any smooth transition, as we'll see in chapter 23. Meanwhile Leadbeater's fellow theosophist Annie Besant is pretty uncompromising when she suggests that a significant proportion of departed spirits spend at least some time in the near-earth plane:[12]

> These... are folk whose interests were bound up in the trivial and petty objects of life, who set their hearts on trifles, as well as those who allowed their lower natures to rule them, and who died with the appetites still active and desirous of physical enjoyment... They are held... in the neighbourhood of their physical attractions. They are mostly dissatisfied, uneasy, restless, with more or less of suffering according to the vigour of the wishes they cannot gratify; some even undergo positive pain from this cause, and are long delayed ere these earthly longings are exhausted. Many unnecessarily lengthen their stay by seeking to communicate with the earth, in whose interests they are entangled.

CAROLINE LARSEN

We saw in chapter 5 that some of the most important early OOB pioneers, such as Vincent Turvey, Oliver Fox and Frederick

Sculthorp, are little remembered but extremely enlightening. Another example is Caroline Larsen. A Dane who moved to Vermont, she had her first spontaneous experience in 1910 when already in early middle age. By the time she published *My Travels in the Spirit World* in 1927 she'd had many, many more spanning the entire spectrum of the afterlife planes, always assisted by the same anonymous guide. Here she explains why it's so easy for the deceased not to realise they're dead:[13]

> One wakes in the astral as one left the material. So far as my state of mind was concerned I was merely continuing earthly existence. So with all spirits. Many of them, because of this condition of mind together with the natural feeling of their astral body, are deluded into believing that they still live in the material and they endeavour to carry on life as they have always done... [They] suspect dimly that something strange has overtaken them but they refuse absolutely to accept the realisation and in order to shut it more completely out of their minds they deliberately continue their familiar activity of the world. Thus with their minds ill-attuned to their conditions they seem unable to reason clearly about their state until by slow degrees they are adjusted to it...
>
> So they all continue in their diverse customary activities of earthly life only to find constantly some inexplicable barriers existing between them and their desires. They live as in that dream in which one attempts accustomed actions only to find oneself bewilderingly baffled in every futile attempt. They are filled with surprise that relatives and friends ignore them, and that their usual aims fail completely... Everywhere in my journeys I found these new citizens of spirit land thronging the streets of cities, passing in and out of houses, travelling on trains and voyaging on steamers. In fact, wherever mortals habituate there are to be found also denizens of the spirit world. So, in reality, there are as many spirits inhabiting this earth as there are mortals. It was a strange sight to me... to look down a busy street and to see spirits and mortals intermingling with one another.

She then goes on to provide specific accounts of various confused or obsessed spirits who've been in the near-earth plane for varying lengths of time.[14] The woman running around at her own funeral, yelling at unhearing ears that she's still alive, and seemingly unable to take on board that it's her body in the coffin; the royal queen unable to understand why she's being ignored; another royal queen who still feels she has unfinished work to do; a man so addicted to alcohol that even in the process of dying he keeps coming out of his body, each time unsuccessfully grasping at a bottle of whisky on the floor, until finally he leaves it for good and staggers off; the young actor who can't catch the attention of the waiters in his favourite New York nightspot; and finally the entire tribe of native Indian warriors who still haunt the basement of a Manhattan theatre, repeatedly going on forays where they furiously attempt to scalp some of the living 'pale faces' who've taken away their land.

Less disturbed, but no less trapped, are the former president and his wife still stalking the corridors of the White House:

> They had prevented themselves from advancing simply because their minds had been and were still securely linked to that environment where they in the flesh had enjoyed so much power and glory. They were jealously regarding everything which had been and was even yet happening in that famous place. Until they develop a more idealistic conception of existence, they will remain in their old limited environment. Yet they were guilty of no great or malicious wrong; they were earthbound simply because of their low ideals.

Similarly the aristocratic lady held fast by her jewellery collection:[15]

> In one room a lady was pacing the floor with slow deliberation. Her stately figure, her aristocratic and refined manner caught and held my attention... Approaching her, I asked, 'Why are you here?' With a graceful gesture she replied with regret, yet with apparent resignation, 'How could I leave these?' I looked down at the point she designated and saw with surprise a wonderful

> collection of sparkling jewels on which she fixed her eyes. I understood: the jewels which she had owned on earth still possessed her soul. They held her now as then, and linked her to earth with a chain that only she could break.

ROBERT MONROE

Moving on to more recent reports, we've already met OOB supremo Robert Monroe in the earlier chapters, and he encounters exactly the same kind of bewildered spirits on his near-earth travels:[16]

> They didn't or couldn't or wouldn't realise they were no longer physical. They were physically dead, no more physical body. Thus they kept trying to be physical, to do and be what they had been, to continue physically one way or another. Bewildered, some spent all of their activity in attempting to communicate with friends and loved ones still in bodies or with anyone else who might come along, all to no avail. Others were held attracted to physical sites in which they had instilled great meaning or importance during their human lifetime... Still others interpreted their change in status as simply a bad dream or nightmare, and were waiting and hoping to wake up soon.

GORDON PHINN

Another modern OOB pioneer is Gordon Phinn, a Scot who moved to Canada. His first book, *Eternal Life and How to Enjoy It*, was published in 2004 and contains an account of the afterlife that his guide Henry began to channel six years earlier.[17] His second, *More Adventures in Eternity*, came out four years later and contains some further channelled material, as well as moving more into his own lucid dreaming and OOB experiences. Because he's best-known as an OOB pioneer we'll include even his channelled material under the former heading.

Here he describes how, while OOB, he sees a local lady who remains stuck in her familiar environment:[18]

> The lady that was living the high life in Casa Loma (a local palatial home, now a tourist attraction) still seems to be there,

and still insists she's doing no one any harm. And as far as I can tell, that is quite true: she has no interest in harassing the living, and is happy to follow the imagined daily routines of the aristocratic lady.

THE EFFECT OF EXCESSIVE GRIEF

This is a topic of huge importance that we introduced briefly in the Preface. For example Gilbert begins by generally stressing how the emotions of the recently departed can be hugely affected by those of the loved ones they've left behind – because in their new environment emotions are felt much more keenly, while the thoughts and feelings of loved ones still incarnate are now laid completely bare, with no pretence possible:[19]

> Let us assume that an average, not very instructed, basically good-hearted person comes over, after a serious illness which has given him warning of approaching death. He opens his eyes and finds himself outside himself, as I did... He looks round and everything appears much as usual, but he soon discovers that nothing is solid: he can glide through a shut door. Very often, he is deeply interested in the behaviour of his family, and this, if he has sympathy and love, is often the first big snag. He finds he can see people's minds working and this may be very confusing if he is not very advanced, because of the tangled blur of thought images – so few people think in a clear-cut way. He gets almost physically the impact of the grief of his loved ones. It is a terrible sensation...
>
> Usually he thinks of someone he has left on earth and if the tie is fairly strong, he finds himself suddenly there, by the dear one's side! Then, sometimes, his troubles begin! There is bitter grief. He sees all the lugubrious details of his funeral. He may see his family squabbling over his bits and pieces. He sees their thoughts and learns far more about them than he knew before.

He then continues with the stark but common warning that the grief of the bereaved can prevent the departed from properly moving on to new and wonderful experiences:[20]

> Great grief, persistent and self-centred on the part of the bereaved, keeps the departed tied up, frustrated and helpless, unless they are spiritually advanced enough to make a thought gesture of separation, of advancement, and even then they are partially tethered.

This may sound harsh, but whether we like it or not we must learn to recognise that prolonged grief *is* self-centred – unless it's on behalf of children, for example, though even then especially younger children can be some of the most resilient in accepting a parent's passing.

Another excellent and very early channelled source of information about the afterlife is *A Wanderer in the Spirit Lands*, published in London in 1896 by A Farnese. Almost nothing seems to be known about him other than that in his preface he indicates he was able to channel several entities via automatic writing. The communicating spirit for this book was a former Italian aristocrat and artist called Franchezzo, and again nothing seems to be known about him now, although in the preface Farnese indicates that he sometimes materialised during séances and was recognised by mutual friends on a number of occasions. In any case, Franchezzo echoes Gilbert's thoughts:[21]

> I saw many mortals who mourned for the dear ones they had loved and lost, weeping most bitter tears because they could see them no more. And all the time I saw those for whom they mourned standing beside them, seeking with all their power to show that they still lived... The living could not see or hear them, and the poor sorrowing spirits could not go away to their bright spheres because while those they had left so mourned for them they were tied to the earth plane by the chains of their love, and the light of their spirit lamps grew dim and faded as they thus hung about the atmosphere of earth in helpless sorrow.

It is heart-rending to hear several of French and Randall's communicants lucidly repeat this concern:[22]

> If only those in earth life knew that their sadness binds and

> holds us, stays our progress and development!
>
> The grief of my people kept me so sad at first that I was not able to see or think of anything but earthly sorrow. That is why grief for departed friends and relatives is so wrong, and is so harmful, both to those on earth and to those who come over. The longer the grief continues and the more hopeless it is, the more those mourned for are kept to earth. Instead of being able to go straight on when they come over, seeing and realising the beauty and wonders of their surroundings, and helping others to see them also, they are kept in a state of helpless grief, which renders them incapable of either helping themselves or others.
>
> This is a beautiful world in which I live, with opportunities beyond your conception. When earth conditions do not bind me I can attend great lectures, and in temples of music hear celestial song. But I am bound to the earth by the sorrow of my father and mother. They brood and weep, and sorrow for me as one dead, and that holds me like bands of steel, so that I can only at times do what other boys do. They don't understand that I am more alive than ever before... I could be so happy and accomplish so much, if they would let me go. Won't you go and tell them what I have said, and change their thoughts? Tell them that death is life boundless and endless, and our sphere is filled with happiness. Please promise.

This latter seems to suggest a particularly frustrating state of partially moving on and partially being held back. In the meantime another interesting channelled source is 'John', a departed spirit originally from England whose *Road of Many Ways* was vocally transmitted via an anonymous Cape Town medium and first published in 1975. Like some other sources he indicates that departed spirits are often energetically 'dragged back' to attend their own funerals whether they want to or not, and corroborates the harmfulness of prolonged and intense grief:[23] 'If only people could see the anguish caused to the departed one by their distress then they would try not to grieve.' But to balance out this section he also emphasises that the calm, genuinely loving thoughts that emerge after initial grief has passed are hugely appreciated by those who have passed on:[24]

> If you send a call of love into this world it will find the one for whom it is meant. It need not necessarily call that person back to you... but if in this world we receive such a thought from earth we magnify it and send it back immediately, thus opening a channel to become a form of communication – it goes on all the time. Because of this we are aware of what our loved ones are doing, are able to listen in and sometimes transmit help. Those thoughts of love, so disturbing to us in the early days, are a great comfort later on. When one knows one has been away for a long, long time, gone so long from sight and almost forgotten, and a thought comes winging its way from earth and reaches us here, then it gives us great joy and makes possible a return visit, perhaps just for a moment, to be near that person. Although we may meet our loved ones in the hours of sleep when they travel to the lower regions of our world, their thoughts mean so much to us for they sustain the contact.

We will return to this idea of meeting up with departed loved ones while we sleep in chapter 26. Meanwhile, from an OOB perspective, both Leadbeater and Besant place great emphasis on similar warnings about intense grief. Yet, like John, they're also clear about the benefits of sending thoughts of love to the departed, and of wishing them a swift and trauma-free transition and a wonderful onward journey thereafter:

> There is another and much more frequently exercised influence which may seriously retard a disembodied entity on his way to the heaven world, and that is the intense and uncontrolled grief of his surviving friends or relatives. It is one among many melancholy results of the terribly inaccurate and even irreligious view that we in the West have for centuries been taking on death, that we not only cause ourselves an immense amount of wholly unnecessary pain over this temporary parting from our loved ones, but we often also do serious injury to those for whom we bear so deep an affection by means of this very regret which we feel so acutely...

> It would be well if those whose comrades have passed on before them would learn from these undoubted facts the duty of restraining for the sake of those friends a grief which, however natural it may be, is yet in its essence selfish. Not that occult teaching counsels forgetfulness of the dead – far from it; but it does suggest that a man's affectionate remembrance of his departed friend is a force which, if properly directed into the channel of earnest good wishes for his progress towards the heaven world and his quiet passage through the intermediate state, might be of real value to him, whereas when wasted in mourning for him and longing to have him back again it is not only useless but harmful.[25]

> Souls, while in this region, may also very easily have their attention drawn to the earth, even although they would not spontaneously have turned back to it, and this disservice is too often done to them by the passionate grief and craving for their beloved presence by friends left behind on earth. The thought-forms set up by these longings throng round them, bet against them, and oftentimes arouse them if they are peacefully sleeping, or violently draw their thoughts to earth if they are already conscious... This unwitting selfishness on the part of friends on earth does mischief to their dear ones that they would themselves be the first to regret... Everyone can help his beloved departed by sending to them thoughts of love and peace and longing for their swift progress through the kamalokic world and their liberation from astral fetters.[26]

Coming more up-to-date, we saw in chapter 5 that Monroe founded his own Institute in 1972 and embarked on a formal program of research into OOB experiences. One of the early explorers in this program was Rosalind McKnight, and her experiences over the next eleven years form the basis of her first book, *Cosmic Journeys*, although it didn't come out until 1999, followed in 2005 by *Soul Journeys*. Her spirit guide provides exactly the same advice about balancing short-term grief with long-term love:[27] 'If the grief continues too long it holds the loved one down in the earth's energies... Truly loving beings will grieve intensely for a brief period of time, and then release their loved ones to go about their new life in the spirit world.'

SPIRITS WHO ATTACH TO LIVING HUMANS

The OOB explorer Waldo Vieira, who we met in chapter 5, provides a clear description of witnessing this phenomenon:[28]

> For the first time, I became aware of several extraphysical consciousnesses riding in cars next to human drivers and passengers. I noticed this in a general manner, as well as specific cases in a gas station and in a dune buggy on the street in which a young couple was riding. Some of the persons passing by were accompanied by one or more intimately connected extraphysical consciousnesses, seeming to be composite persons. A young man, under the impulsive influence of an extraphysical consciousness attached to him, was speaking loudly inside a convertible. It was quite astonishing to witness the cool, overt intrusion. It is incredible how persons can be influenced... Intruders are truly energetic parasites.

I wouldn't wish to alarm people with the idea that intrusive 'possession' by deceased spirits is widespread, although less harmful 'attachments' may be fairly common. Nevertheless we will encounter a couple of rather worse examples of only temporary possession in chapter 18.

15

THOSE WHO DON'T BELIEVE IN AN AFTERLIFE

Let us now take a moment to consider the fate of those who have always believed only in the material world they can touch and feel, and who similarly believe that the death of the physical brain extinguishes all consciousness. As we've already noted this kind of strident, intellectualised materialism has made significant strides in the Western world in recent decades. If only its adherents could be exposed to the warnings that follow – which are so insistent and consistent I've deemed it appropriate to give them their own chapter.

CHANNELLED MATERIAL

TE LAWRENCE (VIA JANE SHERWOOD)

In terms of channelled reports of the various planes, one of the finest sources is the work of the British medium Jane Sherwood.[1] A friend gave her a channelled message purporting to be from her husband Andrew not long after he was killed in WWI and, because it included certain private details about her life since his death, and in any case she missed him terribly, it piqued her interest enough for her to start visiting various mediums in an attempt to make further contact. But it took many years of little success mixed with a great deal of scepticism before she was advised to try automatic writing herself in the late 1930s. The spirit that worked through her first of all soon revealed himself to be none other than TE Lawrence, of 'Arabia' fame, although initially he insisted on anonymity and on being referred to as 'Scott' in any published work. He was soon joined by another discarnate spirit who she simply refers to as 'EK', and also, eventually, by her beloved husband. Their messages were published in two volumes in the early 1940s, *The Psychic Bridge* and *The Country Beyond*, although these were later combined into one book bearing the latter name.

Intriguingly from an evidential point of view, Sherwood's automatic script was completely different for each of the three entities. In fact she provides an example of each in her book, and indicates that she held the pen so lightly she could barely influence the style. In the case of her husband the script was a close match for his handwriting. But more important, not being interested in evidential proofs, she herself made no effort to compare Lawrence's own handwriting with that of Scott. By contrast, armed with the internet and a healthy lack of expectation, I easily found a reproduction of a letter written by Lawrence and was fascinated to find there's a pretty close match (see Figure 1).[2]

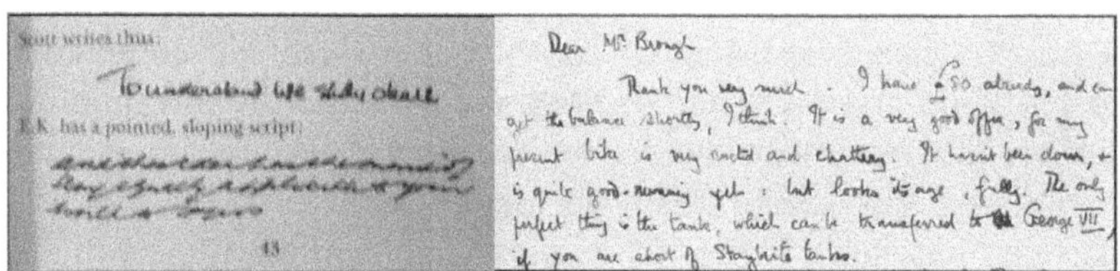

Figure 1: Comparison of Scott's automatic writing on the left with Lawrence's handwriting on the right

It is equally intriguing that OOB explorer Frederick Sculthorp in passing mentions a woman he knew from a spiritualist circle:[3] 'This lady had a remarkable gift of objective clairvoyance, and could describe a spirit in great detail. She once described a spirit, a man in Arab clothes who was with me, but said that she could see that he was not an Arab, but Lawrence of Arabia, and then passed on a message that, although she did not know it, at once proved to me that it was indeed Lawrence.' Quite what Sculthorp's interest in Lawrence was is never made clear but, while this is only anecdotal and not objective proof of anything, it's surely worth mentioning none the less.

More to the point for our current purposes, all three of Sherwood's sources reveal fascinating details of the afterlife, although each is operating from a different plane due to their different stages of post-mortem development. Indeed *The Country Beyond* is relatively unique in that, whereas automatic writing usually involves a medium who in real time is entirely unaware of the messages they're recording, Sherwood seems to remain entirely conscious throughout. This is especially the case during the theoretical interchanges between her three communicants that dominate the latter half of the book, even to the point of her interjecting with her own observations and questions – and sometimes being rebuked for so doing, instead of acting as a 'clear channel'. Yet the use of different handwriting still suggests that an element of automation was involved.

Perhaps most important of all, Lawrence eventually decided to dictate a complete afterlife autobiography, which he insisted should be called *Post-Mortem Journal*, and which was completed in 1959 and first published in 1964. It seems that by this time his further progress meant he no longer cared about anonymity, and in any case the details meant his identity was pretty obvious. His account has such a ring of honesty and authenticity, with its searing insights and complete absence of ego, that it surely deserves to be considered as one of the finest sources of material about the afterlife available to us. So I make no apology for commencing with the following lengthy reproduction of his initial afterlife experience which, despite its sombre tone, is as instructive as it's eloquent and fascinating – and introduces many themes that we'll encounter repeatedly. Indeed perhaps *this*, coupled with the more enjoyable material that will follow in later chapters, turns out to be his greatest gift to humanity.

In the accident that claimed his life in 1935 in rural Dorset, he parted company with his beloved Brough Superior SS100 motorcycle while trying to avoid two boys on bicycles. He never regained consciousness and passed on six days later, but his own account merely opens with:[4] 'A shattering blow, darkness rent with interludes of throbbing agony and finally merciful cessation of pain.' He gradually finds his awareness stabilising, but his is a fine example of someone not initially realising their change in condition, having been of the belief that death is the end of everything. He seems to spend no time at all in the near-earth plane and, after initial drowsiness, his experience immediately has a somewhat depressing and unnerving quality:

> There came a time when I could no longer drowse my fears away. The sense of identity grew stronger and with it came a tumult of emotions and hurried anxious thoughts. Unwillingly I had to awake to a formless world of which I seemed the only inhabitant... Becoming aware of my body I found myself on my feet, surprised to find movement so light and easy, but I was afraid to venture far in any direction because of the shadowy obstacles I sensed around. I fumbled in the dimness, seeking a way out of the grief that enveloped me. Where was I? Even if I had become blind and deaf surely there must be someone around to help me? I tried calling, but there was no response. What had happened?

We saw earlier that the life review is common to most NDEs, and here Lawrence experiences it too:

> At first my mind was entirely occupied with my predicament and the past did not concern me, but as I wandered now one, now another vision flashed across my mental retina. A ribbon of road, boys on bicycles, my cottage, and soon these discrete memories began to coalesce into a continuous series of past experiences. Before long I was racing back along the years faster and faster, helpless to stay the record and obliged to feel as well as to remember as my past unrolled back to the earliest childhood memories. I had come to a stand while this

> disquieting survey held me, and as it checked at the unconsciousness of the infant my own consciousness flickered out. At the very moment of oblivion I gasped with relief and just had time to think: this is really the end.

It is at this point that he realises he's dead yet still very much alive. He begins to discover that time is experienced differently in the afterlife, that his thoughts are instantly affecting his experience, and that he still seems to have what seems like a physical body – even though he feels much lighter and freer than before:

> After a long or short interval – how should I know? – I came to myself again, mildly surprised because I had not expected existence to continue and certainly had as yet no reason to welcome it. The dimness had lifted a little and a world of vague outlines was developing out of the mist; meadows, I thought, hedges and trees. Perhaps the blurred outlines in the distance were houses? A town perhaps, people. I did not want to meet people. For the first time I realised that I was naked, but apart from this embarrassment I shrank from my kind and even preferred the empty solitude. But in thinking of the town and what it might hold I found myself drifting towards it, and thus got my first indication of the way movement here is affected by thought. I obstinately resisted this drift toward the town and turned away to explore the open country.
>
> All this while, the light had been strengthening and the greyness lifting. Soon the dreary place could be distinguished as a gloomy November dusk, and I could move freely without the fear of stumbling into shadows and finding they were substance. I came upon a convenient bank and rested. I was not conscious of cold and forgot my nakedness. As I sat there it became possible to think more clearly and take stock of my position. All my known and familiar world was gone and if this was a nightmare I still had to abide the awakening. The startling impression that this was death became insistent, but if I had to accept that idea what became of my conviction that death ended it all? For I was certainly alive, if you could call it living, and it even appeared that my surroundings were taking

> on more substance and I myself more vitality. So any expectation that this was just a particularly persistent nightmare became unlikely. I felt my body; firm flesh. How odd! I tried to speak but only a throttled ghost of a sound came forth. I arose and walked and realised afresh how light and resilient my limbs felt. So back to my bank to think afresh.
>
> Suppose for the sake of argument that this was death; what kind of world was this? I thought with a pang of 'Sheol', a place of the shade. It was that, all right. Had Charon already rowed me over the dark river and was this the accursed Hades? If so, the Greeks had been right after all, as they nearly always were. My thought seemed as bound by shadows as my surroundings. All life and living was reduced to a monochrome. No sound, no movement, no light, no joy: only a dreary acquiescence in this half-light, half-living. A grievous lassitude invaded me. Existence, endurance: endurance, existence. How much better to have flickered out for good!
>
> How long this weary experience lasted I cannot guess. Weeks? Months? I walked about. I sat. I experimented with my new powers of motion. I even began to make recognisable sounds, and either I had got used to my conditions or my sight was sharpening for my vision was clearing. Moreover, the cloud of depression and despair had begun to lift from my mind and a desire for action began to stir. But what to do in this desert?

At this juncture things become rather more unsettling for Lawrence:

> My thoughts turned towards the town I had seen. If I had to come to terms with this existence I must first find out more about its conditions. In my wanderings I had long ago lost sight of the blur on the horizon and I had no idea of its direction. But as though the wish had the power to direct me, my steps were drawn in the right way and before long I saw the roofs and chimneys of a small town ahead...
>
> I decided to accost someone and ask for information, but the passing faces had in them no signs of friendliness so I wandered on oppressed by my loneliness. True, I could now hear clearly, I could speak and sight was becoming clearer. But

> whether the fault of my vision or a characteristic of the locality, the same dingy murk prevailed and the place and the people were all of a piece; hard-featured women with shrill, harsh voices, and men whose faces were marked by brutality and meanness, came from the houses and mingled uneasily in the streets.
>
> Near panic began to mount in me, and the more my loneliness and fear increased the more menacing seemed my surroundings. My only thought now was to get clear of the place, and no sooner was the decision formed than my feet drew me swiftly back to the outskirts and away from the gloomy place. I did not stop until I had put a considerable distance between myself and the last of the houses.

This grey town contains no incarnates and appears to exist in the lower astral, which we'll come on to properly in the next few chapters. But thankfully Lawrence's visit is only temporary. His account continues as he gradually senses a presence near him, but is confused about why he can't see whoever it is:[5]

> My new friend replied, 'You have got yourself into a very unhappy region and as I can see that you do not belong here I should like to help... You must have been in a wretched state of mind before you came here and that accounts for waking in this part of the world. We must get you into a happier condition before we can help you much.'
>
> As he spoke I saw that a light had diffused itself around us and I smiled with pleasure at the first brightness I had seen in this dreary Hades.
>
> 'Come, that is better already,' he said, and I felt warmth and reassurance stealing over me as he spoke.
>
> 'Now, if you are able, come with me,' he said, and although I thought this might not be so easy since as yet I could not see him, my feet were led and I went, keeping always near to the light and warmth of his presence.
>
> He took me quietly over an ever-brightening landscape and explained as we went that my newly developing senses had to be given time to adjust to their new world, and that this new world would only hold for me what I was capable of seeing in it.

> 'So the gloomy town was only a reflection of my state; or is it an actual place?' I asked.
>
> 'Unfortunately it is actual enough for those who want nothing better. They have not yet developed the power to live in any other way,' he replied. 'They make their own atmosphere by the emanations of their own rather horrid emotions and I see that you found it uncongenial enough to get free of it quickly. They are not very pleasant folk there and they might soon have sensed your difference and resented it, and then there might have been trouble. Not that they could have injured you in the physical way you are thinking of, but a lot of undesirable emotions would have been let loose and you would have suffered from these. To encounter active ill-will is for us a painful experience, but all this will become easier to understand when you know more about this world.'
>
> I explained that I had already discovered that a strong desire could be used as a directing agent, and that my fear and loathing of the place had helped me to get away from it.

This provides a wonderful introduction to the way our thoughts and emotions help to create our environment in the astral. Lawrence then asks his new companion to reveal their identity:

> 'My name is Mitchell,' he said. 'It won't convey anything to you but I work with newcomers and was here when you came into view.'
>
> I felt suddenly constrained and diffident and the change must have been obvious to him for he said: 'Don't do that, for God's sake, or I can't stay. You have to learn that your feelings create an atmosphere about you that alters your relationship to those you meet.'
>
> I shrank away and his light dimmed. In alarm I called to him and he heard me and returned.
>
> 'I think I had better find someone you have known to help you,' he said, but I was ashamed and begged him to stay. So again we went on together and he explained to me that my present body, being of such a light, responsive kind, would express in its colour and emanations every emotion I felt, so that not the slightest change of mood could be hidden.

> 'I begin to understand then, the unstable state of my feelings,' I said. 'I hope you will forgive me. I am raw and prickly all over and it affects me as though physically. I do not know how to adjust to your kindness nor to control the surges of emotion. You must think me a most ungrateful cuss,' I said.
>
> 'No,' he said. 'I understand the difficulty too well. At first one is all over the place. But the less you worry about other people's reactions to you the better; the more happy and at your ease you can feel the easier it will be for you and for us... I shall take you, with your permission, to a kind of sanatorium where I work,' he said. 'There they will go on helping you and giving you the right conditions for health.'

This again emphasises that emotions can no longer be hidden in this environment, and particularly that they affect others of a higher vibration. This is why the astral planes generally are very much associated with emotions, and the astral body is even referred to by some as the emotional body. We will return to Lawrence's progress in Part 4, but their final exchange at this point is equally revealing:

> 'All this is very intriguing, if uncomfortable,' I said. 'It isn't going to be the effortless sort of heaven one would have expected if one hadn't been so stupid as to expect nothing at all.'
>
> 'Is that what you thought?' Mitchell asked. 'It seems very stupid now, as you say. But it helps to explain your difficulties before I found you.'

ANONYMOUS (VIA EMILY FRENCH AND EDWARD RANDALL)

Lawrence clearly didn't really belong in the grey realms he encountered, presumably because his lack of belief in an afterlife wasn't heavily entrenched and he was reasonably open to assistance. But other sources stress that those who have really only ever concentrated on the material world can sometimes be in rather more trouble.

Edward Randall's transcripts of his séances with Emily French provide several specific examples of spirits who don't even realise they're dead.[6] More to the point, one of their communicants describes the potential for spirits who only ever concentrated on the material world to become trapped for far longer:[7]

> In the earth life they never lived on the higher planes; they had little, if any, spiritual development, and so across the frontier they practically live on this material plane although in another way. It will take a long time, and some unusual incident, to awaken these to their true condition. Some men are blind to all but material interests, and the spirits of these are blind to all interests except those embraced within their limited plane... There is no advancement for such men, or for any man, until the desire comes from within.

VARIOUS (VIA JOHN WARD)

John (or more formally JSM) Ward first started to develop mediumistic abilities when his late uncle Henry Lanchester began to communicate with him after his death in 1914.[8] The messages from Lanchester and others were published in *Gone West* in 1920 and came mainly via automatic writing, although sometimes via lucid dreams or 'trance visions' that he had to record as soon as he awoke. These latter can effectively be thought of as OOB experiences, although for simplicity we'll incorporate them with his channelled material.[9]

The majority of Lanchester's messages involve descriptions of the higher planes that we'll come to in Parts 4 and 5, but he does provide corroborative warnings about the potential confusion of those who have no belief in an afterlife:[10]

> The materialistic mind remains materialistic after death. Often it denies that it is dead, and considers its psychic or its spiritual body to be a physical body, so that it is still alive on earth. Even when it realises it has passed through death, it may still deny there is a God and refuse to listen to any who could teach it.

Another departed spirit who communicated via Ward is referred to only as 'WA', but he too admits that he gave little thought to any sort of afterlife and was far more obsessed by his sometimes less-than-honest business dealings, and by his physical and material wellbeing.[11] This is his account of an initial passing that is very different from Lawrence's yet equally harrowing, perhaps even more so:[12]

> Dimly in the far distance I perceived a faint speck of light. It grew brighter and seemed to be approaching me. Suddenly close by me I was aware of a greater intensity of darkness, and then a sensation of something horrible and evil became evident. I trembled and seemed filled with nausea, and turned towards the distant speck of light. But though I could now see what it really was, I was unable to approach it. What I saw was a great and glorious spirit of light, but so far distant that I could form no clear idea of his features and relative size. 'Am I dead?' I shrieked; and an evil voice at my shoulder cried, 'Yes, but fear not. I will look after you, protect you, and guide you.' I shrank from this awful being nevertheless, and turning to the bright spirit tried to approach him, but could not...
>
> Having done little on earth to develop my spiritual faculties, I was at first as one who is blind. After a while I began to be faintly aware of someone weeping. I knew instinctively it was M [his wife], and sought her that I might comfort her, but alas! I could not even see her. After what seemed like an endless age I began to see things dimly, like a man looking through a dirty glass, and the things I saw appeared blurred and indistinct...
>
> Gradually I became conscious of the fact that I was watching some persons place something in a box, and in time realised it was my coffin... Then a vague sensation of my funeral... I followed the mourners back to my house... I was present while men whom I had believed to be my friends devised means by which they might take advantage of my carelessness in drawing up my will. I had left my dear ones at their mercy, and of mercy they would get none. Oh how I suffered, and yet even then I realised the justice of my punishment. I had often taken advantage of another man's carelessness to snatch a mean advantage. I called it 'good business' then, now I saw it in its true light. I drifted away for I found, strive as I would, I could do nothing to influence these harpies, and so fled away dejected and miserable.

He is then delighted to encounter an old friend, only to find her encouraging him to join her in drawing on the energy of an incarnate couple by possessing them – at which point he's repelled by her admission that in the end this would seriously damage the couple, even kill them. This is followed by visits to the homes of various former lovers and friends, none of whom exhibits any great sorrow at his passing, all of which depresses him greatly. Later he adds:

> During almost the whole time I was continually desiring to gratify the old lusts of the flesh. Many times when I was haunting the earth I found myself drifting towards places where these abounded. The whole time a cursed devil was urging me to gratify my desires by obsessing [possessing] someone. Again and again I nearly gave way to the temptation, but each time I heard the warning voice of my guardian angel saying, 'If you do that, you go to hell.'

In chapter 17 we'll find out what happened to WA after this brief sojourn in the near-earth plane.

PHILIP GILBERT (VIA HIS MOTHER ALICE)

Of course Lawrence had done plenty to unselfishly help his fellow man, at least in the Arab world. But Gilbert again emphasises that those who have only ever concentrated on the material world, *and* selfishly on themselves and their own wellbeing, may find themselves rather more trapped:[13]

> So many people, without being in any way 'wicked', have no positive spiritual life, not even any sincere 'religion'. Any sincerely practised religion, however inaccurate some of its dogma may be, is a conscious effort to tune into our world, and so puts the soul in touch, to a greater or lesser extent, with our vibrations... But people who have lived entirely in the material, seeking only earthly and bodily advantages, and with no real love bonds... have created a thick cloud of thought images – a deep rut between high walls – through and over which they cannot see at all when they emerge from the body.

As an example of this he encounters a woman who had been a civil servant and had nothing else in her life but a great obsession for cleaning and polishing the flat in which she lived.[14] After she was killed in an air raid during WWII she didn't realise she had passed on, and couldn't understand why she couldn't prevent the dust from accumulating.

ARTHUR FORD (VIA RUTH MONTGOMERY)

By contrast Arthur Ford turns his attention to those who, rather than just not bothering to think about the afterlife, *proactively* consider themselves materialists as a committed, intellectual stance – although he mistakenly uses the word *atheist* instead:[15]

> For instance, an avowed atheist finds himself waking up over here, after insisting all his life that there was nothing beyond the grave. At first he is astonished, then resentful, because he feels that this is a hallucination and that those who try to help him adjust are fantasies of his imagination. Little by little he grudgingly accepts that he was wrong, however, and as dawn breaks through he is eager, even avid, to learn all about this sphere, which for him had previously been nonexistent.

OOB REPORTS

EMANUEL SWEDENBORG

We saw in chapter 5 that the earliest OOB pioneer to write clearly and in detail about their experiences was Emanuel Swedenborg nearly three centuries ago. We also saw that much of his work is somewhat distorted by a contemporary Christian bias. Nevertheless his views about the pitfalls awaiting those who don't believe in an afterlife are entirely consistent with more modern sources. For example, we see how little things have changed in the intervening centuries when he describes how 'scholars' on earth claim that people who believe in an afterlife are 'simpletons', and adds that 'spirits are heartsick over the fact that this kind of ignorance is still common in the world'.[16] He also provides the following warning:[17]

> Some people in their earthly lives have not believed in any life of the soul after the life of the body. When they discover that they are alive they are profoundly embarrassed. However, people who have convinced themselves of this join up with others of like mind and move away from people who had lived in faith. Most of them link up with some hellish community.

CHARLES LEADBEATER

Charles Leadbeater provides a similar warning, and also makes an interesting suggestion concerning a potential intermediate state of being, not unlike Lawrence's, whereby a departed spirit can initially be caught *between* the near-earth and the astral:[18]

> The type of person who clings desperately to physical life because he has no certainty that there is any other still persists among us. Having been intensely material, having had no ideas, no conceptions of any sort beyond the physical during earth life, he becomes crazy with fear when he finds himself altogether cut adrift from it. Sometimes such men make frantic efforts to return into some sort of touch with physical life. Most do not succeed, and gradually give up the struggle; as soon as they do that, they slip off at once into a natural moment of unconsciousness and shortly awaken in the astral world. But those whose will is strong enough to attain a partial and temporary success, hold on tenaciously to at least some fragments of their etheric double...
>
> While that etheric matter clings around him he is neither on one plane nor the other. He has lost the organs of his physical senses, and he cannot use those of the astral body because he is still enveloped in this cloud of etheric matter. He lives for a while... in a dim grey world of restlessness and discomfort, in which he can see clearly neither physical nor astral happenings, but catches occasional glimpses of both as through a world of heavy fog, in which he wanders, lost and helpless.
>
> There is no reason whatever why any human being should suffer such unpleasantness at all; but he fears that in letting go that shred of consciousness he may lose all consciousness forever – may in fact be annihilated; so he grasps desperately

at this which is left to him... Such people may sometimes be found drifting miserable and even wailingly about the astral plane, and it is one of the hardest tasks of the helper to persuade them that they have nothing to do but to forget their fear, to relax their tenseness, and to let themselves sink gently into the peace and oblivion which they need so sorely. They seem to regard such a suggestion as a shipwrecked man far away from land might receive an order to abandon his supporting spar, and trust himself to the stormy sea.

16

THE LOWER ASTRAL GENERALLY

Whilst in both the lower astral and the near-earth planes the inhabitants display varying degrees of emotional imbalance and confusion, the distinguishing factors are twofold. First, as we've already seen, in the astral generally the departed spirit's vibrations are now fully aligned with their surroundings so they no longer walk through doors and so on. Second, they're no longer sharing the environment with a mass of incarnate humans, although the latter can visit these planes while consciously OOB, or even when just asleep and dreaming.

On that note, OOB explorers tend to learn to avoid or pass through the more troubled realms when left to their own devices. But if they're being guided and protected by benevolent spirits they're often led to these planes so they can report back on what they find there. So the following chapters on the lower realms do contain plenty of OOB reports as well as those from NDEs and channelled material.

As to how spirits arrive in the lower astral, they may have an intermediate sojourn in the near-earth plane before sinking down, as for example did John Ward's WA in the last chapter. Alternatively they may skip this and find themselves automatically attracted to the lower planes, as TE Lawrence was at least initially. Either way a period of sleep or loss of consciousness, as suggested by several sources in earlier chapters, may be involved.

The other alternative is whether they find themselves in a solitary, individual hell that's clearly of their own making, or instead they're attracted to a group environment peopled by spirits with similar temperaments and obsessions. As we noted in chapter 12, the lower astral encompasses a huge variety of what we might term hellish experiences, from the mildly unpleasant to the most depraved and sickening imaginable. Generally speaking the individual experiences tend to be the milder, so we'll commence with these.

As for anyone already starting to become nervous about what might await them in the afterlife, the key point that shouldn't be forgotten when reading the following chapters is that help is *always* available for those who seek it, or are even just open to it.

17

INDIVIDUAL HELLS

CHANNELLED MATERIAL

VARIOUS (VIA EMILY FRENCH AND EDWARD RANDALL)

Edward Randall's transcripts from his group sessions with Emily French provide a number of examples of departed spirits suffering in isolated environments, who they attempt to help whenever they can. The first is relatively mild, but illustrates the fact that just looking after our own is selfish and doesn't guarantee a smooth transition:[1]

> I felt that God had been unjust to take me when I had so much to do, and when I was so needed by my family. I was not satisfied with the place I was in. About me there was a fog, and I started to walk out of it, but the farther I walked the more dense it got, and I became discouraged and sat down by the wayside in deep grief. I had ever tried the very best for those dependent on me. Where was my reward? Then someone approached me, came as it were out of the fog, and I told him of my life work and complained of the condition I was in... He replied, 'Yours was a selfish love; you worked for self. You should have made others happy as well as your own.' He promised to help me in my great trouble, if I would help myself. Together we have worked, and now all is well.

A rather worse case involves a successful but somewhat uncharitable businessman well known to Randall: 'It is so cold and dark… There is around and about me a wall of money, nothing but money, it shuts out the light. It is so dark, and wherever I go I cannot get away from it, around it or over it.' This is a stark warning of the sort of literal environments we can conjure in the afterlife *for ourselves* if we're obsessed. No one else does it, nor is it a punishment imposed on us. Randall's group then help this spirit to see that his condition is entirely self created by his devotion to money.

Another case involves a departed spirit who reports: 'I have wandered for years, searching, searching, and travelled, travelled, travelled. I have found nothing but vegetation, and I am so weary.' It turns out he'd been so unthinkingly religious, and had put so much reliance on the idea that Christ would save him without him having to do anything, that he'd expected to be met by him when he passed – and when this didn't happen he too became obsessive in his fruitless search. Again the group help him to see his situation as it really is. The final case is a rather harder nut to crack, however:

> I was not a good man among men. I was selfish, cruel, took human life and was, as I now know, killed while committing a crime. When I awoke it was very dark and, not knowing what had happened, I called in anger but my companions did not come. My voice echoed back to me again and again, and I began to think I was in a cave. I arose and groped about in the darkness, but I could not find the walls, though I walked for hours… Days and months passed, while I was ever searching for the walls that threw back the echo of my call. Can you imagine the sensation you would have, to be lost in an open forest with the sun in the sky, to say nothing of being lost in darkness? My sensations and suffering beggar description.

Eventually he perceives the light of a spirit rescuer but runs away in fear, and keeps hiding from or rebuffing any effort to help him, not least because he still doesn't accept he's dead – until, eventually, he does accept his condition and the help offered.

Several of French and Randall's communicants also provide

more general but equally bleak descriptions of the lower astral, culminating in a stark warning from one of the group's guides:[2]

> In those spheres that so lock and interface, I saw that the lowest and nearest the earth were dull, coarse, barren spheres, dreary and unlovely, where dark and uninviting beings wander to and fro... The hard cold natures of the wretched dwellers gave out no light, no beauty, no harmony or love.
>
> My first impression was of a descent in the dark, all about me gloom, and to add to the horror, I could hear voices though I could not see any one. After a time... I could see people about me, poor men and women who did not realise they had left the physical body – some shrieking because they could not escape their victims, even though those they had wronged were not there – it was their awakening consciousness that brought such visions... We have as much trouble in making these poor spirit people understand conditions beyond their sight and touch, as you have with earth people.
>
> There are many on the spirit side of life who are so densely ignorant that they have no ambition to become better. They continue on in the same old rut in which they were when on earth... If you were able to see and know the conditions of the spirits in the lower spheres and could contrast their condition with that of spirits in the higher spheres, you would understand how important it is that people should be enlightened upon this subject while they are still upon earth.

WA (VIA JOHN WARD)

After his sojourn in the near-earth plane recounted in chapter 15, John Ward's WA sinks down into the lower astral where he finds himself in a forbidding forest:[3]

> It was a most dreary place, dark, evil-smelling, full of marshes and, worst of all, of savage animals of former ages. Again and again these weird creatures appeared and attempted to attack me. Often they pursued me for what seemed like hundreds of miles. On and on I fled and they followed, but they never caught me or approached any nearer than they were when the

> pursuit began. This was not so strange as it seems, for they willed to hunt me and I willed to fly. My will was not sufficiently strong to compel them to cease hunting me, nor was theirs strong enough to hold me rooted to the spot. After a time their interest in me weakened and they turned their attention in other directions. Then I was able to go on my own way for a time unmolested.

He finally finds himself being encouraged by his guide to act in a compassionate way to help others who are incarnate, in order to help himself to rise higher in the astral planes.[4] First, he helps his former lover who is having a difficult time, but this is none too hard. Next he's told to assist someone he doesn't know at all, so he picks on a young man who's about to falsify accounts and steal from his employer – to whom he manages to appear as a warning spirit, frightening the boy half to death, yet ensuring he doesn't follow such a regressive path. Finally, as a real test, he's told to help an enemy. With reluctance he picks on an old acquaintance who'd swindled him, whose business partner was now intent on doing the same to said acquaintance. Unable to make himself seen to this more materialistic man, he waits for him to fall into a drunken stupor before taking some degree of control of his faculties and forcing him to automatically write a full admission – and to deliver it to his old acquaintance, all while effectively unconscious.

This earns his release to move on to the mid astral. By contrast with TE Lawrence in chapter 15 it's only at *this* point, some way into his astral journey when he's ready to move on, that he experiences the ubiquitous life review:

> On every side, visions of my former life came crowding upon me in a wild chaos, like a hideous nightmare from which I could not escape... Then I prayed, and as I did so the visions ceased to be chaos, and took on a regular sequence. From my earliest childhood up to the hour of my death every act and thought were there shown as a little drama enacted again and again. Not only the evil, but also the good.

ROBERT BENSON (VIA ANTHONY BORGIA)

Robert Benson describes his first visit to the lower realms in vivid terms. He and a spirit friend called Ruth are escorted by their guide Edwin, a fellow priest from his earthly life who, having died earlier, has had more time to develop in the spirit world.[5] First they have to dull down the brightness of their auras in order to not be too conspicuous or blind the inhabitants, after which they traverse a 'great bank of mist' in which they encounter another guide who offers to accompany them. On exiting the mist they find:

> The landscape was bleak in the extreme with, here and there, a dwelling-house of the meanest order. We came closer to one of the latter, and we were able to examine it better. It was a small, squat house, squarely built, devoid of ornament and looking altogether thoroughly uninviting. It even had a sinister look in spite of its plainness, and it seemed to repel us from it the nearer we approached it. There was no sign of life to be seen at any of the windows or round about it. There was no garden attached to it; it just stood out by itself, solitary and forlorn. Edwin and our new friend evidently knew both the house and its inmate quite well, for upon going up to the front door Edwin gave a knock upon it and without waiting for an answer opened it and walked in, beckoning us to follow. We did so and found ourselves in the poorest sort of apology for a house. There was little furniture, and that of the meanest...
>
> We passed into a back room and met the sole occupant seated in a chair... He was a man just past middle years. He had something of an air of faded prosperity and the clothes he wore had been obviously neglected... He rather scowled at the two of us as Edwin brought us forward as new visitors. It was a moment or two before he spoke, and then he railed at us rather incoherently, but we were able to gather that he deemed himself to be suffering under an injustice. Edwin told him in plain terms that he was talking nonsense, because injustice does not exist in the spirit world. A heated argument followed, heated, that is to say, on the part of our host, for Edwin was calm and collected and in truth wonderfully kind.

Afterwards Edwin explains that the man had been a highly successful but ruthless businessman, who had been generous but ostentatious in his donations to his local church – even paying for a new chapel so it could be named after him – and he now felt all the promises the church had made had been misleading. He was struggling to understand that just one small, genuine act of kindness to a stranger would have changed his current situation far more than the largest donation that, under the surface, was selfishly motivated.

FREDERIC MYERS (VIA GERALDINE CUMMINS)

We saw in chapter 5 that Frederic Myers wasn't only a celebrated paranormal investigator and founder of the SPR, but also proactive in attempting to gather proof of the afterlife. So much so that after his passing he was able to communicate his own experiences of these realms via the medium Geraldine Cummins, who we met in chapter 2. These were published in *The Road to Immortality* and *Beyond Human Personality*, published in 1932 and 1935 respectively. This is his brief take on the inhabitants of the lower planes:[6]

> The cruel man who has changed his natural craving for affection into a longing to give pain to others necessarily finds himself in a world here where he cannot satisfy this craving… Until there is an actual change in his cold, cruel soul, he will remain in outer darkness… a darkness of soul, a mental distress, a perverted desire that cannot find its satisfaction. Eventually this individual faces up to his own misery, to his vice; and then the great change comes… His soul or mind becomes gradually purified through his identification with the suffering of his victims.

EK (VIA JANE SHERWOOD)

Jane Sherwood's EK too provides just a brief, general observation:[7]

> Where a man has power of an evil nature he spreads such suffering around him and will attract such suffering to himself that life will be intolerable to him. He will be abandoned by all

> and become an isolated misery until he comes to himself. He will have to work out the inner conflicts which are at the root of his antisocial tendencies, and when they are resolved he will be sane and happy again.

ARTHUR FORD (VIA RUTH MONTGOMERY)

Arthur Ford reports that departed spirits who aren't necessarily 'bad' but have simply made no preparation for the afterlife can become trapped in a kind of 'purgatory' equating to our lower astral:[8] 'They sleep or move about in despondency and make no positive effort to advance, to learn, to recover.' He continues that they may remain in this limbo for a long time: 'They are morose and unhappy, until at last the idea comes through that they are holding themselves back, that no one can do anything for them until they themselves make the effort.'

ASHTAR (VIA JOHN/ANONYMOUS)

This idea that these spirits are punishing *themselves* is very much corroborated in John's anonymously channelled *Road of Many Ways*, which was introduced in chapter 14. Here is his guide Ashtar also emphasising that help is instantly available to them:[9]

> The lower regions do exist, those areas of darkness to which people have projected themselves by their way of living, the place which earth calls hell... [But no one there] has to remain one moment longer than he himself wills it, for he himself pronounces judgment and he alone knows when he is ready to leave... This type of person... concentrates his every thought upon himself. I've seen it so often and it's dreadful to watch. Let him, though, cry out but once, 'God help me'... Messengers are always there waiting for a glimmer of repentance, of self-reproach, and knowing that the lesson has been learnt they move in quickly to bring aid.

SALLY LEHMANN (VIA CYNTHIA SANDYS)

One source of channelled information we've not yet considered is Cynthia Sandys, whose daughter Pat communicated with her via automatic writing after her passing – as did Sally, the daughter of her friend and co-author, the novelist Rosamond Lehmann. In time a variety of other departed spirits used her as a medium as well, most of them family or friends such as her husband Arthur and brother Joe. The first volume of her *Awakening Letters* came out in 1978, the second in 1986. In one of these Sally describes the experience of what she calls the 'don't knows':[10]

> They are left to themselves because they go on wishing [for solitude] so deeply, hugging their old grievances and going on being miserable and lonely to such an extent that no one can penetrate and, if they do, they brush them aside and go on grumbling. But the moment light begins to dawn they are off like me, into a world of light and colour and music.

FRANCES BANKS (VIA HELEN GREAVES)

Like Philip Gilbert and his mother Alice, another channelled source that relied on the use of a telepathic connection already established during earthly life is that of Helen Greaves and Frances Banks.[11] The latter was a strong personality who for many years led a rich and varied life as a Sister in an Anglican Community in South Africa, while at the same time acting as principal of a teacher training college and writing a number of books on education and psychology. She then returned to Britain where she and Greaves became firm friends, not least because of a shared love of Christian mysticism and deep meditation.

In 1965 Banks passed on from cancer aged 72 with Greaves by her bedside, and only three weeks afterwards they were able to re-establish their telepathic bond. Like some other non-professional mediums Greaves had initial concerns about ridicule if the messages she received were published, but her departed friend's forceful personality continued and she was persuaded of their importance. *Testimony of Light* was communicated over a two-year period although in two parts, with a seventeen-month gap in between. In the first Banks remains a spirit helper in the 'rest home' where she finds herself after her passing, of which more in Part 4. But while there she's allowed to join a number of her fellow Sisters on one of their missions to undertake rescue work in the 'shadow lands'.[12]

She describes how they have to lower their vibrations to operate in the lower planes, and generally describes them as 'dark, depressing and as real as the tortured consciousness of the dweller makes them'. She then goes into more detail: 'The shadow land is a very real place indeed; a gloomy murk covers it... squalid dwellings inhabited by unhappy, tormented beings who jeer and mock and pursue their warped existences. Sometimes these poor souls live in hatred and rebellion, sometimes in apathy and sometimes with a fierce denial that there is any other state of existence possible.' But, importantly and like so many others, Banks also makes it clear that their condition isn't permanent: 'The man in these mental torments need stay there no longer than his desires keep him. He is free to resist the hatreds, cruelties, lusts of his lower nature, which he has retained from his earth life and which are keeping him in dark dungeons amid like-minded inhabitants... Always there are souls ready to help, to guide, to comfort and to assist.'

NDE REPORTS

MELLEN-THOMAS BENEDICT

An American artist, Mellen-Thomas Benedict, had a wonderfully transcendental near-death experience after being diagnosed with terminal cancer in 1982. During it he's shown around a variety of afterlife planes, including a brief glimpse into the lower realms:[13]

> I had a descent into what you might call hell, and it was very surprising. I did not see Satan or evil. My descent into hell was a descent into each person's customised human misery, ignorance, and darkness of not-knowing. It seemed like a miserable eternity. Each of the millions of souls around me had a little star of light always available. But no one seemed to pay attention to it. They were so consumed with their own grief, trauma and misery.

OOB REPORTS

CAROLINE LARSEN

By contrast with her descriptions of the near-earth plane in chapter 14 – in which the spirits were trapped but not suffering per se – here Caroline Larsen visits the lower astral where she encounters a society lady reclining on a couch in a most depressed and bitter state:[14]

> She discovered that she was almost totally lacking in the development of those very qualities needed for advancement. She found herself all alone, facing a life of stern realities where everyone carries outside oneself, in full view, the evidence of his or her spiritual qualities and exact state of development in the colour emanated. To add to her distress, she now could see that all her friends of earth life had been false. Not a kind thought from them had followed her and in her bitterness she blamed them to an extent for her sad predicament. 'I hate them all!' she exclaimed, for she had a great many friends and had been very popular. 'With their false and lying flattery they helped to mislead me'... I told her that by setting herself right and by study and by hard work she could develop herself and thus she would eventually succeed and be happy. However, my advice did not seem to be of any avail.

GLADYS LEONARD

In chapter 2 we met Gladys Leonard, who acted as the primary medium for Sir Oliver Lodge's communication with his son Raymond. But in chapter 5 we also saw that her 1931 book *My Life in Two Worlds* reports not only on her channelling work but also on her own OOB experiences. She indicates therein that she visited the lower realms on a number of occasions, the following being an example:[15]

> These lower planes are darker. The very air seems grey. One visit to such a place remains in my mind above all others... I found myself floating over a curious, desolate, rocky country. Dark gloomy rocks, forming caverns and crevices, pools of dark

> water, and an overwhelming feeling of loneliness are what I remember most strongly about this sinister plane... On looking more closely through the murky atmosphere, I saw many human forms moving about, slowly, dejectedly, and others sitting or standing on the rocks and large stones that abounded there. What astonished me was that the people all stood or sat singly. They appeared either to be unconscious of each other's presence, or to be uninterested. The atmosphere of depression and hopelessness was expressed by the very 'cut' of the scenery, the 'air' of its miserable-looking inhabitants.

One other experience in particular seems to have affected her massively and, although it's not strictly relevant to our discussion of the human experience of the lower planes, I cannot help but feel it should be included here:[16]

> I suddenly found myself in a narrow, dark street... Gloomy buildings, like stables, huddled against each other so closely that they almost touched, leaving only sufficient room for one to walk between. Here and there I saw a wider opening, which appeared to lead into a kind of yard, into which the doors of some of the stables opened. I looked in and saw that the yard was crowded with animals – bullocks, pigs and sheep – dead, and yet alive. I knew they were dead, but I could also see that they were alive, too. They moved very slightly, many lay on the ground. I understood at once from their appearance that they had just been slaughtered...
>
> In the very air around me was a most definite feeling of terrible fear, suffering, and blind resentment that was even more tangible than the buildings and walls. My guide told me that it was this awful feeling that was to be deplored, not only because it was an indication of the sufferings that these wretched animals had experienced, but because it affected the spiritual and mental atmosphere of the earth, and had a bad effect on human life and progress.

Fortunately she reports feeling that 'this dreadful place had but a *temporary* existence'. But it's perhaps unsurprising that immediately afterwards, despite having thoroughly enjoyed eating meat up until that point, she and her husband became committed vegetarians. Although I've seen little corroboration of this account from other sources, a certain amount is provided by Frederick Sculthorp, even if the following experience takes place in a higher plane:[17]

> I saw a sheep that was squatting down with head up and its eyes wide open in a sightless stare... Surrounding it on the grass... was a circle of sheep, also squatting, who looked very contented and serene. I sensed that this central sheep was a new arrival in spirit, and that the surrounding sheep were induced by higher minds to be there as some comfort when it became conscious. I felt something sad about it – something about its treatment before passing. I did not want to know more.

ROSALIND MCKNIGHT

Like Larsen, Rosalind McKnight too comes across a trapped and self-absorbed spirit in the lower astral:[18]

> They are taking me into a house. I can see a soul that has left the body. It's an older man. Though the body has died, the soul is exactly the same. This is a mansion. The floors are highly polished and very clean. The soul is walking around the mansion and has no intention of leaving. Much money is involved here. This soul has put so much money into this particular home that he doesn't want to release it... Even while in the physical body, he was already cut off from everything, including himself. He was locked into his own selfishness and will remain there until he seeks help and change – or until a higher level of energy can penetrate his cold and foreboding shell of existence.

GORDON PHINN

Here is one of Gordon Phinn's guides describing the hell her brother is trapped in:[19]

> My brother's building, a dump if ever you saw one, was typical of the worst Saigon neighbourhoods... Dead junkies gravitate to

such places for the same reason other dead types move to their favourite spots, because they feel comfortable there, they feel they belong. That can be a hard thing for a paradise lover to admit, that others actually want to be miserable, but it's true. Maybe it's because that's all they know, but still, at some point in their cloudy past they made a choice.

Picking up on the earlier descriptions in chapter 15, we can now turn to reports of committed materialists who have descended into the lower astral and are still denying the existence of an afterlife. These come from Phinn's guide Henry, who describes 'stepping down his energy level' so he can visit them without 'scaring them by looking like a large floodlight':[20]

> [They] find themselves in some kind of endless dream in landscapes as bleak as their imaginings... The terrain is bleak, rugged and windswept... A slate grey sky of formless clouds that suggest the word November; some ancient stone hovels, crumbling and damp are surrounded by wooden shacks of a more recent vintage.

He goes on to describe how he regularly visits the inhabitants to try to help them escape these bleak surroundings, but they tend to see him as some sort of tormenting but imaginary 'demon' who keeps showing up in their dream-state, talking 'brain-dead drivel' about how they are dead-but-alive in the afterlife. One in particular is a mathematician who died of a stroke but didn't even notice his passing, who now sits wrapped in a blanket, obsessively huddled over his endless calculations – the solution to which he believes will bring him fame and fortune.

Henry then moves to the bottom of a nearby canyon where he encounters various materialists in more of a group setting, although they seem to be individually isolated.[21] He describes them as 'hunched and squatting figures, either looking dolefully into the middle distance or staring disconsolately at their feet'. Most tragically of all he reports that some remain convinced they're still just experiencing the 'random thrashing of brain activity', and are happy to debate 'the complete lack of independent verification of his afterlife theory' with him. Perhaps one should even admire their tenacity in clinging to beliefs that fly in the face of all the evidence to the contrary?

JURGEN ZIEWE

Modern OOB pioneer Jurgen Ziewe, who we met in chapter 10, visits a number of lower astral environments on his journeys.[22] He senses that one of these is a replica of Hamburg except it's neglected, dark and sparsely populated by 'a few lost souls wandering about aimlessly, puzzling over how they got here or how to get home'. In another a very old, thin man resides in a ramshackle hut made out of discarded rubbish which is a 'natural extension of his own character and the pain he feels'. In a third he goes into more detail:[23]

> Especially on the lower level it is easy for people to mistake their often short-lived mental projections and aberrations as realities. I once came across a woman who was imprisoned in a ten foot square cell, made out of whitewashed cement with no doors or windows. I tried to persuade her to leave her prison by suggesting that it was no more than a solidification of her feelings (she was suffering from an intense feeling of self pity), but she rejected this. Angrily she pointed out to me that there were no doors or windows and consequently no way of escaping. She totally ignored trying to explain my appearance. I knew though that eventually her self-pity would be exhausted and the walls of her prison would simply disintegrate.

Perhaps rather more worryingly he suggests that as far as he can tell a person can lead a pretty 'good' and 'moral' life and still find themselves in the lower astral after death if their emotional state has been degraded, especially in later years. He actually illustrates this using the case of his mother.[24] She lived in Germany and had been very warm-hearted but, unbeknown to him, had suffered severe depression in the years before her death due to a controlling partner who cut her off from all her friends. By the time Ziewe found out and got help it was too late and she died shortly afterwards. He visits her in the afterlife on a number of occasions but, much to his dismay, finds her ‘shrouded by a thick blanket of mist’ and totally unaware of his presence. This carries on for some time after her death, but his sad tale does have a happy ending when some years later he sets the intention to find her again and meets her in ‘paradisiacal countryside’ looking young, angelic and happy.

Meanwhile his uncle seems to have been a still worse case.[25] Having been severely wounded in the leg in WWII and constantly in pain, he sank into a life of negativity, pessimism and cynicism and dragged his lovely wife with him. When Ziewe meets him in the afterlife some three years after his death he’s living in a ‘dull, sad place’ and is still full of a sense of injustice. Although he’s aware of his nephew’s presence there’s nothing the latter can do to persuade him that a better life awaits if only he’d change his attitude.

18

THE DEPTHS OF HELL

As we noted earlier, these even more hellish environments in the lowest planes tend to be inhabited by groups of departed spirits who are seriously emotionally disturbed, or who remain obsessed with the basest aspects of the human experience. One of the most obvious signs of this level of degradation is that their appearance becomes horribly distorted by it, so the scenes we're just about to witness are not for the faint-hearted. But, as I indicated in the Preface, it would be remiss to omit them and provide an incomplete picture, merely for fear of upsetting or frightening some people. In the pursuit of truth and balance it's important to recognise that, just as there are sublime experiences to be had in the higher planes, so the opposite is true in the lower planes. Despite the unpleasant nature of these accounts therefore – and please bear in mind what it's been like to wade through so much dark material when researching this chapter – if pulling them together like this helps even one person to avoid such realms, or to know how to escape should they find themselves therein, it will have served its purpose.

Before we start there are a number of things we should remember as we read them. First, no one is placed in these environments except by their own choices. This might sound strange, but it's each individual's own actions, attitudes and makeup, built up during both their earthly life and any time they've already spent in the afterlife, that determines the level they sink to, who they associate with and what they experience. The golden rule in these group environments is that 'like attracts like'. Second, as emphasised many times already, help is always on hand for even the most degraded spirits, even if it may be a long time before they open themselves to it. So these environments are decidedly *not* places where unfortunates are sentenced to *eternal* damnation by a vengeful and all-powerful being who sits in *judgment*. That is, pure and simple, a horrible distortion of the truth, first peddled centuries ago by various orthodox religions who were primarily attempting to keep the masses under control. Third, these aren't the dogmatic rants of Christian preachers, albeit that some of the earlier material can sometimes have a somewhat religious flavour. They are first-hand accounts by incarnates and discarnates who've either visited or even spent time in these realms. Fourth, just as we should attempt to avoid judgment of others in the earth plane, we should try to do the same here. Finally, a few of the following scenes involve attempts at possession in the near-earth plane, but because the spirits involved are more degraded they're included here.

CHANNELLED MATERIAL

FRANCHEZZO (VIA FARNESE)

There are a number of extremely detailed channelled reports of the lower planes. A highly graphic account is provided by Franchezzo, who we met briefly in chapter 14. He seems to have led a selfish and hedonistic existence with no expectation of an afterlife – which, as we've already seen, can lead to problems in its own right.[1] So when he dies suddenly he's amazed to find himself still conscious, but alone and in total darkness. Gradually he becomes aware that he's beside his grave, with his 'beloved' – the only woman he truly loved – strewing flowers upon it, but his attempts to contact her are as usual in vain. Then he hears a voice telling him to look at his spirit body, and he's disgusted to see the effects of his earthly debauchery: 'So awfully changed, so vile, so full of baseness… so repulsive in every feature – even my figure was deformed.' This is our first example of how the astral body projects the true character, without the pretences we're able to adopt in the earth plane.

He wanders aimlessly in almost total darkness, becoming occasionally aware of other spirits, some of whom try and tempt him to possess incarnate humans so they can all satisfy their unchanged cravings. But he gains strength from his beloved and refuses. His agonised wanderings are interspersed with periods of sleep, but eventually he's guided towards much-needed healing in a 'house of hope', which we'll discuss more in Part 4.

After this treatment Franchezzo describes being sent on various rescue and retrieval missions that he insists are integral to his own rehabilitation. This is the first time we encounter the idea that an extremely self-centred spirit might need to *earn* their own reprieve by helping others, and it's one to which we'll return many times. In any case, as part of this he initially visits various lower astral 'lands' as he calls them, commencing with a visit to a 'land of selfishness':[2]

> One place was a great valley of grey stones, with dim, cold, grey hills shutting it in on every side, and this twilight sky overhead. Here again not a blade of grass, not one poor stunted shrub was to be seen, not one touch of colour or brightness anywhere… Those who dwelt in this valley had centred their lives and their affections in themselves and had shut up their hearts against all the warmth and beauty of unselfish love… There were a great many beings flitting uneasily about in this valley, but strange to say they had been so centred in themselves that they had lost the power to see anyone else.
>
> These unhappy beings were invisible to each other until such time as the thought of another and the desire to do something for someone besides themselves should awaken… and through their efforts to lighten another's lot they would improve their own, until at last their stunted affections would expand and the hazy valley of selfishness would hold them in its chains no more.

> Beyond this valley I came upon a great, dry, sandy-looking tract of country where there was a scanty, straggling vegetation, and where the inhabitants had begun in some places to make small attempts at gardens... In some places these were clustered so thickly they formed small towns... This was also a land of selfishness, although not of such complete indifference... therefore they sought for a certain amount of companionship... Many had come from the grey valley, but most were direct from the earth life and were now, poor souls, struggling to rise a little higher... Such miserable hovels as were in this land! Such ragged, repulsive, wretched-looking people, like tramps or beggars, yet many had been amongst earth's wealthiest and most eminent in fashionable life, and had enjoyed all that luxury could give!

He then goes on to describe a 'land of misers' in which 'dark, crooked-looking beings with long, claw-like fingers' are 'scratching in the black soil like birds of prey in search of stray grains of gold', which they then wrap close to their hearts, shunning all company in case they might be robbed of their treasure. This is followed by a 'land of misery' containing cities and towns where the 'once-handsome mansions and fine palaces' are now just slums 'stamped with the same appalling look of uncleanness, foulness and decay'. On the outskirts of one he hears the sound of quarrelling coming from a barn, and inside he finds a large table surrounded by spirits who are gambling over a bag of coins – describing them as 'more like orangutans, with the varieties of pigs and wolves and birds of prey expressed in their coarse, bloated, distorted features... such faces, such misshapen bodies, such distorted limbs... clothed in various grotesque and ragged semblances of their former earthly finery'.

This is in turn followed by a 'frozen land' inhabited by those who had been 'cold and selfishly calculating in their earthly lives'. Here he encounters one of the Catholic Grand Inquisitors from the terrible persecution in medieval Europe, encased in an icy cage. This is imprisoning him, but also partly protecting him from the spirits of a few of his earthly victims who had been 'so crushed and tortured that only the fierce desire for revenge remained', and who would have loved to 'tear him to pieces' if only they could have reached him. It seems incredibly sad, even unjust, that people who were mere victims of something as revolting as the Inquisition should end up suffering in the lower planes, but the consistent message is that this only happens to those who retain a fierce desire for revenge on their persecutors. By that means, unfortunate as it is, they bring it on themselves.

Franchezzo separately describes what he terms a visit to 'hell' itself, which again is part of a mission to retrieve and rescue any spirits he can in order to help his own rehabilitation. He describes it as being surrounded by a 'great bank of smoke and flame' that he and a companion have to 'will themselves through' by effectively forming a tunnel.[3] He continues:

> The heavy atmosphere like a black fog shut in our vision on every side... In some parts there were great, tumbled, jagged mountains of black rocks, in others long and dreary wastes of desert planes, while yet others were mighty swamps of black oozing mud, full of the most noisome, crawling creatures, slimy monsters and huge bats.

He has a variety of experiences in these realms, commencing with a visit to a city that is the degraded counterpart of an earthly city – just as a higher vibratory version of it exists in the higher planes, of which more in Part 4.[4] Herein he finds himself entering the council chamber of a great palace, although there is 'over everything the same stamp of foul loathsomeness' as on the exterior, while the inhabitants 'appear to be eaten up with a loathsome disease like lepers, only even more horrible to look upon'. Intriguingly, though, he suggests that to themselves and each other they look exactly as they had in their earthly lives – beautiful, clothed in finery and so on. In other words for those who truly belong in these lower environments all forms of deception can be carried on with themselves and each other, while it's only visitors from higher planes who perceive them as they truly are.

In any case the ruler invites him to sit down to a banquet,

although 'the food never satisfies the awful cravings of hunger which these former gluttons feel', while 'the wine is a fiery liquid which scorches the throat and renders a thousand times worse the thirst which consumes these drunkards'. But once the pleasantries are over he has to beat a hasty retreat as the mob attempt to set upon him, although he does manage to rescue one man who is ready for salvation.

Worse follows as he next enters a huge cavern where 'horrible reptiles are hanging on the walls and crawling at his feet', while 'great funguses and monstrous plants of an oozy, slimy kind hang in festoons' from the roof.[5] Before him is an enormous fire round which are dancing a 'troop of demons' who are prodding at it with long black spears. He is horrified to find, as he draws nearer, that the fire is composed of 'the bodies of living men and women writhing and twisting in the flames... tossed about by the spears of these awful demons'. He then learns that here the earthly roles have been reversed, and that those who condemned hundreds of their indigenous victims to die on huge bonfires during the conquests of the Americas now find themselves *in* the fire, while those previous victims who remain hell bent on revenge are now the tormentors. With regard to the former he's informed that it's their own thirst for blood and power, their insatiable greed for gold and treasure, and at the same time their complete lack of any shred of pity or human decency, that has placed them there.

Elsewhere he comes upon a party of repulsive looking spirits who are attacked by an equally foul set of opponents: 'They half walked and half crawled on all fours. The faces could scarcely be called human; the very features had become bestial.' Again it's explained to him that these people had been pirates, highwaymen, slave dealers and so on who had completely brutalised themselves and their victims. He subsequently finds himself in a 'land of swamps', which he describes as 'a great liquid sea of mud, black, fetid and stagnant, a thick slime of oily blackness floating on the top', within which are 'struggling human forms wading up to their armpits in the mud' and crying out for help, several of whom he manages to rescue. This time he's told that the inhabitants of this swamp 'had revelled in such low abominations in their earth lives' and, since their passing, had continued to enjoy such pleasures vicariously through incarnate humans, that their increasingly degraded behaviour had eventually caused them to sink into this lower plane – until such time as 'the very disgust of themselves would work a cure'.

This clearly shows that it's not just their behaviour in their earthly life that determines how low departed spirits may sink, but just as much their behaviour in the initial afterlife too – particularly if in the near-earth plane they involve themselves in the insidious pastime of possessing or attaching themselves to others still incarnate. Indeed elsewhere he actually witnesses the 'earthbound spirits of men and women still tied by their gross pleasures or their sinful lives, many of them using the organisms of mortals to gratify their depraved cravings.'[6] We will encounter more of this in due course.

THE OFFICER (VIA JOHN WARD)

The third spirit who communicated via John Ward is referred to as 'the Officer', described by his fellow communicant Henry Lanchester as follows:[7]

> He married a girl and robbed her of her money. Left her behind when he went to India. Seduced a girl there and got her money: murdered a native. They found out about the girl but not about the native. Kicked out of the army. Returned to England. There went in for bogus company promoting. Robbed dozens of poor people of their money.
>
> Finally came under the law. Got five years. While in prison his wife brought an action for divorce and won it. When he came out, set up as a card-sharp. Was discovered and turned out of the various clubs to which he belonged. Then got in with a young fellow who had a new invention. Ran him for a time, finally murdered him and stole the invention. Got it accepted, and as he was going to sign the agreement was knocked down by a bus in the Strand.

The Officer himself then takes up the story. It is a gruesome one, being that rarity or rarities, a first-hand account of a spirit descending to the depths of hell because, unlike for example Franchezzo, he has no focal point for any sort of loving sentiment. But – as he, Ward and Lanchester emphasise – it's a hugely important and salutary tale for those who are still incarnate to take on board, and therefore worth reproducing at some length.

At first after being knocked down he doesn't realise he's dead, and carries on to the meeting as planned.[8] However as so often happens he becomes confused when he seems to walk straight through the doors and the lawyer ignores him – at which point a former acquaintance who had passed over previously appears and informs him of his true situation. Indicating that he needs a drink he's taken to a den in the east end of London frequented by a variety of incarnate drunks, where to his frustration he finds he can't pick up a glass. In a rather more gruesome example of possession in the near-earth plane than those discussed earlier, he then sees how the other spirits satisfy their desire:

> I noticed that many of the others were twining themselves round the men and women who were drinking. I cannot exactly describe how they did it, but they seemed to be insinuating themselves into their carcasses. Suddenly I saw a man who was already fairly tipsy drop in a kind of drunken stupor. At once a spirit who had been twining round began to fade into him and soon seemed to be absorbed into him. He was gone, and lo! the man staggered to his feet and yelled, 'More beer, you ——!' I won't say what. The barmaid gave him some more; but I could see that it was not the drunk man but my spirit companion who was, as it were, shining out of his eyes...
>
> I noticed for the first time that these spirits were divisible into two groups – those who were obviously men and those who were not. The latter had various forms, all more or less bestial. I cannot describe them. They were foul, misshapen things, not human or animal, sometimes composite, with animal heads and human bodies, some heads only, some foul monstrosities with no shape or form.

This seems to suggest that spirits whose degraded appearance shows them to be true denizens of the lower planes can also raise themselves up to revisit the near-earth, something the Officer's fellow communicant WA discusses too. In any case after spending a long time visiting various drinking dens he learns to imitate his fellow spirits, although he indicates how tormenting it is to never be able to satisfy his cravings – and, in retrospect, how foul it is to be dragging down incarnates with him. But eventually, after a seriously unpleasant case of possession in which he manages to ruin a former enemy and have him sentenced to death, his continuing degraded behaviour means he suddenly finds himself sinking into the lower astral proper.

He falls until he finds solid ground underneath him, and follows a dark path to the gates of a great city.[9] He notes that there are many such cities in the lower realms – some, like this one, devoted to cruelty and hate, others to lust and debauchery, and so on; also each tends to be modelled on those parts of a major earthly city in which such influences have predominated at some time. He soon learns to use his strength of will to dominate others, and is told that there are various kings and emperors ruling different districts of the city, all of which are constantly warring with each other.

He visits a coliseum, and sees horrendous torture and suffering inflicted on the prisoners from the most recent war, which only serves to feed his own cruelty. He goes to a theatre where a shocking portrayal of a scene from the Grand Inquisition is played out – as we've seen from Franchezzo above this is unsurprisingly a common theme in the lowest realms – at the end of which he engages in a battle of wills with the Grand Inquisitor himself and conquers him. He takes over a house and its servants by literally throwing its master out of the window. He attracts a band of followers who roam the streets terrorising all they meet, until as expected he's summoned before the emperor of his district, who asks him to lead an onslaught against a neighbouring king. He accepts and assembles a huge army made up of groups from a variety of earthly locations and periods, which engages the enemy forces and eventually defeats them – albeit that, because no one can actually die, it's more a battle of wills between the two armies and between individuals too. As a result he takes charge of his new kingdom, but all the while has to subdue those who would usurp him.

In the end he grows tired of this – not least because, as with every inhabitant of the lower planes, nothing he does provides any real pleasure and only produces an endless sense of unfulfilment. So he links with a human black magician and manages to effect a temporary return to the near-earth plane, where he exacts horrible punishments on the magician's enemies. As a result of this he ends up descending even lower into the depths of 'hell' – and this time his will is no longer stronger than what he refers to as genuine demons that have never been human.[10] Along with other unfortunates he is whipped and goaded, driven to run endlessly and aimlessly with no destination. His description of one of these demons isn't pleasant:

> He was far larger than I, and seemed made of darkness, if you can understand me. Never for two minutes did he look the same; not merely his face, but his whole form seemed to be constantly changing. He was robed in a long flowing robe of black; but even while I looked he became stark naked. Then he changed, and became like a goat, and even while I was struggling with my amazement he became a python. He next resumed his man's shape – man's, did I say? No; no man, however vile, looked as diabolical as this creature did. The face was hideous in the extreme; the eyes were oblong and glittered like a snake's, the nose was hooked like an eagle's beak, the mouth was full and armed with teeth which were pointed and almost like tusks. Malevolence and debauchery seemed stamped on his features – while his hands were almost like talons, they looked so bony. From his body darkness seemed to ooze. Again he changed and became a column of red flame, which yet gave no light.

Eventually he's told by a demon that, if he returns to the level from which he came, and brings a hundred spirits back with him by pretending to offer them greater power over others, he can become a tormentor not a victim. This he does, only to find he's been double-crossed by the demon, his torment only increased by the wrath of the spirits he lied to. As a result he ends up descending further to the very lowest depths of hell, where he's completely alone in a darkness so intense it's 'spongy'. Here he's confronted by all his actions, but because he feels all hope is lost he experiences no real remorse – the Christian doctrine of *eternal* damnation has much to answer for – and actually yearns to return to the torments of the higher levels of hell.

Finally and suddenly, after what seems to him like an eternity, the phrase 'My God, my God, why hast thou forsaken me?' comes to him. And from that moment on the spark of light required for his rescue is kindled. He has to undergo many trials to release himself from the various planes of hell, including being on the receiving end of some of the cruelty he inflicted on others. But each time, sooner or later, he finds the power of prayer is enough to take him on to the next stage. The happy ending comes, even for a spirit who had sunk so low, when we learn that – with echoes of Franchezzo earlier – he now works to help other spirits who are confused after death, especially soldiers.

ARNEL (VIA GEORGE VALE OWEN)

Our next source is a prolific one. Between 1913 and 1914, and then again between 1917 and 1919, the Revered George Vale Owen, the vicar of Orford in Lancashire, received a significant number of messages from departed spirits that he recorded using automatic writing.[11] These were published in four volumes, *The Lowlands of Heaven*, *The Highlands of Heaven*, *The Ministry of Heaven* and *The Battalions of Heaven* in 1920 and 1921. His main sources were his mother, Emma; Kathleen, a young Liverpool seamstress who passed on in her early twenties and acted as surrogate mother to Vale Owen's daughter Ruby, who joined her aged only two; Astriel, who in earthly life had been headmaster of a Warwickshire school in the mid-eighteenth century; Zabdiel, who described himself as Vale Owen's guide but disclosed nothing about any earthly life; and Arnel, an experienced spirit who had been an English art and music teacher exiled to Florence to escape religious persecution during the early Renaissance.

Interestingly an example of Vale Owen's channelled scripts, recorded at an average of 24 words per minute, shows the words and sentences were written with no breaks between them, except when Vale Owen recorded a question of his own. This suggests that, like Jane Sherwood as discussed in chapter 15, he was conscious of their contents in real time – yet as with her it still seems an element of automation was involved in his writing.

In any case, rather like Helen Greaves in the last chapter, because of his own doubts he went to great lengths to assure himself that the messages were genuine and originated from the sources claimed, and only published them under great pressure from his communicants. What is more, despite the worldwide attention that accompanied their release, he continued as a committed and much loved vicar, and refused to accept a single penny of the money raised from book sales for himself. The only downside, particularly with the messages dictated by his mother, is that perhaps unsurprisingly they contain a heavy Christian bias, with a number of references to Christ appearing in elaborate afterlife ceremonies.[12]

For our current purposes it's Arnel who provides a lengthy description of a rescue mission to the lower astral:[13]

> We saw that there were many ruined buildings, some in clusters and some solitary. Decay was all about us. There were trees also, some very large, but mostly leafless, and those with unattractive leaves... spiked with lance-like teeth... Here and there we crossed a waterway full of boulders and sharp stones and with little water, and that water thick with slime and stinking. And at long, long last we came within sight of the colony we were seeking. It was not a city, but a cluster of houses, some large and some small. They were scattered

about, here and there, and not in any order. There were no streets in the city. Many dwellings were merely mud huts, or a couple of slabs of stone to form a shelter. And there were fires about the open spaces to give light to the inhabitants. Round these many groups were gathered, some sitting in silence looking at the flames, others loudly brawling, others wrestling in their anger one with another...

At last one arose and looked about him in the mist and gloom uneasily. He was a tall, gaunt figure, with knotted joints and limbs, bent and bowed, and his face was pitiful to see, such lack of hope and fullness of despair was there upon him, and found expression throughout his frame... He and I had lived near one another on earth. Indeed, he was a magistrate in the town nearby my home...

From that colony we went further into the regions of gloom... And as we went we felt about us a growing power of evil... Thus we came to a large city, and entered through a massive gateway where guards marched to and fro... Filth and mockery was rife all around us. Even the buildings in their plan and ornamentation shocked the eye whichever way we turned... We willed ourselves into such a condition so that we could be seen by the inhabitants, and entered the gate of the dark palace of evil...

Opposite us there rose a great flight of steps from floor to balcony. All the crowd which filled the hall sat around and faced it. Upon the lower steps and half-way up there were coiled, in different attitudes, all unbeautiful, men and women in loose and scanty clothing, which, nevertheless, made pretence to grandeur... Upon the stairs, just above them, stood the speaker. He was of giant stature, bigger than them all, as he also dominated them in his wickedness... They had elected him governor, but that was in fear of his great power of evil. And now that he called those poor, misshapen, half-frenzied men noble, they applauded him in their servility for the self-same reason. Those poor hags, the women in their squalor of finery, he called fair ladies, and bade them follow him as sheep their shepherd, and in fear they too cheered approval and arose to go with him as he turned to mount the great flight of stairs.

At this point Arnel and his fourteen companions spiritually overpower the wicked governor, and his followers are immediately released from their bondage and assisted by others into the light of the mid astral. In the meantime Arnel and company, assisted by a guard who is ready to be rescued and so recruited to act as their guide, continue on to a 'city of mines' in an even deeper level of the lower astral:[14]

> The city itself was built about with a strong wall, and it was large in area... We passed through some streets where single-storied houses were placed in no regular line or pattern, but gaps were in between, and waste places where grew no herbs or vegetation, or only coarse, dank grass, or shrubs with stems and branches blasted as if by the sirocco breath which came about us, now we were within the city and its high enclosing walls. It came in chief part from the mines which we were now approaching. These were the hovels where the slaves took rest of short duration, with long periods of labour in between. These we left behind us, and shortly came upon a place where there opened out to us a large cave mouth which led into the bowels of that region. We drew close and there came forth, in gusts, a wind of odour so foul and hot and fetid that we drew back and paused awhile to call for strength. This done, we steeled our hearts and went within and downward...
>
> So we continued our descent... And now we came to a stairway cut into the rocky earth, and at the bottom of it a heavy gateway... Through a grid a hideous face appeared and demanded who stood outside and knocked. It was a human face, but with much of the savage animal in it, large mouth, enormous teeth and long ears. Our guide gave some short answer, speaking as one to command, and the gate was opened inward and we passed through. Here we found ourselves in a large cavern and, before us, an opening through which a ruddy, murky glow came and but barely lighted the walls and roof of the place in which we stood. We went forward and looked through this opening and saw there was a steep dip, about the height of six men.
>
> From our vantage point we looked about and, as our eyes

> became more used to the gloom, we saw that before us there lay a large stretch of territory, all underground. We could not see how far it reached, but there were passages leading off the main cavern, here and there, which disappeared into what seemed black darkness. Figures went here and there, to and fro, with a furtive tread, as if afraid some horror should be found in their pathway when they were most unaware. Now and then the clanging of chains came up to us, as some poor fellow shuffled on his way in fetters; then a weird cry of agony and often a mad, wild laugh and the sound of a whip. All was sad both to hear and see. Cruelty seemed to float in the air as one sufferer gave vent to his agony by torturing another more helpless...
>
> I said we would descend and see what was there, by nearer viewing of the chamber directly below us... I was resolved to fathom the misery of these dark regions to the uttermost... At last we came to the mine itself. A large heavy gateway gave on to a plateau. Here I could see no roof. Above us was blackness. We seemed to be now not in a cavern, but in a deep pit or ravine, the rocky sides rising up until we could not follow them, so deep were we below the land surface. But tunnels here and there penetrated deeper still and most were in pitch darkness, except where at times a light flickered and went out again... Oh, the desperate anguish of the helplessness of those poor souls – lost in that immensity of darkness and with no guide to lead them out. But although they must have felt so, yet every one is noted and registered in the spheres of light and, when they are ready for help, then help is sent to them, as it was even now.

Arnel and his companions now start to sing a song of the delights awaiting these poor slaves in the mid astral, and first a trickle, then a flood of these poor, frightened wretches come out from their tunnels and signal their willingness to be assisted and saved from their awful plight.[15] At this point the leader of the city enters the mine having heard what's going on, and this gigantic, misshapen being thunders down to halt the rescue operation. But he and his remaining followers are spiritually no match for the powers of Arnel and his group, after which thousands of the inhabitants of the mining city are led to safety.

ROBERT BENSON (VIA ANTHONY BORGIA)

Robert Benson too provides several graphic and corroborative accounts of various group environments in the lower astral. The following is a description of a first visit in which he's accompanied as always by his guide Edwin and, on this occasion, a friend of his:[16]

> Our nostrils were at first assailed by the most foul odours; odours that reminded us of the corruption of flesh in the earth world. They were nauseating... Here in these dark lands all is bleak and desolate. The very low degree of light itself casts a blight upon the whole region. Occasionally we were able to catch a glimpse of the faces of some unfortunates as we passed along. Some were unmistakably evil, showing the life of vice they had led upon the earth; some revealed the miser, the avaricious, the 'brute beast'. There were people here from almost every walk of earthly life, from the present earthly time to far back in the centuries...
>
> Both Edwin and his friend told us that we should be appalled at the catalogue of names, well known in history, of people who were living deep down in these noxious regions – men who had perpetrated vile and wicked deeds in the name of holy religion, or for the furtherance of their own despicable, material ends. Many of these wretches were unapproachable, and they would remain so – perhaps for numberless more centuries – until, of their own wish and endeavour, they moved however feebly in the direction of the light of spiritual progression...
>
> Their bodies presented the outward appearance of the most hideous and repulsive malformations and distortions, the absolute reflection of their evil minds. Many of them seemed old in years, but I was told that although such souls had been there perhaps for many centuries, it was not the passage of time that had so dealt with their faces, but their wicked minds... The multitudinous sounds that we heard were in keeping with the awful surroundings, from mad, raucous

> laughter to the shriek of some soul in torment – torment inflicted by others as bad as himself.

Elsewhere Benson then recounts a second visit that is more disturbing still:[17]

> As we climbed down through one of the numerous fissures in the rocks, I could see and feel the loathsome slime that covered the whole surface of them, a dirty green in colour and evil smelling... After we had journeyed downwards for what seemed to be a great distance... we found ourselves in a gigantic crater, many miles in circumference, whose sides, treacherous and menacing, towered above us. The whole of this area was interspersed with huge masses of rock... In our present position we were well above this sea of rocks, and we observed a dull cloud of poisonous vapour rising from it, as though a volcano were below and upon the point of erupting... Dimly, we could see through this miasma what might have been human beings, crawling like some foul beasts over the surface of the upper rocks...
>
> We walked closer to one of the sub-human forms that lay sprawled upon the rocks. What remnant of clothing it wore might easily have been dispensed with, since it consisted of nothing but the filthiest rags, which hung together in some inconceivable way, leaving visible great gaps of lifeless-looking flesh. The limbs were so thinly covered with skin that one fully expected to see bare bones showing forth. The hands were shaped like the talons of some bird of prey, with the finger nails so grown as to have become veritable claws. The face upon this monster was barely human, so distorted was it, and malformed. The eyes were small and penetrating, but the mouth was huge and repulsive, with thick protruding lips set upon a protruding jaw, and scarcely concealing the veriest fangs of teeth...
>
> He had spent the greater part of his earth life inflicting mental and physical tortures upon those who had the misfortune to come into his evil clutches. Every crime that he had committed against other people had, at last, reverted to and descended upon him. He now had before him – he had

> done so for hundreds of years – the memory, the indelible memory of every act of evil he had perpetrated against his fellows... Had we been able to detect one tiny glimmer of that light – it is a real light that we see – which is an unmistakable sign of spiritual stirrings within, we might have done something for this soul. As it was, we could do nothing but hope that one day this dreadful being would call for help in true earnestness and sincerity. His call would be answered – unfailingly.

They then descend further to some flatter ground, where they witness scenes of such degradation that Benson is loath to actually describe them in detail:

> The inhabitants were variously occupied: some were seated upon small boulders, and gave every appearance of conspiring together, but upon what devilish schemes it was impossible to say. Others were in small groups perpetrating unspeakable tortures upon the weaker of their kind who must, in some fashion, have fallen foul of their tormentors. Their shrieks were unbearable to listen to... Their limbs were indescribably distorted and malformed, and in some cases their faces and heads had retrograded to the merest mockery of a human countenance.
>
> Interspersed throughout the great area of this dreadful region were pools of some sort of liquid. It looked thick and viscid, and inexpressibly filthy... We were horrified to see signs of movement in some pools, and we guessed... that frequently the inhabitants slip and fall into them... We witnessed all manner of bestialities and grossness, and such barbarities and cruelties as the mind can scarcely contemplate... We had by no means reached the bottom of this foul pit, but I have given you quite sufficient details of what is to be found in the realms of darkness.

At this point we must accept that between them Franchezzo, the Officer, Arnel and Benson have painted a quite horrible picture of what might await truly degraded spirits in the afterlife. Anyone might be forgiven for supposing that, even if these messages do come from genuine discarnate spirits, they merely represent the rantings of those who, in their nineteenth-century and even earlier earth lives, had all been thoroughly indoctrinated by – or at least exposed to – Christian ideas of hell, demons and divine retribution. But actually there's a similar explanation that operates in quite the reverse manner.

We briefly introduced the law of attraction in chapter 8, whereby our thoughts, our beliefs and even more our expectations create our reality in all planes. Imagine then the collective power of so many incarnate humans down the ages believing in, for example, Christian ideas of heaven and hell. Would that not be enough to actually create a whole plethora of such environments in the afterlife planes, with those who believe in them then being attracted to them in ever-increasing numbers as millennia pass? Indeed we will see exactly the same concept in operation with regard to illusory religious heavens in chapter 25.

In any case we will shortly come onto many more recent and less Christianised, yet still corroboratory, reports of the lowest realms from other sources. But let us first conclude this section with one other, briefer, channelled account.

DAVID PATTERSON HATCH (VIA ELSA BARKER)

Elsa Barker was an American author and poet with a passing interest in spiritual issues, who had occasionally attended séances just out of curiosity and been persuaded to briefly attempt automatic writing.[18] Then one night while staying in Paris she felt strongly impelled to write down a message, the contents of which she doesn't disclose but which was signed 'X'. She could make little of it, but the following day a friend identified the author as a well-known, elderly lawyer, student of philosophy and author with whom Barker had been friends before she moved to Europe. It then emerged that he'd died only days before that first communication.

With some degree of initial reluctance but much encouragement from her friend, Barker made more successful attempts to channel X, and over the next three years compiled in excess of 130 letters contained in the three volumes of *Letters from the Living Dead Man*, published between 1913 and 1919. She decided to keep his identity secret, but he was later revealed to be well-known Los Angeles judge David Patterson Hatch, who himself had published books on occult and mystical subjects. It is also interesting to note that, having commenced with conventional automatic writing, Hatch and Barker switched to pure telepathy – as used by Philip Gilbert with his mother Alice, and Frances Banks with Helen Greaves – from about Letter 20.[19]

As regards hells, Hatch indicates that there are many such, most created and inhabited by single discarnates intent on punishing themselves as related in the last chapter. But he also makes an albeit brief reference to visiting a 'hell of fire and brimstone such as Dante must have seen', although he provides no details.[20] But he does go into more detail about a visit to a 'gin palace' in the near-earth plane where he witnesses a similar revolting scene to the Officer above:[21]

> A young man with restless eyes and a troubled face... and threadbare clothes... was leaning on the bar... Close to him, taller than he and bending over him, with its repulsive, bloated, ghastly face pressed close to his, as if to smell his whisky-tainted breath, was one of the most horrible astral beings which I have seen in this world since I came out... The hands of the creature were clutching the young man's form, one long and naked arm was around his shoulders, the other around his hips. It was literally sucking the liquor-soaked life of its victim, absorbing him, using him.

NDE REPORTS

GEORGE RITCHIE

George Ritchie's journey through the other realms, the beginning of which we discussed in chapter 14, continues with him being taken to a crowded bar near a Navy base in the near-earth plane, where he witnesses a similar disturbing scene to those reported by the Officer and Hatch above.[22] In amongst the incarnate humans are a multitude of discarnates who are desperately fighting over drinks on the bar, even though they can't actually lift the glasses. But then, just like the Officer, he's shocked by what happens when one young man falls down in a drunken stupor:

> I was staring in amazement as the bright cocoon around the unconscious sailor simply opened up. It parted at the very crown of his head and began peeling away from his head, his shoulders. Instantly, quicker than I had ever seen anyone move, one of the insubstantial beings who had been standing near him at the bar was on top of him. He had been hovering like a thirsty shadow at the sailor's side, greedily following every swallow the young man made. Now he seemed to spring at him like a beast of prey... Twice more, as I stared, stupefied, the identical scene was repeated. A man passed out, a crack swiftly opened in the aureole round him, one of the non-solid people vanished as he hurled himself at that opening, almost as if he had scrambled inside the other man.

This experience is followed by a trip to a genuinely hellish realm inhabited only by discarnates:[23]

> They were the most frustrated, the angriest, the most completely miserable beings I had ever laid eyes on... Everywhere people were locked in what looked like fights to the death, writhing, punching, gouging... Although they appeared to be literally on top of each other, it was as though each man was boxing the air; at last I realised that of course, having no substance, they could not actually touch one another. They could not kill, though they clearly wanted to, because their intended victims were already dead, and so they hurled themselves at each other in a frenzy of impotent rage... These creatures seemed locked into habits of mind and emotion, into hatred, lust, destructive thought patterns.
>
> Even more hideous than the bites and kicks they exchanged were the sexual abuses many were performing in feverish pantomime. Perversions I had never dreamed of were being vainly attempted all around us. It was impossible to tell if the howls of frustration that reached us were actual sounds or only

> the transference of despairing thoughts... What was keeping them here?.. Perhaps in the course of eons or of seconds, each creature here had sought out the company of others as pride-and-hate-filled as himself, until together they formed this society of the damned.

It is worth noting at this point that several sources, particularly the Officer, emphasise that the mere *willing* of pain onto another, and the *expectation* of it on the part of the recipient, is enough to replicate a human punch, stabbing, gunshot or whatever. Of course because there's no lasting damage, the torment can be continued ad infinitum. Ritchie also reinforces the message that suffering in the hellish realms is at least as much about perpetual frustration at no longer being able to satiate various appetites as about anything else.

HOWARD STORM

One of the most renowned, hellish NDEs is that of Howard Storm.[24] As a professor of art at the University of North Kentucky he seemed to 'have it all', but was inwardly deeply sad and something of a control freak. One afternoon in 1985 while on a trip to Paris, he was suddenly taken ill with a perforated small intestine and rushed to hospital. As he awaited an operation the following morning he was in such intense pain that, drifting in and out of consciousness, he suddenly found himself standing by the side of the bed looking at his own body.

He admits that his utter confusion at this point was at least partly due to his avowed rejection of any sort of afterlife – here we find a materialist having a difficult time again – but emotionally he was also angry and upset. So when he realises his wife can't hear him screaming at her, and then hears voices saying they can help him, he reluctantly follows them out of the door and into a 'hazy fog'. He has the impression of walking for a very long time, while the silhouetted figures with him become increasingly aggressive. When he tries to turn back they push and shove him, and then start clawing and biting. As fast as he pushes them off more arrive, all of them wanting to cause him pain, seeming to feed off his misery.

In the midst of all this fear and turmoil an inner voice tells him to pray and, despite the reluctance of his still 'rational' mind, he starts to chant the Lord's Prayer. His tormentors go into a frenzy, screaming and yelling but at least backing off, until he finds himself alone. Yet he still feels utterly hopeless until, in his desperation, he cries out to Jesus to save him. At this point a small dot of light begins to approach, growing and growing until it surrounds him with an incredibly radiant and healing love and compassion. Just as with the Officer above, this demonstrates the power of prayer – although of course it can be *any* prayer, to *anyone*, as long as it's a heartfelt cry for help.

EBEN ALEXANDER

We saw in chapter 4 that prior to his NDE Eben Alexander too was a fully paid-up member of the materialist school, coming as he did from the medical and scientific community. Now we have a chance to examine some of the details of his experience and, although at the outset he finds himself in a 'pulsing, pounding blackness' that doesn't unduly bother him, things then take a turn for the worse:[25]

> The longer I stayed in this place, the less comfortable I became... a feeling like I wasn't really part of this subterranean world at all, but trapped in it. Grotesque, animal faces bubbled out of the muck, groaned or screeched, and then were gone again... The more I began to feel like a me – like something separate from the cold and wet and dark around me – the more the faces that bubbled up out of that darkness became ugly and threatening. The rhythmic pounding off in the distance sharpened and intensified as well – became the work-beat for some army of troll-like underground labourers, performing some endless, brutally monotonous task. The movement around me became less visual and more tactile, as if reptilian, wormlike creatures were crowding past... Then I became aware of a smell: a little like faeces, a little like blood, and a little like vomit. A biological smell, in other words, but of

> biological death, not of biological life. As my awareness sharpened more and more, I edged ever closer to panic. Whoever or whatever I was, I did not belong here. I needed to get out.

In a similar way to TE Lawrence earlier, this knowledge that he didn't belong was enough for Alexander to be rescued from this horrific experience by a 'light' reaching down into the darkness and providing an escape tunnel for him.[26] But again it seems that his lack of belief in an afterlife had a significant bearing on the unpleasantness of his initial experience.

MAURICE RAWLINGS

If we turn now to more general NDE research, most exponents only rarely report negative or hellish experiences. The main exception to this rule is US cardiologist Maurice Rawlings, who provided some of the evidential cases in chapter 4. His work is usually somewhat dismissed as that of a fanatical Christian who lost his objectivity, and admittedly his conversion from typical medically trained sceptic and materialist appears to have been swift, complete and very much biblically driven.[27] No surprise then that *Beyond Death's Door* contains a great deal of Christian proselytising – nowhere more than when he reminds us that, although many NDEs involve some sort of 'figure of light', Satan loves to disguise himself.[28]

But even if some of his interpretations are open to question, that shouldn't entirely detract from the evidence he presents. His conversion came as a result of witnessing a cardiac patient having a hellish NDE in the midst of repeated resuscitation – an experience so terrifying that the patient blocked all memory of it afterwards and could only recall certain more pleasant aspects.[29] So Rawlings' suggestion that the reason most other researchers don't report hellish NDEs is because they're only interviewing subjects some time after the event, by which time they may have blocked the unpleasant elements, has a certain plausibility.[30]

Disappointingly his chapter that concentrates on hellish

experiences quotes a number of cases from other sources, and nearly all of them contain some sort of description of a 'fiery underworld' in keeping with the biblical training of their subjects.[31] A fine example is that of Kenneth Hagin, who was raised in a highly orthodox Southern Baptist setting. He had an NDE aged only fifteen due to a malformed heart, during which he entered the very 'fires of hell' but was rescued by the 'word of God' loosening his demon attendant's grip. He went on to become a Baptist minister. Although we've seen that some environments in the lower astral can have a fiery element to them, remember it's also true that prior expectations and subjective interpretation tend to play a more significant role in NDEs because by their very nature they're one-off experiences.

Having said that Rawlings does cite several less Christianised cases from his own portfolio. They make for pretty harrowing reading, although in each the subject is 'saved' by some sort of intervention:[32]

> The next thing I remember was entering this gloomy room where I saw in one of the windows this huge giant with a grotesque face that was watching me. Running around the windowsill were little imps or elves that seemed to be with the giant. The giant beckoned me to come with him. I didn't want to go, but I had to. Outside was darkness but I could hear people moaning all around me. I could feel things moving about my feet. As we moved on through this tunnel or cave, things were getting worse. I remember I was crying.

> I was going through this long tunnel and I was wondering why my feet weren't touching the sides. I seemed to be floating and going very fast. It seemed to be underground. It may have been a cave, but the awfullest, eerie sounds were going on. There was an odour of decay like a cancer patient would have... Some of the workers were only half human, mocking and talking to each other in a language I didn't understand... There are a lot of other things that may have happened that I don't remember. Maybe I'm afraid to remember!

In another case witnessed by a colleague, a girl of fourteen who has attempted suicide is being resuscitated when she keeps crying out, 'Mama, help me! Make them let go of me!' The doctors think she means them, but in the immediate aftermath she explains it was 'those demons in hell, they wouldn't let go of me, they wanted me, I couldn't get back, it was just awful!' As with Rawlings' own initial case, and to a lesser extent the subject quoted above, she subsequently repressed these terrifying memories.

He never wrote a follow-up, but in that first book he suggests that the number of hellish cases in his portfolio is 'accumulating rapidly' – presumably due to him attempting more real-time questioning before memories could be blocked.

BRUCE GREYSON AND NANCY BUSH

In a 1992 paper written for *Psychiatry* magazine, Bruce Greyson and Nancy Bush begin by backing up Rawlings' conclusions. They cite multiple studies indicating that unpleasant or even hellish NDEs are significantly more prevalent than the mainstream books on the matter tend to suggest, along with further convincing arguments as to why they're probably under-reported.[33]

They then describe how over a ten-year period they themselves managed to collate some fifty distressing or even terrifying NDE reports from contributors writing to them both spontaneously and as a result of an advert they placed.[34] Many of their correspondents had never heard of NDEs before, had no particular religious affiliations and were scared to tell even their loved ones about what had happened to them.

These cases were placed in three categories: typical experiences involving a tunnel and light that were nevertheless interpreted as distressing; experiences of total darkness, nothingness or a void, often accompanied by mocking voices suggesting that human life is all an illusion; and a smaller number of genuinely hellish experiences involving dark locations whose inhabitants were being tortured or were in constant pain.

OOB REPORTS

EMANUEL SWEDENBORG

The third part of Emanuel Swedenborg's *Heaven and Hell* is devoted to the innumerable dark realms he was allowed to visit on his travels, although the sense is that he was allowed to 'look into them' rather than fully immerse himself in them as most of our other sources seem to have done.[35] Equally unusual is that his heavy Christian bias seems to imply that there's no salvation for those who descend into hellish realms.[36] Despite this he's at pains to point out that 'after death it is we, not the Lord, who cast ourselves into hell', and stresses again and again that, just as in the earth plane, spirits are drawn to others of like mind – all of which is thoroughly in keeping with our contemporary view.[37]

Like so many others, Swedenborg also describes the grotesque appearance of spirits in the lower astral as being an outward reflection of their inner state:[38]

> One can tell instantly what their nature is not only from their faces but also from their bodies, and especially from their speech and behaviour... Some of their faces are black... some with huge ulcerated sores... in many cases there is no visible face, only something hairy or bony in its place.

Like Franchezzo he also suggests that *to each other* they appear as they would want to appear, for example beautiful and clothed in finery, the inference again being that it's only visitors from higher planes who see them as they truly are. Rather more unique is his suggestion that the 'hellfire' often reported in the Bible and elsewhere isn't necessarily a literal fire or flame, but the way in which the noxious emanations from these spirits and their abodes is often perceived by visitors.[39]

Swedenborg's accounts of the hellish realms aren't particularly vivid or detailed – indeed sometimes he deliberately shies away from describing the awfulness of what he's seen. But he does talk about the varieties of scenery, first in terms of the entrances to the different hells:[40] 'Some are under mountains, hills and cliffs; some are like caves and caverns; some are like large chasms and quagmires; some like swamps; and some like stagnant ponds.' As to what is found within:

> Some looked like the lairs or dens of wild animals in the woods, some like the vaulted chambers and crypts found in mines... In some you can see what look like the ruins of houses and cities after a fire... In the milder hells you can see crude huts, sometimes grouped in something like a city, with alleyways and streets. There are hellish spirits in these homes, with constant quarrels, hostility, beating and violence. The streets and alleys are full of thieves and robbers. In some hells there are nothing but brothels, foul to look at and full of all kinds of filth and excrement. There are also dark forests where hellish spirits roam like wild beasts; and there are underground caves there where they flee when they are being threatened by others. Then there are desert areas where everything is barren and sandy, with rugged cliffs here and there with caves in them, and huts scattered around as well.

In terms of the behaviour of the inhabitants there is again a strong correlation with some of the more detailed elements of Franchezzo's experience – not mentioned earlier – when Swedenborg describes the initial falseness and subsequent attempts at enslavement that form the modus operandi in many of these hellish realms:[41]

> They are accepted cordially at first and think they have arrived among friends. This lasts only a few hours, though. All the while they are being probed to find out how crafty they are, and therefore how powerful. Once this probing is complete the attacks begin in various ways, getting more and more severe and intense... After these attacks, the malevolent spirits begin to torment the newcomers with punishments until finally they are reduced to slavery.

ANNIE BESANT AND CHARLES LEADBEATER

Annie Besant describes the lowest regions of the astral in similar terms. Moreover, like the Officer, Hatch and Ritchie, she provides descriptions of desperate discarnates attempting to attach themselves to or even take possession of – or in her terms 'obsess' – their human counterparts in the near-earth plane:[42]

> The atmosphere of this place is gloomy, heavy, dreary, depressing to an inconceivable extent. It seems to reek with all the influences most inimical to good, as in truth it does, being caused by the persons whose evil passions have led them to this dreary place. All the desires and feelings at which we shudder find here the materials for their expression; it is, in fact, the lowest slum, with all the horrors veiled from physical sight parading in their naked hideousness. Its repulsiveness is much increased by the fact that in the astral world character expresses itself in form, and the man who is full of evil passions looks the whole of them; bestial appetites shape the astral body into bestial forms, and repulsively human-animal shapes are the appropriate clothing of brutalised human souls. No man can be a hypocrite in the astral world, and cloak foul thoughts with a veil of virtuous seeming...
>
> Men here show out their passions in all their native hideousness, their naked brutality, full of fierce unsatiated appetites, seething with revenge, hatred, longings after physical indulgences which the loss of physical organs incapacitates them from enjoying, they roam, raging and ravening, through this gloomy region, crowding round all foul resorts on earth, round brothels and gin-palaces, stimulating their occupants to deeds of shame and violence, seeking opportunities to obsess them, and so to drive them into worse excesses.

We can only assume as before that such degraded behaviour will lead to the perpetrators sinking down into the lower astral proper, if it hasn't already – remembering that those spirits who haven't sunk to the absolute depths of the lower realms may still be able to return to the near-earth on occasion. She does however end with a now familiar, more positive refrain:

> It is well once again to remember... that we have here no arbitrary punishments inflicted from outside, but only the

> inevitable working out of the causes set going by each person... Further, we may cheer ourselves in contemplating these unhappy brothers of ours by remembering that their sufferings are but temporary.

Charles Leadbeater provides similar descriptions of degraded spirits attempting to influence and even possess incarnates in the near-earth plane:[43]

> If men's earth-lives have been low and brutal, selfish and sensual, they will be conscious to the fullest extent in this undesirable region; and it is possible for them to develop into terribly evil entities. Inflamed with all kinds of horrible appetites which they can no longer satisfy directly now they are without a physical body, they gratify their loathsome passions vicariously through a medium or any sensitive person whom they can obsess; and they take a devilish delight in using all the arts of delusion which the astral plane puts in their power in order to lead others into the same excesses which have proved so fatal to themselves...
>
> One whose psychic sight has been opened will often see crowds of these unfortunate creatures hanging round... public houses, or other even more disreputable places – wherever the gross influences in which they delight are to be found, and where they encounter men and women still in the flesh who are likeminded with themselves.

He also suggests that classical myths – such as that of Tantalus, whose raging thirst could never be quenched; and of Sisyphus, condemned to forever roll the rock up the mountain only to see it slide down again – are warnings about this afterlife state of endless unfulfilment.[44]

SWAMI PANCHADASI (A.K.A. WILLIAM WALKER ATKINSON)

Yet another early OOB pioneer who is often overlooked in modern literature is William Walker Atkinson.[45] In the early twentieth century he edited and wrote articles for a number of magazines devoted to the 'New Thought' movement that had sprung up in the US, a key element of which was the crucial importance of the law of attraction – which we've already discussed.[46] But as an occultist more in the theosophical vein he was not long behind Vincent Turvey in publishing an account of his OOB travels. What is more, unlike Turvey and other early OOB pioneers such as Oliver Fox and Sylvan Muldoon who seem to have restricted their travels to the near-earth planes, he ventured further afield.

In his far-reaching *The Astral World*, published in 1915 under one of his several Hindu-sounding pseudonyms, Swami Panchadasi, he describes the inhabitants of some lower astral planes as 'so low in the scale as to seem almost beast-like, rather than human'.[47] He goes on to describe similar near-earth scenes to those already discussed:

> On all sides... they see their kind in the flesh eating, drinking, gambling, engaging in all forms of debauchery and brutality – and while they eagerly cluster around, they cannot make their presence felt under ordinary circumstances, nor can they participate in the scenes which they witness. The lack of the physical body is indeed a very hell to them, under such circumstances... Occasionally, they are able to influence some earth companion, who is so saturated with liquor, or overcome by drugs, that he is physically open to such influences.

Again, though, he balances these descriptions by emphasising that 'even the lowest rises in time'.

YRAM (A.K.A. MARCEL FORHAN)

Electrical engineer Marcel Forhan similarly wrote under a pseudonym, Yram, and his *Practical Astral Projection*, originally published in French in 1925, reflected fourteen years of OOB experiences.[48] He too 'travelled from dimension to dimension', including into the lower planes:[49]

> I noticed that a 'being' was coming towards me. He was dressed in a cloak whose dark grey colour did not inspire confidence in me; yet, despite my mistrust, I went on my way with him. Soon I found myself in the centre of a town, being chased by men in black. Passing through the forms which were

> being built up around me, hiding in one house and then another, I found myself shut up in a kind of small cavern from which there was no exit. Mentally, I called for my guide. Immediately I was freed from the illusions created by these beings. All traces of houses or town had disappeared.
>
> I was in space, surrounded by about fifteen persons who were quite incapable of hiding their malevolent thoughts. My curiosity aroused, I contemplated their envious and sneering faces and made the protective sign of the cross. They staggered back slightly, but once more came forward laughing and talking foully. I made this an opportunity to try out the value of the so-called magical signs: triangles, pentagons, divine names, etc.. Not only did these have no effect, but they mimicked my gestures, laughing and sneering at me all the while. They even managed to catch hold of my arm to stop me. The result was that I lost my temper... I came hurling back into my body, furious with rage, my teeth clenched, but luckily unharmed... I have learned since that the best and most powerful protection is a thought of love, which may be symbolised by the sign of the cross.

Elsewhere he reports:[50] 'In a world which was lower than this one I observed a group composed of voluptuaries and slaves to animal passion. The dwelling places in certain cases would be no more than a stable smelling strongly of urine.' But he then adds the familiar refrain: 'Those beings who are more advanced lead, little by little, those individuals who show the necessary desire to a state of consciousness above that of their existing one.'

CAROLINE LARSEN

Caroline Larsen provides a number of reports of visits to the lower realms that could be individual or group hells – but they're included here because of the level of degradation of their inhabitants', whose inner characters heavily influence the outer form they project:[51]

> I entered a house and found that room led on to room in a straight and seemingly endless line... Many of the dwellers

> were strange and terrible. In one room sat the squat and ugly form of a woman who on earth had kept a house of ill fame. She had been the ruin of the body and soul of many an unfortunate girl. Now, though in the spirit world, her one horrible desire was to continue her former infamous career... I shuddered as I hurried from her presence to another room, where I found tenants of many types, pathetic, or repulsive, or horrible...
>
> One of [the inhabitants] particularly attracted my attention because he was such an unusually horrible specimen of this type of spirit. Evil seemed to have actually deformed him. His face was ill-proportioned – far too wide for its height. There was hardly anything one could call a nose, and the mouth stretched from ear to ear. The ears, abnormally large, hung below the chin. Beneath an extremely flat forehead, nearer the temples than the nose, was set a large pair of eyes that shone with a diabolical malice which froze the very spirit within me. His face expressed only evil, low lust and ruthless hatred. I clung to my guide for protection. The arms of this misshapen spirit dangled loosely from his grotesque frame. His fingers, gnarled and rough, resembled the claws of an eagle... My guide explained to me that such a spirit spent most of his time on the earth, endeavouring to win over mortals to a life of sin and evil such as he had himself indulged in.

Here we can see her corroborating the idea that at least some of these denizens of the lower astral seem to be able to return to the near-earth plane to harass and attach themselves to incarnate humans, a point she reiterates elsewhere:[52] 'On earth these spirits had no vision of spiritual things and they were wholly absorbed in material pleasures, worldly success or base desires... Those whose desires were evil strive to attract others, both spirits and those still in our world, to their own false standards. With them life does not advance, but only futilely repeats itself.' She then describes being led into a 'desolate, vast enclosure' containing:[53]

> ...those spirits who arrived with minds clouded or shattered by the use of drugs or liquor, or by indulgence in their evil

> passions on earth. Here their minds, and often their astral bodies, remained crippled as on earth. On couches, on the floor, or huddled in corners lay or crouched these wrecks of humanity, blind of spirit and shrivelled of limb, often entirely unclothed, with stupor or dull hopelessness written in their eyes. The atmosphere of death, desolation, and despair filled my soul with anguish. My woman guide suddenly stopped. Here before us on a bench lay a shape twisted and deformed. Its motionless silence seemed horrible; the face was terribly distorted; and the limbs a random heap.

FREDERICK SCULTHORP

Frederick Sculthorp reports a number of visits to the lower planes but, apart from the final quote below, none of them involve the distortion of features and so on usually found in the most hellish realms. However from the following description of their general tenor, and the fact they're more group than individual environments, again they're included here rather than in the previous chapter:[54]

> When I arrived on a lower plane I would at once know the nature of the place. The spirit body is very sensitive and at once picks up the thoughts of the people there. The result is a sickening harshness which is indescribable. The most depressing moments on earth cannot compare with it... However, if I had to stay awhile to witness something in these lower states, my spirit helper would neutralise these vibrations in some way. On most of these dull astral planes I am invisible to the people there. The lower spheres are quite earth-like. There are cities, towns, villages, etc., which seem to be replicas of existing localities on earth, and sometimes the conditions are similar to those on earth. They are quite 'solid' when the spirit body assumes the same wavelength. I have read that these localities are formed naturally and automatically by the minds of people who have passed to spirit life and expect to see their familiar surroundings. This seems to be true.

He then continues by recounting specific experiences.[55] On one particular visit with his ever-present but anonymous guide, he finds himself in a town where everyone is attracted to quarrelling with each other:

> Many of the lower states are inhabited by people with similar predominating thoughts or tendencies, who gravitate to the same approximate wavelength in spirit. This 'main-thought' is very strong and noticeable when entering such a state. One of my most distasteful visits was to a town inhabited by those unfortunate people with quarrelsome habits. I was put down in a street, and as usual sensed the quality of the place. It was dreadful and as I looked round, invisible to them, I saw people violently quarrelling. As my awareness became more of the state, my spirit body received their thoughts. They were vicious, pitiless and murderous.
>
> It was a hopeless place to be in, as each individual's nature was worsened by the collective thoughts of the whole. I could not stand it and said: 'Take me away.' My guide at once moved me and we arrived at the outskirts of the town, a bare, gravelly place, and there I saw a collection of hutches for pets like mice and rabbits. Asking what these were for, I was told that these people had no love for their fellow humans, but would sometimes be fond of a pet. They were encouraged (impressed) to keep pets in the hope that some sort of love would grow from it.

On another excursion Sculthorp is taken to what he calls a 'land of low thoughts':

> I saw what appeared to be a dreary endless marsh... The place seemed to smell like a town's sewage works. Here and there were sad-looking people, some slowly walking, some standing still. The vibrations of this place were wretched and I... was not kept long... There are many such places in the lower vibrations and their description is depressing, but the facts should be known.

Despite his adverse reaction he's then taken on a third trip to an even lower plane than before:

> I appeared to be nearing the lowest depths of the place and no one was visible. I was halted in front of what appeared to be a grey-looking warehouse with a door. This opened, and I was made to go forward, but was halted by the awful vibrations that met my spirit body. Inside I saw a number of individuals, perhaps a hundred, who were slowly walking about. Their clothing, which was nondescript, hung around them like festoons of dirty cobwebs and their faces were dull grey. The inside of the place was also grey; there was no colour and only a dim light penetrated from above. Wretched as the scene was, it was mild compared with the vibrations I felt. Each entity was walking slowly with bowed head taking no observable notice of anything. All their thoughts had the same dreadful tenor: 'We are here forever; there is no hope for us!'

This last again reminds us just how much the Christian doctrine of *eternal* damnation has to answer for in that, in removing hope from those who sink into the lower planes, it tends to at least temporarily blind them to the possibility of assistance and rescue that's *always* available to *everyone* at *all times*. Meanwhile Sculthorp finally reports distorted appearances when, during another journey, he's actually attacked by a group of demented spirits:[56] 'I thought that some of my attackers were boys until I noticed their faces and saw that they were shrivelled men. Such stunted spirit bodies are the result of the low mentality. The chief one was of normal size with a long purplish face with deep cracks in it – another spirit effect.' Needless to say his guide soon comes to his rescue.

Having said that, he too reminds us that help is available as soon as any of the unfortunate denizens of the lower planes open themselves to it:[57] 'These minds are fixed on earth conditions until at long last an inward questioning will gradually alter their weary round and they are open to the help that was previously ignored.'

ROBERT MONROE

Coming more up-to-date, Robert Monroe doesn't describe a great deal of lower astral travel in his various books, but here he describes the densest region of 'Locale II' that he sometimes has to pass through on his journeys:[58]

> It is a grey-black hungry ocean where the slightest motion attracts nibbling and tormenting beings. It is as if you were the bait dangling in this vast sea. If you move slowly and do not react to the curious 'fish' who come to investigate, you pass through without much incident. Move violently and fight back, then more excited denizens come rushing in to bite, pull, push, shove.

Then in a later projection he finds himself in the midst of a seriously debauched, lower astral environment:[59]

> I found I was standing a few feet away from an enormous pile of writhing forms. It reached up, slanting back as high as I could see. In each direction, right and left, it swept off into the distance. It reminded me of nothing so much as the interweaving of huge fishing worms in the bottom of a can after being left there overnight. The motion was continuous, thousands upon thousands, each wet slippery form wiggling in and out among the other in the pile, searching, trying to do something... but never achieving satisfaction. Three perceptive shocks hit me simultaneously. The forms were not worms, they were human! Second, the incredible staggering radiation of sexuality, both male and female, that emanated from the seething mass. Third, they were all physically dead... [I felt] intense compassion for those trapped in this undulating mass, so focussed and intent on seeking sexual satisfaction they were unaware of any other existence.

Here Monroe provides us with a timely reminder that we shouldn't judge the inhabitants of these realms, however odious or degraded we might find their behaviour. Instead we should exercise compassion. We will return to this issue in chapter 20.

GRAHAM DACK

Modern British OOB pioneer Graham Dack, who we met in chapter 5, provides us with a brief but heart-rending glimpse of what appears to be a similar environment to that in Sculthorp's third trip above:[60]

> All of a sudden, the ground opened up beneath me! I felt myself falling, projecting into what seemed to me to be the bowels of the earth. Further and further, faster and faster, until my descent eventually levelled out and before me I perceived a terrible spectacle. I was flying low over rows upon rows of naked people. Men and women standing naked, and frozen, in lines that stretched as far as my eyes could see, in every direction. They were alive but lifeless, holding hands in some semblance of unity, their faces drawn and blank, their bodies shivering in hopelessness. Between each row was a mere eighteen inches of space, their skin was a horrible shade of white, and a kind of blue mist swirled around them.

BRUCE MOEN

Bruce Moen, who attended the Monroe Institute and who we also met in chapter 5, describes visiting a former acquaintance of his joint-exploration partner Rebecca in the lower astral. This was a man called Max who had been a psychotherapist but also an out-and-out emotional sadist – for example he loved to set people up against each other and watch the fireworks, albeit that he did this in an extremely clever and subtle way.[61] No surprise then that they found him surrounded by those of his own kind, still setting up horrible encounters for others – but now with the added challenge that others in this environment were even more clever and sadistic, so that quite often he ended up as victim rather than perpetrator. This was truly a hell of his own making.

What is more Moen quite rightly warns that, whereas in the earth plane he had examples of people who led a kinder and more loving life that he *could* have followed, now there were no role models to show him a way out. As always Moen also reminds us that he would only escape when he allowed even the slightest doubt about his behaviour to create a chink in his armour, at which point help would be able to find a way in. Unfortunately when Moen saw him no such chink was in evidence.

GORDON PHINN

Gordon Phinn's guide Henry describes a slightly less unpleasant but nevertheless group environment that's perhaps reminiscent of Lawrence's grey town:[62]

> There is a level where souls are petty, mean-spirited, vindictive and gossipy in a back-stabbing sort of way, but never quite criminal in the conventional sense. Most of them know they're dead but seem not to care, carrying on with their spiteful, resentful grouchiness. Of course they end up with the same nasty quarrelsome neighbours they had on earth, as that is just what they deserve... To walk down a street in one of their towns is to know the scowl, the averted gaze, and the whispered suspicion.

He also describes similar near-earth scenes of obsessive attachment and possession to those mentioned earlier.[63] One in particular involves three discarnate drug addicts who start off by climbing into an incarnate dealer's car and squabbling like 'ravenous raptors' to see who can get closest to him and his stash of heroin.[64] Once it has been handed over to a surprisingly refined, middle-aged lady in a classy apartment, one of the discarnates waits until she has slipped into an almost comatose state then swoops straight into her prone form to try to vicariously enjoy the high.

JURGEN ZIEWE

Finally Jurgen Ziewe corroborates the idea of like-minded spirits flocking together:[65] 'People who were out to take advantage of their fellow human beings, to the extent of causing misery and destruction: fraudsters, rapists, murderers, psychopaths... tend to meet their match in the next life simply because of the laws of attraction.' He also echoes the other reports of deformed appearance:[66]

> In the absence of any redeeming qualities the inhabitants' appearance can be dramatically affected, producing a Gollum-like character, someone whose appearance is stunted,

> deformed, ugly and hideous, even down to torn and shabby, ragged clothes. Their dwelling places may be no better than a hut, or simply holes in the ground... They scuttle, bent over as if carrying a tremendous burden. All of which is simply the expression of the contents of their minds and an absence of humane qualities. Fortunately, people functioning on such low mentality as to warrant existence on the very lowest level are in the minority.

This latter is a timely reminder that the experiences reviewed here in Part 3 almost certainly aren't the norm for the *majority* of departing spirits. Nevertheless we'd be fooling ourselves if we tried to gloss over the fact that they appear to affect more than just a tiny minority.

19

MORE ON RESCUE AND RETRIEVAL

As we saw in the last chapter, both Howard Storm and Eben Alexander were saved from their hellish NDEs by being surrounded by light – which almost certainly means a rescuer from the higher planes helped them to escape, but because they were so unaccustomed to such high energy they were unable to work out what was really going on. In chapter 15 we also saw TE Lawrence being helped to safety by his rescuer Mitchell not least because, like Alexander, he knew he didn't really belong in such a grey environment. This isn't dissimilar to the relatively swift and decisive assistance offered to those who find themselves dazed and confused in the near-earth plane. Here help is always on hand – for example, we saw in the last chapter that this is exactly the work the Officer turns to after his own hellish experiences, and we'll encounter many more departed spirits who engage in it in Part 4. Moreover many departed spirits accept this help with little resistance and move on, as we'll see in chapter 21. But some take rather longer, and these are the ones we refer to as *trapped* and in need of more serious rescue and retrieval.

SPIRITS TRAPPED IN THE NEAR-EARTH PLANE

We saw at the outset that these kinds of departed spirits tend to cling tenaciously to earthly possessions or settings, or remain unconvinced they're even really dead. As an example, we introduced Cynthia Sandys' *Awakening Letters* in chapter 17, and in one a departed friend describes accompanying a spirit from the higher planes – who takes the form of a Crusader from the Middle Ages – on a mission to rescue former slaves from the dungeons of a castle in Cyprus, where they'd been trapped for centuries of earth time:[1]

> I was amazed by the number of unawakened 'ghosts'... still lurking in the lower part of the castle. Lots... were still earthbound mainly owing to past deeds of violence and injustice combined with a complete lack of desire to change or to improve their lot. I... was told that rescue work had always been going on, but until they were ready for help it was useless.

In another Sandys' brother Joe describes being taken by his similarly discarnate son to a pub on the earth plane to re-experience the joys of Christmas.[2] Although the astral inhabitants aren't anything like the ravenous alcoholics encountered in the last chapter, they nevertheless discover that one old man has been trapped for some time. He admits he's becoming somewhat bored and had expected something rather more from the afterlife, although he didn't know what, at which point Joe and his son whisk him away to the mid astral so he can start to begin his journey proper.

Nor is help only provided from the spirit planes. For example, the group led by Emily French and Edward Randall often conduced séances that were deliberately targeted at freeing trapped spirits, sometimes large numbers at a time, by helping them to recognise they've passed and can now move on.[3] This work was usually undertaken in conjunction with spirit helpers too. Meanwhile Gladys Leonard describes exactly the same thing:[4] 'Many rescue circles are held where mediums and sitters are specially developed so as to help and advise the unhappy spirits that are brought to them by guides whose mission it is to do this work.' It is also worth noting that in his 1945 book *Lychgate* none other than Lord Hugh Dowding, head of RAF Fighter Command during WWII's 'Battle of Britain', describes his and his wife's close involvement with a spiritualist rescue circle.

Similarly in his anonymously channelled *Road of Many Ways* John emphasises that with harder cases than his own it's often easier to enlist the help of human rescue circles, because their vibration tends to be closer to that of the departed than that of the spirit helpers themselves. From this perspective, two of his fellow communicants found themselves sufficiently lost and confused that they were guided towards his human circle in Cape Town.[5]

The first is Ken, a US soldier involved in the Korean War who finds himself face to face with an enemy soldier firing a burst straight at him. Yet he carries on retreating with a few comrades, unable to understand how he wasn't hit. Over several days they fall right back to the coast, expecting to be re-engaged by an enemy who never appear. One by one his comrades seem to just disappear until he's on his own, totally confused and disoriented. Eventually he senses that he's in a room with people he doesn't know, who turn out to be John's circle. They ask Ken if he has anyone he was close to who has already passed over, and he finally becomes aware of the presence of his older brother Joe, who takes him off to a place of recuperation because he's suddenly very tired. It turns out that his bitterness at the loss of Joe during WWII, coupled with his hatred of the enemy in his war, had so distorted his outlook that he'd remained trapped in the earth plane for nearly two years. In a rather wonderful twist his rehabilitation really begins when he meets Ho, the Korean soldier who shot him but has also now passed and wants to be of service. They find they get on well by telepathy even though neither can speak the other's human language.

The other is Lillian who, although she doesn't remain trapped for too long, has a desperately difficult earth life. After her own mother dies she falls out with her stepmother, then starts seeing a young soldier during WWII and has a daughter by him. Not only does her child only survive a few days, but she then learns he too has died. Her whole life devastated she ends up selling herself on the streets. One night she's standing at her normal corner touting for business when she sees a car heading straight for her out of control. She thinks she's managed to dodge out of the way, but when she later goes home she's perplexed to find her landlady and a friend going through her belongings and refusing to take any notice of her. The same happens when she goes back to the street corner and her former co-workers ignore her too. She urgently prays for help and a man appears who guides her to John's rescue circle, who again help her to realise she's dead and to move on with the man. In something of a daze she finds herself reviewing her life and feeling somewhat ashamed and concerned at what will happen next, but she then finds herself in the courtyard of a beautiful building – where she's overjoyed to be reunited with her long-departed mother and baby girl. When they go inside she also finds a warm welcome from many other friends who had predeceased her, none of whom are judging her at all.

From an OOB perspective, Caroline Larsen reiterates the widely expressed view that help is always available for those trapped in the near-earth plane:[6]

> Finally there linger here... earthbound souls – those whose minds are open only to desires and influences of earth, having no wish for spiritual development... Helping spirits are to be seen everywhere and are easily recognised, for their aura envelops them in a ball of white light which indicates their high spiritual state... Before assistance can be given, the seeker must possess a sincere desire for improvement.

Meanwhile Robert Monroe describes receiving strong signals during the latter stages of his OOB journeying, which he learns are calls for help from trapped spirits – albeit that during his early attempts he seems to keep losing them after the initial rescue.[7] But these experiences spurred him on to introduce the 'Lifeline Programme' to his Institute, which was deliberately developed so that OOB participants could assist spirits who had only recently passed or become trapped. Bruce Moen became an enthusiastic member of this programme and describes assisting several trapped individuals to move on.[8] One is an elderly lady who suffered from Alzheimer's for many months before her passing, who then remains sitting, disoriented and confused, in a familiar chair in her kitchen. Another is a lady who experienced a long illness treated with extensive drugs, which seem to have dulled her consciousness considerably. This tends to confirm the suggestion, found in many spiritual writings, that our emotions and experiences in the *lead up* to our passing can also have a significant impact on our initial afterlife experience.

Finally Jurgen Ziewe indicates that he too involves himself in rescue work, and confirms the extent of assistance available from spirit helpers:[9]

> I have had plenty of practice helping other people when out-of-body and I know for sure that there are many discarnate 'social workers' having their work cut out for them giving a helping hand to people who simply haven't managed to deal with their mental turmoil.

SPIRITS TRAPPED IN THE LOWER PLANES

Even harder to rescue are the long-term residents of the lower planes – who may again remain unconvinced they're even dead, or may be so caught up in self-pity or guilt that they're unable to perceive anyone outside of themselves, or may have sunk low enough to be surrounded by like-minded spirits who may even drag them lower still. We saw in the last two chapters that Franchezzo engages in rescue missions to help these unfortunates as part of his rehabilitation, while Frances Banks' fellow Sisters do likewise purely out of love and a desire to help others. But we repeatedly encounter reports of such missions from a variety of other sources too.

For example, John Ward states:[10] 'The spirits in this plane devote themselves very largely to helping their fellow-men, especially in hell, and continuously journey down to that place to save those who are in bondage.' Better still, Lawrence rightly extols the virtues of his guide Mitchell in repeatedly tackling those cases that are far more difficult than his own:[11]

> This rescue work is his passion and when one understands the hazards he runs to make these difficult contacts, and the hurts and injuries sustained by his body in braving the harmful emanations, one can better appreciate the heroism of this work. I have known Mitchell fail when some desperate case has refused his help and drifted back into dark and misty regions where it is almost impossible to reach it. But I have never known him to give up, and again and again he will go out and scout on the borderlands to bring in the stragglers, always hopeful that sooner or later the lost one will return within his range again. He is, of course, not the only one engaged in this sort of work; there are many other devoted souls able to penetrate the depths according to the toughness of their make-up and the consequent length of time they can safely stay down there.

Lawrence also recounts the wonderfully redemptive tale of the rescue of a friend called Edgar:

> In a moment of frenzy he killed his wife and the law then sent him to death with all the usual accompaniments of shame and violence. I can well imagine the impossible conditions into which at first he drifted. His own shame and despair drew him to the darkest regions of the lower planes and his plight there was awful. He hid himself among the debased and brutal population of a town of ill repute, afraid that his victim would find and reproach him. Here he lived in a dark hell of his own making, a prey to fear and remorse. There are certain devoted souls who managed to penetrate to these regions in search of any who can be helped, and they found Edgar eventually and persuaded him to face his problem, come out of hiding and find his wife.
>
> She also had suffered. Anger and hatred of him had

> prevented her progress, but by degrees she was helped to see and understand the real situation for which she had been partly responsible, but which had been hidden from her by the mists of her own anger. These two poor souls were still bound to each other by wrongdoing which seems to make nearly as strong a bond as love itself. Until they had cleared the anger from their souls and the blindness from their eyes they could not get free. They neither of them wished to remain together, or so they thought at first; yet when, by the help of those who are skilled in bringing about such adjustments, they did at last face the evil in themselves instead of condemning it in each other, the change in their whole condition produced a strange solution. They each laid hold again upon their essential innocence; they renewed the long-lost appearance of youth and charm; and to their own surprise they found that the bond which really held them together was love.

Similarly Banks continues her description of her visit to the shadow lands in chapter 17 by describing how she witnesses the rescue of an artist.[12] He apparently had no little talent but squandered his gift in drink and drugs, and was eventually killed in a knife fight with a fellow painter. She finds him seated in a narrow street outside his dark, foul-smelling hovel, and his paintings are 'all dark, all hideous, all primitive and almost evil... all exceedingly ugly'. As so often, having had no belief in an afterlife he's angry and believes himself to be in some sort of illusory dream from which there's no escape. It is clear he's been visited unsuccessfully by rescuers before, and initially he continues to refute the fact that he's in a hell of his own making and that other, lighter realms exist. But eventually he's persuaded to accompany one of Banks' accomplices to find pastures new where he can rediscover his ability to paint beautiful scenes, and his rehabilitation can begin.

Meanwhile by the time of his later messages Philip Gilbert is himself involved in 'welfare work', and describes his creative approach as follows:[13]

> My work in the lower astral... goes on and on: it seems endless, the number of people needing help. Our control department

> has lists of them, running into millions – yes, literally!.. I usually, by a certain power I have acquired – a power of imagining myself into other people's minds – make myself part of his illusion first, and then, I act as my intuition prompts me. That is why the job suits me: it is never monotonous. Each case is different... Also there are long periods when I deliberately train my thought force by meditation and by practising the creation of thought images. I can do the oddest things when I really set about it and this faculty is a joy to me. I astonish some folks and try to shake them out of their set environments by doing this.

By their very nature NDE reports don't tend to involve much in the way of rescue and retrieval except of the subjects themselves. But on his journey through the realms George Ritchie does mention that various beings of light hover over the hellish planes just waiting for the chance to help any of the unfortunate inhabitants – albeit that sadly most are far too self-preoccupied to notice.[14]

Similarly most OOB pioneers tend to concentrate on helping those who have only recently passed, as we'll see in chapter 21, or on those trapped in the near-earth plane, as we've just seen. However Gordon Phinn provides brief descriptions of undertaking rescues while OOB in what appear to be lower planes.[15] He reports that localised despots similar to earthly drug barons resent losing any of their acolytes and can make life difficult. So the response he's developed is to literally 'zap' any who show signs of being ready to move on with 'white light', which immediately lifts them out of that level of vibration so he can work with them.

We will encounter more passing references to rescue and retrieval missions in chapter 21.

WHY ARE RESCUE MISSIONS NEEDED?

We have seen that every trapped spirit will eventually break free, and that none is lost for good. So the question arises: why are deliberate rescue missions so widespread? Why not just wait for each unfortunate spirit to be ready and to ask for help – especially given that, as we've seen, elapsed time is experienced differently in the afterlife planes? Robert Benson provides perhaps the most obvious answer:[16]

> Every spirit hates the lower realms for the unhappiness that is there, and for no other reason. And for that reason great organisations exist to help every single soul who is living in them to rise out of them into the light. And that work will continue through countless ages until every soul is brought out from these hideous places.

Gilbert raises my very question, but then gives a somewhat different answer:[17]

> If it is all from the point of view of eternity, so temporary, why is it of supreme importance to dig these people out of their trouble? Because it is cumulative. The more muddled, miserable there are who when they get here give up and go under to the ever insidious forces of the vacuum, the more these forces grow in power... Also the advanced people are, I am told, affected to an extent by very great waves of misery and malice.

This hints at a somewhat outdated 'good versus evil' conflict. But it may still contain a kernel of truth that, from an OOB perspective, Monroe builds on:[18]

> As a group, they are the major blockage in the flow of the human learning experience. Until they are reached and assisted, or some glimmer of awareness occurs, they remain in this locked-in state for years, perhaps centuries... Evidently there are methods by which rescues are achieved individually and on a relatively large scale – and the process is ongoing.

Meanwhile Waldo Vieira makes a similar point:[19] 'Sick individuals make up a large part of the extraphysical population and are a burden to our school/hospital/planet... The cleansing projection is one of the greatest opportunities for the projector to make himself or herself useful.'

To be somewhat more specific, I've come across suggestions that concerted efforts at rescue and retrieval are a vital part of the 'shift in consciousness' on our planet that many spiritual commentators have been discussing for some decades now. This is said to be precisely because the existence of so many disturbed and confused spirits who are trapped in the near-earth and lower planes is potentially something of a blockage to this process.

We have just seen that plenty of modern OOB pioneers deliberately undertake such rescue work. But there are also suggestions that many normal, incarnate humans are engaged in such missions at night, when asleep and projecting OOB – something we'll discuss more generally in chapter 26. This despite the fact that most remember nothing of this important work when they wake up. Again, it seems they're sometimes better placed to assist those in the lower planes than more high-energy spirits. In fact Gilbert suggests his mother is one such.[20] More recently Rosalind McKnight describes this as a widespread process.[21] As does Vieira, who even witnesses gatherings of sleeping OOB projectors being instructed by spirit helpers as part of rescue programmes involving specific problem areas in the cities they're from – coordinated programmes that are apparently in operation all over the world.[22] Indeed, even as far back as the early twentieth century, Charles Leadbeater was providing instruction for incarnates who wished to provide general assistance to confused spirits making the transition.[23]

IS THE SITUATION GETTING BETTER OR WORSE?

Concerted attempts at rescue and retrieval in all the forms we've just mentioned should on the face of it be reducing the overall numbers of spirits trapped in the near-earth and lower planes. But to what extent are disturbed or degraded spirits who have only recently passed counteracting this by continuing to swell their ranks?

Monroe, for example, is in no doubt:[24] 'Their numbers increase constantly and will continue to do so as long as the physical human values that generate the condition remain unchanged.' So is he right?

This is no easy question to answer. On the one hand our apparently increasing obsession with appearance, celebrity, material possessions and so on might be expected to increase the numbers of those who never even bother to think about the afterlife, or simply don't believe there is one. Not that such behaviour hasn't always attracted a certain kind of person down the ages, but it used to be more restricted to the elite, whereas nowadays it's spread across the entire spectrum of society. Having said that one might equally argue that in the modern world people generally are increasingly ready to spread love amongst their fellows, and to help those less fortunate than themselves – certainly to the extent that life is no longer the 'nasty, brutish and short' experience it has been for most of our existence on this planet.

So, on balance, this must remain an unanswered question.

20
CONCLUSION

Let me open my concluding remarks by repeating that my aim in Part 3 has absolutely *not* been to scare. Rather it has been to attempt to achieve some sort of balance in reporting on what can await us on the other side. It could be argued that too many modern spiritual commentators skip over the darker elements and present an unduly rose-tinted view, but as we've seen this isn't representative of the evidence – and nor, I would argue, is it healthy. Gladys Leonard, who as we've seen visited the lower realms repeatedly when OOB, describes how she wrestled with the same problem and came to the same conclusion:[1]

> I feel it cowardly to shirk truth because it is unpleasant, and it seems a very poor policy always to present one side of a picture, and purposely to ignore the other, when one knows it exists. Let us dwell on the happy, hopeful aspects of life as much as we will, but we must not imagine there are no evils to be cleared away. While we pretend there are none, or purposely avoid discussing or trying to tackle them, we help them to accumulate, just as one would by ignoring the presence of dirt or dust in a room, because one didn't want to raise trouble by making an onslaught on it.

What is more, if someone is already in a 'good space' about their life, then nothing I've presented here should be able to alter that. But for those who have doubts, potential unpleasantness and even suffering can be avoided by confronting our less savoury sides now, while in the earth plane, rather than leaving it till later. So if any of the warnings herein prompt such a response it's surely all to the good.

At this point it's also important to repeat that, as far as the more unpleasant experiences of the lower planes are concerned, these are *not* punishments imposed by higher entities who are waiting to judge us. The inhabitants are either judging themselves or are directly attracted to those realms by their very natures. One of Franchezzo's guides emphasises this point:[2]

> In those hells which you have seen all has been the outcome of men's own evil lives – the works of their own past – either upon earth or in its spheres. There is nothing but what has been the creation of the soul itself, however horrible may appear its surroundings to you. However shocked you may have felt at the spiritual appearance of these beings, yet you must remember that such as they are have they made themselves.

He then adds the crucial rider that hellish experiences do *not* last for eternity, and hope should always remain:[3]

> To all is given the inalienable birthright of hope, and to each will come at last the hour of awakening, and those who have sunk to the lowest depths will arise even as a pendulum swung to its farthest limit will arise and swing back again as high as it has sunk low... Not one atom of the immortal soul essence which has been breathed into man and become a living conscious individuality is ever again truly lost, wholly doomed either to annihilation or eternal misery.

THE IMPORTANCE OF COMPASSION

Speaking of judgment, from my own experience it's sometimes easy to allow this in when reading through this kind of material, especially some of the earlier reports that tend – whether intentionally or not – to have a more unsympathetic, Christian, good-versus-evil tenor. But, as difficult as it is for some people to accept, one of the corollaries of Supersoul Spirituality – and indeed of other more enlightened spiritual approaches – is that there's *no such thing* as 'good' or 'bad' per se. Any attempt to categorise actions or attitudes in this way will always rely on some sort of moral code developed by different cultures in different ages with very different ideas of what is 'right' and 'wrong', meaning there simply are no moral absolutes.[4] Instead, as we saw in chapter 7, there's only *experience*, because that's how consciousness expands. The corollary is that, however acutely painful some experiences in the earthly and lower planes might be, ultimately we're all just engaged in a game as actors in a play, and no permanent damage can ever be inflicted on our underlying essence.

Admittedly, at least in our human hologram, love-based experiences are far more rewarding to the individual and more expansive for the general consciousness than fear-based ones, and we'll return to this subject shortly. But let's not forget that, as we saw in chapter 8, we all come into the earth plane with different 'birth givens'. So how can we *judge* the subsequent adult behaviour of, for example, the poor unfortunate child born into orphaned squalor, with no love or affection to alleviate their suffering, just a constant battle for survival from an early age? Or the equally unfortunate one born into a life of intolerable sexual abuse from a family member or friend? Of course they don't *have* to turn out to be disturbed adults, and those who don't have passed the severest of tests their supersoul can set them. But if they *do* turn out to be even horribly disturbed, and end up trying to inflict their own torment onto others, is it any great surprise? Can we *really* stand in judgment on them, never having walked in their shoes?

Moreover we've already mentioned that for most of human history life has involved levels of cruelty and deprivation that we can scarcely even imagine today. *That* is why, as degraded as some of the descriptions in the preceding chapters are, *all* inhabitants of the lower astral deserve our compassion, not our judgment. What is more we would do well to remember this when we get to the other side.

THE CONSISTENCY OF THE REPORTS

What about the reliability of the information presented here in Part 3? We have certainly seen that there's incredible consistency between the various reports of the near-earth and lower astral planes. Even if a sceptic attempted to explain this away as what departed spirits and others *expect* to see, this is no solution because, as we've seen, that's exactly how these realms work. Human expectations built up over centuries help to *create* the plethora of afterlife heavens and hells that departed spirits are then attracted to. So it's not good enough to blithely suggest that Swedenborg and other more conventional Christian commentators set a tone in the eighteenth and nineteenth centuries that all others since have followed. It is much more likely that these are genuine, independent experiences obtained from different fields of research over more than a century – if we include Swedenborg over nearly three – that strongly corroborate each other.

Let us take a moment to review what these remarkable consistencies are, while recognising that even this is probably not an exhaustive list:

- The state of confusion after death, especially for those who don't believe in an afterlife, along with the failure to understand or accept what's happened.
- The attempts at attachment to and possession of incarnates in the near-earth plane, and the potential for sinking into lower planes as a result.
- The individual hells for the punishment of self, and the isolation of those who remain entirely wrapped up in themselves, often living in hovels, huts or caves.
- The group hells for those attracted to others of like mind, which sometimes form entire towns and cities whose very buildings and streets announce their degraded nature.

- The dominant obsessions of degraded environments, whether they be selfishness and greed, or the desire to subjugate and control others, or argument and conflict, or trickery and subterfuge, or bitterness and revenge, or various combinations thereof.
- Alternatively debauched environments where earthly obsessions with perversion and lust, or with gluttony, drink and drugs remain insatiable, leading to never-ending torment and frustration.
- The potential for the progressive worsening of the spirit's condition in group environments where degraded and obsessive behaviour is encouraged, or even required for survival.
- The grotesqueness of outward appearance reflecting the inner character, and the often bestial resemblance to animals, even half-human, half-animal hybrids.
- The grey bleakness, sometimes even blackness, and the rocky, or desert, or barren, or swampy or cavernous terrain, accompanied by an absence of vegetation and of colour.
- The reptiles and other foul beasts and tormenting demons inhabiting caves and swamps.
- The smell of decay and excrement.
- The attempts to ridicule, intimidate or even attack NDE or OOB visitors.
- The help always available to those who open themselves to it, however little, especially using the power of prayer.
- The importance of showing kindness and love to others in all planes, and the rehabilitation available thereby.

CONTEMPLATION AND REVIEW

There is strong evidence that when we pass over we'll experience the ubiquitous life review already mentioned several times in Part 3. This is found in many channelled accounts and most NDE reports, which we'll focus on in chapter 22. But for the moment one of the reasons why the contemplation of our own lives *now* is so important is because, if we *don't* do it while on the earth plane, we'll clearly be forced to do it in the afterlife – and as we'll find out this can be a real shock to the system. Sometimes this process is more akin to having an instantaneous, panoramic memory of every detail or our earthly life, or even just an instant awareness of our true nature, laid bare with no pretence or masking.

So we should be taking time to consider how we've behaved during our life as honestly and objectively as possible, and also to contemplate what lies beyond. However it's also important to stress that in the modern world the majority of people are just too busy 'getting on with it' to spend much time in such contemplation. I would like to think that for the great many who lead unselfish lives, always willing to lend a hand to neighbours or even strangers, their experience when they pass on will be broadly positive – even if they might suffer a degree of initial confusion.

WHAT DRIVES OUR AFTERLIFE EXPERIENCE?

To sum up, we've seen that there are four main determinants of the kind of experience we'll have, at least initially, when we pass into the afterlife realms:

1. Our expectations of what will happen, if any.
2. Any major obsessions or addictions, whether to a substance, a person or an activity. If strong enough the latter will continue to dominate our thinking after passing, whether we remain alone or are attracted to a group environment.
3. Our particular emotional state at the time of or in the run up to our passing – such as shock if it's sudden, a desire for revenge if it's unpleasant, a sense of unfinished business, or a dulling of the senses due to a lengthy illness.
4. Our reaction to having our true nature laid bare by life review or panoramic memory, which can lead to self-inflicted punishment.

TE Lawrence wonderfully reinforces the importance of being

aware of these various factors:[5]

> Much of this earlier nightmare could have been avoided if I had known how to avail myself of the help that was freely offered... I took [carried] over a very difficult make-up full of powerful repressions and tangled complexes, all of which caused me much suffering before they were straightened out. My own obstinacy and pride were largely to blame for my plight. This was purgatory, if you like, but unavoidable unless one has done the job beforehand.
>
> I think I really had the maximum difficulties: an attitude of blank unbelief in any future life, a repressed and powerful emotional state, and the shock of a violent death. So this was not the normal passing but just a difficult and painful personal experience. I am satisfied that it was a just necessity and that I had made it inevitable by my wilful ignorance and scepticism. 'Whatever a man sows' you know.

Philip Gilbert corroborates this view:[6]

> I think it is primarily essential for you people to get a clear, helpful line on the next phase of existence after 'death'... It helps (1) if you know intellectually something of what to expect, as then you can set to work at once to study new conditions and (2) if you have refrained from cluttering up your thought images with earthly obsessions or hate and greed, as these tie you up... What is wanted is for people to realise that they have got to go on, in a new form which is at first strongly affected and moulded by their physical life.

Australian Robert Bruce has been having OOB experiences since he was four years old and his *Astral Dynamics*, first published in 1999 and heavily revamped ten years later, is regarded as a classic practical manual. Although he doesn't talk about visiting the lower planes per se, he adopts a very similar stance:[7] 'There are many variations on how the afterlife transpires for individuals. What happens depends upon how much life pain, emotional baggage, and beliefs concerning death are carried into the afterlife. These are the things that generate the afterlife environment.'

PRACTICAL ADVICE

So let us now build all this into some practical advice that people can follow both before and after passing:

- We should try to come to terms with the life we've led before we pass over. If we can we should try and make amends for our less desirable actions. If we feel we've been going down a less than ideal or even destructive path, we should change our approach. It is never too late. We will return to what a more constructive path might be shortly.
- We should try to imagine our ideal heaven world, picturing it as vividly as we can and having an expectation of finding it after passing, although retaining an awareness that even this may only be a temporary sojourn.
- In the lead up to our passing we should try to remain as calm and positive as possible in the circumstances. In particular we should avoid the tendency to hang on to earthly life at all costs, irrespective of its quality, just because we're afraid of what does – or doesn't – lie on the other side.
- If we do find ourselves in any sort of unpleasant environment after passing we should immediately ask for help in whatever way suits us best, and *know* that it will come. We should also make it clear *to ourselves* that we don't belong here and we aspire to something better. If there are other spirits around, hopefully our vibrations are different anyway so we can ignore them just as we would a deranged person on a train or bus, or someone trying to cause a fight in a bar.
- If the above doesn't work straight away, it either means we're punishing ourselves in some way, or our emotional make-up is attracting us to a lower plane. We should try and work out what's going on and again ask for help, although accepting that we might require a short sojourn in a lower plane before we can properly move on.

Looking at it from the other side of the coin, as hard as this may sound in our modern world, we should try not to grieve for loved ones who have passed on with too much intensity, at least not for too long. Instead we should try to send them on their way with love and good wishes, accepting our own loss and not unduly wallowing in it – even if someone has seemingly been taken 'well before their time'. A certain knowledge that any passing is a new beginning and not an ending should surely help with this process.

Finally, of course, we can pass this simple advice on to others if we think they'll listen and it will benefit them. In particular we might try to help less ardent materialists to allow some sort of spiritual possibilities into their mental orbit, just in case they turn out to be wrong.

THE LAW OF KARMA AND ATTRACTION

One of Franchezzo's guides makes the clear point that 'there is not one thought we think but lives for good or ill, not one act whose image shall not live to torture or to solace the soul in the days of its release from its earthly form'.[8] Similarly Gilbert again gives us a stark warning when he echoes my earlier comments about the rose-tinted view adopted by many spiritual commentators. Even though he was communicating in the 1940s, arguably his comments are even more apposite now:[9]

> Education of everyone in a sensible instructed way about post-death possibilities would help enormously... The less salubrious aspects of my [rescue] work... do occupy a good deal of my time... too little stress is laid on this by the average spiritualist, with his often syrupy wishful thinking. The sooner people have it rammed into them that 'as ye sow, so shall ye reap' is the unmitigated truth, the sooner things will improve.

In traditional spiritual or religious circles this idea of 'sowing and reaping' is associated with karma, and of it being carried from one life to another. But we saw in chapter 8 that there are good reasons to question the traditional notion of reincarnation as one life *after* another, because instead it seems likely that all the life personalities projected by our supersoul are operating *alongside* each other, irrespective of the human era involved, in the 'eternal now'. So instead we might assume that it's more important to apply this maxim *within* our single earthly life as we go along – as in what we do one day or week affects what happens to us the following day or week. This is all well and good. But Gilbert is clearly suggesting that it's even more important to think in terms of what karma we carry into our *afterlife* – because *that's* where it will determine the experience we have, and where everything we've done in our earthly life has to be faced.

I have always shied away from talking about any sort of *law* of karma, because I felt the way it might be passed from one life to another in a traditional context was far too varied and dynamic to be regarded as an inviolate law. But now, in this new context, to suggest that what we have sown in our earthly life must be fully reaped in our afterlife starts to make some sense. What is more using *this* context we can now strip away the jargon and recognise that the law of karma and the law of attraction are effectively one and the same – they both involve cause and effect, reaping what we sow, getting back what we put out, or creating an experience that mirrors our inner state – but *not* judgment by others.

These laws operate in two obvious ways in the afterlife. First, all of our earthly actions and intentions will be fully laid bare and must be fully faced as part of the panoramic life review, and this may directly *cause* guilt and self-inflicted punishment. Second, the way we've led our earthly life will have a huge bearing on the plane, conditions, fellow spirits and experiences we're *attracted* to in the afterlife. This might mean we find ourselves in a lower astral environment, but it could just as easily lead us to one of the effectively *illusory* heavens in the mid astral, which we'll discuss more in Part 4. So even for those who avoid the lower astral there may be little cause for complacency.

Those sources who talk about such ideas tend to refer to just one, all-encompassing law. Here are Emanuel Swedenborg, Annie Besant, one of Emily French and Edward Randall's communicants, Henry Lanchester, Gladys Leonard and Frances Banks:

> Our nature after death depends on the kind of life we led in the world.[10]

> [The astral] does include conditions of suffering, temporary and purifactory in their nature, the working out of causes set going in his earth life by the man who experiences them. These are as natural and inevitable as any effects caused in this world by wrongdoing, for we live in a world of law and every seed must grow up after its own kind.[11]

> Upward and onward ye must go; and only by such a ladder as ye shall have built can ye mount. So it is well that ye build wisely and with care. Let the rungs be of good deeds, and ye shall mount quickly and joyously to great and splendid heights; but if ye are careless and slothful in the building, and heed not nature's laws – and they are writ that all may read – your advancement will be delayed by your failure, for each rotten rung must be replaced; and O ye of earth! If ye could but know the weariness of such undoing and redoing, more heed would ye give as ye rush onward through life.[12]

> We stand self-condemned. Our spirit cannot rise to higher realms than those for which it has fitted itself. There is no necessity to enforce any law, for the law is self-acting.[13]

> The power that a man will have, the position he will occupy, the place where he will live, all depend upon what he has made of his soul body while on earth. He cannot 'will' or 'choose' where he shall live in the spirit world; he goes to the place that he has fitted himself for during his life in the physical body.[14]

> By man's thoughts and inspirations he weaves for himself his future place in this dimension. This is logical law… The intensity and power with which light illumines the inner life are objectified here; the newly transported soul graduates always to its rightful place, to the place it has earned and prepared.[15]

To close this section, Swami Panchadasi suggests that the lower realms are exactly the sort of 'purgatory' – or 'place of the burning out of desires of a low kind' – described in many religions, and that this idea must have originally come from astral experiences.[16]

BUILDING UP SPIRITUAL CAPITAL

Another of French and Randall's communicants adds an interesting perspective:[17]

> Everyone knows what a handicap the lack of capital is in your world. Well, exactly the same thing applies here. Folks arriving here in the spiritually destitute condition before mentioned have just as hard, if not a harder, struggle to make their way in the spiritual life as anyone who is left without means on earth. People placed in the latter condition may and very often do receive financial help from friends and relatives, or societies which deal with that sort of thing, but there are no charitable institutions here. That is to say, no spirit ever gets something for nothing, or without effort on his part. Though we old spirits can and do help newcomers, we cannot give them spiritual riches – we can only show them how they may acquire them for themselves.

This indicates that there's no sense of divine *retribution* in the afterlife, but what does predominate for those unfortunates in the lower realms is the much more constructive idea of *rehabilitation* – in particular by building up spiritual capital or wealth. So how is this done? We have repeatedly seen references to them needing to open themselves up to becoming aware of and helping others as a way out of their predicament. More particularly we've seen that the Officer, after all his trials and tribulations in hellish realms, ends up helping others who have just passed. By contrast Franchezzo doesn't really spend time in the lower astral at all, except in that he's directed towards rescue and retrieval work as part of his rehabilitation. French and Randall's communicant quoted above continues by confirming this approach:

> Such wealth is not easily acquired, even here, but it is possible for any and every spirit to become possessed of it in time, if he only desires it sufficiently and is willing to work hard to get it. This may sound as if selfishness is encouraged here, but that is not so. Spirits can become possessed of the wealth here spoken of only by loving and unselfish conduct towards others.

> They must learn to work gladly and without thought of reward before they can hope to enjoy the fruits of their labours.

FINAL IMPLICATIONS FOR OUR EARTHLY LIFE

Several of French and Randall's other communicants translate these ideas of rehabilitation into their implications for our behaviour on the earth plane:[18]

> You cannot realise all each good, generous, noble thought will mean to you someday, even if it never grows into an act.
>
> Let me impress upon you that of all the pleasure I have received on the spirit side of life, the most came from those to whom I had previously done some act of kindness. If I had my earth life again, I would spend every hour doing good – I would spend my life in doing acts of kindness.

Arthur Ford expands on this using the example of a reasonably positive life review:[19]

> The veil is withdrawn, and we are able to see clearly where we erred and where we chose rightly and thus advanced perceptibly. There is a great joy as we realise that some of our most insignificant deeds, forgotten by ourselves, loom large in that advancement; the helping hand, the good deed done without personal gain, the sympathetic letter which helped a stricken person, the smile which we gave to strangers who were low in spirit. All these tiny, forgotten acts help us to advance more than one showy act of assisting... We equally find, with disappointment, that some of the things we were sure would help us advance here, in fact, retarded our progress. We hand out advice freely and think that we are helping. We overdo our profusive praise or flattery. We tell people proudly of what a great thing we did to help somebody.

Similarly George Ritchie makes a brief, general point that was impressed upon him by his NDE:[20] 'How we spend our time on earth, the kind of relationships we build, is vastly, infinitely more important than we can know.'

All of this reminds us of something only briefly mentioned when we were talking about compassion above. It is that, beyond the general objective of adding to our supersoul's database of experience, the over-riding objective of our time in this human hologram – or version of the game, or whatever we want to call it – is to choose love over fear as often as possible, sometimes against the odds. Our sources have made it very clear that all thoughts or actions driven by pettiness, selfishness, anger, jealousy, resentment and so on will be relived, often from the other person's point of view, and the pain fully felt until we come to terms with who we really are and work to transform ourselves. By contrast, as pointed out above, all loving, selfless, compassionate acts store up huge spiritual capital for the afterlife. Indeed, as suggested earlier, it seems likely that even a relatively materially oriented person who does much to help others will build up far more than the person who spends plenty of time contemplating the afterlife while remaining relatively selfish.

So now we can see that choosing love over fear, and helping others, is how we follow a constructive or expansive path rather than a limiting, constricting, even destructive and degrading one. We won't always get it right. But simply by being aware of this issue, and by cultivating an 'observer self' who helps us to notice what we're doing rather than just blindly reacting to events, will make a huge difference.

To close, Yram makes this beautiful observation:[21] 'In this evolutionary process there are no privileged people. Whatever one's social position, the law is at the disposal of everyone. All that has to be done is to love a little more each day.' Or, as Neale Donald Walsch so aptly says in his *Conversations With God*, when faced with any given situation, ask yourself: 'What would love do now?'

PART FOUR

PLANES OF TRANSITION, RECREATION & ILLUSION

You must remember that these worlds, which are different from the true or divine vital, are full of enchantments and illusions and they present appearances of beauty which allure only to mislead... Their heavens are more dangerous than their hells.

Sri Aurobindo, 'The Integral Yoga'

21

ASSISTANCE, HEALING AND ACCLIMATISATION

In Part 3 we were primarily concerned with departed spirits who become trapped in the near-earth or lower astral planes. But all the evidence suggests that sooner or later they'll open themselves up enough to ask for help to transition to the mid astral, where they'll need some degree of rest, recuperation and healing before they can move on. Meanwhile the majority of people, being less damaged, should transition directly to the mid astral. But even so, those who've been traumatised by, for example, long-term illness or a sudden passing will require considerable healing, while pretty much all departed spirits experience greater or lesser degrees of initial confusion as they try to orient themselves to their new surroundings. Indeed, as suggested in the Preface, it seems very few of us are properly prepared for our transition. Nevertheless, as we've just seen in our conclusion to Part 3, those departed spirits who expect to have some form of afterlife and have had time to prepare themselves for it are likely to make the easiest transition, and in rare cases might even be directly attracted to the upper astral – although we won't be discussing the latter until Part 5.

As we'll find out there are multiple sub-planes or layers within the mid astral just as there are in the lower, each corresponding to a different level of vibration, and departed spirits will be attracted to that layer that most resonates with their energy – that's to say with their emotional and psychospiritual makeup.[1] What we can assume is that the greater the healing and acclimatisation required, the lower the entry level will be, and the more the departed spirit will need sometimes prolonged periods of sleep or unconsciousness to assimilate the changes that are occurring. This chapter therefore deals with the lower levels of the mid astral, while the remaining chapters in Part 4 will take us to somewhat higher levels that may be thought of as more heavenly – although with reservations, as we'll see.

INDIVIDUAL ASSISTANCE

Because nearly all transitioning humans require some degree of healing and initial acclimatisation, assistance is always available, just as it is for those who find themselves trapped in the near-earth or lower planes as discussed in Part 3. This assistance will usually come from a departed friend or family member, or from a spirit helper or guide, or a combination of the two.

HENRY LANCHESTER (VIA JOHN WARD)

We have heard from John Ward's uncle Henry Lanchester before, but now some general remarks about his view of the mid and upper astral are called for. His values are very much of his time, and in particular he's very keen on order and structure, indeed on minutely categorising everything he experiences. For example, he maintains that all the world religions are represented in the afterlife, but that believers in each are kept separate until they've progressed some way into the afterlife planes. He similarly reports segregation between men and women. Even if we accept that these are his genuine experiences, and those of the spirits he associates with, all the evidence suggests they're not more generally representative. But remember all shades of every type of belief and expectation are represented in the afterlife. Nor should this be allowed to detract from his more general corroboration of various elements of the experience.

Here he is then, providing a fascinating description of being taken to watch as his fellow communicant via Ward, the Officer – whose terrible suffering in hellish planes was described in detail in Part 3 – is helped up out of the lower realms and into the relative light of the mid astral:[2]

> Suddenly out of the darkness beneath us a ball of light began to emerge and, rapidly mounting, we saw it was a glorious spirit of light. As he rose from the depths the darkness seemed to fall from off him... Having climbed over the edge of the cliff on to its top, he lay down and stretched his arm down into the darkness. It vanished up to the shoulder; but gradually he withdrew it, and soon we saw his hand grasped that of another. The newcomer's hand was not bright and shining like his, but dark and dirty, with a pallid, unhealthy tinge. Soon there struggled up beside him, slowly and painfully, a most miserable object. His eyes were covered with a kind of bandage. He fell to the ground beside his guide, who rose to his feet and gently helped him to rise... 'Oh, this terrible light,' he moaned. 'I can see it even through this bandage.' To us it was a very murky light, most like that seen in a London fog.

DAVID HATCH (VIA ELSA BARKER)

Similarly we quoted from David Hatch's letters channelled via Elsa Barker in chapter 18, but now it's time to admit that in general they come across as somewhat lacking in humility when compared to most other such material – although maybe this is to be expected from a former judge. What is also clear is that he deliberately stays very much in the lower regions of the mid astral to make communication with Barker easier.[3] But in doing so his experience contrasts strongly with other sources in some respects.[4] For example, he continues with human behaviours like breathing quite far into his afterlife journey. He also spends much of his time in the near-earth plane travelling to different parts of the globe. He even insists that in the astral he still experiences day and night but as the opposite of their earthly counterparts.

All that having been said, as with Lanchester, Hatch does corroborate what our other sources have to say in some areas. For example, as regards the initial assistance of spirits making the transition:[5] 'There is even a large organisation of souls who call themselves a league. Their special work is to take hold of those who have just come out, helping them to find themselves and to adjust to the new conditions.'

EMMA VALE OWEN (VIA HER SON GEORGE)

George Vale Owen's mother Emma reports on an example of assistance being given to recently departed spirits in the near-earth plane who don't yet realise their situation:[6] 'A band of missionary spirits had returned from their period of duty in one of the regions bordering on the earth sphere, where they had been working among souls just come over who did not realise that they had crossed the borderline between earth and the spirit land.' She also provides several lengthy examples of herself helping departed spirits who, like the Officer, are finally emerging from the lower astral.[7]

PHILIP GILBERT (VIA HIS MOTHER ALICE)

We saw in chapter 19 that Philip Gilbert is generally involved in welfare and rescue work, and sometimes adopts unusual tactics to shake departed spirits from their lethargy – for example, taking on familiar or unexpected forms as the situation dictates. The following case doesn't involve a trapped spirit, only one in transition, but it amusingly demonstrates his point:[8]

> I actually found a man yesterday, just over, who had been a Bible class leader of a very narrow type – but his heart was good. When he waked after death, his mind was as usual in its own illusion. He was seeking the kind of heaven he visualised... I was with a group of our band, all gay and 'young', and we were indulging in a little recreation, whizzing and whirling for sheer joy of speed, and I was creating a few thought images... of a slightly absurd nature to amuse... some new arrivals. How that solemnsides managed to impinge on our 'aura' I don't know: I am still often puzzled at the working of these magnetic vibrations.

> Anyhow, he saw us and was utterly aghast. He at once tried to organise us into a prayer meeting! We were very nice to him and I did a quick change, increasing my vibrations till I began to glow – and then he wanted to worship me!! I had to put a strong break on my sense of humour. Eventually a glimmer of truth came to him; he was in a type of new world, not heaven or hell, but in a new type of existence. We showed him a few laws and helped him to find someone whom on earth he had misjudged, and then left him to sort himself out.

He adds more generally: 'One of the pleasantest aspects of this new work of mine is to see the joy and change in the face of some poor muddled creature when I have succeeded in penetrating his illusion and putting him into the way of sensing and visualising that light. It is all worth my trouble.'

JOHN AND ALAN (VIA ANONYMOUS)

In chapter 19 we saw that in *Road of Many Ways* several of John's fellow communicants became trapped in the near-earth plane and needed the help of his human rescue circle in Cape Town to move on. But his book also contains descriptions of transitions straight to the lower-mid astral, albeit that assistance is still required from a spirit helper – and the first is actually his own.[9] During a battle in Asia during WWII he's hurled to the ground with a huge shrapnel wound in his back, and briefly passes out before coming back round to what he feels is a receding battle. He lies in the mud for some time, unable to move, but in the end a kindly Japanese soldier who has passed over some time before tells him to try to flex his legs and stand up – and reassures him that it's *he* who has moved on while the battle is still raging all around them. We will find out what happens to John next shortly.

The second example is Alan, an Australian soldier again killed in the fighting in Asia during WWII.[10] He suddenly finds himself staring down at a face that looks very familiar and realises it's his own, with a bullet hole through the forehead. He is confused but then a British officer reassures him he's dead, puts an arm round him and tells him to shut his eyes. In what seems only a moment he reopens them to find they're emerging from a bank of mist and walking up a hill, where he's overjoyed to be joined by an old friend. But, although he's never really thought about an afterlife, he's worried that he's being taken to a place of judgment and that he'll be ordered to descend to hell. The officer reassures him that, although he doesn't realise it, he's already judged *himself* as they travelled through the mist bank – and now he can move on to his idea of heaven. As they crest the rise he sees a coastline just like one he loved south of Sydney, and they walk down to a little village where he meets more former soldier friends who have a glass of cold beer waiting for him. He later finds out this is really just somewhere for him to rest up, a 'decontamination centre' where they all need to forget all thoughts of war and fighting before moving on. This shows that even the sudden death of someone who's never thought much about the afterlife doesn't *have* to lead to huge trauma during transition, as long as some assistance is on hand and they're fairly emotionally balanced. Having said that, as we'll shortly see, assistance for soldiers dying in battle tends to be even more readily available because multiple casualties are expected.

John also emphasises that there's no coincidence in what happens at passing:[11] 'We know… when a person is due to arrive here. The whole operation is then laid on, usually through the aid of a very close relative or friend or someone who has been a guide to that person during his or her lifetime.' However I don't think we should interpret this as meaning that everyone's point of death is entirely predetermined, merely that in the afterlife planes a different perspective on time and on events on earth is available, as we'll see in chapter 23.

JOE SANDYS (VIA HIS SISTER CYNTHIA)

In one of Cynthia Sandys' *Awakening Letters* her brother Joe describes helping a rich tycoon to move on:[12]

> His poor old wife couldn't face life without him. He'd always done everything and now she was alone. I sensed that they had

> no children, and he'd been so successful that he'd alienated most of his contemporaries, and there he stood outside his body, a grey, frightened individual, completely alone.

Joe explains to the man that he's passed on, but he insists it's just a dream from which he'll soon emerge. Not long afterwards Joe returns, finding the man still trying in vain to reassure his wife he's not dead. Finally he's persuaded of his true situation and asked if there's anyone he cares about – at which point he thinks of a departed friend, who appears immediately and calms him to sleep, promising Joe that he'll look after him when he awakes.

In another letter a departed friend describes her rather more challenging passing, which this time does seem to be at least partly due to her lack of expectations of an afterlife:[13]

> My heart gave out and that was that. I fell into a coma, and woke up to find myself in a curious light... different from any light I'd ever seen. I tried to go to sleep again but the light was rather disturbing, and to this were added voices, laughter and talking... I got up, but instead of feeling tired and ill I was perfectly all right... Then suddenly I saw Pat, and I felt I must hold onto her. I said, 'Stay with me, I don't feel very well.' She sat down at once and explained just why I was feeling so muddled and insecure. It was a horrid feeling. I came over to this plane with no idea of what I should find. It was all half light and half shadow.

However in due course this woman is able to progress in the afterlife, with help and encouragement from Sandys' daughter Pat.

OOB REPORTS

Turning now to OOB reports, we've already seen in Part 3 that incarnate pioneers get involved in the rescue and retrieval of trapped spirits. But they can often be of assistance in initial transition as well. One explorer we've not yet mentioned is Peter Richelieu, whose experiences commenced just a few days after he was devastated by the loss of his younger brother early in WWII. Living in Colombo in what is now Sri Lanka, he was apparently visited by an unnamed Indian sage who himself appears to have been an incarnate OOB adept. His account of his experiences, *A Soul's Journey*, was first published in South Africa in 1953 under a different title, and it alternates between lectures by the sage and accounts of actual OOB expeditions. On several of these the two are together, but in the intervals Richelieu also practices journeying at night on his own, and remembering and recording what happens on his return. The entire book only covers a period of about one month in 1941, although one can only assume his exploits continued thereafter – not least because during that month he was able to rekindle his relationship with his sweetheart, who passed on before he could propose marriage.

Of particular interest here is that on one of these journeys his sage comes to the aid of a confused young pilot who has just died in a dogfight above London, and also describes the multitude of 'astral helpers' who assist the recently deceased to move on.[14] Moreover in due course Richelieu himself becomes involved in such work, aided by a spirit helper called Jim.[15]

We saw in chapter 19 that his more illustrious successor Robert Monroe engaged in some initial rescue attempts before setting up the Lifeline Programme at his Institute, which was specifically designed to assist both trapped spirits and those just in transition. But in his own later journeys he describes working as part of his group soul – which he typically labels his 'EXCOM' but we would call his supersoul – to assist with transitions:[16]

> Many of our tasks involved helping through... after the physical death process. In most of these instances we became what we were perceived to be: father, mother, departed friend, even some 'heavenly being'.

As with Gilbert above, this again shows the inventiveness and flexibility of spirit helpers when they're deciding what appearance to adopt to most help the departed spirit. Monroe also describes his first visit the 'reception centre', which would come to be used by many of his Lifeline protégées to help departing spirits:[17]

> I ended up in a park-like surrounding, with carefully tended flowers, trees and grass, much like a large mall with paths crisscrossing the area. There were benches along the paths, and there were hundreds of men and women strolling by, or sitting on the benches. Some were quite calm, others a little apprehensive, and many had a dazed or shocked look of disorientation. They appeared uncertain, unknowing of what to do or what was to take place next. Somehow I knew that this was a meeting place, where the newly arrived waited for friends or relatives. From this place of meeting, these friends would take each newcomer to the proper place where he or she 'belonged'.

In a similar way to Monroe, Gordon Phinn's guide Henry and several of his helper colleagues provide a number of reports of taking the form of someone else to help with tricky transitions. Indeed during Henry's own passing in a car accident he's met by his own guide, Jack, who for his own amusement is disguised as a middle-aged golfer – although apparently he also impersonates rabbis, sports heroes and politicians.[18] Then when a young drunk is murdered by robbers outside a seedy Seattle bar and doesn't realise he's dead, Henry takes the form of a prostitute to try to get through to him – even conjuring up a bright red Corvette Stingray which he then flies into the air until they meet the boy's departed sister, who then takes over.[19] Elsewhere an unhealthy man with no concept of the afterlife dies slumped over his desk and can't understand why he's looking down at his body, until a call goes out to a spirit helper called Hester who impersonates his mistress so well that he follows her into the mid astral.[20]

Meanwhile Jurgen Ziewe movingly describes assisting a torture victim to pass on:[21]

> I was led into a sparse room where a man had been tied to a chair and was being tortured. He was a victim of a brutal regime. The henchmen serving the punishment received a cruel satisfaction from their evil deed, but their victim was my focus. To my relief my guide indicated that his ordeal was nearly over and that I was there to ease his distress and to prepare him to

> move as gently as possible into the next dimension. He said there was a real danger that his state of mind could be so severely unbalanced by the ordeal that it could catapult him into a very dark place, which he didn't deserve.
>
> Every time pain was applied to his body I knew he could see us. My invisible partner had generated a soothing light around the man: when he passed out from the pain, the light was there to comfort him... I compensated for his pain with warmth and love, reassuring him with thoughts of the beautiful world I told him he would enter... The man's face relaxed and he smiled. Then he returned to his body for the last time. He didn't even feel the pain of the blow which killed him. My guide took over and carried him away. I returned to my body.

This neatly brings us on to the fact that when someone is going through a sudden or difficult death that could involve severe pain and trauma, their spirit *can* depart before the body itself completely gives out.[22] It is also interesting to hear how Bruce Moen deals with an elderly man in a hospital bed who doesn't have long to live, by showing him how to travel OOB to Monroe's reception centre.[23] He then finds that the man practices going in and out of body a number of times to get used to the process before he finally passes. Anecdotally a lot of especially elderly people seem to get glimpses of where they're going, and even to practice the same sort of 'in-and-out' manoeuvres. Indeed in later life my own father suffered from dementia for several years and, when I visited him around three days before his full passing, his eyes had a glazed look – as if his essential self was absent.

MAJOR DISASTERS AND BATTLES

Generally speaking those who die suddenly and *en masse* in battles, wars or natural disasters may in fact have a less traumatic experience than those who die suddenly and alone, because at least they're surrounded by others in the same situation. As suggested above it also seems that assistance is especially proactive in such circumstances.

ANONYMOUS (VIA EMILY FRENCH AND EDWARD RANDALL)

One of Emily French and Edward Randall's communicants provides the perspective of a departed spirit involved in a battle:[24]

> I had no conception of a hereafter... So you can imagine how startled I was to awake as from a deep sleep; bewildered, I got to my feet, and looked down and saw my body among many others on the ground... Then I remembered the awful battle; still I did not then realise I had been shot... I looked about; others of the seeming dead moved, seemed to stir. Then many of them stood up, and like me seemed to emerge from their physical bodies...
>
> Soon I found myself among thousands in a similar mental state. Not one among them knew just what had happened... While the passing out of the old body was without pain, it is a terrible thing to drive a strong spirit from a healthy body... About us all was gloom, not a ray of light... and we waited in fear and silence; we seemed to feel one another's thoughts... or to hear one another think. How long we remained in this state I cannot now tell, for we do not measure time as you do.
>
> Soon there was a ray of light that grew brighter each moment, and then a great concourse of men and women with kindly faces came, and with comforting words told us not to fear; that we had made the great change... That we would live on forever, and by labour reach a higher mental development.

LANCHESTER (VIA HIS NEPHEW WARD)

Here is Lanchester again, describing the early days after the outbreak of WWI:[25]

> Huge crowds of spirits are pouring over, most of them still convulsed with hate, nearly all having died a violent death, and you can easily imagine the condition there. Many indeed do not even realise that they are dead, but ascribe their changed condition to some wound which has temporarily clouded their brain... A great call has gone forth for more enlightened spirits to come to the aid of the newcomers, and already countless hosts are pouring down to help.

ROBERT BENSON (VIA ANTHONY BORGIA)

Robert Benson describes the state of readiness those in the higher planes increasingly have to be in due to ever more devastating human warfare:[26]

> As the earth world progresses in civilisation – in its own estimation – the means and methods of waging war become more devastating and wholesale... The earth world, in its blind ignorance, hurls hundreds of thousands of souls into this, our land. But those who dwell in the high realms are fully aware, long before it happens, of what is to take place upon the earth plane, and a fiat goes forth to the realms nearer the earth to prepare for what is to come. These dire calamities of the earth plane necessitate the building of more and ever more halls of rest in the spirit world.

JOHN (VIA ANONYMOUS)

John himself spends quite some time after his passing involved in helping WWII soldiers make the transition, as part of a group working under a guide called Oshito – showing that spirits don't have to be hugely experienced to undertake such work.[27] In fact he only occasionally returns to the little cottage he calls home to have some much-needed rest and recuperation before continuing, but eventually the war ends and Oshito insists it's now time for him to properly enjoy and explore his new home. He returns only to find a whole host of the spirits he has helped waiting for him, and the outpouring of love is just reward for the selflessness and devotion he's shown in helping others ever since his own passing.

Elsewhere he makes it clear that the human circle in Cape Town that he goes on to work with at a later stage are regularly involved in mass transitions – particularly, for example, of Korean war victims.[28] He also describes how he and a team of spirit helpers head to an imminent plane crash, although in fact they're not needed because one of the passengers – a man with an interest in spiritualism – takes control and calms all the others down, getting them to pray to be led into the light.[29] When they reach it, those who aren't too traumatised are met by a departed friend or family member, while others are escorted to a place of 'rest and recuperation'.

ARTHUR SANDYS (VIA HIS WIFE CYNTHIA)

Sandys' letters provide a number of examples of mass transition. In the first she asks her departed husband Arthur, a former Lieutenant Colonel, to visit the astral environs of Knossos in Crete – and while there he comes across some 'etheric army barracks':[30]

> On stepping inside in my usual brusque way, I found a sergeant in charge of the orderly room. He looked up and welcomed me in a semi-army way... I asked what he was doing. 'Running the camp, sir, and keeping the mess going for the duration.' I said, 'But the war ended eighteen years ago. What do you mean by the duration?' He laughed and said, 'Not that duration, sir. We are rather 'out-back', but not so far! We are keeping this place going for the chaps who can't get settled into the new life. They come over so quickly. Some have gone home – no-one recognised them. They'd never thought about a future life and they just didn't know what on earth to do with it. So we decided to build a camp on army lines, and let them all make a base here until they found their feet. Many of them enjoyed it all so much we can't get them to move on; but there's no hurry... As the other battlefields set up similar bases, some chaps came and visited us and we got them circulating.'

Nevertheless this same departed spirit then describes how scared he and his fellows had been on first passing over, precisely because they simply didn't expect anything of them to survive bodily death:

> 'I didn't come over like you, sir, knowing a lot. I came over very green, and was I frightened when I found myself out of my body, drifting about? I hung on to earth, it was all I knew, I wasn't going to lose touch if I could help it. Hundreds of others felt the same. We were like drowning men searching for anything we could hold on to that was familiar. We have wonderful spirits here at times. They come and teach us how to

move, and think, and use our new powers. It's all very interesting. I'm quite happy to stay on for a bit longer, but I'm beginning to feel a desire to go on.'

In the second example, a departed spirit caught up in the Summerland fire disaster on the Isle of Man in 1973 gives us the fascinating real-time perspective of one of the victims.[31] He describes trying to reach his children in the amusement area, finding several others instead and helping them to try to crawl to safety when a huge beam falls on them:

> It was so sudden I was knocked out instantly and so were the children. The next thing I knew I found myself standing outside on top of the wreckage. It was burning furiously but it didn't touch me, and one by one the children joined me and we cowered close together. We were all standing on the glowing embers, but we weren't being burnt. I couldn't understand it... Some queer draught, I thought, had taken the heat from the spot where we were... I told the children to stay quite still and wait... Others joined us, seeing that we were unhurt, and we became quite a large group. Then suddenly we heard voices calling us, 'Don't be afraid, walk out. Lift yourselves. You are free of the fire.' We took no notice at first – how could we lift ourselves out of the fire?

Then one of the group realises she can float around in mid air, and the others join her, although the narrator remains convinced they're all caught in an updraught caused by the fire. They float on upwards and hear more voices telling them to relax:

> I began to see we were in a large party being escorted... Then my hand was seized by a firm grip, and before I knew what was happening, we were among trees and flowers and standing... on firm ground in a sort of garden... Suddenly, in front of me, I saw the form of a man. He seemed to grow into my vision. At first only a blurred object, which crystallised into human form.

He is informed they've all passed on, and that the other victims are all 'sleeping off the exhaustion of this tremendous experience'.

He realises he too is 'dead beat', so he and the children with him do likewise.

The third example is provided by a departed friend of a friend.[32] She describes attending the site of a boat disaster with Pat, Sandys' daughter, who is an experienced spirit helper. They find much confusion and many spirits who don't yet realise they've passed, so Pat takes on the form of a uniformed seaman and instructs them all to 'come aft for coffee'. This calms them sufficiently that they fall asleep, and can then be taken away and dealt with properly.

OOB REPORTS

As part of the research for Monroe's Lifeline Programme, Moen describes attending the aftermath of the earthquake in India in 1993 that claimed 68,000 lives.[33] Spirit helpers had set up a kind of refugee camp and the dazed and confused victims were streaming towards it in a never-ending line. They were given astral water, bowls of food and blankets to make them feel at home, then directed to an opening in a nearby cliff where they were whisked up a tunnel straight to the reception centre. During a debrief he and other members of the research team subsequently agree to meet up while OOB and pool their resources to act as 'bait' in attracting victims and funnelling them to the reception centre – not least because, as we've seen before, those still incarnate on the earth plane are often more easily visible to the recently departed than spirit helpers, even if they're operating OOB. He also describes 'getting the call' to assist with the aftermath of the Oklahoma bombing in 1995, where he again guides a number of the victims to the reception centre.[34]

Phinn's guide Henry describes similar cooperation between incarnates and spirit helpers in mass transition work:[35] 'There are several teams who circle the globe constantly looking for trouble, as it were. Their numbers are made up of a rotating population of astral and physical plane dwellers who specialise in what you might call anguish and terror management.' He then goes on to describe how he and an OOB Gordon give assistance at a major flood disaster in Central America, where the mainly Catholic victims are easy fodder for Henry appearing to them as a radiant angel. On a slightly smaller scale he also describes meeting a group of spirits who departed in a major road accident involving multiple vehicles.[36] Even though they've left husbands, wives and children behind, because plenty of assistance was available at the crash site they're all now happily ensconced in one of several lakeside resorts, playing tennis and generally enjoying themselves – even though it's only been a week since they passed. This suggests serious recuperation isn't necessary for everyone, or at least that a period of relaxation may be in order before departed spirits start to tackle more demanding challenges.

Phinn himself also used tapes based on Monroe's Lifeline Programme to start doing his own retrievals.[37] Specifically, for example, he describes assisting in the Beslan school hostage drama in Russia in 2004 in which over 300 people died, ferrying a number of children and adults to the reception centre while working alongside many spirit helpers.[38]

SLEEPING

We have already seen numerous examples of departed spirits sleeping through at least some of the transition process, or effectively losing consciousness completely for periods of time. This can occur whether they're transitioning into the lower or mid astral. Indeed Annie Besant specifically suggests that those who aren't too emotionally disturbed and have led a reasonably balanced life will still spend some time in the lower planes where they shed the denser energies of their earthly life, but they tend to remain unaware of this and only regain consciousness in the mid astral.[39] We will see this seemingly born out in the next chapter.

Randall's transcripts of his sessions with French are full of references to how confused spirits who aren't ready for the afterlife can spend a long time just sleeping, and can also be very hard to wake up.[40] Meanwhile most of Sandys' communicants describe regular periods of deep, restful sleep during their initial transition.

Moen describes one particular case where the departed spirit of a man remains predominantly asleep for a lengthy period before being able to make the transition proper.[41] This appears to be mainly because the long-term disease that killed him had conditioned him to think he'd never get better, and in his comatose state he'd completely missed his actual passing. So it was only by his departed mother sitting patiently talking to him, especially whenever he woke up, that he was finally brought to a realisation of his true condition.

It is also the case that these periods of sleep sometimes occur in special healing environments, as we'll now see.

HEALING ENVIRONMENTS

We have seen a number of references to these already, but now we can concentrate on various more detailed accounts.

TE LAWRENCE (VIA JANE SHERWOOD)

As previously I make no apology for commencing this section with a further lengthy extract from TE Lawrence's communications with Jane Sherwood – because here he provides a detailed, first-hand perspective of the healing experience which is, as always, wonderfully enlightening.[42]

Picking up from where we left him in chapter 15, he's taken over by tiredness after his first meeting with his guide Mitchell, whereupon he lapses into unconsciousness for a time before being taken to a communal 'home' where he has a room of his own. He desires solitude because his intense emotions are still getting the better of him, and he needs to learn to both work through and moderate them. Mitchell, who appears to work in this place, diagnoses that he has repressed way too many emotions and desires during his earth life. This is what led to him being so very driven in some areas, but also more latterly to him living a somewhat monkish existence, which is why he's now like a volcano waiting to erupt. Mitchell's recommended cure is for him to 'go on a spree' to release some of these hidden tensions and desires.

As a result he's directed to a meeting place where spirits who had little experience of relationships and sex in human form are learning to express themselves with each other. Here he pairs off with a girl called Winifred who is initially just as tentative as him:

> We wandered away together absorbed in comparing our earth experiences and soon we became friendly and comfortable together. I was charmed by the ease of this feminine comradeship: we were both curious and expectant; we both admitted freely our lack of experience and our need to remedy it, yet we shared a great diffidence and a sensitive approach. I did not return to the home for a long while. We two have wandered happily in an enchanted land exploring the delights of an intimate companionship crowned by the magic of union. She is very lovely; at her heart is an innocence, joined to a flame-like ardour and between us we create a burning bliss of union. I am intoxicated with happiness and for a time have forgotten all my problems and difficulties. Without sorrow we both begin to feel the beginning of the inevitable withdrawal and we have discovered that neither of us had expected a permanent relationship. This has brought no disappointment but rather gratitude for a perfect experience shared.

On his return a further discussion with Mitchell reveals significant improvement but also a deep-seated arrogance and disdain for lesser mortals that has carried over into the afterlife. This leads to a brutally honest and hugely revealing exchange that again points towards the high degree of authenticity of this communication:

> 'Your big difficulty is a scorn of slowness and impatience of mediocrity and, if you will forgive me, a really horrible feeling of superiority to most of the pleasant and ordinary people you are meeting here. They cannot avoid recognising your reaction to them and so they keep away from you. Now how are we to get that right? I think you really feel that you ought to be able to find and meet the great people of the past whom you would

perhaps regard as your equals, but my dear fellow, you are not yet fit to come near them. Look at yourself!'

I looked. Either I saw myself through his eyes or in some kind of immaterial mirror, but this is what I saw: shafts of keen blue light struggling to issue from a core of dark and muddied colour – a tumult of angry, murky shadow at the centre and, as a response to his merciless criticism, angry dartings of red flying off from it. It was not a pretty sight.

'You see,' he said gently, 'we have to clear all that before you are ready to go on.'

The shock broke me down. All my pride and unconfessed arrogance were shattered. I saw myself as less worthy than the least of these to whom I had been condescending and they must have seen it and known it as clearly as I was doing. At this crisis I fought one of my hardest battles. I subdued the angry response and begged Mitchell to go on helping me and to deal mercilessly with the faults he saw in me. A great flood of affection, warm and healing came from him to me as he replied.

'Thank you for taking it like that. I knew you were big enough to stand the treatment.'

For the first time I was beaten, not by anything exterior – that can happen to anyone – but by an intimate revelation of what was within. I was reduced to a state of helpless penitence and pride slunk out of sight. Mitchell was wise and has left me alone to recover from this collapse. Eventually I have regained some balance but only by climbing down for good from my false pedestal and painfully accepting myself as I am, a mess, a travesty of what I might have been.

The storm has a little subsided and a strange sense of relief has come out of this abasement. I feel a new dignity and a truer integrity than I have ever known. Perhaps I have reached rock bottom now, and there is rest and peace in that thought.

Realising that his desire for solitude has in part been due to this arrogance, he goes on to describe his need to learn to socialise in this new environment, and the difficulties he encounters in so doing:

> My emotions still shake me dangerously and I have to learn also to take the emotional impact of other beings with equanimity. I have become wary of impatience and anger; their manifestations are too repulsive. The slightest shift in feeling makes a corresponding change in appearance, as well as in one's own feeling of well-being. Relations with people, when nothing can be hidden, become a high art requiring control and a larger sympathy than is ever needed on earth, where its absence can usually be covered by the conventional word or action. It really amounts to this, that one is not safe in this plane until all the twisted, negative emotions are cleared out of one. Then it will be possible to live fearlessly and freely, knowing that one cannot send out any harmful motion.

Of course he recognises that those who don't learn to control and eradicate emotions such as anger and fear run the risk of being drawn back to environments such as the grey town he visited when he first passed over – which is more than enough incentive for him and his fellow inmates to strive to progress.

FRANCHEZZO (VIA FARNESE)

To return to a chronological review of the channelled material on healing, in chapter 18 we briefly mentioned that Franchezzo is treated in a hospital-type 'house of hope' not long after his passing.[43] He refers to it as being in a 'twilight land' that could easily be on the boundary of the lower and mid astral, and initially he can see nothing of the building or its inhabitants, and is only aware of 'an appalling, enshrouding gloom' that 'crushes his spirit as nothing else could have done'. But, motivated solely by the memory of his former love, he gradually improves to the point where he can sense his surroundings:

> It was a great building of dark grey stone with many long passages, some long, large halls or rooms, but mostly composed of innumerable little cells with scarcely any light and only the barest of furniture. Each spirit had only what he had earned by his earthly life, and some had nothing but the little couch whereon they lay and suffered... It was a house of

> sorrow, but also a house of hope, for all there were striving upwards to the light... Each had his foot planted upon the lowest rung of the ladder of hope by which he should in time mount even to heaven itself. I spent my time in resting or meditating in my cell, and going with those who, like myself, soon grew strong enough to hear the lectures which were delivered to us in the great hall.

These lectures turn out to be like extended versions of the life review, where the patients are encouraged to look at the consequences of their selfish and unkind actions, and to consider their full effect on the person on the receiving end. As part of his own salvation he also learns how to help others having a difficult transition by 'magnetising' them, under the guidance of more advanced spirit healers and doctors:

> Being myself possessed of strong magnetic powers, I was set to help an unfortunate young man who was utterly unable to move, and who used to lie moaning and sighing all the time. Poor fellow, he was only thirty years old when he left the earth body, but in his short life he had contrived to plunge into such dissipations that he had prematurely killed himself, and was now suffering such agonies from the reaction upon the spirit of those powers he had abused, that it was often more than I could bear to witness them. My task was to make soothing passes over him, by which means he would obtain a little relief, till at stated times a more advanced spirit than myself would come and put him into a state of unconsciousness.

Unfortunately he also reports that, as their strength grows, many of the patients succumb to the temptation to go back to earthly haunts for greater or lesser periods of time, usually returning in an even more 'exhausted and degraded' state than before. But, of course, the doors are never closed to them. As for Franchezzo himself, it's not long before he graduates to a 'land of dawn', which is a lighter – although hardly bright – environment in which he makes a new home, and from where he embarks on the rescue missions to the lower planes discussed in chapter 18.[44]

ANONYMOUS (VIA FRENCH AND RANDALL)

One of French and Randall's communicants briefly describes how they are engaged in 'impressing crippled children with the thought that they are no longer crippled... teaching them little dance-steps, observing their joy as they realise they can use their legs'.[45]

WARD (WITH LANCHESTER HIS UNCLE)

During one of his OOB-style trance visions Ward visits a 'school for the regenerate in hell' with Lanchester, which seems to be in a similarly low-vibration environment to Franchezzo's 'house of hope':[46]

> Having entered the building, we passed down a passage and through a door into a classroom. This was filled with light from the teacher; but what shall I say of the pupils? Picture the lowest and most degraded men reduced to the size of tiny children. Imagine them misshapen and idiots for the most part, with a low, cunning expression on their wizened faces. This will give you but a faint idea of what I saw. They were ever trying to play some stupid trick or other either on their neighbours or on the master. In addition to him, there were two other spirits who stood behind the form while he taught from the front. All three were needed, firstly, to keep the room sufficiently light, for from each of the 'children' there seemed to exude a kind of darkness which appeared to be burnt up by the light. Further, they were needed to keep the pupils under control. They did this solely by a kind of hypnotic power, by the exercise of their will and of their mentality. If for a moment they relaxed their concentration, at once several of the boys broke out into disorder.

By contrast in this next extract the pair visit a 'mental hospital' that's almost certainly centred in the mid astral, as are the remaining reports in this section.[47]

> We entered a room and found a hypnotist at work. He was making passes over someone. As soon as he saw us he bowed and explained that this patient could not eliminate from his

> mind the remembrances of a terrible accident for which he was to a certain extent responsible. The remembrance of this had turned his brain on earth, and the ill effects were not yet entirely removed from his mind. 'I am hypnotising him for a time, so as to compel him to forget this terrible experience, and so by degrees we shall restore peace to his troubled mind.'

VARIOUS (VIA VALE OWEN)

Vale Owen's mother Emma discloses that she works in a rehabilitation home herself.[48] Elsewhere she reports on seeing children bathing in a broad stream, and being told that 'the waters are electrically charged and give strength to them, for many come here very weak and require such nourishment'.[49] Similarly her fellow communicant Kathleen describes departed spirits bathing in the 'water of life':[50]

> You have read of the water of life. That phrase embodies a literal truth, for the waters of the spheres have properties which are not found in the waters of earth, and different properties attach to different waters. The waters of the river or fountain or lake are often treated by high spirits and endowed with virtues of strengthening or enlightenment. Sometimes people bathe in them and gather bodily strength from the life-vibrations which have been set up in the water by the exercise of some group of angel ministers.

Similarly Kathleen also reports on a 'healing temple' where departed spirits are treated with water, colour and sound:

> They are immersed in its vibrations of colour, bathed in the streams and fountains of water which are within, or swathed in the web and woof of music, the while, their natures responding, they are strengthened in the parts where strength is lacking, or enlightened in those other parts where intellect is dimmed.

BENSON (VIA BORGIA)

Benson describes being taken to visit a 'home of rest' by his guide Edwin:[51]

Edwin told us that it was a home of rest for those who had come into spirit after long illness, or who had had a violent passing, and who were in consequence suffering from shock... It was white in colour as far as the materials of its composition were concerned, but immediately above it there was to be seen a great shaft of blue light descending upon and enveloping the whole building with its radiance, the effect of which was to give a striking blue tinge to the whole edifice. This great ray was the downpouring of life – a healing ray – sent to those who had already passed here, but who were not yet awake. When they were fully restored to spiritual health, there would be a splendid awakening, and they would be introduced into their new land.

I noticed that there were quite a number of people seated upon the grass in the grounds, or walking about. They were relatives of those who were undergoing treatment within the hall of rest, and whose awakening was imminent... They were all supremely joyful, and very excited... An outer vestibule led into a lofty hall of considerable dimensions... Occupying the whole of the floor space were extremely comfortable-looking couches, each of which bore a recumbent form, quite still and obviously sleeping profoundly. Moving quietly about were a number of men and women intent upon watching the different couches and their burdens...

I learned that all the 'patients' in this particular hall had gone through lingering illnesses before passing over. Immediately after their dissolution they are sent gently into a deep sleep. In some cases the sleep follows instantly – or practically without break – upon the physical death. Long illness prior to passing into the spirit world has a debilitating effect upon the mind, which in turn has its influence upon the spirit body. The latter is not serious, but the mind requires absolute rest of varying duration. Each case is treated individually, and eventually responds perfectly to its treatment... The patients resting upon their couches looked very peaceful. Constant watch is kept upon them, and at the first flutterings of returning consciousness, others are summoned, and all is ready for the full awakening. Some will

> wake up partially, and then sink back again into slumber. Others will shake off their sleep at once, and it is then that those experienced souls in attendance will have, perhaps, their most difficult task.
>
> Until that moment, in fact, it has been mostly a matter of watching and waiting. In so many cases it has to be explained to the newly awakened soul that he has 'died' and is alive. They will remember usually their long illness, but some are quite unaware that they have passed over into spirit, and when the true state of affairs has been gently and quietly explained to them, they often have an urgent desire to go back to the earth, perhaps to those who are sorrowing, perhaps to those for whose care and welfare they were responsible. They are told that nothing can be done by their going back, and that others of experience will take care of those circumstances that are so distressing them. Such awakenings are not happy ones by comparison with those who wake up with the full realisation of what has taken place.

He then continues with the kind of stark warning we've already heard in Part 3, but its repetition is entirely appropriate:

> Were the earth more enlightened, this would be the more often the case, and there would be a great deal less distress to the newly awakened soul. The earth world thinks itself very advanced, very 'civilised'. Such estimation is begotten of blind ignorance. The earth world, with all things appertaining thereto, is looked upon as of the very first importance, and the spirit world is regarded as something dim and distant. When a soul finally arrives there, it is quite time enough to begin thinking about it. Until that time comes there is no need even to bother about it. That is the attitude of mind of thousands upon thousands of incarnate souls, and here, in this hall of rest, we witnessed people awakening from their spirit sleep. We saw kind and patient spirits trying so hard to convince these same people that they had really 'died'. And this hall of rest is but one place out of many where the same service is being carried on unceasingly, and all because the earth world is so very superior in knowledge!

VARIOUS (VIA SHERWOOD)

Sherwood's EK provides an equally stark warning about those who haven't built up a strong and emotionally balanced astral body in preparation for the afterlife experience:[52]

> When the average man lays by his physical form… very little is left to face a new life. His resulting form is often so tenuous that he needs a long period of rest and treatment before his new body is fit. The less he has trained and controlled his emotional nature the less formed will his astral body be, and the longer time he will need for preparation. His astral body, so poor, so weak and unformed is now the only outward form he possesses and its condition depends entirely on the building up of his desires and emotions in his earth life. So frequently the emotional life has been either starved and neglected, or else allowed to become chaotic and diseased. It may even be deformed because of habitual indulgence in evil desires and feelings.
>
> These facts should be widely known and taken into serious consideration in order that a worthy astral form may be built up there. So much depends on the man's actual condition when he comes here. The state of his astral body judges him and decides the future of his after-death experiences. One needs no worse hell than the torment of living in a diseased and suffering astral body.

Her husband Andrew, who specialises in helping others with their transition, echoes EK's comments:[53]

> What I want to emphasise is that in the undeveloped soul the astral body is inclined to be formless with undeveloped organs of sight and hearing and may be quite incapable of living on our planes. Such people are born here in utter helplessness and a long time must elapse before they are strong enough to live normally among us.

This would explain why so many departed spirits report that they struggle to *see* anything properly when they first come over. Elsewhere Andrew continues:[54]

> If you were suffering from an unsightly disease, which made you objectionable to your friends and abhorrent to yourself, you would take any possible means to cure it. That is literally the case with people who come here suffering from faults of disposition and temper, from fears and anxieties, from old angers and envies. For their own sakes as well as for the sake of others they must be cured, or they cannot bear to live among us where their disease must be seen in ugly auras, harmful emanations or noxious odours.

He then goes on to describe in some detail the healing process he uses:

> All these radiations are the results of certain rhythmic activities. Where these are in conflict, as in the unhappy emotions, the rhythms given off are jangled and out of harmony. They therefore enter the body [of the healer] as painful shocks and dislocations of its own ordered rhythms. The healthy body has to absorb these disharmonies and to neutralise them. Now there is a scale of these rays and, as in physics, the finer and keener the rays the more they will be able to coordinate and control the faulty rhythms they encounter [in the patient]. They work in with the disorder and gradually smooth out its inequalities so that a new and better rhythm can be established. You will not be surprised that the finest, keenest ray of all is emitted when love is felt. This is the master rhythm. It can sort out and re-harmonise any and every conflict in the astral body and it is our only means of cure. It may take many forms; sympathy, understanding, and the will to help and heal. But these rays can only be given off by the healthy part of the astral body, so while one's own nature retains dark, conflicting emotions one is less effective as a healer.

GILBERT (VIA HIS MOTHER ALICE)

Gilbert corroborates the fate of departed spirits who did little to develop their spiritual side while incarnate:[55]

> Most people, so far, are earth-minded. I don't mean bad, or

> gross, but just preoccupied with their incarnation conditions. They build up almost no spiritual body, which is what functions here... You do not automatically create a well-equipped thought body by the act of throwing off the physical, any more than you are born into earth full-grown. You may have to start again as ignorant as a young baby.

As well as being involved in rescue and welfare work it appears he sometimes works in a hospital environment too:

> We have been working hard on some of our patients – this time in a kind of hospital... It is a spot of space on which some concentrated rays are focussed to create a shower of energy and general toughening up. People stay there for very long periods; they are half drowsy and feel that they are in a sort of dreamy trance amidst brilliant colours.

FRANCES BANKS (VIA HELEN GREAVES)

As regards Frances Banks' own passing from cancer, she describes waking up in a rest home staffed by Sisters and Fathers she knows from her earth life in South Africa:[56] 'I am now lying in a bed, high up on a terrace, that looks out over a vast sunlit plane. It is a beautiful scene, and so restful. I am recuperating from the illness which brought disintegration to my physical body.' Like so many departed spirits her conscious periods are interspersed with frequent slumber, and she's also drawn to attend her funeral and various memorial services – in the last of which she manages to make her presence known to a number of those present.

She soon makes her mind up that she wants to remain in the rest home, which she learns is only one of many, to help those less fortunate than herself:[57]

> I suppose you could call this a hospital, a home of rest upon the way and a kindergarten teaching-centre. All these terms would be correct. The weary souls, the frightened souls, the ignorant and fallen souls, together with those who have been rescued from the land of shadows, require understanding and explanation of their sore states, and there are some to whom

> survival has to be explained, even demonstrated. Many will not accept the fact of death, or prefer to consider that they still dream.

She also graduates to having a little home of her own, with a wonderful garden that she recuperates in and also brings patients to.[58] One such is a man who was 'brutal and bitter' to his wife and family: 'He has spent a long period of your earth time... in being tied to the places and people where his cruelty and his bitterness had been exercised. Now he is here, and trying to go on. But the film reel of his life appalled him; and he has become completely immobile.' Here she's making a reference to the initial life review process that we'll come to properly in the next chapter – but the good news is that the transformative energy of her garden starts to bring him more to his senses.

Another patient is a well-known WWII Nazi leader who committed suicide and then spent twenty earth-years wandering in the lower astral before graduating to the home:[59]

> I was apprehensive as we went towards a separate ward at the far end of the home. But not prepared for the sight that met us. The ward was dark and gloomy, very different from our usual light and sunny rooms. A pall of murky twilight seemed to hover over it. Only slowly did it become apparent to us that 'something' lay on the bed. I looked away quickly from the repellent sight. The poor creature's body appeared to be covered with sores and scars. Various of the attendants began to focus healing energy onto him, and were soon joined by the shimmering light of a 'celestial being', after which the room became lighter and the patient slept soundly.

Yet another patient she describes as being a 'locked up soul' who is struggling to adapt:[60]

> He is willing and helpful, but he cannot seem to get past his dogged beliefs, nor to adapt himself to the new life here. He 'works' about the home; his limited intelligence has not yet even realised that he needs not go to call the Sisters, or dig to plant the flowers... We talk to him and try to persuade him to

> accept this new phase of life... He appears to have become static... He is perfectly content with being where he is and is not at all aspiring to anything more real.

Perhaps Banks' most heart-rending yet uplifting story is that of a sweet-natured girl called Jeannie who suffered from polio in her earth life, leaving one leg shorter than the other – which put paid to all her ambitions to be a dancer.[61] When she passes over aged twelve she's initially unable to accept that her leg is fine and strong again, but eventually she's persuaded to try to stand – and her incredulity and joy are something to behold. In time Banks becomes her closest companion, and they enjoy long, rambling walks where Jeannie runs, dances and frolics as she'd never been able to on earth. In due course she's told that soon she'll be able to graduate to the 'halls of beauty' where she'll join all the greatest dancers who've ever lived, and her pure, innocent excitement is unbounded. Not long afterwards a 'man of light' with the form of a perfect dancer appears on the edge of the garden and beckons her to him, whereupon she happily joins him in the light.

JOHN (VIA ANONYMOUS)

John describes leading a young man away from a battlefield medical station on the earth plane, and emphasises the need for initial continuity:[62]

> We carried the unconscious form of our young friend with us on our journey to the reception centre, one of many such that are always in use – similar to hospitals... We laid him on a bed to rest. It could have been any room in any hospital anywhere upon the earth, and those who worked there wore nurses' and doctors' uniforms. The awakening new arrival must not, at first, notice any difference. He must see what he expects to see. He does not know of his passing. He does not know of the new life that awaits him.

VARIOUS (VIA SANDYS)

Returning to the water theme introduced by Vale Owen's

communicants above, three of Sandys' – who remain anonymous, and none of whom had given any thought to an afterlife – report on being urged by unseen voices to receive healing in a lake environment.[63] The first describes this as the 'colour-bath treatment' and bathes in a series of lakes, all of different colour and with a different energy:

> All the time a queer lightness was coming over me. I felt the same only stronger, but my body seemed to be of different texture... Nothing in all the world can take from one the inspiring moment when every cell in one's body becomes flooded with light. That is the sensation. All weight and confusion, all darkness of mind and body literally melt away... I may have been disappointed by the brevity of death, but the wonder and beauty of the resurrection is beyond all explaining. I ceased to be, and yet I became more completely myself – plus so much more.

The second finds himself in just one lake: 'In the centre radiating outwards on all sides were beautiful coloured rays, flashing such bright colours that by the time we reached the centre I was feeling terribly giddy... I was sandwiched above and below between two belts of mesmeric blue.' He then notices that others are being brought to bathe in the lake, most of them asleep and with 'crippled, twisted, etheric bodies' that are straightened out before they wake up. The third again immerses herself in a single lake, at which point:

> I knew I was experiencing real life for the first time. I found ecstasy in that lake. The power of movement and the sense of force within me were beyond anything I could ever imagine... Then a tiny network of sound emerged. It grew until I could define notes, and then gradually the whole orchestra of heaven burst forth.

OOB REPORTS

Various OOB pioneers report on visiting healing environments during their journeys, starting with Frederick Sculthorp who is, as always, accompanied by his anonymous guide:[64]

> We entered a hall which I felt was a rest home where people who had passed over recently, perhaps after physical sufferings, were gaining strength before wakening to full consciousness of spirit life. They were seated around the hall, accompanied by a relation or helper patiently waiting to assist them when they awakened. As we went round the hall they appeared like people enjoying an afternoon siesta, and some had their eyes slightly open.

Elsewhere he visits a more specialised hospital dealing only with young women:[65]

> I was shown over this hospital, which was for young women who had passed early in life... As I passed between the tables I contacted their auras. Many contained the shock of accident, fear, illness and worry... A few had slight red patches on arms, necks and faces, which I sensed were the marks of earthly accidents and still held by their mental recollections. None looked ill and there was a general air of cheerfulness in the hall, with feelings of vitality and well being. This, I knew, was being continuously infused in some way by the advanced people in charge, and was the treatment necessary in these particular cases.

He also mentions 'a seaside resort, where spirits were regaining strength and becoming acclimatised', and a place where 'coloured rays are used on children... some defects appear to be carried over at first, as they are held by the mentality by force of habit, and the correct ray has an effective power to correct them'.[66]

Moen describes being taken to an operating theatre in a 'healing centre', with a viewing gallery all around and above it.[67] A severe burns victim is wheeled in, his astral body still wrapped in bandages. The spirit 'paramedics' accompanying him had helped his passing by giving him an astral pain-killing injection as a placebo. The spirit 'surgeon' then offers him either instant or more prolonged healing, and of course he chooses the former, at which point the entire gallery beams unconditional love into his astral form. The surgeon then theatrically removes the bandages and the patient of course finds himself with no burns, at which point his real acclimatisation can begin.

Phinn's guide Henry reports on being taken to a form of guest house just after his own passing, where he benefits from a refreshing sleep before an old college friend comes to show him around his new surroundings.[68] It is also explained to him that many spirits who have departed due to illness or accident, and who placed great trust in the medical profession, tend to need the reassurance of a hospital-type atmosphere to ease their adjustment.[69] Elsewhere when he's more experienced he takes Phinn on a tour of one of a number of new and different healing centres, this one having been deliberately set up to cater for AIDS victims.[70]

On one of his journeys Waldo Vieira comes across a colony where senile departees are convalescing, and especially receiving music therapy:[71] 'The delicious sound waves, which could be felt but not heard, constituted music therapy taken to the extreme. It is capable of restoring the memory, the imagination and the judgment of those still traumatised by human experiences. It dissolves conflicts, apprehensions, doubts, regrets, fixed ideas and opinions.' He also mentions a children's healing and education centre.[72]

Ziewe refers generally to 'health and welfare centres', and describes visiting one where several nurses are assisting a couple who have just passed in a boating accident.[73] He is somewhat surprised to see them wet through and covered in seaweed, until one of the nurses reports that they 'cried out for help as they drowned so we picked them up and brought them here'. He then adds with no little pride: 'Sometimes we have to put on a bit of a show to provide continuity from one state to the next... We quickly adjust to a situation and do what is required to give these guys a smooth transition.'

Finally Robert Bruce corroborates much of what we've already heard:[74] 'I have visited astral rest and recovery realms many times.

The hospital-like scenario and atmosphere is consistent, but the appearance of individual rooms varies. These reflect the personality and life conditions of each patient.'

EARTH-LIKE ENVIRONMENTS

As if we've not already found enough ways for people to move into the afterlife, we also find reports of earth-like environments in which departed spirits seem to carry on almost exactly as they did before their passing. This topic can become somewhat confusing, so bear with me as I try to present it as logically as I can.

Sculthorp provides many accounts of these, and he sums up the difficulties encountered by the OOB explorer – and indeed all of us, departed spirits included – in knowing exactly what type of environment is being experienced, and in mapping the afterlife terrain generally:[75]

> At the beginning of these accounts of travels to the spirit world, I stated that my intention was to bring back a true picture of life in the next world as seen by one still living on earth. As my description had to include so many and different states of existence, we can now see how some of the information given by returning spirits is also varied. This makes it difficult for those on earth who are trying to compose a mental picture of spirit life. During my twenty years of spirit travel I have at times been amazed at this variety. I have seldom been to the same place twice, and each emits a different vibration which the sensitive spirit body at once notices.

The first point to be made, then, is that reports of earth-like environments are found far more in OOB than in channelled material. This raises the possibility that they *could* be the sort of parallel-earth environments discussed in chapter 7 that are populated by *incarnate* humans, whereas channelled messages can only come from departed spirits reporting on genuine afterlife environments. However one thing that points towards the *astral* nature of at least Sculthorp's visits to earth-like milieus is that he repeatedly encounters deceased relatives – most obviously his wife and one of his daughters, but also his parents and others.[76]

Moreover, as he says, experienced OOB explorers tend to be pretty good at sensing the different vibrations of different planes, so we should probably take most of them at their word when they report on these as being *afterlife* planes inhabited by *discarnates*. But we must allow for the possibility that *some* of the reports that follow *may* involve experiences of parallel-earth environments – or even different *theoretical* versions of the earth game that exist only as potentialities, as also discussed in chapter 7. As such they wouldn't strictly belong in this study.

To the extent that we *are* talking about reports of genuine afterlife environments, however, we should clarify that they're not in the near-earth plane that we discussed in chapter 14 because they're completely devoid of incarnate humans. Nor are they in the lower astral because the inhabitants clearly aren't suffering any form of torment – indeed they may often be perfectly contented. Instead we must assume them to be in the lower reaches of the mid astral, where departed spirits who remain very much attached to earthly life find an easy and familiar existence.

Having said that, in these closely earth-like environments the inhabitants, for example, continue to work, shop and use money – completely ignoring their potential new powers of creating by pure thought, as introduced briefly in chapter 8. There is a clear distinction between these and what are perceived to be more heavenly realms that we'll be considering in future chapters, even if these latter can bear some similarities to earth. The other factor that distinguishes any lower-mid astral environments is that they tend to be rather uninspiring, not to say gloomy – in other words of a lower vibratory level and less filled with light.

REPLICAS OF EARTH CITIES

Some of the reports we're going to consider, although by no means all, are reported to take place in specific astral replicas of earth environments, such as major cities – although they're not always exact reproductions of the versions we know in our current time. We saw a few degraded examples of this in respect of the lower planes in Part 3, and the similar existence of such mid astral replicas is fairly widely reported in OOB literature.

For example Richelieu's sage briefly mentions departed spirits living in 'the astral counterpart of London', because 'to begin with they want to remain in touch with something they understand' and 'have a perfect home where they can entertain friends as before'.[77] Sculthorp also mentions in passing that there exist 'etheric counterpart of places which are, or once were, on earth'.[78] Swami Panchadasi meanwhile goes rather further:[79] 'There are regions, points of space, places, kingdoms, countries etc., on the astral just as on the material plane. Sometimes these astral regions have no connection with any on the material plane, while in other cases they have a very direct connection with and relation to material places and the inhabitants thereof.' Similarly Phinn's guide Henry:[80] 'For every physical North American city there are at least two, if not three, astral counterparts, catering to the various levels of spiritual attainment.'

This latter reinforces the point that, while some of these counterparts exist in the lower-mid astral planes and will therefore be considered here, others appear to exist in more heavenly realms so we'll save them for chapter 24.

WHERE THE INHABITANTS DON'T KNOW THEY'VE PASSED

In a couple of the reports of these earth-like environments it's clear that the inhabitants still don't actually know that they've passed, yet for reasons I'm unable to fathom they haven't become trapped in the near-earth plane. Almost uniquely from a channelled perspective Vale Owen's mother Emma asserts the existence of such places:[81] 'Those who come over after living an unprogressive life on earth find themselves in spheres of so gross a character as to be, to them, indistinguishable from earth itself. That is one of the reasons why they are not able to realise that they have changed their state.'

To pick up on the fact that the inhabitants may exhibit confusion, turning back to an OOB perspective here is Caroline Larsen:[82]

> At last light appeared in the distance, and soon we set foot in a world, dark and dull compared with the sphere I had just left, but not unlike this world in which we live, with its open country, its cities with streets and buildings, and its life moving in familiar paths...
>
> I found myself in a city of gigantic size, its streets running between continuous buildings in seemingly endless lines, save where they led on to great open squares. The traffic was denser than in any earthly city. Throngs of spirits hurried past in every direction. Multitudes and more multitudes of them pushed by the spot where I had stationed myself. They were, I learned, newcomers. They seemed to me confused, disturbed, endlessly seeking. On their faces I read bewilderment, agitation, and vague desire as if they were set upon reaching an uncertain goal. Most of them, still unaware they had left this earth, were seeking to discover why they were suddenly surrounded with strangers in a city like any earthly city, yet somewhat more than strange. Puzzled surprise, wonder, distress, incredulity, and a dawning apprehension, peered from these passing faces. A few who understood or suspected their state sought only confirmation and to reach their destination, as yet unknown... Thus this plane seems as a kind of clearing house for the newly arrived.

Just to clarify, it's the reported *traffic* that gives this away as a closely earth-like environment. By contrast during one of his journeys Ziewe finds himself talking to a group of youngsters in a similarly earth-like environment where, although none of them recognise they've passed, they exhibit no confusion and treat him with disdain when he tries to explain their condition.[83] He rightly conjectures that some discarnates may simply adapt themselves very quickly to a new environment as long as it feels very familiar, and may ignore or even dismiss any apparent evidence of a new state of being. I would add that this will be more likely if, first, they find themselves in an earth-like environment that's *not* being shared with incarnate humans; and, second, if they die in a group who all know each other.

WHERE THE INHABITANTS DO KNOW THEY'VE PASSED

More common are reports of earth-like environments where the inhabitants *do* realise they've passed on, yet remain entirely fixated on continuing their earthly lives in exactly the same context as they did before. Only two channelled sources report on such environments. The first is John:[84]

> Many here are living very close to the earth... Their world is so little removed... that they are unable to relinquish their former mode of living and so conjure up similar surroundings. Some still go daily to their jobs (or what appears to them to be daily). They even drive motor cars. They live in homes, in flats, in rooming houses.

Meanwhile, unusually, many of Sandys' departed family seem to spend much time in the near-earth plane after passing, not because they're trapped but because they're drawn to and enjoy investigating key energy spots where they spent time in their earthly lives – such as the Scottish island of Iona. But they also make references to the astral equivalents of these places. For example her nephew is reported by her brother to have made 'the Scarba on this plane into his earth base'.[85]

Turning to the more numerous OOB references to such environments, the earliest seems to come from Yram:[86]

> I once noticed, whilst I was in the astral world, a region in the ether where, after death, those people go who are neither good nor bad, and who know of nothing but their daily work, with its pleasures and difficulties... In this state each one will devote himself to his work, and familiar habits: technical work, administrative work, commerce... As I saw it, space had been divided into sections in which were placed people of similar affections. Everyone was happy. I watched a certain class of workmen draw their wages and contrive important economies.

> Had they but known it they had but to think of it to become multi-millionaires...
>
> In this ideal town I could see the trams working without an accident ever happening. I visited several factories without noting any other difference from those on earth than a general happiness and wellbeing among all the workmen. It was in the dwelling places, created by different individuals, that I observed the most curious facts. By examining them I was able to follow the nature of the thoughts and feelings of their occupants. Some were simple, sober and in good taste, others large and luxurious. Many were furnished oddly, all the shapes corresponding with the mentalities of their creators.

Sculthorp Similarly reports on departed spirits continuing with manual work:[87]

> Many spirits seem quite contented, as they feel well and do not tire, but their minds do not seek for or know of anything better, nor can they be pushed forward. The spirit law seems to be that the urge must come from within, which will happen in time. As the ingrained thought of many is their livelihood, this habit continues and I have seen all manner of occupations – road-making, factory work, bridge building – I have even seen coal-miners riding on their small trucks and singing cheerfully. In one factory I watched a welder at work. His 'arc' was a small spot of light needing no eye-shade, but he 'thought' he was welding...
>
> On two occasions in this world, where thoughts are things, I have seen butchers' shops. In a land where the slaughter of animals is not possible, this may sound surprising even to those with some knowledge of spirit. They are purely the result of thought and looked just as substantial as anything else... They were simply the earthly life ambitions of the butchers to have a well-stocked shop, capable of satisfying all their customers' demands.

Elsewhere too he talks about spirits going shopping – whereas, of course, in more refined astral planes there would be no need, because the inhabitants create whatever they want by thought.[88]

More recently, Phinn's guide Henry describes a visit to 'one of the slightly less glamorous mid astrals':[89]

> It perfectly fits the bill for that type of soul who's always figured on an afterlife but is sure they've put in a less than spectacular performance and are not worthy of heaven's glories – yet... The communities are small, drab towns plunked down in bleak prairie landscapes under ominous, cloudy skies which occasionally break for a burst of inspirational sunshine. Churches, libraries, and theatres are well attended, and the inhabitants are polite in a hopeful way, although their burdens of regret and self-criticism are all too obvious.

Meanwhile Ziewe encounters a number of lower-mid astral environments on his journeys. The first finds him in an unidentified town centre:[90]

> By this time I had adapted to my surroundings and was clearly visible to other people. Looking around, trying to find familiar features, I felt slightly disappointed that this town was not much different to any town on earth. The atmosphere, however, appeared to be less intense... As I moved through the town I noticed some of the houses looked rather neglected. One district I strayed into looked decidedly bleak. Other parts were much more friendly, with restaurants, shops and pubs. I was surprised by the fact that the nice and not so nice parts of the town were not that far apart, just like on earth... People were socialising in the streets. Although the atmosphere was very earth-like, it was also quite different. There seemed to be more interaction between the people than on earth, and there was a rather more lethargic attitude to the place. Yet so far I had not come across anything that would make this town a particularly attractive place to live.

He asks a woman how long she has been there and she replies, 'For ages... I do get a bit bored sometimes, but I don't know where else to settle. It's not the most exciting place.' He then enters a block of flats and meets another woman who was actually 85 years old when she passed but now looks younger, and is therefore enjoying a new lease of life with her somewhat uninspiring, middle-aged boyfriend. He continues:

> I wondered whether the little old lady had lived most of her life in a block of flats, maybe in London, and I could see why, in this case, she felt comfortable... Although I knew this place was... limited in scope, she had managed to create for herself and her boyfriend a pleasant enough environment, maybe nicer even than her flat on earth. I couldn't see any reason why someone who had lived happily all their life in a large block of flats would want to change anything after they died.

A second finds Ziewe in an uninspiring supermarket, where he's taken into a rather rundown staff room by the checkout girl and meets various workers who seem jovial enough.[91] He asks what he assumes to be the manager if he's happy living in this relatively mundane place and receives a fairly terse response: 'You probably belong to the kind of people who think they are better than everyone else.' Looking out of the window he then sees a somewhat gloomy harbour with countryside stretching off beyond, before making his exit. Afterwards he feels sure he's seen some sort of lower-mid astral equivalent of Shoreham in Sussex, although the layout wasn't exactly the same as its earthly counterpart.

In a third he visits the lower-mid astral equivalent of Boscombe in Bournemouth, where he's living at the time:[92]

> The environment appeared to be very 'down-to-earth'... My first impression was that everything revolved around more or less earth-like activities. People here... had settled more or less into pursuing similar interests that they had when alive, but with added pleasures that leisure has to offer when you have enhanced abilities to fulfil your desires. These people were able to create very agreeable environments... Presently I was walking down the higher dimensional counterpart of Christchurch Road... It wasn't the landmarks that made me recognise the place, rather the atmosphere. Although I knew the road I was in, the buildings were all different. There was an

> unhurried quality of life here. It was friendly and peaceful... There were bars and 'shops', which were more like little galleries where the owner could display their creative skill...
>
> Attracted by loud noise and a jovial atmosphere, I strayed into a nearby pub. I thought it would be good to get more involved with the locals... The people here had taken enjoyment onto another level altogether. They interacted free-spiritedly and were amazingly relaxed around each other... I saw people frolicking and flirting provocatively in front of everyone else without any self-consciousness whatsoever. The absence of inhibition and a prevailing feeling of solidarity, friendship and intimacy was something I had never experienced before. There was certainly a feeling of sexuality in the air... There was something liberating about the absence of any scruples. This was a group where everyone was in agreement... My conclusion was that these people had no problems enjoying their body and sexuality. They were all in it together. There was nobody who would object, because they were attracted to each other simply by functioning on the same level...
>
> However, there was something about this place, despite the good time I was having, which was rather at odds with how I felt... Despite all the wealth of pleasures and amusement to be had here, the limitations of this world suddenly became very apparent. There as an absence of any spirituality, which made me feel like a stranger. This was a basic world with rather crude emotions.

Just to prove that help is always on hand as soon as any resident has had enough, Ziewe also describes finding a young woman looking very downcast in the porch of a large building in one of these environments, and she tells him she's bored and unhappy but doesn't know how to go anywhere else.[93] He decides that he'll break through her psychological barrier by taking her up the stairs to the attic, where he starts tearing away at the plaster on the ceiling, until he's made a hole large enough for her to escape into a beautiful open field where she happily skips away. Elsewhere he makes the general observation:[94]

> In these dimensions everything is still very much more physical than one would expect from a nonphysical level and, instead of manifesting simply by thought, as in the higher dimensions, there still seems to be an element of effort involved... Physical laws, habits and behaviours are still very much in evidence and the people are quite content to continue to live the lives they have been used to.

Meanwhile Bruce briefly alludes to what are probably the lower levels of the mid astral as 'like a mishmash of shopping malls, roads and buildings, and parks and open spaces, teeming with millions of people'.[95]

We conclude this section with two highly pertinent observations. The first comes from a pioneer we briefly met in the Preface, William Buhlman, who has been journeying since the 1970s, is probably the best-known successor to Monroe, runs regular workshops at the Institute and has written three books: *Adventures beyond the Body*, *The Secret of the Soul* and *Adventures in the Afterlife*, published in 1996, 2001 and 2013 respectively. The second comes from Ziewe:

> If you were born and lived your entire life in a crowded city apartment, it is likely that this is the reality you may find comfortable after death. It appears that many people's concept of heaven is often limited to their physical conceptions of reality... Be aware that if we have accepted mediocrity or lack in any form as our norm in this life, we will likely continue to experience the same sort of reality when we make the transition of death.[96]

> The environment we move into after exiting from the physical dimension is a reflection of our state of mind. If we experience our life as repetitive, dull and uninteresting then there is no reason why things should be different on the next level. If we are excited about life, inspired, positive and cheerful, then the environment on the next dimension will reflect this.[97]

Which seems like a good time to turn our attention to the slightly more elevated dimensions of the mid astral.

22

SMOOTH TRANSITIONS AND LIFE REVIEWS

This chapter looks at transition for those who are less damaged and in need of assistance, and whose experience is therefore relatively easy by comparison with those just discussed. It also provides more details on the ubiquitous life review already mentioned many times in Part 3.

SMOOTH TRANSITIONS

Having seen the potential trauma that can await departing spirits if they're unprepared or emotionally unbalanced, let's open this chapter with some general reassurance from several of our sources that for the majority of people the transition into the afterlife shouldn't be too difficult. Starting with channelled material, here are George Vale Owen's mother Emma, TE Lawrence, Andrew Sherwood, Philip Gilbert and Arthur Ford:

> In the case of those who are more enlightened, they realise immediately that they are passed into the spirit land, and then our work is easy.[1]

> Not all souls have to pass through Hades as I did; many are better prepared and come straight through to the light.[2]

> Even without special knowledge the average man can be well prepared for the change if he leads a decent life, is morally

> sound and not too selfish.[3]
>
> The average decent sort of chap senses light at once: a distant glamour of light which pulls at him.[4]
>
> Sometimes the step across is so gentle as to seem like the wafting of a summer breeze. This was so in my case, because I knew enough of what to expect to welcome the shedding of the husk which was my ailing body. The pain ceased, the spirit departed, and here I was amid such beauty as you cannot dream.[5]

Similarly from an OOB perspective we have Emanuel Swedenborg, Caroline Larsen, Robert Monroe and Bruce Moen:

> People who are prepared... need only to slough off their natural uncleanness along with their bodies and are immediately taken into heaven.[6]
>
> Those most highly developed spiritually on earth pass almost directly to higher spheres.[7]
>
> Very large numbers accept their transition without difficulty.[8]
>
> Not everyone who dies gets isolated or stuck... This happens when fears or beliefs interfere with the natural process of dying... From my experience I'd say most of the dying are met by friends, relatives and helpers when they move into the new world of the afterlife.[9]

Despite these reassurances, though, our main message still stands – which is that it would surely be as well to be as prepared as possible for the afterlife, rather than leave it completely to chance. This is not least the case because we've seen that, while we can make some general observations, for any one person it's not always easy to tell what their transition will be like. Someone whose earth life suggests they might be in for a difficult time may end up having a smooth ride, while the same *can* operate in reverse – although hopefully this is less likely. This again relates to the fact we can't always accurately judge the character of another human being from the outside. As to the benefits, this is what Ford has to say about those who are properly prepared:[10]

> Having made the transition with full consciousness and knowing what to expect, they realise they are no longer in the body and cannot be seen by their loved ones there. Often they attend their funeral to pay a sweet farewell and then, unless sorely needed by grieving ones, are able to step into the new role without taut strings to their earth life. They are the ones who make truly rapid progress here.

JULIA AMES (VIA WILLIAM STEAD)

Our earliest channelled source, which hasn't yet been mentioned, is a series of letters transmitted using automatic writing by the American temperance reformer Julia Ames via the pioneering English journalist William Stead.[11] He had just started to discover his talent in this regard when Ames died young in 1891, shortly after he met with her for the first time, and her communications lasted for some six years – sometimes coming through daily, at others only after a lengthy gap. As with other spiritualists involved in public life he risked all his hard-earned journalistic reputation when he published them first in 1897, then republished them under the new title *After Death: Letters from Julia* in 1905. Her surname was deliberately not included, but in time her identity was established. As for Stead, he was one of the many unfortunates who perished in the Titanic disaster of 1912.

The letters are short and simple, and carry two over-riding messages to which Ames repeatedly returns. First, that the incredible state of love that is the default in the higher reaches of the astral needs to be brought down into earth as much as possible. Second, that Stead needs to establish a 'bureau of communication' between the inhabitants of the astral and earth planes.

It is worth noting that Ames repeatedly becomes impatient with Stead for not putting as much effort into this latter endeavour as she deems he should, even when she herself is expressing reservations about its possible misuse.[12] Moreover she's often sharp with him for interjecting his own thoughts and questions – meaning that, as we saw in Part with Jane Sherwood and George Vale Own, he's perfectly conscious while he's writing – instead of acting as a clear channel and not getting 'in the way'.[13] One might argue that this adds to the authenticity of the messages, but equally her sharpness somehow feels rather out-of-kilter with her message of universal love. Indeed there's none of the tenderness often encountered between departed spirits and their human channels – these two almost seem to interact like a long-married couple who've had enough of each other. All that having been said, even if it's possible that Stead's own conscious or even subconscious mind is coming into play on occasion, there's no question that Ames provides useful corroboration of other sources in some areas, not least in her account of her initial passing – as described in a letter to a close friend on earth called Ellen:[14]

> I found myself free from my body. It was such a strange new feeling. I was standing close to the bedside on which my body was lying; I saw everything in the room just as before I closed my eyes. I did not feel any pain in dying. I felt only a great calm and peace... Then I felt as though a great warm flood of light had come into the room, and I saw an angel... who came to me and said: 'I am sent to teach you the laws of the new life... We must go.' We went at first through the streets, then we went through the air, till we came to the place where we met friends who had passed on before... They told me much about the spirit world. They said I must learn its laws, and endeavour to be as useful as I could.
>
> Then I began to be sad about you, and I wanted to go back; the angel took me swiftly through the air to where I came from. When I entered the death chamber there lay my body. It was no longer of interest to me, but I was so grieved to see how you were all weeping over my worn-out clothes, I wished to speak to you. I saw you, darling, all wet with tears, and I was so sad I could not cheer you. I very much wanted to speak and tell you how near I was to you, but I could not make you hear. I tried, but you took no notice of me.

Despite this relatively straightforward transition it's clear that longer term she will need time to heal, because she later adds:[15] 'We have brought with us all our [emotional] diseases. We get cured.'

VARIOUS (VIA EMILY FRENCH AND EDWARD RANDALL)

One of Emily French and Edward Randall's communicants describes the well-known scene of being met by a welcoming party on passing:[16] 'I was aware that I was in new surroundings, most beautiful. Then I became conscious that I was in the midst of a company of fellow souls whose voices were filled with happiness, all welcoming me, and others whom I had temporarily lost while upon the earth plane.' Another incorporates many of the themes we'll expand upon shortly when describing their transition:[17]

> The last physical sensation that I recall was one of falling, but I had no fear – it seemed so natural. At the same time I heard voices speaking words of encouragement, voices that I recognised as those of loved ones that I thought dead. For a time I had no recollection. Then I awoke in this spirit sphere, and never will I forget the joy that was mine. My body appeared as usual except lighter and more ethereal. I was resting on a couch in a beautiful room filled with flowers. I looked through a window and saw the landscape bathed in rose-coloured light. There was a quiet that was impressive, then music, the harmonious vibration of which seemed to rise and fall softly. Then someone appeared and, though she spoke no words, I seemed to understand and answered. In this thought language she told me that she had been my guardian while in the old body.

HENRY LANCHESTER (VIA HIS NEPHEW JOHN WARD)

Henry Lanchester describes his initial passing as relatively simple, although shortly we'll find that he then had a rather painful surprise in store:[18]

> I became unconscious and after a time recovered, or so it seemed. Indeed, my mind suddenly became clear, but I began

> to feel a heavy weight. Gradually I realised that this weight was slipping away from me, or rather, I was sliding out from it, as if someone were drawing his hand out from a wet glove. Then I began to feel free – at one end, so to speak – and then I began to see again. I saw once more the room and the people in it. Then I was free! Free! I saw myself lying stretched out on the bed, and from my mouth came, as it were, a cord of light. It vibrated for a moment, then snapped... At that moment someone said, 'I think he has gone'... Then I realised what I looked like for the first time. How different from what I had always seen in my looking glass!..
>
> I was aware of a presence. How can I describe him, this glorious being?.. He shimmers and shines and flashes, and seems as if he were made of fire. His robes, his face, his whole form is as it were fire. Yet that word gives but a faint idea, nor would the word light be any nearer. All colour, too, is there. This glorious one is my teacher.

Elsewhere Lanchester provides a heart-warming report on being present at the passing of someone he describes as 'a saint':[19]

> Suddenly the room became full of beautiful spirits... 'Who are these?' I asked. 'All the fair souls he has helped to save... All these have come to welcome their pastor and friend.' Then I was aware of a still more glorious being... 'Who is he?' I whispered. 'He is the teacher and ruler of that realm. He comes to take him home. Look!' Slowly from the body a light seemed to rise, strongest at the head. It was almost golden, but had a touch of blue in it. Gradually it seemed to take the form of a head and shoulders, and slowly I saw this figure of light draw out from its fleshy covering. Soon it was clear, and at once a glad cry broke from the lips of the hundreds who were present. 'Father, your children greet you with joy and gladness,' they seemed to say...
>
> The spirit turned and blessed those earthly ones who were watching by the bed. Then the cord of flame, which had been growing longer and longer, snapped, and I heard a wild cry of sorrow from the mourners below; but it was quite drowned by the song of rejoicing which burst from the lips of the spirit

throng. The great spirit took him by the hand and seemed to say: 'Well done, thou good and faithful servant... now thou shalt rule over many.'

ROBERT BENSON (VIA ANTHONY BORGIA)

Here is Robert Benson describing his own passing, and being met by his former friend and colleague, now guide, Edwin:[20]

> I saw my physical body lying lifeless upon its bed, but here was I, the real I, alive and well... I could still see the room quite clearly around me, but there was a certain mistiness about it as though it were filled with smoke very evenly distributed. I looked down at myself wondering what I was wearing in the way of clothes... I was extremely surprised to find that I had on my usual attire, such as I wore when moving freely and in good health about my own house...
>
> At no time was I in any mental distress, but I was full of wonder at what was to happen next, for here I was, in full possession of all my faculties and, indeed, feeling 'physically' as I had never felt before... The new sensation of comfort and freedom from bodily ills was one so glorious that the realisation of it took a little while to comprehend fully... All idea of a 'judgment seat' or a 'day of judgment' was entirely swept from my mind in the actual procedure of transition. It was all too normal and natural to suggest the frightful ordeal that orthodox religion teaches we must go through after 'death'...
>
> [Edwin] told me to take hold of his arm firmly, and to have no fear whatever... I at once experienced a sensation of floating such as one has in physical dreams... The motion seemed to become more rapid as time went on... After a short while our progress seemed to slacken somewhat, and I could feel that there was something very solid under my feet. I was told to open my eyes. I did so. What I saw was my old home that I had lived in on the earth plane; my old home – but with a difference... The house itself was rejuvenated... rather than restored.

He also reports that his friend Ruth experienced a similarly smooth transition:[21]

> Her transition had been a placid one, and she had consequently awakened, after a very brief sleep, calmly and gently... She had then found herself in a delightful house, small, neat and compact, and all her own. An old friend was beside her, ready to help in the inevitable perplexities that accompany so many awakenings in the spirit world.

This latter comment shows that, even with a smooth transition, time and assistance is needed to understand the new astral conditions we find ourselves in – which we'll examine in more detail in the next chapter. In the meantime Edwin too describes his own easy passing into spirit:

> Making myself 'comfortable' upon a couch, I sank into a delightful state of semi-sleep, in which I was fully conscious of my surroundings, yet at the same time I could feel a downpouring of new energy, which coursed through my whole being. I could feel myself becoming, as it were, lighter, with the last traces of the old earth conditions being driven away for ever. How long I remained in this pleasant state, I have no knowledge, but eventually I fell into a gentle slumber from which I awoke in that state of health which in the spirit world is perfect.

This again shows that even with a smooth passing we nevertheless need to discard any earthly emotions and energies that are too heavy to allow us to operate in the mid astral, and to strengthen our astral body itself, and that an element of this may be achieved by some sort of automatic, energetic, healing process carried out while we rest or sleep – probably using similar methods to those described in the last chapter.

EK (VIA SHERWOOD)

Sherwood's EK provides an interesting general description of a 'normal' transition that backs up my comments above:[22]

> The normal experience is neither unhappy nor difficult... Where death comes gradually and naturally like this, one wakes quietly in the new conditions after an interval of a few days...

> Actual death is followed by a period of unconsciousness which lasts for some time; this gives way to a kind of awareness but not a consciousness of one's environment. The new senses have not yet begun to function so there is nothing, or at best a misty, unreal setting, fantastic and dreamlike. During this interval the memory seems to be stimulated so that one lives through a résumé of the lifetime just past. Then one sinks into a second period of unconsciousness which should give place to a full awakening in the new world.

Note that he seems to be suggesting there's a brief, automatic, initial life review, presumably followed by a far more in-depth and considered process later.

BRADSHAW (VIA JOHN/ANONYMOUS)

By contrast with the examples provided for the last chapter, one of John's fellow communicants in *Road of Many Ways*, Bradshaw, has a much easier passing.[23] An English businessman who is happily married with two children until he contracts terminal cancer, he has always had spiritualist leanings and knows he will pass on to pastures new. Yet he loves his wife and family so much that he fights hard to survive, which he does for far longer than expected. But eventually, bed-ridden in hospital, he wakes up to see his departed father and an old friend showing him the beautiful green valley to which they'll soon lead him. Some time later he says goodbye to his wife then, feeling just a slight touch on his forehead, finds himself lifted away from his body and standing above the valley with his father and friend. He drifts into a deep, painless sleep, only to wake up in bed surrounded by many more former friends, who urge him to come home with them.

VARIOUS (VIA CYNTHIA SANDYS)

One of Cynthia Sandys' letters is from Andrew Glazewski, a Polish priest and polymath who helped to set up the excellent Scientific and Medical Network that's still going strong today. Here he eloquently describes his passing after illness:[24]

> The ecstasy of dying is something I can never express. It is

> suddenly like becoming light itself. It is so wonderful... It is clarity of vision and understanding. It is like a clap of divine thunder, and hey presto, there I am out of my tiresome old body, leaping about in the glorious ether... This is the most transforming experience any mortal can attain. I am overcome with joy, pure joy. May I write down exactly what I experienced?
>
> The pain grew suddenly so bad that it seemed to break or burst something inside me – and I was suddenly free... I was above my body... So I accepted death, and as I did so the whole world changed. The room blazed with light. The books on the table, the chairs, even the carpet and the curtains, everything in that room was alive with love power. I stayed quite still, quite close to my body, but I couldn't see it any longer... I felt like a piece of blotting paper that was being saturated with light... I became tireless in my power to receive.

He is then joined by a close former friend and fellow priest from Poland, who now appears 'god-like', and takes him away to be welcomed by many other departed friends before he falls into a deep and restful sleep. Meanwhile her brother Joe not only reports on his own passing, again after illness, but also provides a timely warning for those who might be tempted to cling on to life at all costs, whatever its quality:[25]

> Death has been made such a bogey that it is only through suffering and great discomfort that we are persuaded to let go and cooperate with death. The body fights to retain life on any terms: it is the inborn instinct of the body brain so we have to re-educate this body brain to the point when it will accept and relinquish its power without waiting for the spirit to be wrenched away through pain and disease... I told you that I had experienced a strange feeling of power that seemed to be drawing me out of my body during the last few days of my illness. I was hopelessly ill, and I knew it, so I welcomed this inrush of new life and let go very willingly. That was why I did not linger... Be ready to receive the power that draws you quite painlessly out of your body. It's the most beautiful and glorious

> thing. I see that so many people are prolonging their lives quite unnecessarily.

He then experiences his life review before attending his funeral. Meanwhile the unnamed spirit who attended the boat sinking with Sandys' daughter Pat in the last chapter has a wonderful transition, despite having been seriously ill for several years:[26]

> When I left my body I was instantly fee of pain – just like that. It was so simple, so beautiful and so life giving. I became young again immediately. I was slender and agile and gay... I felt myself bathed in the love of God. There is no other way to describe this sense of ultra wellbeing.

ERIK MEDHUS (VIA JAMIE BUTLER)

Most of our channelled material for this book dates from the 1970s and before. As we noted in the Preface, since then many books have been published containing the wisdom of supposedly higher entities, but the practice of channelling ordinary humans who have passed over and can tell us all about their experience of the afterlife has all but died out. All that remains is the continued use of mediums to pass on personal messages to loved ones in spiritualist circles. However, thankfully there are two channelled sources we haven't yet discussed who completely defy this trend.

The first is Erik Medhus. In 2009, having suffered from severe bipolar disorder throughout his teens, he shot himself in the family home in Houston, aged just twenty. Some time after the initial shock his mother Elisa started to accept that he was trying to communicate with her, and began her 'arduous journey from sceptical physician to a believer without so much as a shred of doubt'.[27] She set up the *Channelling Erik* blog and wrote about her experiences in her 2013 book *My Son and the Afterlife*.

But what is really useful for our purposes is Erik's own memoir about the afterlife, *My Life After Death*, which was channelled through the medium Jamie Butler and came out in 2015. She found she could see Medhus as well as hear him, and unusually spoke his messages word-for-word in real time rather than waiting for a sentence or idea to be completed then repeating it.[28] In other words the process was very similar to most automatic writing. She was initially shocked by his regular use of bad language, and I must admit that when I first started reading his accounts I too found that distasteful, and totally at odds with the older material I'd become used to.[29] Yet he insisted he wanted his words to be totally authentic and to show that he was still exactly the same person at heart, and in time one comes to accept there may be some value in this.

So let's begin with his transition. After his death he's somewhat confused to find himself looking down at his body, trying to pick the gun up and failing, watching the hysteria as it's found, seeing it being carried away in a bag and so on.[30] He then spends several days doing the rounds of his family and friends saying his goodbyes, trying to reassure them that he's still very much alive and ok.[31] Moreover, unlike most departed spirits who just get upset because their loved ones can't see or hear them, he understands he has to communicate with them energetically and insert ideas into their thoughts – although some are more open to this process than others. All this means he stays in the near-earth plane until his funeral, which he attends and enjoys, delighted to find he meant so much more to people than he'd realised.[32]

It is worth pointing out that many religious approaches – and indeed some of our sources for this book – adopt the approach that suicide is the ultimate betrayal of the gift of life, and that the perpetrator will inevitably suffer. This has never gelled with me, at least partly because I take the view that we have complete free will to do what we want with our lives, and that by definition this must surely extend to when to end them. Medhus' case seems to confirm this because his suffering ends with his death. He does of course realise that he's hurt his family and friends hugely by his suicide, and does everything he can to comfort them. But he also has a degree of emotional detachment, and feels that, for him at least, it was the only way out.

Let us be clear that neither of us are *encouraging* suicide, because there are examples of departed spirits reporting that they regretted their actions when they were shown just what their life could have been if they'd stuck it out. But nor are we *condemning* it outright. As for supposed selfishness towards those left behind, as always the bereaved are responsible for their *own* reaction. So, while suicide can be incredibly emotionally complex, it's certainly not a clear-cut issue.

In any case, after this Medhus finds himself in total blackness that feels like having a 'spiritual car wash'. He is then bathed in a bright white light and met by a multitude of departed spirits welcoming him – and projecting a love so intense that it quite overwhelms him, and reassures him that, whatever happens, everything will be ok.[33] Two of the spirits make themselves known as his aunt and grandmother, and they take him through a 'Disneyesque landscape but even more colourful and vibrant'. We will find out what happens to him after this shortly, but it's also worth pointing out that later on he realises a spirit guide he never saw, and was only occasionally aware of, was actually with him during the whole of his transition.[34]

More generally, he asserts that 'each spirit creates the version of their transition that resonates best with them, whether they're aware of this or not' – which explains why it's such an individual experience, but with some commonalities.[35] He also confirms that 'how you get into heaven will be based on the belief system you maintain while you're alive'. In particular he observes that initially materialists may just experience the blackness of zero expectations, but if they ask for help it will be forthcoming. As for him, he admits to having been agnostic – not expecting nothing, but having no preconceived ideas, which is why his experience is fairly 'freeform'.

BILLY COHEN (VIA ANNIE KAGAN)

Our other contemporary channelled source is Billy 'Fingers' Cohen – his self-awarded nickname reflecting the fact he was a bit of a 'wheeler-dealer' who lost the top of one of his digits in an accident as a teenager. Published in 2014, *The Afterlife of Billy Fingers* tells his post-mortem story, as dictated to his sister Annie Kagan – a songwriter based in New York with no previous history as a medium. Initially she could only hear him, but like Butler above in time she learned to see him too. The messages began only three weeks after his death at the age of 62 when, homeless and in an alcoholic stupor, he ran out in front of a car. He had lived a varied life, but its main theme was that of a perennial drug addict and small-time dealer who was in-and-out of both jail and rehab from an early age. Yet it seems he was also a good-looking charmer who women fell for, and a genuine guy who would always try to help others when his mind was clear.

The book is a combination of Cohen's messages interspersed with commentary from Kagan, chronicling her initial disbelief and the many ways in which her brother proved he was real – particularly by accurately forecasting small events in the near future involving her friends, and giving her other synchronistic signs. It also reveals her initial reluctance to be a channel for publishing his account of the afterlife, feeling that humans 'aren't meant to know' such things, which she eventually overcame.[36]

His experience is highly unusual and arguably sheds important new light on the afterlife. For a start his transition is extremely smooth after such a sudden death. However this makes more sense when we later learn that he thought about spiritual and esoteric topics a great deal during his life, and towards its end had a huge although entirely nonreligious love of God – indeed that he ended it deliberately because he'd had enough of suffering and trials and was ready to 'embrace the light'.[37] So, while his transition includes some healing in a 'chamber of thick, silvery blue lights', the process appears to be instantaneous and all-encompassing:[38] 'It wasn't just the wounds from my car accident that were being healed. In the first nanosecond that the lights touched me, they erased any harm I suffered during my lifetime: physical, mental, emotional or otherwise.' We will return to the other elements of his enigmatic experience in due course.

OOB REPORTS

For obvious reasons our OOB sources don't tend to discuss actual transitions, with one exception. Swedenborg claims that he was allowed to experience being taken OOB as if he was passing on properly from the earth plane.[39] From this he deduced that there's an intermediate state between heaven and hell that he refers to as the 'world of spirits', which in our schema probably corresponds to the lower reaches of the mid astral. From here he suggests that departed spirits either progress upwards into heaven, whose inhabitants are all described as 'angels', or downwards into hell.[40]

Here he is, then, describing the acclimatisation assistance that's always available:[41]

> Angels... do everything for us as newly arrived spirits that we could ever wish in that state. They tell us – at least to the extent that we can grasp it – about the realities of the other life. However, if our nature is such that we do not want to be taught, then once we are awakened we want to get out of the company of angels. Still, the angels do not leave us, but we do leave them. Angels really do love everyone. They want nothing more than to help people, to teach them, to lead them into heaven. This is their highest joy.

LIGHT AT THE END OF THE TUNNEL

The description of a 'light at the end of a tunnel' is the most commonly reported aspect of the typical NDE. Here is leading researcher Peter Fenwick's take on the phenomenon:[42]

> The person may enter darkness, usually a dark tunnel. They seem to pass very rapidly through this without making any physical effort. At the end of the tunnel they see a pinpoint of light which, as they approach it, grows larger and larger... For many people, the light is one of the most significant parts of the experience. Nearly always it is described as white or golden, a very brilliant light but not dazzling, so that it doesn't hurt your eyes. Very often the light seems to act almost as a magnet, drawing the person towards it.

Fenwick adds that invariably this is followed by a meeting with some sort of 'being of light'. A fine example of both these phenomena is provided by Dannion Brinkley, a 25 year-old American working in military intelligence who was struck by lightning while on the telephone in 1975 – and was on his way to the morgue before he returned to his body. As he reports in his 1994 book *Saved by the Light*, his experience commences with him finding himself OOB in his home and then in the ambulance:[43]

> I looked toward the front of the ambulance to a spot over my dead body. A tunnel was forming, opening like the eye of a hurricane and coming toward me... There was the sound of chimes as the tunnel spiralled toward and then around me... [It] engulfed me completely... I looked ahead into the darkness. There was a light up there, and I began to move toward it... The light became brighter and brighter until it overtook the darkness and left me standing in a paradise of brilliant light... I looked to the right and could see a silver form appearing like a silhouette through mist. As it approached I began to feel a deep sense of love that encompassed all of the meanings of the word. It was as though I were seeing a lover, mother and best friend, multiplied a thousand fold. As the being of light came closer, these feelings of love intensified until they became almost too pleasurable to withstand.

So how does all this relate to the conventional transition into the mid astral? Although channelled sources commonly report on moving into a much lighter and brighter environment at some point during their passing, they don't tend to mention the tunnel experience, so it's clearly something relatively unique to NDEs. My own view has always been that this represents a mistaken human attempt to describe in spatial terms what's actually happening in energetic terms, as their awareness and consciousness expands into a higher vibratory plane and many of their earthly concerns fall away. OOB pioneer Rosalind McKnight also tends to this view:[44]

> For many who come over temporarily, and experience a movement through a tunnel and see the light at the other end,

> this is merely a change in the rate of vibration within the self. It is experienced as movement through space, but it is really movement through the vibrations of the inner self into higher vibrations, and therefore higher light-levels of energy.

As for the being of light, the experience of one of French and Randall's communicants seems to suggest that the light at the end of the tunnel may at least in part *stem from* this being:[45]

> Presently a faint light began to peer through darkness, first blue and grey, then white, and then rose. The light, so sublimely luminous, gradually condensed into matter, and in a moment a celestial being of beauty, richly wrapped up in pure white and silken robes, stood before me... I beheld the same figure transforming into an almost manly and commanding attitude, with radiant face and brilliant eyes now turned toward me.

Another example of all this is provided by American Bettie Eadie, who temporarily died after a hysterectomy operation in 1973, aged only 31. Although her Christian upbringing didn't turn her into a committed devotee it's perhaps no surprise that, as we saw with Maurice Rawlings and George Ritchie in Part 3, it gives her experience a distinctly Christian flavour. For example her best-selling *Embraced by the Light*, first published in 1992, contains plentiful references to the temptations of Satan.[46] But as the following extract shows, her initial experience is almost identical to Brinkley's except for one major difference – she's absolutely convinced that the being of light she meets is none other than Christ himself.[47]

> I saw a pinpoint of light in the distance. The black mass around me began to take on more of the shape of a tunnel, and I felt myself travelling through it at an even greater speed, rushing toward the light... As I approached it, I noticed the figure of a man standing in it, with the light radiating all around him. As I got closer the light became brilliant... I saw that the light immediately around him was golden, as if his whole body had a golden halo around it... As our lights merged, I felt as if I had

> stepped into his countenance, and I felt an utter explosion of love... There was no questioning who he was. I knew that he was my saviour, and friend, and God. He was Jesus Christ, who had always loved me.

This is actually very similar to Ritchie's experience, where he's confronted by an 'impossibly bright light like a million welders lamps all blazing at once', which then resolves itself into the form of a man:[48] 'I got to my feet, and as I did came the stupendous certainty: you are in the presence of the Son of God... I knew that this man loved me. Far more even than power, what emanated from his presence was unconditional love... A love beyond my wildest imagining.'

This is not uncommon in Western NDEs, although in other parts of the world the being of light is often identified as Mohammed, Krishna or whoever. But, and without wishing to cause offence by questioning such clearly powerful and transformative experiences, other evidence suggests these identifications may be flawed – however convinced the subjects themselves are. For example, Gordon Phinn's guide Henry actually describes one of his fellow guides helping an NDE subject who, on his return and just like Ritchie and Eadie, testifies in church how he's been saved by Jesus.[49] Meanwhile, as far as permanent rather than temporary transitions are concerned, Henry reports that he deliberately appears as an angel during the Central American flood disaster. We also saw in the last chapter that Gilbert deliberately makes himself glow when he encounters one religiously oriented departed spirit, at which point the man wants to worship him, while Monroe talks about taking the form of a 'heavenly being' to aid transitions. Moreover in chapter 25 we'll encounter further examples of spirit helpers deliberately pretending to be Jesus to try to persuade people to leave various religious heavens.

Albert Taylor, a former NASA engineer who began having consciously directed OOB experiences in the early 1990s, makes the following pertinent observation is his 2000 book *Soul Traveller*:[50] 'A person who is unfamiliar with the creative magic that is always present on the astral plane may impose his own visual images onto another being. This will likely contaminate the journey and prevent the traveller from having a dogma-free experience.'

All this suggests that possibly *any* permanent inhabitant of the mid astral will appear to someone having an NDE as a being of incredible radiance and light. Which is why, as I indicated right at the outset, one-off NDEs shouldn't be taken too literally because the subject tends to be overwhelmed by subjective impressions of an environment with which they're completely unfamiliar. Nevertheless they can definitely add to our stock of knowledge if treated with caution.

GUIDES AND GUARDIANS

Talking about beings of light in NDEs brings us onto the more general topic of spirit guides and guardians, and we've already encountered the idea of them assisting our transition into the afterlife on a number of occasions. Usually guides seem to have had a human life on earth so that they can empathise with our problems, but they vary hugely in their levels of experience. We have seen examples of some of our own sources who, although still relatively new to the afterlife planes, begin to help newcomers where they can. On the other hand some guides clearly have a far more expanded consciousness, and are often described as possessing a far larger astral body. Here, then, is a selection of more detailed descriptions of them.

Ames initially perceives that her 'guardian angel' has wings, which is unusual because most of our sources scoff at this overt religious symbolism – which probably originated in ancient NDE and OOB subjects reporting on beings who could 'fly' through space with them in tow. But she later reports:[51] 'They were scenic illusions useful to covey the idea of superiority to earth-bound conditions... I was glad my guide had wings. It seemed more like what I thought he should be, and I was at once more at ease than I would otherwise have been.' This again fits in with the idea that guides project whatever image best suits the individual situation.

By contrast here's Franchezzo describing the guide who not only accompanies him during his visits to Farnese to dictate his book, but also appears regularly to counsel and help him:[52]

> He was a tall, majestic-looking man with long, flowing, white garments... His complexion was that of an Eastern, of a pale, dusky tint. The features were straight and beautifully moulded... His eyes were large, dark, soft and tender as a woman's, yet with a latent fire and force of passion in their depths... A short, silky, black beard covered his cheeks and chin, and his soft, wavy, black hair hung somewhat long upon his shoulders... The spirit was strangely like an earthly, mortal man, and yet so unlike in that peculiar, dazzling brightness of form and feature which no words can ever paint, nor pen describe, that strange and wonderful ethereality, and yet distinct tangibility, which only those who have seen a spirit of the higher spheres can truly understand... Like myself of a warm and passionate nature, he had learned during long years of spirit life to overcome and subdue all his passions, till now he stood upon a pinnacle of power whence he stooped down ever to draw up strugglers like myself... One who had never himself fallen would have spoken to us in vain.

This spirit has clearly achieved a high state of emotional equilibrium. Meanwhile during one of his OOB-style trance visions Ward sees his uncle's guide, who appears to be of a similarly expanded level of consciousness:[53]

> Something was placed over my eyes for a moment, and I could see nothing. The 'something' was removed and, behold, I could see more clearly. Behind HJL [his uncle] stood a great spirit form made of light. His robes kept changing colour and seemed to run through all the colours of the rainbow. He was far taller than HJL, and large in proportion, being perfectly made... No words can describe the majesty and beauty of this being. I can quite understand whence the ancients drew their inspirations for their gods. Then I thought, 'This is doubtless an angel,' and I looked instinctively for his wings, but he had none.

In terms of somewhat shorter descriptions of guides, Lawrence reports that Mitchell is 'tall and dark with deep-set, kindly eyes', and that 'raying out from him light in warm tones enveloped and comforted me'.[54] While Cohen describes his guide Joseph as 'a smiling radiant man with silver hair... an elder although he's not old.'[55] Elsewhere he adds:[56] 'He is better looking than the best-looking actor you've ever seen. His face has experience and goodness etched right into it. His attitude about everything is not at all serious; it's light-hearted and wise... He doesn't impose rules or give me opinions unless I ask. He doesn't dominate me in any way, and that's a beautiful thing.'

Male sources often seem to perceive their guides as male too, but here Larsen describes a female guide she meets during one of her journeys:[57]

> Her flowing dress was shining white, her head covering fell gracefully down her back; and her hands rested on her breast. In form and face she was very beautiful, and a bright white aura enveloped her with radiance. But it was of her spiritual qualities that I was chiefly conscious. Purity, love and sympathy seemed to emanate from her as the perfume from a flower. Strength of intellect and high authority clothed her in dignity.

In fact the general consensus seems to be that the more we progress in the afterlife planes the less we identify with one or other human gender, becoming much more androgynous. We might still *project* ourselves as having the gender of our earth life in certain situations where it's deemed helpful, particularly when dealing with denizens of planes beneath us, but essentially we become sexless – which is, after all, what our true soul essence must be.

Before we close this section, although it's not directly relevant to the afterlife, the idea of guidance being provided during our *earthly* lives is common to most spiritual literature. It is therefore deserving of further, albeit brief, attention. Benson discusses this topic, and starts by clarifying why so many earth-oriented spirit guides seem to have stereotypical human backgrounds:[58]

> They are drawn from every nationality that exists upon the earth plane, and they function regardless of nationality. A great many of them are drawn from eastern countries, and from the North American Indians too, because it has always been the case that dwellers in those regions of the earth world were and are already possessed of psychic gifts themselves, and are therefore aware of the inter-relationship of our two worlds.

He then turns to the thorny issue of the potential impact of guidance on our free will:

> It must never for one instant be thought that the influence of the spirit guide negates or violates the possession or expression of free will. If, upon the earth plane, you were to observe somebody about to take a false step into a stream of traffic upon the road, the fact that you put out your hand to stop him would in no way impinge upon his exercise of free will. A spirit guide will try to give advice when his advice can be got through to his charge; he will try to lead him in the right direction solely for his own good, and it remains for his charge, in the exercise of his free will, to take that advice or reject it. If he does the latter, he can only blame himself if disaster or trouble overtakes him. At the same time, spirit guides are not there to live a person's life for him. That he must do himself.

To clarify why this is such a thorny issue, we saw in chapter 8 that one of the fundamental precepts of Supersoul Spirituality is that 'the law of attraction reigns supreme' – in other words, once we become adults we're entirely responsible for creating our *own* experience in the earth plane using our free will. Now, while I like the way Benson *attempts* to assert that guidance cannot impinge on our free will to create whatever experience we choose, I've maintained for a long time that the two – guidance and free will – simply *cannot* be compatible. I do this precisely because commentators like Benson are always forced to use phrases such as 'leading us in the *right* direction', or 'guides know best what is *good* for us'. But what does this mean if, as we saw in chapter 7, all experiences – supposedly good and bad – usefully add to our supersoul's overall database? Indeed what if, as we saw in chapter 20, the whole idea of good and bad is a relative human concept that has only qualified spiritual relevance?

Of course the context in which most spiritual commentators place the idea of guidance is that all of us have some sort of 'life plan' agreed before our birth, so that all our guides are doing is trying to 'keep us on our path'. But this implies a traditional reincarnation pattern of one life *after* another, rather than the idea of all lives happening at the same time, which is what underpins Supersoul Spirituality.

What I *can* accept though is that, first, they may well try to influence us to make the correct universal choice of love over fear in any circumstance; second, they'll almost certainly try to respond to any of our prayers or requests for help, where possible; and third, and related, I can conceive that they might interfere to bolster the workings of the law of attraction to help a fervently held wish to manifest in the earth plane. But further than this I cannot go. I certainly don't hold with the idea that guides are constantly trying to proactively direct our lives in potentially different directions from the ones we're choosing of our own volition.

LIFE REVIEWS AND BALANCING

We have seen that the idea of experiencing a life review is one of the best-known aspects of transition into the afterlife. At the very least we've all heard of the idea of our whole life 'flashing in front of us' as we die. So let's examine this in more detail, starting with some theory.

Scientific evidence suggests that we don't use most of the capacity of our human brains, and that every single minute detail of what has happened in our lives is stored in our subconscious – or 'on disc' as it were. But we have to filter out most of this detail otherwise our human brains would be overloaded and unable to cope. The trick in our human lives is then to be able to access any given piece of information on disc and retrieve it into our conscious or 'working' memory to be able to use it. Of course this is one of the problems associated with age and particularly dementia, although for some reason long-term memory seems to be relatively unaffected. In any case what if, when our consciousness or disc is released from the confines of our human brain, all these details are instantly available to us without any conscious effort at recall? In other words, what if our memory *automatically* becomes panoramic, as suggested by Sherwood's EK above and various other sources.[59]

This raises the question of whether *every* departed spirit experiences this automatic expansion of memory on passing, especially those who remain trapped in the near-earth or lower astral planes? Clearly some do, because this is what can cause them to punish themselves. But it seems that the majority of those trapped in these lower planes aren't *consciously* punishing themselves at all – they just continue to be blindly obsessed in the same way they were in their earthly life. One might argue then that such high degrees of obsession acts as a block to the otherwise automatic expansion of memory. But it also seems that the latter may be more generally tied in to the level of consciousness or self-awareness the individual has already achieved in their earthly life – albeit that it seems outside agents such as guides might be able to stimulate the process too.

There is more than just the completeness and detail of the panoramic memories we're suddenly confronted with, however. Most accounts of the life review suggest that the process uncovers our true motivations for various actions too, which we may have tried to hide even from ourselves. Not only that but we're also placed in the shoes of others we've upset or hurt so that we feel their reaction and pain as our own – this being information that must derive from outside our own consciousness. These additional elements can deliver such a jolt to the system that they lead to guilt, feelings of unworthiness and even self-inflicted punishment.

It is no surprise then that, following on from any initial expansion of memory and associated life review, many departed spirits need to time to assimilate what they've uncovered – even those who had relatively smooth initial transitions and needed minimal initial healing. This is because very few people can spend several or more decades in our earth system without being tainted by it, however 'saintly' they may appear. Choosing love over fear again and again, consistently throughout one's life, is hard, hard, hard. The corollary to this is, as we'll see in the next chapter, that those who pass on as children have had far less time to become corrupted, and therefore need far less healing and balancing on their return to the spiritual planes. But for the rest of us, the ongoing assimilation and balancing of our emotions as a result of possibly repeated reviews is likely to take some time and involve much literal soul-searching – maybe even, as we've seen, a period of rehabilitation that involves helping others.

Overall, then, we can see that the life review isn't necessarily a one-off *event*, it's much more like an ongoing *process*. The objective, though, is to return ourselves to what is in fact merely a state of *equilibrium*, in order that we can then actually start to *progress* in the afterlife planes.

FRANCHEZZO (VIA FARNESE)

In addition to the life review elements of his time in the 'house of hope' recounted in the last chapter, Franchezzo's guide advises him to visit a 'land of remorse' to develop further self-knowledge:[60]

> You will see displayed in all their nakedness the actions of your past, actions which you have already in part atoned for but do not yet see as the eyes of the higher spiritual intelligence see them... In that land men's lives are stored up as pictures which, mirrored in the wondrous spiritual atmosphere, reflect for them the reasons for many failures, and show the subtle causes at work in their own hearts.

Following on from this general description, he continues with his own actual experience – and remember as an Italian aristocrat he led a pretty selfish and dissolute life:

> As I passed slowly on there rose before me pictures of my past… Like dissolving views they appeared to melt into one another and give place to fresh scenes. Through them all there moved the friends or strangers whom I had met and known, and the long-forgotten, unkind thoughts and words which I had spoken to them rose up in an accusing array before me – the tears I had made others shed – the cruel words (sharper and harder to bear than any blow) with which I had wounded the feelings of those around me. A thousand hard, unworthy thoughts and selfish actions of my past – long thrust aside and forgotten or excused – all rose up once more before me, picture after picture, till at last I was so overwhelmed… that I broke down and, casting my pride to the winds, I bowed myself in the dust and wept bitter tears of shame and sorrow.

Subsequently he finds himself in an equally uncomfortable but instructive environment:

> The thought-creations of my earthly life… like haunting ghosts of my past, were rising up in accusing array against me. The suspicions I had nursed, the doubts I had fostered, the unkind, unholy thoughts I had cherished, all seemed to gather round me, menacing and terrible, mocking me and taunting me with the past, whispering in my ears and closing over my head like great waves of darkness… They showed me what my heart had been. I had had so little faith in goodness, so little trust in my fellow man. Because I had been cruelly deceived I had said in my haste that all men and women too are liars, and I had sneered at the weakness and the folly around me, and thought it was always the same thing everywhere, all bitterness and disappointment.

Fortunately his guide indicates that this somewhat disturbing process isn't necessary for those whose 'errors have been merely trivial, daily weaknesses such as are common to all mankind'.

VARIOUS (VIA FRENCH AND RANDALL)

One of French and Randall's communicants describes their life review as follows:[61]

> Sometimes a spirit gravitates, as mine did, to some lonely, church-like hall, a quiet place of inner rest and contemplation, where the past resolves itself into shadowy pictures which come and go, mapping out the minutest event, thought, or word of past earthly life. I saw that ineffaceable record, which every soul must read again and again, as the past returned with its appropriate judgment.

Notice however that, as we saw in Part 3, this judgment is coming from no one but the departed spirit *themselves*. No gods or other wiser beings are passing judgment *on* them, as so many of our earthly religions would have us believe. This point is well made by another of their communicants, who also refers to the review only occurring when the spirit is ready rather than automatically – suggesting that the opening up of panoramic memory can be delayed, either by the spirit's consciousness being insufficiently expanded, or perhaps by guides deliberately blocking it:[62]

> When a spirit is able to comprehend, its past life comes before it like a panorama. The good thoughts and their results are ranged on the one side; the evil thoughts and their results on the other. Then begins heaven and hell. The poor soul realises, perhaps for the first time, how much evil he has wrought, and his spirit is in torment, for he thinks there is no reparation. When this phase of his punishment is over he is shown how, by influencing thought in earth life, he may wipe out the consequences of each sin. Then comes peace from the torture of remorse. I am speaking of the average man, with the average conscience. Some there are who have led lives that need very little of this punishment. Others must wallow for a long time in the mire of their own sad sins.

We must remember that this message was communicated in a far more orthodox Christian era, but note again that any 'punishment' is *self*-inflicted after introspection, not imposed by other agencies. As for reparation, we've already seen that there are many other ways to achieve this than what's reported above – for example, engaging in rescue and retrieval work. But again this isn't imposed, the departed spirit chooses their own 'path to equilibrium' – I would suggest this is a far better and less loaded word than *salvation* – and then engages in the work gladly.

LANCHESTER (VIA HIS NEPHEW WARD)

Ward's WA described his life review in chapter 17. But here his fellow communicant Lanchester reports that, after his relatively smooth initial passing as related above, he experiences a review that he at first finds extremely unpleasant:[63]

> Like a hideous nightmare, on every side visions seemed to press me round... I saw them not with mortal eyes; I perceived them with my whole being. I call them visions, but they were in real bodily form, like tableaux, moving and acting again before me all my past. My past deeds crowded before me, not in any order, but like a dream, all at once. Oh! the anguish as once more rose up deeds long since forgotten. Little or great, nothing was now forgotten. At last, after what seemed countless ages, an inspiration seemed to seize me, and I prayed... Slowly the wild chaos began... to sort itself out. It... took a kind of chronological order, and the scenes took the form... of a street which stretched far away, far beyond my ken... Among them I saw many visions which came as a relief to my tired soul, little acts of kindness which I had long forgotten, times when I had resisted temptation.

Two things stand out here. First, the way in which any anguish caused by unkind deeds needs to be set against pleasure at deeds lovingly undertaken – and, as we saw at the end of Part 3, often it's the apparently trivial kindnesses involving complete strangers that attract most attention and provide the greatest pleasure during reviews. Second, the experience is often reported as not just like watching a cinema film, but as actually being involved once again in the real-time action.

BENSON (VIA BORGIA)

This idea of gaining a balanced perspective is repeated by Benson, picking up the thread from his initial passing as related above:[64]

> I have said that my mind was alert. That is an understatement. I discovered that my mind was a veritable storehouse of facts concerning my earthly life. Every act I had performed, every word I had uttered, every impression I had received, every fact I had read about, and every incident I had witnessed, all these, I found, were indelibly registered in my subconscious mind. And that is common to every spirit person who has had an incarnate life... The subconscious mind never forgets, and consequently our own past deeds become a reproach to us, or otherwise, according to our earthly lives. The recordings upon the tablets of the real mind cannot be erased. They are there for all time, but they do not necessarily haunt us, because in those tablets are also set down the good actions, the kind actions, the kind thoughts, and everything of which we could justly be proud. And if they are written in larger and more ornate letters than those things we regret, we shall be so much the happier.

VARIOUS (VIA SHERWOOD)

Sherwood's EK describes his more in-depth life review as putting the emphasis on the emotional content of earth experiences:[65]

> The scenes and events of the past life begin to come vividly back in terms of their feeling content and in a manner never experienced before... The impressions of people, events and acts which now come crowding back are far more real and comprehensive than when they were actually experienced. The difference in this presentment of the past is that included in it now is the reaction of other people... As an incident comes back to one's mind it brings with it the actual feelings, not of oneself alone but of the others who were affected by the event. All their feelings have now to be experienced in oneself as though they were one's own. This means that the effects of deeds on the lives of others must be experienced as intimately as though to do and to suffer the deed were one. Where sorrow and wrong have been inflicted, sorrow and wrong must be felt, not merely known to exist.

Here for the first time we see the perspective of others coming into play. In terms of ongoing balancing, he adds:

> It is a purely natural process, set going by the astral body itself which thus works to rid itself of impurity and disease... I am only in the middle of this retrospect myself and have some way to go before all my earth experiences have been seen and known fully in the light of reality. I judge that by this process one is gradually emancipated from earth and, having repented and accepted the truth about oneself, is free to continue in other spheres the proper development of the being. You must realise that all this recollection does not take place in a void; it is the subjective side of life, but ordinary objective living goes on with it side by side... [This] is full and happy unless the retrospective process is too fraught with suffering.

The important point here is that ongoing balancing doesn't take place in a vacuum. Ordinary spiritual life and pleasures can still carry on – just as human life doesn't stand still merely because we're in therapy, for example. Sherwood's husband Andrew then provides his own highly eloquent perspective on the process:

> Anger against oneself is useless, and shame and guilt come to be known as false attitudes due to pride. There is nothing for it but to accept the thing and recognise one's full responsibility... All one can do is be humble about it. In effect one says: 'Yes, I did that. I am like that, more's the pity. I am not the fine fellow I thought myself, but now I will eradicate that fault, strengthen that weakness, clear out that anger.' It becomes a process of stripping off all the pretensions with which one deceived oneself and others, and of facing at last the real man. Very small beer he is too, when one actually comes face to face with him.

Turning to Lawrence, we went through the initial element of his life review in chapter 15 and then, in the last chapter, saw that his sense of superiority was laid bare by Mitchell. His next hurdle is a more lengthy review of all the less desirable actions in his earthly life that are now also revealed and have to be assimilated:[66]

> This is the longest and most painful part of our progress. How to think rightly of what in our ignorance and hardness of heart

> we have done amiss; how to reconcile ourselves to the wounds we have dealt others and now have to feel in our own being? This is the new aspect of wrongdoing which we have to face, for inasmuch as I have injured another I now have to suffer his pain. It is really an illustration of the solidarity of mankind and proof that every deed affects the whole as well as the part.

This idea that in hurting others we're ultimately hurting ourselves is rightly brought to the fore here, and it's an argument used in earthly spiritual circles to support the view that 'we're all one'. This is of course entirely healthy, provided it doesn't lead to the belief that there's no such thing as the individual soul or spirit – which idea is, I hope, proved blatantly incorrect by this very book. In any case, after discussing the particular pain of a court martial he felt honour-bound to carry out himself but then rather botched, Lawrence carries on in his usual self-effacing way by echoing some of the observations made by EK and Andrew above:

> Submission to this justice has brought to me a special peace and stability. I know that a dark place in my being has been cleansed and the remorse lurking there has been purged away. I realise with reflected agony what I did, I see myself as the criminal idiot who could do a thing like that, and through this abasement I have gained a truer knowledge of myself. I do not know how to describe adequately the relief, the lucidity, the new vigour that has succeeded this purgation. I am finding out what it is to rest on a basis of humility with all pretensions to superiority, cleverness and wisdom burnt out of me.
>
> Of course there are many other unhappy things in my past that I shall have to know, suffer and accept in the same way. Each will bring its own measure of retributive suffering; each will teach me the measure of my real stature and bring me nearer to humility and peace... All this process is going on in the context of everyday living. We are not always sorrowing for our sins, yet the memories of our past recur in consciousness and we cannot escape from them for long. We have to get them into proper relation with our estimate of ourselves, to expiate wrongdoing by our own pain, and to integrate the whole

> experience into the new self we are building up. This for me means the destruction of the false self and the facing and acceptance of the real. When all scores are cleared we shall be free to go on.

He also reports that this rebuilding process cannot be rushed, and carries on for the equivalent of a number of earth years. We will find out what happens to him next in chapter 24, but it's worth noting that elsewhere he admits to having an intensely introspective, brooding nature.[67] In his earthly life this was fuelled by his guilt because he deliberately sought fame in Arabia, then promised things to the locals he was unable to deliver as well as causing many people to die – even though these latter clearly *weren't* deliberate. So his guide Mitchell advises that he should engage more in the life around him. All this means that his painful experiences as narrated here may be rather more exaggerated than those of many other departed spirits.

FREDERIC MYERS (VIA GERALDINE CUMMINS)

Frederic Myers makes the following brief but corroboratory comment about the life review:[68]

> We become aware of all the emotions roused in our victims by our acts... No pain, no anguish we have caused has perished. All has been registered, has a kind of existence that makes us sensible of it once we have drifted into touch with the web of memory that clothed our life, and the lives of those who came into contact with us on earth.

FRANCES BANKS (VIA HELEN GREAVES)

Like French and Randall's communicant above, Frances Banks suggests that the life review doesn't have to occur straight away, but that when it does it can be painful and cause a temporary backward step:[69]

> There is no compulsion... to review one's past life on earth as soon as one arrives and the new life here begins. Some take a long time to tackle the problem. They dread to see the effects

> of mistakes and failures... The whole cycle of your life term unfolds before you in a kaleidoscopic series of pictures... Yours is the judgment... This is where quite a few souls have become immobilised. Their pictures were too searing in their exposures. So we try to help them along, but only when they have made the inner desire to right their wrongs.

She adds that at some point this must be followed by a longer, secondary process of review, and describes how her own is assisted by a guide:

> The mind works slowly... backwards through one's experiences... Now, as you ponder, work out, go over, tabulate and judge what you did and why and what were the results (good or bad) you are gloriously aware of this great being beside you, giving strength, peace, tranquillity and helping with constructive criticism. This is a wonderful experience, though harrowing at times. But very cleansing and bringing new hope.

She then continues with her own ongoing and lengthy process of assimilation and balancing:

> Sometimes we have a round-table conference [with the other Brothers and Sisters in her rest home]... where I put all the questions that bother me to wiser minds than mine... I am exactly the same person now. I still have to go over and over again in my mind the possibilities I had when on earth, the failures and mistakes I made... But here one does not waste effort in regretting blindly. There is too much to learn in a positive manner and to apply to one's future progress. And always there are souls in far worse predicaments from whom lessons can be learned.

Later she adds that, despite having a marked impatience to progress to higher planes, she recognises that the process of attaining equilibrium cannot be rushed:[70]

> I retire more and more to the deep joy and peace and rest of my garden amongst my flowers... I revel in light... I rest in that light and am healed from my many mistakes... I become

> uplifted and eager, so very eager, for that succeeding stage. Yet I know that I have to remain where I am and do just what I am doing until I have shed more of the 'shadow-covering'... And there are three ways in which to carry it out here. By self-judgment, and true assessment of experiences; by service to one's fellows; and by aspiration.

MEDHUS (VIA BUTLER)

Medhus experiences a very particular form of life review after the events recounted earlier in this chapter. His aunt and grandmother guide him to what he perceives as a bright, white room, where six tall spirits with intense energy and projecting a sense of huge wisdom are arrayed behind a crescent-shaped table.[71] They are also projecting compassion rather than judgment. This is remarkably similar to the descriptions of a 'council of elders' that are commonly found in contemporary books about reincarnation and the interlife, although whether Medhus had ever been influenced by any of these during his earth life is unknown. In any case here's what happens next:

> The table changed shape, morphing into what seemed like one of those theatres where the screen wraps around you... All of a sudden, everything from when I was a tiny, tiny baby to the moment I died – the good, the bad and the ugly – came flying at me from all directions... As my entire life unfolded before me, I was not only experiencing every single moment I ever lived, but I was also observing and feeling what everybody else in my life went through in reaction to whatever I said or did to them. I felt their joy, their hurt, their disappointment... Not only could I feel the emotions they had in response to my actions, but I could actually see things from their perspective. It was like I was them.

He emphasises that all this was experienced *simultaneously*, like an 'instant download from beginning to end'. He then discusses something again found in modern reincarnation literature but not mentioned by our other sources:

> My life review also allowed me to see every possible outcome for every choice I'd ever made in my life, and as you can imagine the possibilities are infinite.

Medhus is also unusual in that often, as we've seen, the life review leads to a period of introspection – whereas he concludes that the instant-recall process itself significantly aided his healing by allowing him to stop judging and to forgive himself. He adds: 'My life review made me feel like I had been cast in a role and played it... As a human I was playing myself. As a spirit I truly *am* myself, and I'm looking back at the part I played.' Nevertheless, after this process he does find himself in the company of a guide who helps him with ongoing therapy and balancing.[72]

COHEN (VIA KAGAN)

Cohen's account of his transition is again unusual in that, after his healing in the 'blue chamber' reported earlier, he immediately sheds any sense of having a body – indeed he 'glides right out into the glorious universe', where he 'drifts through space amongst stars and galaxies', surrounded by 'higher beings' who he can sense but not see, the whole blissful experience capped off by a 'soothing hum'.[73] As we'll see properly in the final chapter it seems as if he graduates directly to the superconscious planes, bypassing the astral and mental completely. Nevertheless at this point he does experience a life review that involves 'deep learning' over a prolonged period, so it's included here for comparison purposes.[74]

First a ring of crystals appears around him, which then turns into a 'cosmic projector' with the 'circular movie playing all at once and holographically'.[75] He continues:

> I'm watching my whole life from my birth to my death. I'm looking here, looking there, fast-forwarding, rewinding, zooming in and out. I see the paths I took, and the ones I didn't... I can follow all the different paths I didn't take when I was alive and see how they would have turned out. What's surprising, though, is that it doesn't seem like one way is more valuable than any other. I don't have a preference. It's all

> fascinating, and I have no regrets... I did a lot of things that most people would call mistakes, big mistakes. But the way I look at it, I had a great life. It was all great, even the hard parts... I'm watching from a distance, so all the ups and downs, all the dramas, seem like they're happening to someone else.

Later he adds that the life review includes seeing other people's own intentions towards us, which of course aren't always what they seem:[76] 'You get to see everything – who loved you, who hated you, what they did for you, and what they did to you when your back was turned... You spend a lot of time viewing what you did on earth, so be sure to make it interesting.'

We can see from all this that Cohen corroborates Medhus' idea of seeing all possible courses of action and also, like Medhus, seems to experience little guilt or remorse. Given that, for example, as a drug addict he often stole from those nearest and dearest to him, this is perhaps somewhat out of step with the reports of the majority of our other sources. But we must accept that everyone has a different path and experience, both in earth life and after it. Nor can we exclude the possibility that this *may* represent a generational shift in the attitude of departed spirits and therefore in their life reviews. That is to say, maybe more recent generations are generally less wracked with guilt and have fewer regrets – not least because they're less likely to follow a narrow religious path – and in the afterlife tend to understand better that they were just playing a part in their earthly life. Certainly Cohen, having undertaken plenty of spiritual and esoteric study, may fall into this category.

NDE REPORTS

The life review is commonly reported during NDEs, presumably because the subject's consciousness is being temporarily released from the constraints of the human brain. We went through Ritchie's in chapter 14, but here Eadie reports briefly on hers:[77]

> My life appeared before me in the form of what we might consider extremely well-defined holograms, but at tremendous

> speed... I not only re-experienced my own emotions at each moment, but also what others around me had felt... I understood all the suffering I had caused, and I felt it.

However her Christ-guide then makes her concentrate on the positives too. Meanwhile Brinkley carries on from above as follows:[78]

> The being of light engulfed me, and as it did I began to experience my whole life, feeling and seeing everything that had ever happened to me... This life review was not pleasant. From the moment it began until it ended, I was faced with the sickening reality that I had been an unpleasant person, someone who was self-centred and mean.

He then carries on to describe a fascinating element of the experience that is, as far as I'm aware, quite unique in the literature currently available to us:

> The depth of emotion I experienced during this life review was astonishing. Not only could I feel the way both I and the other person had felt when an incident took place, I could also feel the feelings of the next person they reacted to. I was in a chain reaction of emotion, one that showed how deeply we affect one another.

As an example he describes reliving an episode when he delivered weapons to a Central American country to support the US fight against Russian involvement in the region. In earth life he did the drop then left. But in his review he's forced to stay with various of the weapons as they go to their eventual destinations, and are used to kill and maim not only enemy soldiers but innocents as well. Although this exposure to the full *chain* of events is quite unique, it's perfectly understandable given the fact that *everything* that happens on the earth plane is clearly interconnected, and that all the memories from our human system are stored and can be accessed when appropriate.

At the conclusion of his review Brinkley is reminded of one of the central messages already discussed above, but it's well worth repeating: 'Good isn't usually accomplished in bold actions, but in singular acts of kindness between people. It's the little things that count, because they are more spontaneous and show who you truly are.' What is more, despite the harrowing nature of his review, rather like Medhus and Kagan he reports: 'Instead of feeling shame and anguish, I was bathed in the love that embraced me through the light.'

There are other elements to his experience that we'll consider in Part 5 but, after coming back to a body that was totally shattered by the lightning strike, he eventually teams up with celebrated NDE researcher Raymond Moody and turns his life around completely. Perhaps even more important he makes up for his misspent early years by performing countless unsung 'small acts of kindness': for example, he devotes many hours to helping people approaching death in hospices, when he's already working flat out on other projects. Eventually all this catches up with him, and in 1989 he has *another* NDE when his already-damaged heart can't cope any more.[79] Again he experiences the tunnel and being met by his being of light, and undergoes another life review.[80] But this time, although he still sees the first 25 'bad' years, he's able to derive a strong sense of pride from his subsequent behaviour.

OOB REPORTS

Having not experienced life reviews themselves, OOB pioneers tend to only make passing comments thereon. The main exception to this is Swedenborg, who refers to witnessing departed spirits being confronted with the error of their ways via instantaneous recall from perfect memory.[81]

However Jurgen Ziewe recounts an interesting episode from one of his journeys that incorporates elements of both life review and subsequent balancing.[82] Initially he finds himself in a city that can only be described as an astral 'tourist attraction', with ultra luxurious hotels, monuments, markets, shops and 'amusement on steroids'. In one hotel he meets a waiter called Kay and can immediately and telepathically 'see' his past, which Kay then admits hasn't been a pleasant one – his having been a self-admitted 'outright evil bastard' in his earthly life, who thought nothing of causing pain and even committing murder.

Ziewe then sees that after Kay passes he finds himself in a 'dark, foul and despicable' lower astral environment where he's surrounded by those of even worse disposition, all incessantly fighting, arguing and tormenting each other. When it all gets too much it doesn't matter how far he tries to run, he can't escape the baying mob. Until, of course, he cries for help and a spirit rescuer arrives. Over time the latter gains Kay's partial trust, but insists that if he's to escape he has to face up to the life he's led on earth. This however generates even more torment as he reviews what he did to his many victims, and on many occasions he makes a little progress but then runs away because the process is too hard – until finally he recognises it's the only way out.

With echoes of the rehabilitation of Franchezzo and of the Officer from Part 3, the helper then assures him that the best way to make amends is to serve others with a glad heart – and that's how, after a long and tortuous road of gradual improvement, he comes to be waiting on others in a tourist hotel. Here is Kay himself closing the episode in a rather beautiful way:

> The only thing that makes me happy is looking after their needs and not expecting anything in return... I like nothing more than feeling the flame in my chest grow slowly and steadily with every day. I never knew that people showing appreciation could mean so much. One day, when I am fully recovered from my madness, I will go back to my dark haunts to meet my old comrades I fought with, and they won't recognise me. I will then try to pay the helper back by doing for them what he did for me.

On that ultimately redeeming note, let's now move on to more universally positive reports of what those who are reasonably prepared for the afterlife can look forward to.

23

THE MID ASTRAL GENERALLY

This chapter looks at the general conditions to which all must become accustomed in the mid astral. Many of them in the various sections have already been encountered in previous chapters, or are corroborated in future chapters, but in contexts where they're not the main issue at hand. Much of this information is presented simply by providing a list of sometimes-brief, corroboratory quotes – which come by default from our channelled sources, but adding in any NDE or OOB reports where appropriate.

FEELING MORE 'REAL' AND 'VITAL'

We have come across this idea a number of times in passing in the last few chapters, but now we can focus on it. Here are, in turn, Julia Ames, two of Emily French and Edward Randall's communicants, David Hatch, Jane Sherwood's EK, Frederic Myers, Frances Banks, John, his fellow communicant Bradshaw and Erik Medhus – all starting to give us a flavour of just what we have to look forward to:

> You don't know what a prison the body is until you leave it. I exulted, I was so well, so free, so happy... There was the increased sense of vitality – doubly and trebly delightful after my illness – and a great feeling of restful absence of fret... The

> memory appears to be quickened rather than dulled. The mind sees more clearly.[1]

> Life on your plane seems like a dream, and now the only time I have really lived.[2]

> I was free, and in the place of weakness and pain and sickness, I had a virility and a vigour which I had never known upon the earth plane.[3]

> I feel considerably younger than I have felt for a long time.[4]

> My body felt quite different... vigorous and ready for anything, as if I had stepped back into youth.[5]

> One is sensible of an extraordinary exhilaration and of an increased mental vigour.[6]

> I felt light, and there was a new sense of freedom that was bewildering. I was the same – yet not the same!.. I could both see and hear as before, only now in a more intense way.[7]

> I was more alive now than I had ever been.[8]

> I look and feel so brimful of energy, so alive, so vital.[9]

> I had heightened awareness and was able to absorb all the details of what was going on in the room.[10]

NDE survivors often report this phenomenon too – for example, George Ritchie:[11] 'Our consciousness becomes keener and more aware than ever.' While if we turn to our OOB pioneers, here are Emanuel Swedenborg, Frederick Sculthorp and Jurgen Ziewe:

> We see and hear and also think more discerningly than when we were in this world.[12]

> With full consciousness and in tune with a plane in spirit, the sight is keener than the best earthly eyes can ever be. There is a more stereoscopic effect and things stand out in greater clearness and colour, even to the most minute details.[13]

> [I often feel] super alive, super awake, with a clarity of vision, hearing and consciousness that is breathtaking.[14]

DIFFERENT PERCEPTION OF TIME

We saw in chapter 8 that one of the fundamental precepts of Supersoul Spirituality is that 'everything is happening in the now' – in other words, the apparent past and future don't exist as a continuum. Another way I like to express this is that time is 'a discrete series of now-moments'. This is extremely hard, bordering on impossible, for our human brains to comprehend, and it's equally difficult for departed spirits to describe their new perspective. Nevertheless let's see what they have to say.

First Banks simply states that ultimately time doesn't really exist:[15] 'There is no such thing as time... Each moment holds in itself all of the past and of the future.' Both Philip Gilbert and John reiterate this, but add that in the astral they do feel some sense of continuity:[16]

> You must realise that though in infinity time does not exist, yet in our aspect of existence we do feel it, in the form of rhythm.

> It is hard to describe time where there is no time; space, where there is no space. One is aware of events approaching, taking place, and passing. Therefore there is some concept of time; but since it has no meaning, since one grows no physically older by it (nor is there any sense of urgency) time, as you know it, does not exist.

Similarly, from an OOB perspective, Swedenborg states that 'even though things keep happening in sequence and progressing in heaven the way they do in the world, still angels have no notion or concept of time and space'.[17]

By contrast both Henry Lanchester and Robert Benson emphasise the difference in the perspective of elapsed time between the earth and astral planes:[18]

> We are in the same world as you, but not subject to the same laws. For example, time and space don't exist... This was the first time I realised the huge difference between our method of reckoning time, or rather our escape from time, and your subservience to it. In those three earthly days [in spirit] I had

> made apparently many [earth] months' progress, and had learnt much about spiritual things.
>
> Those of us in the spirit world who live in the realms of happiness and perpetual summer will have no cause to find time hangs heavily. In this sense we are simply not conscious of the flight of time. In the dark realms the reverse is the case... A period of existence within these dark regions, amounting to nothing more than a year or two of earthly time, will seem like an eternity to the sufferers... Some people... have returned to the earth world for the very purpose of satisfying their curiosity as to the number of years they have been in the spirit world. I have spoken to some who have made this journey, and they were all amazed to discover the unsuspected scores of years that had passed by since their transition.

TE Lawrence corroborates this before concentrating on the way time speeds up as we progress through the planes, until we reach a point where everything is timeless – and adds that as he himself progresses it becomes harder to slow his vibrations down enough to be able to still communicate with someone on earth:[19]

> The sense of duration, which is each individual's measure of passing time, is checked and regulated on earth by exterior standards set according to earth movements and position with regard to the sun, hence time is a highly formalised concept which over-rides the individual sense of duration. Here the exterior checks are absent and we begin to realise that our sense of duration is a function of our kind of consciousness and alters as the scope of that consciousness widens. In other words, the rate of experiencing quickens as we as ascend, and so the change over from time to timelessness comes about gradually as we are fitted to adjust to it.
>
> My experience here has already shown me the beginning of this gradation. Up to the present – and you must remember that I have not yet progressed far – I have reached a stage of consciousness where I am aware of a great difference between my rate of living and the tempo of all my activities and those of men still on earth. Granted that men vary in their tempo even

> on earth, but taking one's experience in working with a medium as a guide, I find that I can only with difficulty slow down my rate to work with a mind still subject to earth conditions. It is tedious and fatiguing and sometimes I think nearly impossible, but it can just be done.

Jane Sherwood's EK echoes Lawrence but introduced the fact that both space *and* time effectively expand as we progress through the planes, which is why those in higher realms hold awareness of a much broader span:[20]

> The sequence of states of consciousness flows quietly by gathering still more of the future into the present. There is a lucid flow of being which alters one's sense of duration and adds beauty to the mere passing of time as it collects to itself the lovely future and passes it into the still lovely past... Each plane shows this contraction effect for space-time values... So it amounts to a progressive enlargement of experience. Thus each plane should provide a vantage ground in regard to those below it. From the higher, one should be able to survey a larger area of time and space in the lower.

George Vale Owen's Astriel makes exactly the same point by inviting us to compare 'a state of four dimensions to a state of three' as follows:[21] 'The former, being of greater capacity than the latter, covers at any moment a wider range of view, as to time and sequence of events, than the latter can do.' Meanwhile Arthur Ford corroborates this by suggesting he can visit any moment in earth time:[22] 'Time, of course, is different. There's no such thing as clock time here, for we are able to eliminate time as well as space, since we are able to will ourselves to be anywhere at any moment of earth time.' Even more in keeping with my opening comments in this section, Erik Medhus repeatedly talks of things happening simultaneously rather than in a linear fashion, and adds:[23] 'Every moment is stacked on top of each other, not laid out in a straight line.'

Moreover, from an NDE perspective, Eben Alexander entirely backs up this view:[24]

Because I experienced the nonlinear nature of time in the spiritual world so intensely, I can now understand why so much writing on the spiritual dimension can seem distorted or simply nonsensical from our earthly perspective. In the worlds above this one, time simply doesn't behave as it does here. It's not necessarily one-thing-after-another... A moment can seem like a lifetime... But... that doesn't mean it's jumbled, and my own recollections from my time in coma were anything but.

TRAVELLING BY THOUGHT

Picking up from the above, departed spirits soon learn that space doesn't exist in the same way as it does on earth either, because they only have to *think* of somewhere or someone and – once they're fully acclimatised – they're immediately there. Here are Ames, Franchezzo, one of French and Randall's communicants, Hatch, Vale Owen's mother Emma, John and Medhus briefly making the fundamental point:

> You have only to think to be anywhere... It is thought-transference of yourself.[25]

> If we were in a great hurry to go anywhere our wills seemed to carry us there with the speed almost of thought.[26]

> Another condition that impressed me was that all time is now, and all distance annihilated. We live in the present always, and if we desire to enter another condition within our zone, or go to a place on your plane, we concentrate our thoughts, and we are there.[27]

> If we think intently of a place we are apt to find ourselves there.[28]

> Distance has a different aspect from what it wears on earth... If [a spirit] wished to leave the summit on which he stood and go to some point near the horizon, or even beyond, he would do so by means of his will, and it would depend on the quality of that will, and his own nature, whether he went fast or slow.[29]

> One does not actually travel from one point to another. There

> is no 'here' or 'there', only mind. Where the thought is, there is the means of transport.[30]

> We just think of where we want to go and – poof! – we're there.[31]

As so often, Benson goes into rather more detail by providing a highly revealing report of what it's like for him and his friend Ruth, as newcomers, to get the hang of 'thought-travel':[32]

> The question came to our minds: should we walk, or should we employ a faster method? We both felt that we should like to try exactly what the power of thought can do, but as before, in other circumstances, we were both devoid of any knowledge of how to put these forces into action. Edwin told us that once we had performed this very simple process of thinking, we should have no difficulty whatever in the future. In the first place, it was necessary to have confidence, and in the second, our concentration of thought must not be a half-hearted affair. To borrow an earthly allusion, we 'wish ourselves' there, wherever it may be, and there we shall find ourselves!
>
> For the first few occasions it may be required to make something of a conscious effort; afterwards we can move ourselves whithersoever we wish – one might almost say, without thinking! To recall earthly methods, when you wish to sit down, or walk, or perform any one of the many earthly actions that are so familiar, you are not conscious of making any very definite effort of thought in order to bring about your desires. The thought very rapidly passes through your mind that you wish to sit down, and you sit down. But you have given no heed to the many muscular movements, and so on, involved in the simple action. They have become as second nature. And so it is precisely the same with us here. We just think that we wish to be in a certain place, and we are there.

Meanwhile Sherwood's EK describes one version of the actual process as follows:[33]

> From my hillside I look across the valley to a house on the other side, surrounded by trees. My immediate view shifts slightly,

> gets vague to me and goes through modifications by way of which it dissolves into this other. The distant house is now large and plain and I am standing at the door... The dissolving of one view into another is not a sudden or startling experience.

From an NDE perspective Alexander confirms the idea:[34] 'In the worlds above, I slowly discovered, to know and be able to think of something is all one needs in order to move toward it.' As do most OOB explorers who report that, on any plane, setting the deliberate intention to visit a particular person or place will invariably and immediately take them there.[35] To close this section, a guide that Bruce Moen meets provides an interesting perspective on the process:[36] 'Getting from point A to point B is an act of creation. It requires no time or movement. One instant you're in one place, in the next instant you're created in another.' But perhaps the earliest of all our OOB pioneers, Emmanuel Swedenborg, explains it best:[37] 'All motion in the spiritual world is the effect of inner changes.'

COMMUNICATING BY THOUGHT

We have already encountered many examples of departed spirits using telepathy to communicate, whether they're in each other's company or not. It seems that some take longer to get used to this new faculty than others – here, for example, is Banks' perspective as a relative newcomer:[38] 'There is no mask even for thought, one's inmost thought, and sometimes I shudder at the realisation that our fellows here can read us, as we read books on earth.' Others such as Lanchester, Hatch, Benson, Banks and Medhus report more generally on this new ability:

> You know that some people have learnt of things which are happening to their friends at a distance. We all can do so here, and that is the way we communicate with each other; speech does not exist with us. This explains those sayings in the Bible about nothing shall be hid. You cannot tell lies here or be deceived.[39]

> I find, as time goes by, that I converse more and more by powerful and projected thought... [But] it is not true that we cannot keep our thoughts to ourselves if we are careful to do so. We can guard our secrets if we know how.[40]

> One of the first things to be done upon arrival here is to realise that thought is concrete, that it can create and build, and then our next effort is to place our own thoughts under proper and adequate control.[41]

> In this further life speech as sound is not needed. Vibration is everything. It is sufficient that we formulate and 'breathe out' a strong thought for this to communicate itself to other minds.[42]

> There's a universal language here that everyone speaks. It's a language of energy, and it's instantaneous. Whatever I need to communicate to anyone here is understood immediately.[43]

Meanwhile Lawrence and Medhus go into more detail about the fuller potential extent of this nonverbal communication:

> One never needs to express in words one's feeling for another. It is always apparent in the immediate reaction of one's body and cannot fail to be read correctly... The transmission of meaning involves not the emotional body alone but the as-yet imperfectly formed spiritual body. Where there is affinity of spirit and closeness of emotional regard, meaning is often carried between friends without the clumsy intervention of words. It 'jumps the gap' and is immediately and fully apprehended as it could never be if it had to be trimmed to fit a pattern of words.[44]

> When I touch other spirits, I get their thoughts, their emotions, their intentions, and all their stories – past, present and future – and in that moment I'm sharing and exchanging the deeper levels of myself too. There are no secrets – no privacy – but that's not a problem here... Heaven is like a naked beach, no bathing suits necessary – no covering up emotions, no lying about how you feel.[45]

This latter seems very similar to the way in which Ziewe reads

Kay the waiter's past in the last chapter. In any case if we now turn to communicating at a distance, often merely thinking of another departed spirit means they'll suddenly appear. Here are Benson and John again, followed by Myers and, from an OOB perspective, Swedenborg and Rosalind McKnight:

> If we can move ourselves by the power of thought, then it follows that we should also be able to send our thoughts by themselves, unhindered by all ideas of distance. When we focus our thoughts upon some person in the spirit world, whether they are in the form of a definite message, or whether they are solely of an affectionate nature, those thoughts will reach their destination without fail, and they will be taken up by the percipient.[46]

> Thoughts of those near and dear to her, who have already made the crossing of death, fill her mind; she desires their presence, and her urgent thought sounds like a voice... Swiftly they appear; for they have loved her dearly, and so are in tune with her mind and may hear its thoughts if directed towards them.[47]

> A thought travels on its journey and reaches the recipient almost simultaneously, and one knows instinctively where one must go to answer that thought.[48]

> In the other life, whenever we think about someone... the other is called to us.[49]

> [Referring to one of her spirit friends] Just by sending out the thought, five people suddenly appeared on the spot.[50]

By contrast Lawrence describes how much joy he gains from communicating at a distance with, and learning from, others in higher planes:[51]

> The experience of sharing the thought of others who are not present with me opens up a whole vista of new possibilities. Think of it! One is part of a great universe of thought which can be tapped without the mechanical interchange of words, either heard or read. It fascinates me more than any of the new

> powers of this wonderful life... It gives me a pure and endless source of joy because at rare intervals my world opens into vistas of a larger, freer life and experience – a wonder of light and joy beyond telling.

Actually this seems to be a forerunner to the kind of communication that operates in the upper astral and even mental planes, as we'll see in Part 5. Meanwhile, from an OOB perspective, Robert Bruce provides some general corroboration:[52] 'Communication here is a kind of telepathic, metaphorical imagining, full of empathy and intuition... Normal speech is superfluous.'

To close this section, Sculthorp provides an amusing story of being caught out by telepathy:[53]

> On one occasion my wife took me to a concert on the other side. There was the usual stage or platform, and one of the performers was a singer, a man. I liked his voice but I thought his gestures were rather overdone. As I thought this he glanced quickly in my direction and modified his movements... After he had finished, he walked to the front of the stage and stared at me with a look of annoyance. Much to my relief, we got up and left the hall, but in a rather thoughtful mood, and outside I suddenly realised that the singer had received all my thoughts. I'm afraid that earthly habits like this must take time to correct.

By contrast Ziewe provides a slightly different perspective. On many of his journeys he seems to encounter especially alluring girls and women, and in one in particular he struggles to hide his sexual desire, despite being happily married in his earthly life. However the girl just shrugs it off, and he concludes:[54]

> I became aware of an easy intimacy here in stark contrast to our physical ways of social interaction. People seemed to be less inhibited in showing their feelings, probably because feelings here are much harder to disguise. On earth we can simply pretend and try to pull the wool over each other's eyes. Here people have to own up to their thoughts and emotions. Consequently they make allowances and are much more open.

TRANSPARENCY

This naturally brings us onto the fact that earthly status is as nought once one arrives in the astral, because spiritual worth comes from within and – even if as departed spirits we can sometimes learn to cloak our thoughts – our basic nature is fully transparent to all. Indeed if this book could serve the single purpose of reminding our celebrity-obsessed earthly culture of this fact, it would have more than done its job. Moreover, of course, all of this ties in to not judging people by appearances either in the earth or the lower planes, as we discussed in chapter 20. Here then, to start us off, is Ames:[55]

> There are men here who seemed to be vile and filthy to their fellows [on earth] who are far, far, far superior, even in purity and holiness, to men who in life kept an outward veneer of apparent goodness while the mind rioted in all wantonness... Hence the thoughts and intents of the heart, the imaginations of the mind, these are the things by which we are judged; for it is they which make up and create the real character of the inner self, which becomes visible after the leaving of the body... Money, rank, worth, merit, station, and all the things we most prize when on earth, are simply nothing.

Of course when he first passes over Franchezzo is a fine example of how earthly and spiritual status can be completely reversed:[56] 'Through my mother I was allied to the great ones of earth whose ambitions had moved kingdoms to their will; and now the lowest, humblest, poorest beggar of my native streets was greater, happier than I.' Meanwhile Vale Owen's mother Emma opens by making the following brief observation:[57] 'The spiritual body here... is patent to all and, being a perfect index of the spirit, shows forth its characteristics.' Elsewhere she provides the salutary example of 'a very learned writer who had published several books' being instructed in spiritual matters by 'a lad who in his earth life was a stoker in a gasworks':

> He was glad to learn, too, for he had partly learned humility;

> and the curious thing was that he did not so much mind sitting at the feet of this young spirit, as going to his old friends here and owning up to his mistakes and his vanity of intellect in his past life. This, however, he will have to do sooner or later, and the lad is preparing him for the task. It is also whimsical to us to see him still clinging to his old pride, when we know all about him, and his past and present status, which latter is rather low, and all the time he thinks he is hiding his thoughts from us.

But as so often it's Benson who elaborates most on this issue of transparency:[58]

> We have left our earthly importance behind us, and we do not refer to it except to show, by our own experiences, to others still incarnate, just what to avoid. We do not revive our memories for the purpose of self-glorification, or to impress our hearers. Indeed, they would not be in the least impressed, and we should only succeed in making fools of ourselves. We recognise the truth here, and our true worth is for all to see. It is spiritual worth, and that alone, that counts, irrespective of what we were upon the earth plane. Perspectives and view-points are completely altered when one comes into the spirit world. However mighty we were upon the earth plane, it is spiritual worth only that takes us to our right place in the spirit world, and it is the deeds of our life, regardless of social position, that at our transition will assign to us our proper abode. Position is forgotten, but deeds and thoughts are the witnesses for or against us.

He then tackles the fascinating subject of meeting famous people in the afterlife:

> In living in these realms one is inevitably bound, sooner or later, to encounter some person whose name is known to all upon the earth plane. But these famous folk have no attachment to the earth world. They have left it behind them... Discretion is something we soon learn to exercise, and it is embodied in our never prying into the facts and circumstances of other people's earthly lives. That does not mean to say that we are debarred from discussing our earthly lives, but the

> initiative always comes from the person concerned. If he wishes to tell anyone of his life on earth he will ever find a sympathetic and interested ear awaiting him.
>
> You can see, then, that our earthly lives are very strictly our own. The discretion that we exercise is universal among us – we show it and we receive it. And whatever our former position upon earth, we are united in these realms, spiritually, intellectually, temperamentally, and in such human traits as our likes and dislikes. We are one; we have achieved the same state of being upon the same plane of existence. Every fresh face that enters these realms receives the same heartfelt welcome, without reference to what he was upon earth.
>
> Several of the earth world's famous people have spoken to me of their awakening in the spirit world, and they have told me of the shock of revelation they received when they beheld themselves for the first time as they really were. But oft-times greatness of earthly position does go hand-in-hand with greatness of soul, and thus spiritual progression and development continue without intermission from the moment of dissolution.

Lawrence, who of course was himself a famous personage on earth, echoes Benson's warning:[59] 'All the nonsense of social standards is lost sight of here because we have to see the true nature of each one, and to recognise that social grade has very little to do with it. In fact the queen and the peasant sometimes, though not always, have to change places. How cleverly good looks and social standing often mask a poverty stricken and desiccated soul on earth!' Moreover his guide Mitchell, Banks, John's guide Ashtar and, from an OOB perspective, Swedenborg and Peter Richelieu's sweetheart, all reinforce the point:

> The basis of all relationships here is purely emotional. One does not think how handsome nor how plain another person is, but judges them entirely on the quality of their aura or emanations.[60]

> In the earth life man can build a facade about himself. Here he has no such mask. He is known here for what he is, and for

> what his inner subjective life has made him.[61]
>
> Here there are no secrets, nothing is hidden. Each accepts the other for what he truly is, not as he appears as so often happens on earth.[62]
>
> In heaven no one can conceal inner character by facial expression and pretend, much less lie and deceive others by guile and hypocrisy.[63]
>
> Any striving to live up to the standards of others is unnecessary. People here become themselves.[64]

CREATING BY THOUGHT

We have already seen from the testimony of Lawrence and others in Part 3 that as spirits in the astral planes we affect or even *create* our surroundings via our thoughts, expectations and so on. In this section we'll find plenty of further confirmation of this idea. To start us off, here are Ames, four of French and Randall's communicants, Lanchester, Hatch, Vale Owen's mother Emma, Myers, Gilbert, Banks, Ford and Medhus:

> The idea with us is creative. We think, and the thing is.[65]
>
> Our home may be said to be space and what thought makes it. We simply create the different conditions about us by thought.
>
> I marvelled at what could be done by thought. The home and its environment were thought-creations, and in a little time, by concentrating my thought and visualising things desired, they took form and appeared, seemingly out of the invisible, but to me tangible and real. Thus I furnished my room, and hung on the walls thought pictures of those I love.
>
> Our life is merely the condition of mind which each one has. We create images in thought, and have the reality before us, just as tangible as your houses and building are to you. You do not have any conception of the great power and force there is, or may be, in thought. It dominates all conditions and makes us what we are.

Thought is a fluid, which becomes substance to us when once it is formed into an expression. It is a vibrating, living thing, and should be recognised as such and controlled accordingly.[66]

You create things by thought.[67]

When next I met the teacher I told him of my wish to wear a toga of my own making, and he carefully showed me how to create garments such as I desired: to fix the pattern and shape clearly in my mind, to visualise it, and then by power to desire to draw the subtle matter of the thought world round the pattern, so as to actually form the garment.[68]

When we think anything very intensely our wills are able to produce an outward manifestation which is really objective to those who behold it.[69]

They were able to create out of their fine, sensitive imaginations surroundings that appeared quite material in character, yet were in every respect the creation of their mind and inspiring spirit.[70]

I am learning to create a set of surroundings for myself. Once, still clinging to some incarnation wishes, I made a complete and perfect car, and I got into it and began to drive, but it did not work at all well... It was a thought-creation which could only function effectively in dense physical conditions.[71]

Here one's thoughts return to one like boomerangs, potent and immediate in their effects. As a thought, negative or positive, comes into mind, it is crystallised into immediate action... As one thinks, so one is – in environment, in appearance and in company! We have to learn to live in this new frequency; to guard the door of our mind; to anticipate the boomerang action of negative emotions.[72]

There is nothing we want that we cannot think into being... We are able to live in houses of thought-forms, or on sunny slopes beside streams, or wherever we like to think of ourselves as being.[73]

I can manifest things instantly just by wanting them.[74]

Although creating by thought doesn't seem to be a skill that most NDE subjects possess, a few do report on it – Alexander, for example:[75]

> Emotions are different up there. All the human emotions are present, but they're deeper, more spacious – they're not just inside but outside as well. Imagine that every time your mood changed here on earth, the weather changed instantly along with it. That your tears would bring on a torrential downpour and your joy would make the clouds instantly disappear. That gives a hint of how much more vast and consequential changes of mood feel like up here.

By contrast OOB pioneers are very much aware of this phenomenon, and learning to control their emotions and thoughts is a big issue for them too. With initial basic corroboration here are Charles Leadbeater, Swami Panchadasi, Yram, Albert Taylor and Ziewe:

> In this astral world thoughts and desires express themselves in visible forms though these are composed mostly of the finer matter of the plane.[76]

> On the astral... the astral material is not thrown into shape by physical forces, but is shaped and formed only by the thought and imaginative power of the minds of those inhabiting that plane.[77]

> Thought is creative in these regions of space.[78]

> During the OOB experience the power of thought is a tool that must be handled carefully. Anything you can imagine you will see or experience.[79]

> I have found that matter, once in the next dimension, is easily manipulated by thought; in fact, the main pastime of our dead relatives appears to be the pursuit of creation, and the ease with which this can be accomplished makes it a very attractive hobby indeed... In these regions people feel motivated and at liberty to make almost all their dreams and wishes come true.[80]

Now, of course, it's precisely because the same rules apply in the earth plane that I emphasise the law of attraction as such a fundamental precept of Supersoul Spirituality, as discussed in chapter 8 and in the last chapter. To reiterate we create our own experience even in the earth plane via our thoughts, expectations, beliefs, intentions and so on. The difference is that because our earthly environment is much more subject to the rules of space-time, the delay between thought and manifested result tends to be much longer and the linkage less obvious.

The entire premise of *The Power of You* is that the majority of the best-known, higher sources of channelled wisdom strongly assert this view. But remember here we're dealing with much more ordinary channelled sources with no pretensions to great wisdom. Nevertheless Banks, for example, explicitly confirms exactly this assertion:[81] 'This is a world of thought indeed! So is the earth plane... only there thought is slower in action because all vibration, and hence all results or effects, are slower.' Meanwhile from an NDE perspective a significant element of Betty Eadie's is an apparent transfer of information to her by her Christ-guide and others, and this is one of the aspects covered:[82] 'There is power in our thoughts. We create our own surroundings by the thoughts we think. Physically this may take a period of time, but spiritually it is instantaneous.'

From an OOB perspective, William Buhlman too is clear on this issue:[83] 'Consciousness creates reality. All reality, including matter, is shaped and moulded by thought... Countless nonphysical explorations into the interior of the universe confirm this observation. It's only the density of matter that obscures the truth of this from our physical senses.' As is Taylor:[84] 'I have come to believe that thought is just as powerful in the physical as in the astral plane or beyond. After all, everything around you presently began as a thought in someone's mind; it just didn't manifest instantly as it would have on the astral plane.' Meanwhile McKnight provides a wonderful description of how 'BC' and Ike – a couple of her spirit friends who both worked in construction in their earth lives – invite her to witness the thought-creation of an extension to their astral home:[85]

> BC motioned for us to follow him to one end of the house. He sent out the thought that they were going to add the extra room at that end. Ike had some plans in his hands that he handed to BC. Two other men were there who were going to help create this addition. They all looked down to study the architectural design on the sheet. Then all four walked over, closed their eyes, and held out their hands. As they stood there... in front of us a faint glow began to manifest, and became stronger and stronger. At first it was s smoky substance, which then began to manifest as a wall in front of us. Then a beam of light came down from above and seemed to be putting finishing touches to the wall... 'Okay', said BC. 'Let's take it on up.' The instant after he said that the room was in place, windows and all! It was beautiful and fitted right in with the rest of the house.

It is extremely hard for many people to accept that, at least as adults, we create *every* aspect of our earthly experience – with *no* exceptions – and it's a topic I go into in detail in my other books.[86] But *this* is some of the most compelling evidence that backs my assertion up.

CONSENSUS REALITIES

The power of thought when applied individually in the astral is strong enough. But if an individual creates something and then ceases to use or pay attention to it, it soon disappears again. By contrast when thought is applied *collectively*, especially over a long period of time, its creations acquire a degree of permanence and stability.

From a channelled perspective, Vale Owen's mother Emma makes this point clearly:[87] 'Time has no effect on our buildings. They do not crumble or decay. Their durability depends simply on the wills of their masters and, so long as these will, the building stands.' Elsewhere, similarly to McKnight above but this time from a *communal* perspective, her fellow communicant Kathleen describes the thought-construction of a temple in some detail:[88]

> We assembled therefore and, after a silence by way of harmonizing our personalities into one endeavour, we concentrated our minds creatively on the foundations and, gradually and very slowly, raised the stream of our willpower from the ground upward and higher until we came to the dome-like roof... The first stage was the outer building in completeness, but faint in outline and of transient duration. So, resting a while, we once again set about our task and, starting at the foundations as before, we strengthened each pillar and gate and tower and turret as we ascended slowly, until the dome again was reached. This we did many times, and then left the structure standing, the outer shell alone, but still completed in form...
>
> Now, when the outer part was done and confirmed, there remained the work of greater detail within – the fashioning of the chambers, halls and shrines, the setting of the pillars in rows... the perpetual flow of the waters of the fountains... and many other matters of detail. First we stood outside and concentrated on the supporting pillars and walls of partition, and when these were placed, we went inside and viewed our handiwork... So we took up our abode within, and... daily went about from chamber to chamber, hall and corridor, and fashioned each, little by little, after the original plan and scheme, till all was done and finished off by beautifying the whole.

Gilbert makes a similar general point:[89] 'People of a fairly advanced type who have common interests and have learned the art of thought-creation, have united their thought-force to form little worlds... which are almost indestructible because there is a constant stream of new power brought by fresh arrivals, to hold it firm and clear and to improve it.' Like Kathleen he then provides an example of the thought-construction of a communal building, this time a hospital:

> We have been inaugurating a new hospital, a great and new

> thought-creation achieved by the advanced... The creation of a new and 'permanent' thought image is a solemn process and takes time. A number of the group get together and after thinking carefully over the details – our hospital is to use colour-sound as treatment – they have a combined meditation on an inner picture presented to them and as they do this, gradually the image takes shape and becomes visible. But it is motivated mainly from intense concentration on a high level – built from those powerful thought rays of the advanced. Yet the group who work for them also contribute. It is a vast combined effort. It has been known, in order to bring in some of the new arrivals here, to create for them bricks and mortar so they actually work on the building, or think they do.

Medhus is in complete agreement:[90] 'If I create a beautiful park and a bunch of other spirits end up really liking it, using it and thinking about it a lot, it stays put energetically. I've learned that the more spirits focus on something, the more stable it becomes in our world. Sometimes I work with other spirits to create something we all want.'

From an OOB perspective, Leadbeater corroborates this view:[91] 'Here the people are living in imaginary cities of their own – not each evolved entirely by his own thought... but inheriting and adding to the structures erected by the thoughts of their predecessors.' Elsewhere he adds: 'In the summer-land men surround themselves with landscapes of their own construction, though some avoid that trouble by accepting ready-made the landscapes which have already been constructed by others.' Therefore, what we saw in action in the lower planes in terms of spirits being attracted to either individual or collective hells, also applies to the more heavenly realms.

Modern OOB pioneers refer to more collectively created environments as 'consensus realities', or what Robert Monroe terms 'belief system territories', which he defines as follows:[92] 'Where many humans reside after completing physical life experiences. Each is attracted to a particular segment in accordance with a deep attachment made during the life just finished to a seemingly powerful belief... The greater the number holding to a belief, the more powerful the system.' He also refers to this area of the astral as 'the rings' and adds: 'You could spend thousands of years in the rings and never explore all aspects of them... I was told that whatever man can think of is somewhere in these rings; thus more is being added constantly as man thinks more.'

In exactly the same way Gordon Phinn's guide Henry talks about there being an almost infinite number of consensus realities corresponding to people's different interests and beliefs in their earthly life.[93] As an example he describes being taken to a 'beach of endless fun' by his own guide Jack, where bronzed young surfers are truly in paradise and have no intention or desire to move on. He also talks about the fact that, whereas in the past many of these realities were religiously based – as we'll discuss further in chapter 25 – now many new ones are springing up in the astral based on the plethora of different interest groups emerging in the earth plane. As an example he discusses several new LGBT-based afterlife groups. It seems that the inhabitants of each reality, whatever interest or belief it's based on, tend to keep themselves to themselves and only mix with those of like mind.

Meanwhile Ziewe provides an OOB perspective on the thought-construction process:[94]

> Building structures such as houses still demands focus and concentration and we will find there is still a call for architects and builders and any possible trade who find it easier, simply because their minds have been habituated and skilled by the experience of their learned profession, to manifest. I visited whole cities of such architectural magnificence that it defied belief, and I realised at once the advantages of creative thought in a region which does not have to deal with issues such as gravity, inertia and the economics of supply and demand, but only the creative skill and desire to manifest and realise.

Because of this understanding, modern OOB pioneers often experiment to see to what extent they can create new aspects of, or alter, the environments they find themselves in – in order to establish how consensual they are. This is because the more an afterlife environment has been created by the thoughts, desires and expectations of *multiple* entities – sometimes both incarnate and discarnate – the less easy it is to manipulate. For example, here's Buhlman again:[95]

> Some nonphysical environments are easily moulded by thought while others are extremely resistant... When a group of individuals maintains the same image or beliefs, the group creates, moulds and maintains a consensus reality. In effect group thought-energy forms, stabilises and actually solidifies nonphysical energy. The larger the group – some number in the millions – the more stable the immediate energy environment becomes.

To illustrate the complexities facing the intrepid OOB explorer, Ziewe reports on visiting an astral print works and being shown the interior of a press – and being amazed to find it contains full working machinery.[96] He subsequently notes that perhaps it should have been empty because that's what *he* expected, but then recognises that it was already fully established before he arrived. Similarly when he tries to add some architectural detail to a building that's already in consensus existence in the astral, the detail appears but doesn't last long before fading away. From the perspective of a departed spirit, Gilbert reports on the same principle in operation the other way around:[97] 'We can dissolve our images by thought. But if a number of people have united to form a set of images... one single average entity cannot destroy them.'

Apart from the delaying impact of space-time, then, this is the other reason why our creation of our own experience in the earth plane is harder to detect. Ours is a hugely consensual reality, fabricated and reinforced by huge numbers of people over millennia. So people of ordinary creative power – that is, the vast majority of us – can't immediately alter their natural surroundings or the buildings around them and so on just with the power of their thoughts, as they would in a personal reality in the astral. Nevertheless the argument runs that our emotions, beliefs, intentions, expectations and so on will still attract the *people* we encounter and the *experiences* we have into our lives, and all this will ultimately impact the entirety of the environment we experience. The most important implication of this, although it's the one many people find hardest to accept, is that when someone else using their own free will appears to do something *to* us that in no way whatsoever would we *consciously* desire, nevertheless it must be an experience that our *subconscious* beliefs and expectations have attracted to us.

To close this section, two of our OOB pioneers provide further reflections on how and why creations in the astral can often be incredibly detailed. First, Sculthorp provides a fascinating insight into how, for example, astral clothing may be recreated from our own perfect memories:[98]

> The mind has a photographic memory capable of reproducing all the details... Regarding this creative power of unconscious thought, I was once talking to a teacher in spirit, and he asked: 'Where do you get your clothes?' I tried to remember my tailor's name on earth and could not, but this was not what he meant. He said, 'Look', and pointed to my clothes. I looked down and saw that I was wearing my everyday clothes, reproduced in every detail, even down to a small stain that was on them, the result of a too vigorously squeezed tube of toothpaste, which I had not been able to completely remove.

But Ziewe then makes the equally fascinating observation that universal blueprints exist for everything that has ever been created or even thought of in any detail in any plane – provided one has the right attitude to be able to access them:[99]

> If I had manifested a luxury car, would it be all shell without engine, powered by thought alone? The answer would be negative. The moment you looked under the bonnet you would find a fully functioning, twelve-cylinder engine, an exact replica of its £200,000 earthly counterpart.

I noticed that everything ever designed, invented, created, thought of is engraved into a 'universal matrix'. This can be compared to a universal computer hard drive. The moment the right creative trigger or request is sent to the central processing unit the hard drive releases the information on the screen, though in this case it is a three-dimensional object. The only requirement is that to request the information, or in this case the object, the energy current has to be of the right frequency, which demands positivity... But this is not always as easy as it sounds. Energies which have been built up over a lifetime, such as the desire for an unaffordable expensive car, are more likely to manifest, but only if they have the right kind of positive energy behind them.

THE DEGREE OF PHYSICALITY

Given that objects are created in the astral planes by thought alone, are they more insubstantial than on earth? As we saw in chapter 9 and in the last few sections, the answer is that they'll appear completely 'solid' to those whose vibrations are in tune with that level. Only visitors whose vibrations are either higher or lower will see them as vague or fuzzy, at least initially and until they adjust their vibrations to suit. In addition it seems that, for visitors to a plane, objects and environments created by consensus may have greater solidity. Here, then, are one of French and Randall's communicants, Lanchester, Hatch, Vale Owen's mother Emma, Benson, Lawrence, Myers and Gilbert:

> Your earth and all the things of your earth have their exact counterparts in the spirit world, just as real, just as tangible, just as substantial to the inhabitants of this world, as material things and forms are to the inhabitants in mortal form upon your earth.[100]

> I suppose all that I see are forms, and being a form myself, they seem as solid as myself... Here the earth on which we stand, though immaterial to the physical world, seems real and material to us.[101]

> Objects here, objects existing in tenuous matter, are as real and comparatively substantial as with you.[102]

> Our bodies here are as solid and real as those we have laid aside... We have real, solid houses and streets and mountains and trees and animals.[103]

> So many souls of the earth world are almost shocked to be told that the spirit world is a solid world, a substantial world, with real, live people in it![104]

> Once one's new senses have developed and are adjusted... our earth is as solid and actual to our senses as the earth is to its denizens.[105]

> This country is not real. It is a dream. But to Tom Jones it is as real as was his office desk and the alarm clock that roused him in the morning.[106]

> People here who are only one step from the earth vibration... all is solid or real to them.[107]

Similarly, from an OOB perspective, here are Swedenborg, Leadbeater, Panchadasi, Sculthorp, Ziewe and Bruce:

> As 'spirit people' we enjoy every outer and inner sense we enjoyed in the world... We smell and taste and feel things when we touch them the way we used to.[108]

> Your friend would still see the walls and the furniture to which he was accustomed, for though the physical matter of which they are composed would no longer be visible to him, the densest type of astral matter would still outline them for him as clearly as ever.[109]

> To the dwellers on the astral, their scenery, buildings etc. are as solid as are those of the material plane to the dwellers thereupon.[110]

> My lessons about conditions in the spirit world had begun. We are 'solid' to others on the same plane or vibration in spirit... Objects and places in spirit look the same as on earth and just as solid.[111]

> We are conditioned during physical life to believe that the world we live in is solid or real. This conditioning is maintained once we cross over into the next dimensions. The world around us appears to be as solid as on the physical... at least on the lower levels.[112]

> This place feels more real than the physical dimension.[113]

PERSONAL APPEARANCE AND AGE

Our channelled sources make a number of observations about this. Generally they tend toward the view that, quite unlike in the lower astral, as we acclimatise to the mid astral we move increasingly towards an appearance representing the 'peak' of our earthly life. However it seems we can also assume any age or appearance we want related to that life, especially for purposes of identification by others. To start us off, here are Ames, Franchezzo, Hatch, Vale Owen's mother Emma, Benson and Lawrence:

> We can, when we please, assume the old bodies or their spiritual counterparts as we can assume our old clothes for purposes of identification, but our spiritual bodies here are young and beautiful... [Elsewhere, referring to meeting her little sister again in the astral] I saw before me the semblance of her childhood, just as she was in the long years ago... But she was only assuming the child-form to gain recognition. After a time... she revealed herself to me... as a spirit who is a grown woman. There is no difficulty in our assuming whatever form we need for the purpose of the moment.[114]

> [After shedding his previously disfigured appearance] I am young again... a man of about thirty or thirty-five... as I had been in my prime on earth... As a spirit grown more highly developed in his intellectual powers, the appearance becomes more matured, till at last he assumes that of a sage without, however, the wrinkles and defects of age in earth life, only its dignity, its power and its experience.[115]

> After a time an old person forgets that he is old... the tendency is to grow young in thought and therefore young in

appearance... Children grow up out here, and they may even go on to a sort of old age if that is the expectation of the mind; but the tendency is to keep the prime, to go forward or back towards the best period.[116]

Souls who have just come over... are of various ages, for the old have not progressed yet in becoming youthful and vigorous again, and the young have not progressed to complete stature.[117]

The spirit body is, broadly speaking, the counterpart of our earthly bodies. When we come into the spirit world we are recognisably ourselves. But we leave behind us all our physical disabilities... Any supernormal or subnormal conditions of the physical body, such as excessive stoutness or leanness, vanish when we arrive in these realms, and we appear as we should have appeared on earth had not a variety of earthly reasons caused us to be otherwise. There is a stage in our lives on earth which we know as the prime of life. It is towards this that we all move. Those of us who are old or elderly when we pass into spirit will return to our prime-of-life period. Others who are young will advance towards that period... We suffer from no ailments – that would be impossible in the spirit world. Therefore our bodies do not require constant looking after to maintain a state of good health.[118]

An amusing circumstance and one that is giving me much secret satisfaction is that I appear to be approaching my 'proper' age... It seems that every human being has a true meridian of age at which his being is unfolded at its peak of achievement... Whichever manifestation of the being was most full and characteristic, at this age the man or woman rests. So it matters not at what age in earthly reckoning a man dies, he reverts by degrees to his ideal age when he comes here. Most of the persons I meet seem to be young but there is an admixture of the mature and elderly.

My own experiences have been stormy and troubled but, now that I'm finding peace and fulfilment, I am intrigued to see that I am definitely becoming younger, not only in appearance but in feeling and in my way of relating myself to others... I

> have achieved equilibrium at about twenty-eight and shall stay there very thankfully. I am young and have the vigour and enthusiasm proper to what is obviously my real age, and now can hardly envisage being any older.[119]

Lawrence then carries on by backing up Benson in regards to the potential loss of less-desirable earthly characteristics:

> Another astonishing change has reconciled me to any loss of the prestige of a riper age. A small man suffers from his lack of inches and is influenced by it in many undesirable ways. He is impelled to try and compensate for it and often does so ruthlessly, to his own and other people's hurt. However great in spirit, he will hardly ever feel safe enough to forego the defences he builds around his puniness. In my own case, my proper growth was stunted by an accident in youth and so my small stature was only incidental to my form. To my great joy this disability is removed and I have now attained a normal height. Only one who has endured this handicap will realise what a deep satisfaction this is to my vanity.

Turning more now to clothing, Banks reports on experimenting with hers as a newcomer:[120]

> Here I look relatively as I did on earth but I am free to refashion this body by thought... We create that which clothes us from the residue of our thoughts, words, acts and aspirations which we have brought over with us... During the first stages of this new and rather exciting consciousness, the pleasure of creating costumes and colours fulfils a need and is often much enjoyed. On the other hand, a dress which had acquired meaning on earth will be assumed, sometimes for the satisfaction of the soul, sometimes as a penance, and sometimes for the joy or peace the wearing of it had afforded the soul.

Similarly John is told it's time to get rid of the military uniform he's been wearing since he passed over while he's been helping soldiers with their transition, and to 'think' himself into the appropriate spiritual 'robe'.[121] Indeed many of our sources refer to those who have acclimatised to the afterlife wearing robes of different colours depending on their level of consciousness and awareness. In any case John is reminded that he can put his uniform back on any time he thinks it's appropriate, or adopt any other kind of appearance for that matter. On another occasion he's taken to meet his parents who, as an orphan, he never knew except from a photograph. It is a joyous encounter even though they are now radiant beings whose appearance is even younger than his own.

From an OOB perspective, although Swedenborg mentions only female spirits in the following quote, we can assume he means male ones as well:[122] 'Women who have died of old age... come more and more into the flower of growing youth.' Meanwhile Sculthorp meets his deceased parents regularly when OOB and reports that normally his father projects an easily recognisable, 'earthly appearance'. But on one occasion the latter tries to test him by projecting 'his progressed form with fine features and the same height as myself, whereas he was shorter on earth'.[123] Similarly with his mother: 'She looked very young, between 20 and 25 years of age, although she passed over at the age of 74, and I sensed that she was now in a higher plane and had to manifest in this way.' Also his departed wife: 'She appears young and has the finely formed features of spirit.' Meanwhile Bruce regularly meets up with a large group of departed friends, all of whom are 'just as they were in physical life but at their most magnificent... glowing ecstatically with inner light, ablaze with happiness and joy'.[124]

To close this section, most departed spirits seem to spend much of their time in the mid astral with friends and family from their earthly life, or more generally to mix with people who lived in more or less the same era. Then, as they progress and wear robes, the era in which they lived becomes less apparent or indeed important. Nevertheless Lawrence provides us with a wonderful report of a friend from a different era:[125]

> I have a special friend who belonged to a knightly family in the middle ages. He went on crusade and eventually lost his life in Palestine. We have found much in common in our knowledge

of and love for the Near East. Glimpses of the real campaigns of those days that I get from his accounts are a wonderful corrective to the inaccurate romancing of the history books. His first-hand knowledge makes nonsense of the usual methods of research. His language also delights me. I found it hard to follow at first with its strong admixture of Norman-French, but when words fail us we can always get on by the exchange of thoughts.

His interest in modern conditions and modern campaigns is as keen as mine in those of the past, so we are intensely pleased with each other's company. He is a simple soul whose creed of fighting loyally, feasting royally and thinking rarely or never has kept him in the lower planes for a long while, where the fantasies of battle and feasting could continue. A gradual emancipation from these illusions freed him and he is now learning to adjust himself to a world where fighting is an anachronism, but his restless energy often has to be worked off by long expeditions to the East. Imagine visiting the desert in company with a fully armed Crusader! He keeps the fashion of his clothing and the accoutrements of his day, as most people.

EATING, DRINKING AND SLEEPING

Of course the astral planes have no night and day, and the astral body doesn't need food, drink or sleep – although elsewhere our sources report they sometimes like to at least rest from their labours, and it also appears newcomers may take time to realise they no longer need these things. Reinforcing the basic message, here are Ames, Lanchester, Hatch, Benson, Sherwood's EK, Lawrence and John:

> We never weary, and do not need sleep as we did on earth; neither do we need food or drink... Save that which we can draw in with the air we breathe.[126]

> At this point I should add that here there is nothing comparable to night and day, nor is there any sleep. This is, of course, evident if you think for a moment, for the spirit never sleeps even upon earth; it, unlike the body, needs no rest.[127]

As time goes on even the habit of demanding nourishment gradually wears off. We are no longer bothered by hunger and thirst... And we are no longer harassed by the thousand-and-one petty duties of the earth.[128]

Here there is no night and day by the alternation of which time can be measured. It is perpetual day. The great celestial sun forever shines... Neither do we have the many other indications of time that force themselves upon the earthly consciousness – such, for example, as hunger and fatigue. Nor in the more lengthy passage of time such as the ageing of the physical body and the dulling of the mental faculties. Here we have no recurrent seasons of spring, autumn and winter. Instead we enjoy the glory of perpetual summer – and we never tire of it!..

It is impossible to convey, even in a small measure, this exquisite feeling of supreme vitality and well-being. When we are living upon the earth plane we are constantly being reminded of our physical bodies in a variety of ways – by cold or heat, by discomfort, by fatigue, by minor illnesses, and by countless other means. Here we labour under no such disabilities... There is therefore nothing that can possibly create any unhappiness, unpleasantness or discomfort.[129]

Almost unconsciously, we infer that the light which pours down on our world is a kind of life. It renews our being, and satisfies and feeds us; in fact, we need no other food. This light shines continuously... renewing our life in vigour and joy.[130]

Day and night, cold and heat, inescapable hunger and thirst – all these have vanished out of existence... The fact that no one needs food or any particular kind of clothing or housing removes the tension and fear from living altogether.[131]

I had been concentrating on my work so much that it was only then it struck me I had not eaten for days or had anything to drink. Of course! These things were no longer necessary.[132]

It is clear then that, compared to the earth plane, life becomes an awful lot easier and less stressful once we're acclimatised to the mid astral. Moreover, as far as pleasures are concerned, a few of our sources say they occasionally and deliberately enjoy the delicious flavour of various astral foods and drinks.

For example, at his home in the lower reaches of the mid astral Franchezzo treats himself with 'delicious fruits which melt in your mouth as you eat them', and 'wine like sparkling nectar, which does not intoxicate or create a thirst for more'.[133] Similarly, despite his earlier comments, Benson makes a visit to an astral orchard:[134] 'I saw every kind of fruit known to man, and many that were known only in spirit. I sampled some of the latter, but it is impossible to give any indication of the delicious flavour of them because there is no earthly fruit that I know of with which comparison can be made.'

From an OOB perspective Richelieu describes his surprise at being shown the *kitchen* at his sweetheart's home, where she 'enjoys making snacks for parties' because apparently 'old habits die hard'.[135] While McKnight's guide provides an almost identical report:[136]

> There are quite a few people who cannot drop their old habits instantly after first arriving here, so they continue to create the foods that they liked while on earth. They have no active digestive systems, of course, but the foods get absorbed into the intensified atmosphere. Gradually, such newly arrived souls eat less and less. When they get really involved in learning and growing here, they forget about food and don't eat any more – other than a few of our luscious, heavenly grapes every now and then.

To close this section, we saw in Part 3 how obsessive spirits can attempt to get their fix by, for example, hanging around bars. In a somewhat similar but less harmful way, and providing his usual added insights, Medhus describes how he doesn't eat in the afterlife planes – but he can visit the near-earth plane and temporarily 'merge his energy field with someone who is eating pizza', whereby he tastes it 'all over and inside his spirit body'.[137] Even more unusually he suggests he can do the same by merging his energy with that of the pizza itself.

SOUND, COLOUR AND NATURAL BEAUTY

We saw earlier how after passing spirits feel more vital and energised, and everything seems more real. But it's in this section that departed spirits' awe at the magnificence and intense beauty of their new astral surroundings really comes to the fore, and they start to describe an energetic 'connectedness to everything' that, sadly, we only tend to glimpse on the earth plane.

We will start with Franchezzo briefly describing 'plants of most lovely hues, like flowers of earth but much more lovely, more fragrant than words can convey'.[138] Followed by one of French and Randall's communicants, who expands somewhat:[139]

> This is a wondrous land of light where the beauties of nature, as seen on the earth, are brought to perfection. Here we have sea, sky, hills, mountains, valleys and grassy plains, in all their beauty of form and colouring, but without blemish... There are forests of noble trees, great rivers, waterfalls, lakes, streams of all sizes, all crystal clear, and lovely meadows carpeted with the most beautiful flowers, over which hover myriads of gorgeous butterflies. There are countless numbers of the most beautiful birds everywhere... It is one vast panorama of loveliness, for those who have eyes to see.

Another introduces the concept of 'heavenly music', which is reported by virtually all sources as underlying everything:

> Let me speak of the music here, of those harmonious vibrations that touch the soul, that universal appeal that is understood by all races, regardless of the language they speak. The music of your world is crude, indeed, compared to celestial compositions and songs. Here we have harmonious vibrations, expressed in what is called music. It elevates the soul, and we devote much time to its cultivation.

Vale Owen's mother Emma makes a similar point:[140]

> Then we began to sing and, although I could see no instrument, yet instrumental music blended with our singing and became one with it... The music... did not seem to come from any one

> point. That is a faculty of music here. It seems very often to be part of the atmosphere.

Elsewhere she describes how flowing water seems to have intrinsic musical qualities in the astral:

> When we had gone some way we entered a large square, where beautiful trees grew on lawns of the greenest of green grass, and fountains played a harmony together; that is to say, there were perhaps a dozen fountains, and each had a tone of its own, and each was composed of many smaller jets of water, each being a note. These are manipulated, on occasion, so that a fairly complicated piece of music can be played, with an effect such as that produced by an organ with many stops.

Benson takes this a step further, as always eloquent in his description of the energy pouring forth from the natural astral world, and how it's intricately bound up with musical harmony:[141]

> It was the gardens round [my house] that attracted my attention more fully. They appeared to be quite extensive, and they were in a state of the most perfect order and arrangement... It was not merely the flowers themselves and their unbelievable range of superb colourings that caught my attention, but the vital atmosphere of eternal life that they threw out... in every direction. And as one approached any particular group of flowers, or even a single bloom, there seemed to pour out great streams of energising power which uplifted the soul spiritually and gave it strength, while the heavenly perfumes they exhaled were such as no soul clothed in its mantle of flesh has ever experienced. All these flowers were living and breathing and they were, so my friend informed me, incorruptible.
>
> There was another astonishing feature I noticed when I drew near to them, and that was the sound of music that enveloped them, making such soft harmonies as corresponded exactly and perfectly with the gorgeous colours of the flowers themselves... Everywhere there was perfect harmony. Already I was conscious of the revitalising effect of this heavenly garden to such an extent that I was anxious to see more of it... As with

> the flowers, so with the trees. They live for ever incorruptible, clothed always in their full array of leaves of every shade of green, and forever pouring out life to all those who approach near them.

He then expands on the energy given off by the flowers in his garden:

> As I moved my hands towards a beautiful bloom, I found that the flower upon its stem moved towards me! I did as I was instructed, and I instantly felt a stream of life rushing up my arms, the while a most delicate aroma was exhaled by the flower.

Elsewhere he introduces the common theme that colour and sound are inextricably linked in the astral:

> Colour and sound... are interchangeable terms in the spirit world. To perform some act that will produce colour is also to produce a musical sound. To play upon a musical instrument, or to sing, is to create colour... It must not be thought that with all the vast galaxy of colours from the hundreds of sources in the spirit world, our ears are being constantly assailed with the sounds of music... The music is there, but we please ourselves entirely whether we wish to... listen to it. We can completely isolate ourselves from all sound, or we can throw ourselves open to all sound, or just hear that which pleases us most.

Elsewhere again he describes how water, like everything else in the astral, feels alive and even 'friendly' as he bathes in it:

> The revivifying force enveloped my whole body, pouring new life into it. It was delightfully warm and completely buoyant. It was possible to stand upright in it, to float upon it, and of course to sink completely beneath the surface of it without the least discomfort or danger... But beyond this magnetic influence there was an added assurance that came from the water and that was its essential friendliness, if I may so call it. It is not easy to convey any idea of this fundamentally spiritual experience. That the water was living one could have no doubt. It breathed its very goodness by its contact.

Benson concludes:

> Those of us who have returned to earth to tell about our new life are faced with the difficulty of trying to describe in terms of the earth what is essentially of a spirit nature. Our descriptions must fall short of the reality. It is difficult to conjure up in the mind a state of beauty greater than we have ever experienced upon earth. Magnify by one hundred times the beauties that I have told you about, and you would still be far short of a true appraisement.

After his initial period of sleep and acclimatisation, Sherwood's EK finds himself in 'the lovely air on a sunny hillside'.[142] He continues:

> There was a light on things and in them so that everything proclaimed itself vividly alive. Grass, trees and flowers were so lighted inwardly by their own beauty that the soul breathed the miracle of perfection... The air itself had a light in it, a sense of being life in itself... I am almost at a loss to describe the heavens as I saw them from my hillside. The light radiated from no one direction, it was a glowing, universal fact, bathing everything in its soft radiance.

His fellow communicant Lawrence starts with some brief general observations:[143] 'Grass, trees and flowers are of a finer texture and a more lucent beauty.' Then he expands on the emotional connection he feels with his surroundings:

> It must not be forgotten that one's new body is emotional in its very nature and that therefore its new powers will be based on emotions. The total reaction to all that is seen or heard – the keener awareness, the swifter response, involves the whole emotional being. For instance, when I see a bush or a tree I am not able to perceive it simply in visual terms; I have to reckon on an emotional response to it. I like it, I value it or even love it, or if I am not yet beyond a negative response I may dislike it or even hate it; but there will be a strong feeling reaction in either case... We have to see, hear and understand with our feelings and this gives a keener and more personal edge to all

impressions... I think the nearest approach to our normal response is the spontaneous feeling of wonder, joy and almost worship which can be felt on earth when something utterly innocent and beautiful is seen and grasped by the emotions.

Meanwhile Banks describes how gardening works in the more energetic environment of the astral, while Ford, John and Medhus corroborate some of the earlier comments:

I have a corner of flowers... golden and glowing. At least they do not always glow. I have to keep them glowing by gardening. That is, I pour light and love into them and over them, rather in the same manner as watering and nourishing them; and they respond by growing profusely and gloriously golden.[144]

The light here is pure and unceasing, since the sun does not control it. The mountains are eternally capped in halos of their own making. The trees are magically attuned, so that each seems to speak with a voice of its own. The songs of insects and birds are beautiful, and from out of the vastness of the universe come vibrations too harmonious to be conceived by the mind of a physical person.[145]

Every species of flower grows in this realm, of every colour and shade; some you know, but many are not seen on earth. How can one describe flowers that are beyond earthly imagination? And colour, where colour is sound? If you have a mind to you can hear the soft, gentle music of the flowers. Their redolent perfume fills the air.[146]

I was in a clearing surrounded by dense forest... Unlike on earth, everything seemed like it was painted with vibrant colours, even the clouds in the sky. Even the air. Everything. And there were colours that I'd never seen or ever could have imagined before. They made the colours on earth seem incredibly drab in comparison. Think about the colours on earth and multiply their intensity by ten, a hundred, a million – and not only were heaven's colours in high definition but they were also three-dimensional. Colours here move and live and breathe as if they have a life of their own... I had these instant

> connections with whatever item I was looking at... There were huge trees that were alive... and there were sounds coming from them... I saw other landscapes like deserts, snowy fields, coastlines and grassy plains.[147]

With an echo of Lawrence's comments about total responses above, in one of Cynthia Sandys' *Awakening Letters* Sally, the daughter of her co-author, provides a fascinating description of how the perceptions of the astral body are multi-faceted and linked:[148]

> We found ourselves in another land of exquisite beauty. The scents of this plane were like the most wonderful garden you've ever known, and I began to sense the colour and scent all over me. My feet were sensing the same things independently. Now this kind of 3D, 4D, 5D, 6D consciousness was very disturbing at first. It's so much easier to smell only with your nose, and not with your ears and toes and everything else thrown in. I gasped at the enlarged awareness of my body, and felt quite staggered by it.

Meanwhile Medhus entirely corroborates Sally's comments, also making reference to the earthly concept of synesthesia:[149]

> I can go up to a flower and merge with its energy, and I experience its smell... I got a little overwhelmed at first because I could see everything at once – and I mean everything – but eventually I learned to narrow my focus to see one thing at a time and put everything else in the periphery... Sound is more like a vibration, and my body resonates with whatever frequency the sound vibrates at... I just absorb the energy with my entire body... Every sensation is all over and in me.
>
> What's also really cool is that all these senses overlap and get jumbled together. When I see something, it comes with a taste, a smell and a sound. Kind of like how synesthesia works for people who have it. When I hear, taste, feel, see or smell something I get a symphony of other sensory input as well, and when I clap my hands together I can actually see the sound waves coming out.

Turning to NDE reports, after her initial exchange with her Christ-guide Eadie is taken on an astral tour by various different guides, although she admits she doesn't recall all of it.[150] At one point she finds herself in a garden, and her wonderful description contains almost all the elements reported by our other sources:

> I saw mountains, spectacular valleys and rivers in the distance... But what filled me with awe in the garden more than anything were the intense colours. We have nothing like them. When light strikes an object here it reflects off that object in a certain colour. Light in the spirit world doesn't necessarily reflect off anything. It comes from within and appears to be a living essence. A million, a billion colours are possible. The flowers, for example, are so vivid and luminous with colour...
>
> A beautiful river ran through the garden not far from me, and I was immediately drawn to it. I saw that the river was fed by a large cascading waterfall of the purest water that dazzled with its clarity and life. Life. It was in the water too. Each drop from the waterfall had its own intelligence and purpose. A melody of majestic beauty carried from the waterfall and filled the garden, eventually merging with other melodies that I was now only faintly aware of. The music came from the water itself, from its intelligence, and each drop produced its own tone and melody which mingled and interacted with every other sound and strain around it... The overall effect seemed beyond the ability of any symphony or composer here. In comparison, our best music would sound like a child playing a tin drum. We simply don't have the capacity to comprehend the vastness and strength of the music there, let alone begin to create it.

To round this section off, here's the OOB perspective of Caroline Larsen, Richelieu, Sculthorp, McKnight's guide, Ziewe and Bruce:

> The place was like a great garden, with bushes and shrubbery of gorgeous hues, and stately trees, some like magnificent palms, others of forms unknown on earth... The landscape charged the dazzling air with beauty.[151]

It was the most beautiful valley I have ever seen. It was partly wooded and the ground was covered with thick heather of varied colours... but soft to the touch; intermingled with this, wild flowers bloomed in profusion... I'm sure no variety was missing, for the ground near and far was a veritable carpet of colours of breathtaking beauty.[152]

A poet or writer could fill chapters with descriptions of the beauties of these idyllic scenes and it would still be incomplete because, as always, there is the sensitivity of the spirit body which is infused by the vibrations of the sphere.[153]

Music and colour are the two main energies that propel... our systems. Music and colour are abundant in everything... Even elevated spirit soil gives off melodious sounds when you hold it in your hands and drop it through your fingers.[154]

What attracted my attention was that the forest appeared to be luminous, and as I descended I discovered that all the vegetation glowed with a subtle, iridescent light. It was not just the light that made my heart soar, but the sheer richness and abundance of the plant life. There was no way I could identify any particular species: everything I looked at had an extra dimension to it, the most prominent of which was its luminous aura – the life pulsating in the light streaming up the stems and out through the leaves and petals. The brightness and frequency of the pulsing light differed from plant to plant, and so did the colours, which were of qualities I had never seen or even imagined before. There were so many hues – thousands more than on the physical earth...

I simply cannot do any of this justice with words. I feel almost pathetic in attempting to describe it – it's like trying to pick up a butterfly with a bulldozer... I say to the people back home, 'Beware of all the beauty; prepare yourself for the day you die so that your heart is big enough to hold a fraction of it...' It was only when I attuned to the tranquil scene that I relaxed utterly, and became witness to the symphony of sound, which penetrated my being in the subtlest of ways, totally unobtrusively, working its way finely to harmonise every part of my soul.[155]

> Music fills the air and resonates my being. Delicate notes are plucked on my heartstrings. My spirit soars. Angelic voices sing in the distance... It is incredibly beautiful here. It is so alive and vibrant and I am invigorated.[156]

These wonderful, effervescent descriptions from so many of our sources should by now be starting to clarify just how much we have to look forward to – if we prepare ourselves properly for life to carry on in the astral plane.

SPIRITUAL PARTNERSHIP AND UNION

As we saw in the last chapter, as we progress in the afterlife planes we increasingly morph into the androgynous form of our true soul essence. But while in the astral planes we retain not only our earthly personality but also our human gender – albeit that the flexibility of astral conditions means we can take the other form, or enter into the experiences of someone of the other gender, any time we like. This of course raises the issue of relations between the sexes. It seems that couples don't *necessarily* pair off, although some may prefer this arrangement, whether temporarily or for the longer term. In these instances they may or may not have been together in their earthly life, because choices made in human form aren't necessarily replicated in the afterlife unless both parties desire it.

For example, Vale Owen's guide Zabdiel reports on one departed male spirit being overjoyed to find his beautiful, young wife waiting for him in a replica of their Dorset home, even though she had exited her earth life as a grey-haired invalid.[157] By contrast his mother Emma reports on another being told by his guide: 'Your wife, who came over here some years ago, is in a higher sphere than the one in which you will be placed when you have at length got the correct perspective of things.'

Similarly Swedenborg and Lawrence have this to say about former earth partners, along with Andrew Sherwood when talking to his wife Jane:

> It often happens that married partners... welcome each other joyfully. They stay together as well, but for a longer or shorter time depending on how happily they had lived together in the [earth] world. Ultimately, unless they had been united by real love... they separate after having been together for a while.[158]

> It is true that there can be great distress when a man and woman are united again here only to find their disaffinity and that their future course cannot run together. One may be unable to get beyond the early planes and the other may be for onward... Many of the ties made on earth seem to be of this evanescent nature. Sentiment and loyalty keep people together for a time who have no real affinity, but as soon as they are strong enough to face reality they can part happily and go on to find their real mates.[159]

> Affinity and equal development constitute nearness for us, and their opposites mean that we are parted by actual spatial distance. For instance, you and I may have to wait a time before we can be literally together in the same plane, unless you achieve a good development on earth and so catch up.[160]

Indeed, just as on earth, staying together because it's convenient and familiar, rather than because it genuinely enhances both individuals, is likely to lead to stagnation rather than progression. On the other hand we saw in chapter 19 how Lawrence's friend Edgar sadly killed his wife, but when they stopped blaming each other their true love was rekindled. At the end he adds:[161] 'He and his charming wife are happy and useful members of our community, and when the time comes it looks as though they may be ready to go on together.' Meanwhile both Sherwood's EK and Myers emphasise that ideally attitudes towards love and relationships need to shift in the afterlife:

> There is less specialisation in human relationships and no sense of possession in even the more intimate relationships... The barriers we set up on earth to protect our special rights of possession are no longer necessary. Life has come of age, you see, so love can come of age also.[162]

> There exists in the higher regions... a harmony and freedom that may not be the lot of true lovers when their minds are dulled, and they are weighed down and oppressed by a heavy material body. On these planes such love changes in character, the conditions of life and consciousness being very different.[163]

Having said that there are plenty of reports of departed spirits experiencing the sort of 'union' that makes earthy equivalents pale by comparison. Here, for example, is Lanchester:[164]

> The further we progress, the nearer together the two sexes draw, so that we understand ultimately there comes about a mystic union in spirit between one man and woman. This is the real spiritual union of which marriage on earth is a true symbol or sacrament. This consummation, this blending of two spirit entities, so that each becomes part of the other and yet retains its own individuality, cannot be fully understood even by us, much less by you. The earth marriage at its highest and best does give you some faint idea of what we really mean.

Of course this was transmitted in an earlier age, but there can surely to be no reason to doubt that – in an environment in which procreation is irrelevant and judgment non existent – two essentially male or female spirits would be able to achieve the same union. Indeed the human trend towards some people preferring not to identify with any gender will also translate into the afterlife planes in due course.

In any case Lawrence's guide Mitchell backs Lanchester up with this description:[165] 'If union takes place it is an interfusion of the two bodies, and an ecstatic and satisfying experience far more lovely than anything one could experience in an earthly body.' Similarly Sandys' daughter Pat:[166] 'Through lying together our auras become enmeshed... We feel drawn together as by a magnet, it exhilarates and unites and we become lovers in a higher sense.'

Rather like Lawrence in the last chapter, given that he'd only had one brief relationship on earth Medhus gets together with a spirit girlfriend. He then reports that, once they decide to 'go to the next level', they 'merge their entire energetic beings' so that each knows everything about the other's thoughts, emotions and so on.[167] He adds that a spirit orgasm is like a human one except incredibly more intense: 'It extends throughout our entire being... then travels beyond the energetic body and shines outwards... it just keeps expanding and soaring. It's complete connection, and it's totally addictive.'

Meanwhile it seems that as humans we can get in on the act if we learn to take ourselves OOB. Here, for example, Yram describes merging with his wife while they're journeying together:[168] 'My aura penetrated hers and I had the sensation as if melting into her. So intense were the vibrations I experienced a kind of giddiness.' Finally Phinn's guide Henry provides this description of spiritual union:[169] 'Here, a blending of heart charka energies can be achieved and, when it is, the lovers are blessed with a blissful union in which every cell in their bodies seems animated with an orgasmic flush that surges and resurges until smoothed by a pleasing exhaustion.' Again it seems we have plenty to look forward to.

CHILDREN IN THE AFTERLIFE

To close this chapter on a rather more sensitive subject, let us turn to the fate of young ones in the astral. Any parent who has lost a child will have gone through agonies that never seem to completely leave them. Despite our general comments about prolonged and intense grief for one's own loss in chapter 14, in this situation more than any other it's understandable. Yet if all bereaved parents had access to the information our channelled sources are just about to reveal it would give them huge comfort. Remember this isn't just the wishful thinking of 'they're an angel in heaven now'. Instead it is good, hard, evidential, first-hand reporting by departed spirits themselves. To start us off here are four of French and Randall's communicants, Hatch, Vale Owen's mother Emma, Benson and Banks, providing some beautiful, and in some cases lengthy, reassurance:

There are countless millions of children... who are plunged into this world of ours, and there are millions of women here who have never known motherhood in earth life, who take and care for them, watch and aid their growth.

No mother who loses a wee one need grieve... You would love to see all the happy wee things we have here, some of whom had a very sad time during their brief sojourn on earth. Not one single baby, out of all the millions that come here, ever lacks mothering. They are surrounded by an atmosphere of love and just grow and blossom... The place where they are rings with the sound of their happy laughter.

Children coming here in infancy are given experiences as nearly those of earth life as possible – given those experiences that are needed to form the soil for the plant to grow... They make our best teachers, having nothing to unlearn, and they progress rapidly... I do not think early dissolution is unfortunate, unless the parents grieve very much. If they do, they act as a weight on the little spirit and chain it to them.

[A young boy writes] Dear Mummy, I am learning many things that are necessary in this life, now you are so much happier about me and feel so sure that everything is all right with me... I wish that every boy knew that dying is just like getting a new suit and discarding the old. The real you inside the new suit feels just the same, only we have to learn to think differently about most things. I mean, we must change some of our ideas, but the new ones are much nicer and make living here easier. I wish everyone knew this before he came here and then no one would fear, and everything would be so nice and comfy.[170]

It is easier for children to adjust themselves to the changed life than it is for grown persons... Children come out with great energy, and bring with them the same curiosity that they had in earth life.[171]

We wandered over the grounds and looked at the various appliances for teaching children. One especially engaged my attention. It was a large globe of glass, about six or seven feet in diameter... As you looked into the globe you could see not only the flowers and trees and plants which grew there, but also the different orders from which they had been derived in time past. It was very much like a lesson in progressive botany, such as might be given on earth and deduced from the fossil plants of geology. But here we saw the same plants alive and growing, and all the species of them from the original parent down to the present representative of the same family.

We learned that the task set for the children was: to consider this progression up to this particular plant or tree or flower... and then to try to construct in their minds the further and future development of that same species. This is excellent training for their mental faculties, but the results are usually amusing... When they have thought out their conclusion, they have to make a model of the plant as it will appear after another period of evolution, and fearful and wonderful some of those models are, and as impossible as they are strange.[172]

What of the souls who pass over as children; indeed what of those, even, who pass into the spirit world at birth? The answer is that they grow as they would have grown upon the earth plane. But the children here, of all ages, are given such treatment and care as would never be possible in the earth world. The young child whose mind is not yet fully formed is uncontaminated by earthly contacts, and on passing into the spirit world it finds itself in a realm of great beauty, presided over by souls of equal beauty. This children's realm has been called the 'nursery of heaven'...

The mental and physical growth of the child in the spirit world is much more rapid than in the earth world. You will recall what I told you about the absolute retentiveness of the memory here. That retentiveness begins as soon as the mind is capable of grasping anything at all, and that is very early...

The temperament is carefully guided along purely spirit lines, so that the possession of knowledge in one so young never takes upon it the obnoxiousness of earthly precociousness. The children are trained in strictly spirit matters first, and then they are usually taught about the earth world, if they have not already lived in it or if their earthly lives were very brief.[173]

> A child is so much nearer to the soul life. Even this child's few short years on earth, six I believe, had scarcely separated him from his before-birth contact with divine love... The soul of this child, unpolluted, untainted by the materialism and separation of earth beliefs, was so ready for the heaven world. I can express it best by saying it was like a bud opening into flower here. Please write this and stress it, for it will I feel give comfort to those fathers and mothers who may have been separated by what the earth calls death from their little ones.[174]

Similarly, from an OOB perspective, here are Swedenborg, Larsen, Sculthorp and McKnight's guide:

> Every child who dies... is brought up in heaven, taught according to the divine design and filled with affections for what is good... Children who die are still children in the other life. They have the same kind of childlike mind, the same innocence in their ignorance, the same total delicateness...A child's state is better than others... in regard to the fact that children have not yet let evils take root in them by actually living them... As soon as children are reawakened... they are taken to heaven and given to female angels who have loved children tenderly during their physical lives... They accept these new ones as their own, and the children love them as their mothers... Once I was allowed to see some children with their nurses... in a paradisial garden... When they entered, the flowers over the entrance radiated the most joyous light imaginable... Little children are unaware that they were born on earth, so they think they were born in heaven.[175]

> The place was one vast garden of heavenly splendour, in which stood numberless magnificent buildings, for utilitarian and recreational purposes. Women helpers, who have known motherhood on earth, cared with tender solicitude for the babies and little children. Older children were taught and guided with minute care and that never-failing kindness which, however, does not neglect discipline. Men and women helpers of various qualifications, superintended by superior spirits, carried on their appealing work. Flowers of gorgeous hues in

> beds of rare designs, trees of perfect form and beauty, birds of varied plumage, fruits of delicious flavour are but the more obvious privileges of that delightful land. Paths through shrubbery and across parks divinely planned led to playgrounds where those fortunate children were seen at play beside their helpers and teachers. It was an atmosphere of beauty, obedience and love. I saw that the study of plants and flowers was an eagerly-followed occupation, which was supplemented by the care of gardens in perpetual bloom.[176]

> Those in spirit who do this work have a certain happiness in seeing children respond to treatment, and resume a life under much better conditions than would be possible on earth. Yet there is a sadness when thinking of some distracted parents who have not the slightest idea of what actually happens... Those children who pass over young are tended by suitable ones who are fond of them.[177]

> There are always sensitive souls who love children, and who are here to meet them, along with their guardian angels. And there are always some relatives here even if they are great-great-grandparents. There is so much love and warmth when the child arrives... Some are raised in caring homes, like foster homes on the earth. Some are raised in larger children's homes.[178]

Referring to the phenomenon of human incarnates going OOB while asleep, which we'll discuss properly in chapter 26, Banks then continues:

> Parents often come to be with their babies and young children, especially right after the children arrive in the world of spirit... It helps them to adjust to the loss of their children, and helps the children to adjust more fully to their new life in spirit.

There is nothing I can usefully add to these wonderful, comforting messages.

24

HEAVENLY LIFE

In this chapter we'll expand on what 'heavenly' life is like, by investigating where and how departed spirits live in the mid astral. Even though at times there may appear to be similarities in this chapter and the next with the earth-like environments discussed in chapter 21, the broad difference is that now the inhabitants genuinely believe they've attained their ideal of heaven.

LIKE ATTRACTS LIKE

In passing we've already encountered the idea that like spirits are attracted to each other in operation in all the realms we've so far discussed, including most obviously in consensus realities. But here are a few more explicit observations to reinforce the point that departed spirits are drawn to others of similar nature and interests in the astral as on earth. Here, for example, are Henry Lanchester and one of Emily French and Edward Randall's communicants:

> Men who think and believe alike each fall into sets.[1]
>
> When one comes here he is irresistibly drawn into that condition and company for which he is fitted by character. So the selfish are together; the immoral and cruel have like companionship; thieves and murderers are among their kind. Also the charitable, the kind, the devout, the spiritual are drawn to congenial souls, among whom they work in harmonious accord.[2]

Turning to OOB reports, here are Emanuel Swedenborg, Frederick Sculthorp, one of Rosalind McKnight's invisible helpers and Jurgen Ziewe:

> Kindred souls gravitate toward each other spontaneously, for with each other they feel as though they are with their own family, at home, while with others they feel like foreigners, as though they were abroad... People of similar quality all recognise each other there just the way people in this world recognise their neighbours and relatives and friends.[3]

> A person whose inner nature was friendly and considerate to others during earth life would automatically gravitate to the same wavelength in spirit, even if that person was ignorant of spirit or religion. The state would naturally be bright and the spirit would inherit the greater powers and broader access to knowledge pertaining to that state, and progress would be pleasant and easy. It would be as well to remember that this spirit would not be separated from relations and friends not so progressed, as the higher can always go to the lower.[4]

> The spirit world is that world that each soul creates. Other souls on the same vibration create a similar world. They are in awareness of and in attunement with each other, since the thought-forms are of the same essence.[5]

> The great diversity of mankind finds its greatest expression on the higher levels. Vast regions are allocated to individuals with similar interests and with unlimited ways of expressing them.[6]

But our sources also remind us that at any given time it's our general level of awareness or consciousness, and therefore of energetic vibration, that determines where we find ourselves. It also limits our ability to visit planes of higher vibration, even if we can usually descend to lower planes by making the appropriate adjustments. Here are Franchezzo, George Vale Owen's mother Emma, Robert Benson and TE Lawrence:

> Such as a man is, such will be his surroundings, and the sphere for which he is fitted must ever be the highest to which he can

attain till his own efforts fit him to become a dweller in one higher... Those above can always descend at will to visit or help those below them, but between them and the lower spirits there is a great gulf which the lower ones cannot pass.[7]

We do not always see those messengers who come to us from the higher spheres. They are seen by some better than by others, and are only truly and definitely visible when they so condition their bodies as to emerge into visibility. Now, if we go too far in their direction – that is, in the direction of their home – we feel an exhaustion which disables us to penetrate farther, although some are able to go farther than others.[8]

[If I tried to visit higher realms] I should... find that I was... undergoing sensations which I could not possibly bear. I should not be able to see anything before me... Just as certain light rays are invisible to earthly eyes and certain sounds and musical notes are inaudible to earthly ears, so are the higher realms invisible to the inhabitants of the lower realms. And the reason is that each realm possesses a higher vibrational rate than that below it, and is therefore invisible and inaudible to those who live below it.[9]

The real 'classes' into which we are separated are divided in space because they have to obey the primal law of affinity. Near and far mean likeness or difference in development, and there is a compulsion in the association of groups of similar levels. Each group makes its own conditions and these are for the time being the only conditions in which its members can exist in comfort. Whatever our natural plane be... to go up before one is ready means an air too rarefied and light, too intense to be borne. So each must go to his own place and stay there until development draws him up into a higher sphere.[10]

MEETING WITH FRIENDS AND RELATIVES

We have seen that departed relatives or friends often help with initial transition, but such meetings might well continue for some time. Franchezzo simply makes a brief observation:[11] 'How can I tell of the many friends who came to visit me.' One of French and Randall's communicants enlarges a little:[12] 'We come together in social intercourse, just as you do. Families meet and have reunions, just as you do. Not one particle of love is lost, but rather it is intensified.' Frances Banks refers to meeting her father, mother, sister and brother, but refrains from further comment because it's a 'private affair'.[13] But as so often it's left to Benson to provide colour and depth to the experience:[14]

> To leave the earth world and to take up permanent residence in the spirit world is not such a personal upheaval as some people might be disposed to imagine. It is true that for a great many all earthly ties are severed, but when we pass into the spirit world we meet again those of our relatives and friends who have passed over before us... The meetings with relations and friends are something that must be experienced in order to grasp the full significance and joy of reunion... These gatherings will continue for some while after the arrival of the new resident. It is natural that in the novelty both of surroundings and condition some time should be spent in a grand exchange of news, and in hearing of all that has transpired in the spirit lives of those who have 'predeceased' us.

However he also stresses the point made at the end of the last chapter that 'such meetings will only take place where there is mutual sympathy and affection'. In other words, if they're to meet frequently said spirits must be of a similar vibration and level, which is why we can't guarantee that especially romantic attachments from earth will carry over. Having said that we've just seen that more infrequent visits can be made by a spirit operating in a higher level to one in a lower, unless or until they reach a point where it's too difficult or just no longer desirable.

INDIVIDUAL HOMES

In this section and the next we'll hear about our sources' homes in the mid astral. Just as in the lower planes these can be individual or consensus environments, and we'll start with the former.

Franchezzo describes his first astral home, located in the 'land of dawn', as a room 'by no means luxurious, yet fairly comfortable in appearance', adding that there are 'a few pictures of scenes of my earth life which had been pleasant'.[15] From here he engages in his rescue missions to the lower planes and then, after his extended life-review experiences in the 'land of remorse' as described in chapter 22, he graduates to a home in the 'land of morning'. This is a much brighter environment and clearly in the mid astral proper, and this time he has a simple cottage all to himself, set in a peaceful valley, and from here he again embarks on multiple rescue missions. Finally he graduates to a home in the 'land of bright day', attained by passing through 'gates of gold'. He is met by a host of departed family and friends and joyously escorted to 'a lovely villa almost buried in roses and jasmine, which clustered over its walls and twined around the slender, white pillars of the piazza, forming a curtain of flowers upon one side', which sits 'upon the top of a hill overlooking a lake'. Within this much more spacious accommodation he has a music room; a picture room containing a greater number of pleasant scenes than before, from both his earthly and spirit life; and a library room containing books – some 'recording his life and those of people he has admired or loved', while those on other subjects are 'full of pictures that seem to reflect the thoughts of their authors more than any words'.

We read Benson's description of his astral home and especially his garden in the last chapter, but he adds:[16] 'You will find many people here who do not possess a home; they do not want one, they will tell you, for the sun is perpetually shining and the temperature is perpetually warm. They are never ill, or hungry, or in want of any kind, and the whole beautiful realm is theirs to wander in.'

Meanwhile, picking up from where we left him in chapter 22, TE Lawrence spends some time in the astral counterparts of the deserts of Arabia searching for old haunts and acquaintances, then returns to the astral version of his cottage in Dorset and spends some considerable further time in largely solitary contemplation.[17] But the huge, inner conflict that had always affected him on earth rears its head again – that is, between his intense desire for action and his equally intense frustration when his actions are thwarted, which is what led to him withdrawing into himself in his earthly life. This temptation is still dominant now. But with his guide Mitchell's help he realises that the call to action is still strong and must be fulfilled, as we'll see in Part 5.

John's little cottage that he calls home in chapter 21 turns out to be only temporary. Rather like Franchezzo he's led to a larger home in which he recognises many of his possessions from his earthly dwelling.[18] However, unlike Franchezzo above, he particularly notices some unfamiliar pictures on the wall and realises they depict aspects of his earthly life he would have preferred to forget. His guide reassures him that all astral homes have these reminders, which serve as a catalyst for the departed spirit to work through whatever their shortcomings are as part of their ongoing balancing. What follows, although slightly off-topic, is a fascinating description of how this can work in practice.

One picture in particular grabs his attention, that of a wartime subordinate called Jenkins who had taken to drinking and brawling because his wife was having an affair. John had an intuition at the time that perhaps he was dealing with him too harshly when he gave him increasingly severe sentences, and now the remorse is strong. The eyes in the picture even appear to follow him around the room. Subsequently John is called back into action to undertake rescue work in the Korean War, and while observing events on the earth plane he sees Jenkins, now an officer, leading his platoon with great skill and bravery.[19] Subsequently he sees Jenkins back in his camp giving advice to one of his men who has just found out *his* wife is having an affair, just as Jenkins' had. Not only does the latter deal compassionately with the man, who cannot get drunk as he did, but he also tells him that his own commanding officer had punished him severely when he went off the rails – and it had straightened him out. This of course makes

John feel considerably better, and when he's next at home he finds the face in the portrait is smiling at him.

Meanwhile Erik Medhus describes the astral home he builds for himself to make his acclimatisation easier:[20]

> I wasn't ready to go 100 percent into spirit mode yet, so I thought myself a house... I'd describe it as a log cabin... a bachelor pad... On the first floor a fireplace, some musical instruments and a bar stocked to the hilt with liquor, so it's decked out like a party pad where I can entertain if I want to... On both floors I have a bunch of big windows because I like a lot of light... I also made sure to include some more material possessions to make my place feel more earthlike, like some video games, a skateboard and a motorcycle... It sits on top of a hill in a remote area, and the landscape is really green.

However later on he decides he doesn't need this reminder of earthly existence any more. In fact he himself ends up as a guide to those still on earth and, with an interesting modern twist, uses his mother's internet blog to reach out to people all around the world who are thinking of suicide and need help, or who want to know more about the afterlife, and so on.[21]

In chapter 20 a few of our sources hinted at the idea that incarnate humans are effectively building their spiritual home via their actions while in the earth plane. John seems to confirm this when he talks to a recently departed spirit he's helping about the home she's been building for herself by thought – albeit that she's completely unaware of this:[22] 'Somewhere here is a home that is yours, created by yourself with thought. Everything that you desire in a home is there... Your every thought and action is reflected there... When you have rested and feel that you are finally at peace we will go together and find it.'

Similarly, from an OOB perspective, Sculthorp mentions making repeated visits to his 'home in spirit'.[23] But to take this a step further, members of the Monroe Institute are encouraged to create their own home in the astral, not least to act as a focal point when they want to meet each other or their guides. As an example, Bruce Moen describes his as a 'beach hut' perched at the top of a mountain outcrop, with incredible views over the surrounding mountain ranges, and adjacent to several small lakes with crystal clear water.[24]

HEAVENLY TOWNS AND CITIES

By contrast some departed spirits prefer to live in more community or consensus environments, sometimes of a relatively rural or small-town nature, other times in magnificent astral cites. Franchezzo briefly mentions hurrying through a region containing 'cities and dwelling places that would have tempted him to linger and admire them' had he not been so eager to get to his own new home.[25] Once installed he mentions the 'cities and lovely scenes' he visits that would 'take volumes' to describe. With more detail, here are one of French and Randall's communicants, Vale Owen's mother Emma, Benson and Jane Sherwood's EK:

> I saw white, spirit cities, long bright roads, embowered in groves and waving trees, and outstretched flowery plains, all full of lovely, happy, busy people, radiant with joy and life.[26]
>
> We sighted the city and descended before the principal gateway, by which we entered the main thoroughfare. It ran straight through the city and emerged through another gateway on the other side. On each side of this broad street there were large houses, or palaces, in spacious grounds.[27]
>
> To obtain a wider view, we walked to some higher ground, whence a clear panorama unfolded... Before us the countryside reached out in a seemingly unending prospect. In another direction I could clearly perceive what had all the appearance of a city of stately buildings, for it must be remembered that all people here do not possess a uniformity of tastes, and that... many prefer the city to the country, and vice versa.[28]
>
> Gleaming palaces and temples and beautiful cities built in elaborate form in surroundings of surpassing loveliness do exist. They satisfy the artistic and creative amongst us.[29]

Meanwhile John meets his parents in a city, although it's 'not a jungle of buildings, but each one is perfect, a masterpiece standing well back within its own grounds'.[30]

Turning to NDE material, although we saw in chapter 18 that Maurice Rawlings' reports are normally associated with hellish experiences, several of his subjects provide excellent descriptions of flying over and even entering 'golden cities'.[31] This, I suggest, would be their interpretation of astral environments operating at a higher energy level than they're used to on earth:

> Everything was getting brighter. I noticed that I was crossing over a beautiful city below, and I followed the river like a soaring bird. The streets seemed to be made of shining gold and were wonderfully beautiful. I can't describe it. I descended into one of the streets and people were all around me – happy people who were glad to see me! They seemed to be in shining clothes with a sort of glow. Nobody was in a hurry. Some other people were coming toward me. I think they were my parents.

> After soaring for a while, the angel sat me down on a street in a fabulous city of buildings made of glittering gold and silver and beautiful trees. A beautiful light was everywhere – glowing but not bright enough to make me squint my eyes. On this street I met my mother, my father and my brother, all of whom had died previously.

> Then I walked through the door, and saw on the other side this beautiful, brilliantly lit city, reflecting what seemed to be the sun's rays. It was all made of gold or some shiny metal with domes and steeples in beautiful array, and the streets were shining, not quite like marble but made of something I have never seen before. There were many people all dressed in glowing, white robes with radiant faces. They looked beautiful. The air smelled so fresh. I have never smelled anything like it. There was a background of music that was beautiful, heavenly music, and I saw two figures walking toward me and I immediately recognised them. They were my mother and father, both had died years ago.

> I was floating over this beautiful city, looking down. It was the prettiest city I have ever seen. People were there. All in white. The whole sky was so lit up, brighter than sunshine.

By contrast Eben Alexander describes a more countryside-based yet still consensus environment that is home to multiple departed spirits:[32]

> Below me there was countryside. It was green, lush and earthlike... I was flying, passing over trees and fields, streams and waterfalls and, here and there, people. There were children too, laughing and playing. The people sang and danced around in circles, and sometimes I'd see a dog, running and jumping among them, as full of joy as the people were. They wore simple yet beautiful clothes, and it seemed to me that the colours of these clothes had the same kind of living warmth as the trees and the flowers that bloomed and blossomed in the countryside around them... I know the difference between fantasy and reality, and I know that the experience I'm struggling to give you the vaguest, most completely unsatisfactory picture of, was the single most real experience of my life.

From an OOB perspective, Swedenborg visits various homes and palaces in communal environments:[33]

> Their houses were just like the houses on earth that we call homes, but more beautiful. They have chambers, suites and bedrooms in abundance, and courtyards with gardens, flower beds and lawns around them. Where there is some concentration of people, the houses are adjoining, one near another, arranged in the form of a city with streets and lanes and public squares... I have seen palaces in heaven that were so splendid as to be beyond description. Their upper stories shone as though they were made of pure gold, and their lower ones as though they were made of precious gems. Each palace seemed more splendid than the last. It was the same inside. The rooms were graced with such lovely adornments that neither words nor the arts and sciences are adequate to describe them.

By contrast Swami Panchadasi only briefly notes:[34] 'We find beautiful mountains and valleys, rivers and lakes, cites, towns, villages and country-land.' By contrast Oliver Fox reports on an OOB trip to what he felt to be the astral counterpart of London, where he encounters a colossal Gothic structure that totally enraptures him.[35] He then adds an interesting point about the comparison between astral counterparts and their earthly equivalents:

> I have found that the astral counterpart of a city appears much larger than the earthly one: for in addition to its present structures and features are to be found buildings, monuments, etc., which have no present existence on the earth. Some of these may have existed in the past; and others I suspect to be very powerful thought-forms – or perhaps the astral foreshadowings of earthly buildings yet to come.

Gladys Leonard – who, remember, not only acted as a medium but also experienced her own OOB journeys – makes the following general observation:[36]

> How very much like the earth this other world looks! At least, that portion of it that I have seen when visiting the different friends who have passed away. There appear to be houses, gardens, meadows, woods, lakes... We find, on comparing notes, that there are an astonishingly large number of people who see and remember the same sort of thing while travelling in the etheric world. I have had abundant corroboration from others of many of the scenes I have witnessed in that way.

Peter Richelieu describes being taken to his sweetheart's home in the astral, which lies within a 'garden city' where each home has plenty of garden around it festooned with gorgeous flowers and trees.[37] It is interesting that this particular place seems to contain an eclectic mix of inhabitants, because some are traditional English-style cottages, others French or Italian-style villas, others still more like Eastern homes with domes and so on. Meanwhile Gordon Phinn's guide Henry describes his home as a picture-postcard, English-style cottage;[38] and Robert Bruce mentions the cottage home of an old family friend that is 'much like her home in real life'.[39] Finally, on one journey Ziewe finds himself in what he believes to be the astral counterpart of Hamburg, although again it's far from identical:[40]

> The town was magnificent. All the buildings were of a Baroque architecture... The first thing I noticed... was the sheer scale of them... The details were phenomenal and very elaborate, so much so that I could quite easily have stood in front of any of these structures for many hours to absorb their intricacy and artistic accomplishment, their inherent harmony and expression of character. It is impossible to begin to describe them.

There are plenty of other references to cities – sometimes again the astral counterparts of earthly ones – that contain universities, halls of learning and so on. But these are mainly covered in Part 5 because of the progressive rather than recreational nature of the activities undertaken therein.

HEAVENLY RECREATIONS

Let us now turn to the myriad ways in which departed spirits amuse themselves in the mid astral – and here we can only scratch the surface. To start us off, one of French and Randall's communicants makes the following general point:[41] 'Everything is intensified to a degree you cannot imagine. Your pleasure and amusements can in no way compare to those which we are privileged to enjoy.' Turning to more specific reports, we find that Lanchester plays chess to amuse himself:[42] 'I don't miss my chess because I can still play it. Games entailing bodily skill we cannot enjoy, since we have no bodies, but those entailing mental skill are not in the same position.' By contrast Benson goes sailing with an acquaintance:[43]

> Ships are meant to float and move upon the waters; they are animated by the living force that animates all things here, and

> if we wish to move them over the water we have but to focus our thoughts in that direction... Our host handled his craft skilfully, and by increasing or diminishing its speed could create, by the different degree of movement of the water, the most striking alternations of colour and musical sound, brilliant scintillations of the sea showing how alive it was. It responded to the boat's every movement as though they were in complete unison – as indeed they were.

He and Philip Gilbert also echo Lanchester's comments about the typically 'physical' sports played on earth:

> On the earth plane skill in games is acquired by the mastery of the mind over the muscles of the body, when once the latter has been brought to a healthy condition. But here we are always in a healthy condition, and our muscles are always under the complete and absolute control of our minds. Efficiency is quickly gained, whether it is in playing upon a musical instrument, painting a picture, or in any other pursuit that requires the use of the limbs. It will be seen, therefore, that most of the usual games would lose their point here...
>
> The fact that we can move ourselves through space instantaneously is enough to make the greatest earthly athletic skill recede into insignificance, and our mundane sports and games are in similar case. Our recreations are more of the mind. We find that we have so much to learn, and learning is in itself such pleasure, that we do not need the number or variety of recreations that you do. We have plenty of music to listen to, there are such wonders in these lands that we want to know all about, there is so much congenial work to be done, that there is no cause to be cast down at the prospect of there being few of the earthly sports and pastimes in the spirit world. There is such a superabundant supply of vastly more entertaining things to be seen and done here, besides which a great deal of the earthly recreations appear sheer trivialities.[44]

Some activities are an extension of earth ones – music, painting, mathematics and so on can all be continued from where they are left off. But any activity which depends for its

> impetus on physical body skill or on earth needs such as, say, cricket or the stock exchange, has no equivalent in the reality here, because our way of functioning precludes it… For instance, Grandpa and I once tried to play chess. We easily conceived the men and board, and settled down, and as we could read each other's thoughts the game became a real test of mind against mind. But when three other ex-service chaps and myself tried to play bridge, it was impossible, as we all knew what the others held!..
>
> Things which are of the essence of mind, such as music and musical instruments, function here admirably… A ship can be made to function in a gentle gliding on great glimmering sheets of water. It is a fine sensation when one is wanting to rest… 'Whizzing' round has been one of my greatest pleasures since I came over – that gorgeous sensation of pure speed, and no fear of crashing! I practised for some time just speeding at some solid object like a mountain and passing through it, and this took me a bit of doing at first, because my earth memory was so strong and instinctively I dodged.[45]

To bring things more up-to-date, Medhus talks about 'creating a snow slope with his friends so they can snowboard together', about 'racing motorcycles' and chilling out and having 'pretend beers' with them, and about being in telepathic 'chat rooms' where those of like mind can discuss their shared interests.[46]

Turning to OOB reports, Richelieu echoes how departed spirits tend to be perfect at pastimes that require mental focus:[47] 'He can still play golf if he wishes… but he soon tires of this, for every shot he makes goes to the exact spot he has in mind… The same applies to billiards. There is no fun in making a big break when you can always do it at will.' Also his guide mentions the continuing popularity of cinema and theatre outings, but adds that the directors' potential for creativity is hugely enhanced.[48] Meanwhile Sculthorp reports on witnessing a variety of recreations, starting with a typical beach resort:[49]

> I was taken to a holiday resort in one of these states where people were sitting on a fine sandy beach and a band was

> playing. Others were surf-bathing, and out at sea there were sailing boats. All interests seem to be catered for on this plane by the advanced spirits in charge, and people were able to see things that perhaps they had no opportunity of seeing on earth.

In one environment he reports on astral cars and bicycles being used on roads, but at least in some cases the context seems to be heavenly enjoyment at the creative possibilities rather than mere earthly repetition:[50]

> The countryman prefers the open spaces and the townsman the built-up areas. Some towns I saw were crowded... There is also traffic on the roads, but in this particular state it consisted mainly of those who were road-minded on earth. Once I found it interesting and rather funny, like other onlookers, to watch this passing show of traffic. Among the usual cars there were quite a number that were evidently the result of enthusiastic do-it-yourself builders. As any whim can be exploited to the full without the earthly expense and trouble, there were some strange-looking three and four-wheelers on the road, and all of them 'went' as they were expected to do in spirit.
>
> I saw one man riding a bicycle who was dressed in Norfolk jacket and knickerbockers of about the 1906 period. He had constructed seats like outriggers on either side of his saddle, which were carrying children... There are many different varieties of houses in this state. Some people like to keep to the style that they had on earth, and even have unnecessary things as it is their idea of home, while others knowing the possibilities would have something entirely new.

Sculthorp even reports on the use of astral aeroplanes.[51] He then closes by talking about visiting pubs, although this time it's difficult to tell whether they're in a heavenly setting or just part of an earth-like environment in the lower-mid astral:[52]

> I have been taken to several drinking places in spirit and I do not think that I was visible to the people there. They seem to be habitual meeting places of like-minded people and the drinks did not appear to have any enlivening or intoxicating

> effect. One place I visited was an old tavern on the sea front, which still seemed to have the appearance of the early 18th century. The proprietor was a large, angular-looking individual with a sun-tanned face and buckled shoes who looked like an ex-buccaneer basking in respectable retirement.

One of McKnight's spirit friends corroborates that 'sailing and flying are great pastimes for many'.[53] Meanwhile Phinn's guide Henry confirms Gilbert's view that flying around – *without* a plane that is – is a major basis for recreation, 'from children's games to elaborate sports';[54] so we can only assume that the Harry Potter game of Quidditch must already be a major pastime in the astral. He also confirms our other sources' reports about cars, skiing and so on: 'Vehicles are still maintained by those who love the thought of them... Vintage car lovers have their rallies here just as they did on earth. Horse and buggy fanciers do the same. Skiers ski in the mountains; water skiers do the same on lakes.'

Ziewe adds:[55] 'Anything that can be imagined is a reality here. It is easy to understand the temptation of people wanting to spend centuries in this world in order to explore its infinite possibilities.' So, for example, he finds himself in the middle of something like the Rio Carnival where 'I have never experienced such uninhibited happiness on such a large scale in all of my life'. Then on a beach outside what he identifies as the Welsh seaside resort of Portmeirion he joins a huge crowd watching an incredible 'weather show', where 'bolts of lighting shot down into the mountainous ocean waves, which reared hundreds of feet into the air like giant tsunamis stopping just short of crashing ashore'. Elsewhere he corroborates the idea of flying, before closing with some remarks about celebration generally:[56]

> There is an increase of energy which allows us to soar and fly literally... Here we are carried by the wings of joy and pleasure... There is simply so much reason to celebrate with the absence of the stresses earthly lives had posed. Just imagine what it would feel like to have all your wishes come true. Would you not feel like celebrating?.. There is a feeling of

celebration and enjoyment and, when people talk about your rewards are in heaven, this is probably the place they are thinking of.

Our sources also make plenty of references to going to libraries, galleries, theatres and concerts.[57] However again these are mainly covered in Part 5 because on balance they tend to be more progressive experiences.

We have primarily talked about recreation in this section, but Benson also talks more specifically about the types of occupation available to departed spirits, and indicates that in the astral there's almost no distinction between an occupation and recreation:[58]

> The spirit world is not only a land of equal opportunity for every soul, but the opportunities are upon so vast a scale that no person still incarnate can have the least conception of its magnitude... I want to try to give you some slight idea of the immensity of the range of occupations in which one can become engaged here in these realms... Imagine yourself in a world where no one works for a living, but where everyone works for the sheer joy of doing something that will be of service to others... It is very surprising how quickly efficiency is gained by the stimulus of desire. The 'wish to do' becomes translated into the 'ability to do' in a very short time. Keen interest and predilection for the work are all that are asked... All that we have in our halls and our houses, in our homes and in our gardens, has to be made, to be fashioned, or created, and it requires someone to do it. The need is constant, and the supply is constant, and it will ever be so.

In particular he talks about departed spirits – who might be picking up on an earthly skill or hobby, or adapting themselves to something completely new – acting as gardeners, builders, architects, librarians, artists, musicians, instrument makers and so on; and that's before we start talking about the possibility of acting as spirit guides, helpers, healers and rescuers.

We can now fully see just how much there is to look forward to in the afterlife. Little wonder then that Julia Ames and Benson allow us to round things off with the following proclamations:

> I have never for one passing moment wished to be back in my body again... There is nothing the body could give me that I do not now enjoy.[59]

> In my travels through these realms of light I have yet to find a single, solitary individual who would willingly exchange this grand, free life in the spirit world for the old life upon the earth plane.[60]

And yet... and yet. Ziewe closes his 'celebration' quote above with this remark: 'All this simply pales into insignificance once we evolve to even higher dimensions.' So is what we've been describing in these last two chapters *really* heaven?

25

ILLUSION

For all that we've been treated to some wonderful descriptions of the supposedly heavenly planes in the last two chapters, we must now turn to the tendency towards stagnation that often seems to be predominant in the mid astral realms. This is especially the case for those departed spirits who don't realise they're actually on a lengthy journey – and, moreover, a very long way from their ultimate destination.

RELIGIOUS HEAVENS

In chapter 14 one of Emily French and Edward Randall's communicants described the ongoing religious devotion that can continue to influence those trapped in the near-earth plane. But now we find the same can be true even in the mid astral, and this is just one example of the type of stagnation we're talking about in this chapter.

It may well be that most if not all of the specific religious settings we'll encounter here are closer to the sort of lower-mid astral, earth-like environments we discussed in chapter 21 – but, because they're such fine examples of illusion, *and* because the inhabitants definitely believe they've attained their true heaven, I've brought all the reports together here. Some are quite hard-hitting, and I don't wish to offend anyone by reproducing them. Nevertheless I feel it's important that these messages are provided in unadulterated form so that their validity or otherwise can be properly judged.

So, to start us off, another of French and Randall's communicants describes how he takes a child who passes very young under his wing and in time, when she's nearly grown to womanhood, he takes her to see what conditions are like on the earth plane.[1] She is overwhelmed by the harshness, which is of an order she has never known. Then towards the end of their visit he takes her to a church service:

> The teachings of the minister to her seemed so gross, so false, so out of line with all she had ever seen, heard or read of in the land which had always been her home that she hesitated to remain, but I told her that her future work and welfare required that she learned as much as possible of the earth conditions in which your people live.

This is strong stuff, but once one starts to appreciate the power and divinity that each of us possess as individual spirits, souls or consciousnesses, traditional Christian messages of unworthiness and so on do tend to grate.[2] Next, here are Henry Lanchester, David Hatch and John's guide Ashtar:

> In the lowest division of this realm the spirits are still strong believers in their own particular sect, and there is a marked tendency for them to remain there segregated into narrow communities. Their principal failings are self-complacency and an unwillingness to make any effort to progress higher, being often well satisfied with their surroundings.[3]

> The holders of different opinions on religion are often hot in their arguments. Coming here with the same beliefs they had on earth, and being able to visualise their ideals and actually to experience the things they are expecting, two men who hold opposite creeds forcibly are each more intolerant than ever before.[4]

> There are still religious creeds here. People follow them, they do not easily cast aside what they have been familiar with, what they have learned to understand and love. Men continue to believe what they have been taught and have accepted.[5]

However TE Lawrence suggests that in the higher planes of the astral most religious dogma is shown to be contrary to the reality that departed spirits are actually experiencing:[6]

> Dogmatic teaching about heaven and hell is fortunately corrected by the known facts; freedom from the cramping doctrines of eternal punishment, original sin and predestination is a wonderful release for those who have lived out their lives under such man-made shadows.

But of course it's former priest Robert Benson who has most to contribute on this issue, given his ongoing remorse at the orthodox life he followed and the books he authored while on the earth plane – despite their conflict with his inner voice and his own psychic abilities:[7]

> The very fact that I was lying there where I was constituted a complete refutation of so much that I taught and upheld during my priestly life upon earth. I could see volumes of orthodox teachings, creeds and doctrines melting away because they are of no account, because they are not true, and because they have no application whatever to the eternal world of spirit and to the great creator and upholder of it...
>
> Creeds... do not form any part of the world of spirit but, because people take with them all their characteristics into the spirit world, the fervid adherents to any particular religious body will continue to practise their religion... until such time as their minds become spiritually enlightened. We have here... whole communities still exercising their old earthly religion. The bigotry and prejudices are all there, religiously speaking. They do no harm, except to themselves, since such matters are confined to themselves. There is no such thing as making converts here...
>
> Such being the case, then, I supposed that our own religion was fully represented here. Indeed, it was! The same ceremonies, the same ritual, the same old beliefs, all are being carried on with the same misplaced zeal – in churches erected for the purpose. The members of these communities know that they have passed on, and they think that part of their heavenly

> reward is to continue with their man-made forms of worship. So they will continue until such time as a spiritual awakening takes place. Pressure is never brought to bear upon these souls; their mental resurrection must come from within themselves. When it does come they will taste for the first time the real meaning of freedom.

Nor does he leave it at that, but elsewhere hammers the point home:[8]

> The earth world is to blame. Religious contentions and controversies are at the bottom of all the ignorance and lack of knowledge that so many people bring with them into the spirit world and, if the minds of such people are stubborn and they are unable to really think for themselves, then do they remain shackled to their narrow religious views, thinking it to be all the truth… It is to be so much lamented that, for every one who leaves these misguided congregations forever, another will come to fill his place – until the time comes when the whole earth knows the truth of the world of spirit.

However he's still delighted by a church he comes across in the astral:[9]

> A short walk brought us to the church that I had seen in the distance, and which I had expressed a keenness to visit. It was a medium-sized building in the Gothic style, and it resembled the 'parish church' familiar on earth… We went within and found ourselves in a very lovely building, conventional in design, and containing little that is not to be seen in any such church upon the earth plane. There were some beautiful, stained-glass windows portraying scenes in the lives of the 'saints'… There was a fine organ at one end and the main altar, built of stone, was richly carved.

He also reveals that his guide Edwin specialises in helping those departed spirits who shared their beliefs on earth:[10]

> Edwin then proposed that perhaps I would like to join him in his work, which was principally concerned with taking in hand newly-arrived souls whose religious beliefs were the same as

> we had held upon earth but who, unlike ourselves, were unable as yet to realise the truth of the change they had made, and of the unreality of so much of their religion.

However Benson doesn't just point the finger at orthodox religions, but at more esoteric and occult sects too – for overcomplicating something that is actually very simple:[11]

> Individuals with strange theories find those theories demolished by the simple fact of finding themselves faced with the absolute truth. They discover that life in the spirit world is not nearly so complex as they would have it to be... The student of occult matters is apt to fall into the same error as the student of religious matters. He makes assertions every bit as dogmatic as those that emanate from orthodox religion, assertions that are mostly as far from the truth.

Indeed I too have always maintained that any religion, creed or belief that takes years of study to understand – and is packed with difficult words and concepts, or contains multiple, categorised and numbered hierarchies and sub-hierarchies of planes and beings – is almost certainly a long way wide of the mark. There is no need to overcomplicate the wonderful simplicity of the way consciousness operates in different planes of experience – and arguably those who do are either showing their ignorance in misinterpreting messages from wise, centuries-old sources that would originally have been much simpler, or exhibiting a form of spiritual ego by espousing beliefs that are too complex for most ordinary people to understand.

From an NDE perspective, in chapter 17 we saw that Mellen-Thomas Benedict had a wonderfully transcendental experience. Here he describes being a given a tour of the almost infinite number of belief-based heavens, making it clear that for millennia these have been created, expanded and sustained by the *expectations* of millions of people from all around the world:[12]

> I was given a tour of all the heavens that have been created: the nirvanas, the happy hunting grounds, all of them. I went

> through them. These are thought-form creations that we have created... I saw the Christian heaven. We expect it to be a beautiful place, and you stand in front of the throne, worshipping forever. I tried it. It is boring! This is all we are going to do? It is childlike. I do not mean to offend anyone. Some heavens are very interesting, and some are very boring. I found the ancient ones to be more interesting, like the Native American ones, the Happy Hunting Grounds. The Egyptians have fantastic ones. It goes on and on. There are so many of them.

Turning to OOB reports, Annie Besant reiterates Benedict's observations:[13]

> Here are situated all the materialised heavens which play so large a part in popular religions all the world over. The happy hunting-grounds of the Red Indian, the Valhalla of the Norsemen, the houri-filled paradise of the Muslim, the golden jewelled-gated New Jerusalem of the Christian, the lyceum-filled heaven of the materialistic reformer, all have here their places. Men and women who clung desperately to every 'letter that killeth' have here the literal satisfaction of their cravings, unconsciously created in astral matter by their powers of imagination... Literalists of every faith, who were filled with selfish longings for their own salvation in the most materialistic of heavens, here find an appropriate and to them enjoyable home, surrounded by the very conditions in which they believed... They build astral churches and schools and houses, reproducing the materialistic heavens they coveted.

These ideas are affirmed by Swami Panchadasi, Peter Richelieu's sage and Rosalind McKnight's guide:

> [The astral] may be said to contain all the heavens that have ever been dreamed of in theology and taught in the churches – each filled with devotees of the various creeds. Each of the great religions has its own particular region, in which its disciples gather, worship and rejoice. In each region the religious soul finds just what he had expected and hoped to find.[14]

> People like to continue their religious practices, even though after death they may have found that many of the statements made by their priests and pastors were not entirely correct. The permanent inhabitants build these churches and ex-priests and ex-ministers of religion carry on their old vocations, drawing around them followers, just as they did in the life that has ended.[15]

> Every kind of religious organisation that exists on planet earth exists here... Many of the religious groups that are tightly knit on earth continue to worship together after arriving here, mainly out of habit... But once the members are here for a while and realise that they are already in heaven, they begin to check out other worship options and gradually lose interest in their old belief systems and ways of thinking.[16]

Meanwhile Gordon Phinn's guide Henry describes being taken by his own guide Jack to a scene outside a church on a Sunday morning in the astral version of a small, New England town.[17] The congregation are all white and, despite the pastor's insistence that they accept Baptists, Catholics, Lutherans or Jews into their community, it's clear that Hindus or Moslems, for example, wouldn't be welcomed. Henry gets the impression that Jack likes to 'stir things up' here, although he doesn't on this particular visit. Backing up his report of a fellow guide being mistaken for Jesus by an NDE subject in chapter 22, Henry adds:[18] 'The historically revered figures of religion and culture, the people that everyone expects to see when they get to their version of heaven, can be, and often are, played by actors.' Of course this follows on from Philip Gilbert and Robert Monroe pretending to be religious figures to help with initial transitions, as we saw in chapter 21.

To reinforce this idea, on one of his journeys Bruce Moen discusses 'hollow heavens' that are predominantly religiously based with a former inhabitant called Bill.[19] Again I make no apology for reproducing the latter's story at length, because it's particularly enlightening. On earth he'd been a preacher for a 'small, Christian sect' of only some tens of thousands of followers, and on passing he's drawn straight to its astral counterpart. Here he meets various fellow preachers and worshippers he'd known previously, as well as some of the most legendary, venerated preachers from before his time. He is soon given a ministry again, with his own church and congregation, where he continues to preach the exact same messages as on earth. These always involved a strict set of rules, and the slightest infringement was enough to condemn the errant member to hell, unless they had their sins forgiven by their preacher. Now, even though they've all attained their idea of heaven, the same set of rules remain in force and any repeat offenders are cast out into hell – either privately or during a public service.

Bill finally begins to doubt when he's forced to cast out a couple who are very much in love, purely for the sin of living together and refusing to get married – which they base on one of Jesus' biblical teachings about there being no marriage in heaven. After that a figure that he believes to be Jesus himself appears to him repeatedly in private, telling him that the love of Christ is to be shared by *all*, and even appearing during one of his sermons with the same message, radiating pure love to everyone there. This leads to such doubts that Bill himself is eventually cast out, but intercepted by a spirit helper who turns out to be the one who had pretended to be Jesus. He is taken for deprogramming and eventually goes on to become a spirit helper himself. In this guise he makes appearances not only in his own former religious heaven but in others too, sowing seeds of doubt wherever possible, appearing as Jesus and so on – and then intercepting any followers who leave or are ejected, and taking them to be deprogrammed themselves.

Clearly the inhabitants of these illusory realms will at some point have to come to terms with the fact that they're only at the start rather than the end of their journey if they're to progress. But even more than this I think we must assume that they've somehow bypassed the initial life-review experience that, surely, would otherwise have set them straight. This may be because their obsession with their religion blocks it, or because they're only operating in the lower-mid astral and such reviews only occur on transition to the mid astral proper, or a combination of the two. Given that we know that the outward observation of religious ceremony is no guide to one's true inner state, this in turn means that most adherents to this multitude of beliefs are likely to have to engage in some form of review, introspection, therapy and balancing once they leave the safety blanket of their community – as is suggested by Bill above.

THE 'GOLDEN CITY' FROM THE BIBLE

The pinnacle of George Ritchie's NDE comes when he glimpses in the far distance 'a glowing, seemingly endless city' whose 'brightness seemed to shine from the very walls and streets... and from the beings within it'.[20] He reports that at the time he hadn't read the description of the 'Golden City' of the 'New Jerusalem' described in Revelation 21 and referred to by Besant above, but given that he feels himself to be escorted by Jesus himself it's little wonder he later interprets his experience in that way. Yet in just the same way that his identification of his guide is almost certainly flawed, this too may just be an ordinary mid astral city of the sort discussed in the last chapter, which is operating at a higher frequency than he's used to on earth.

IS EVERYTHING WHAT IT SEEMS?

The foregoing of course leads us on to a more general discussion of the level of illusion operating in the mid astral. That isn't to say that living in an illusion can't be fun, because clearly it can. It is simply to recognise that the mid astral is actually just a staging post on the journey, and arguably not one we should get too caught up in. Here, then, are the thoughts of Hatch, Frederic Myers, Frances Banks and, more briefly, Arthur Ford:

> Life on this side is only an extension of the life on earth! If the thoughts and desires there have been only for material pleasures, the thoughts and desires here are likely to be the

same... This is a great place in which to grow, if one really wants to grow; though few persons take advantage of its possibilities. Most are content to assimilate the experiences they had on earth. It would be depressing, to one who did not realise that will is free, to see how souls let slip their opportunities here... We draw to ourselves the experiences which we are ready for and which we demand, and most souls do not demand enough here, any more than they did in life.[21]

Nearly every soul lives for a time in the state of illusion. The large majority of human beings when they die are dominated by the conception that substance is reality, that their particular experience of substance is the only reality. They are not prepared for an immediate and complete change of outlook. They passionately yearn for familiar though idealised surroundings. Their will to live is merely to live, therefore, in the past. So they enter the dream I call 'Illusionland'. For instance, Tom Jones, who represents the unthinking man in the street, will desire a glorified brick villa in a glorified Brighton. So he finds himself the proud possessor [of same]. He naturally gravitates towards his acquaintances, all those who were of a like mind. On earth he longed for a superior brand of cigar. He can have the experience ad nauseam of smoking this brand. He wanted to play golf, so he plays golf. But he is merely dreaming all the time or, rather, living within the fantasy created by the strongest desires on earth. After a while this life of pleasure ceases to amuse and content him. Then he begins to think and long for the unknown, long for a new life... He realises his own increased intellectual powers and, above all, his capacity for living on a finer plane of being.[22]

We live, or we exist, according to the level of our thought-life; some are content to stay, thinking no doubt that this is the final stage. There must, of course, come a time in the soul's awakening when that belief is proved false, but... some souls settle down in one stage for years – even centuries! While others persist in their former earth surroundings for ages!.. Life is a continuing path towards... one's own progress and onwards into the arc of ascendancy. To me this is a far more heartening

> process than any glory of a static heaven with angels and golden floors.[23]

> Will we want to plunge into a round of festivities and pure pleasures, or will we want to develop our spiritual side?[24]

For a more contemporary perspective, Billy Cohen refers to the 'supra world' of the mid astral that's 'designed for the comfort of the newly dead soul'.[25] Here they can acclimatise, let go of their fears and reunite with others they knew on the earth plane. But he adds: 'This is also the place where the newly dead play out strong beliefs they had about death while they were alive. It's like a spool of ribbon unwinding. The spool gets thinner as the beliefs are played out... As a person gets more familiar with the new atmosphere, these ideas lose their grip.' He accepts that there are many different forms of afterlife experience, and even suggests that he was so ready for ecstasy and bliss that he didn't need to experience the intermediate realms, as we'll see in Part 5.

Turning to OOB reports, Besant makes the following general observation:[26] 'Their creative thoughts fashion the luminous materials of their temporary home into fair landscapes and rippling oceans, snow-clad mountains and fertile plains, scenes that are of fairy-like beauty compared with even the most exquisite that earth can show.' However she's clearly stating that such a home is only *temporary*. Providing more explicit warnings here are Yram, Caroline Larsen and Richelieu's sage:

> Each state of density, or dimensional division of the ether, corresponds to our affinities, desires and preferences. Each one is therefore able to lead the life he wishes. As the majority of people are ignorant of the possibility of living consciously in space, they surround themselves with imaginary creations... For those who know no better, their imagination is a reality.[27]

> Here dwelt those who... gave little consideration to the things of the spirit... Their souls were fallow fields season after season... Hence, though now in a realm where infinite possibilities open ahead, their progress is slow. They live as on

earth in pleasant houses with delightful gardens... In touch with friends to whom they are courteous and neighbourly, dressing as they did on earth... But they are content with their earth-made ambitions, and with the easy virtue of pleasant, unheroic life, unmindful of the spiritual struggle that marks everywhere the upward road.

Sometimes because of mutual sympathy they live together in groups of three or four or more, but more often man is attracted to woman... Here I found living an aunt and a cousin of my own. On earth this lady had long presided over the house of my cousin, a wealthy banker who, like her, never married. Their long and harmonious life together had produced an ease of intercourse that made its continuance natural. So in the spirit world I found them again living contentedly, and reproducing as far as might be the details of their earthly life. Even the good-natured superiority of the aristocratic class that they represented was reproduced in their new life, with its narrow human sympathies, its entire respectability and its rectitude. No atmosphere could well be more hostile to change.[28]

Many people are perfectly happy with this Arcadian existence, particularly those who have had a rather hard time during their earth life... They have the friends, pets, beautiful houses and gardens which satisfy them.[29]

Turning to Sculthorp, he first corroborates the idea of stagnation:[30]

Apart from the lower, dull states there are a number of spheres of normal brightness, earth-like in a better way, where the spirits enjoy themselves, getting accustomed to the many possibilities of the spirit world. It is difficult to describe these easy-going states as they are neither backward nor advanced. Generally speaking, all spirits keep to a habit of thought or way of living for a time, as during earth life.

He then moves on to an account of a consensus environment inhabited solely by former members of the English upper classes, who refuse to take advice when it's offered:[31]

> I was taken to an astral plane of normal brightness, yet I was surprised by the vibrations there. At first glance it appeared to be a pleasant park, with large gates set in stonework and rockeries, ornamental ponds and wooden seats here and there... Then I noticed that there were no plants or shrubs of any kind in this park. There were a few people about. Some were walking and others sitting on the benches. They appeared to be smartly dressed but each was assuming an attitude which was supposed to represent the very height of dignity and elegance that only an exclusive set should have. Those on the benches were sitting stiffly and formally, with set faces, as if fearful of being caught relaxing by a society photographer. The women wore hats which were mostly an exaggeration of the fashion of their period, but all had a look of frozen nonchalance ingrained by their habit of thought on earth.
>
> Presently I saw a man enter through the gates... I could see at once that he was an advanced teacher, and he began to address the people in the park. His voice was clear and ringing, but he had hardly started to tell them of other places much better than this, than two of the men gently escorted him out through the gates. Immediately he re-entered the park and again started to speak, and again he was taken out. They were very gentle with him, as if they were saying: 'Really, old chap, park oratory is hardly the thing for our class of people; do be a good fellow and step out.' This is a strange state. These people were quite all right in their dealings with their fellow men and they were causing no harm, hence the normal brightness of their locality; but it was shown how difficult it is to penetrate the hard shell of their unnatural affectations. The spirit law is perfect and simple. It demands a simple sincerity.

Meanwhile the basic message is thoroughly reiterated by Moen, Phinn's guide Henry, Phinn himself, one of Jurgen Ziewe's guides and finally in two separate quotes from Ziewe himself:

> In a sense they are stuck too, since their own beliefs bring and hold them there. But they are not isolated and alone, suffering in fear or pain.[32]

These heavens, after all, are paradises of personal and cultural fulfilment, and only a few tire of such terminal bliss. The tales of the formless but sentient systems that lie beyond often fail to charm the conventional soul... On the mid astral... it is not commonly realised that the habits they most admire and promote are the very ones that they will have to relinquish if they wish to make further progress. The upper reaches of heaven... are quite formless and the houses, gardens, personalities and cultures we so carefully cultivate on our way up... must be ruthlessly cast aside in order to participate in the new ballgame of pure mind. Naturally I do my best to illuminate these thorny issues, but as the mid astral is filled to the brim with competing belief systems and agendas, and many of these believers see the glorious worlds of form to be the ultimate achievement, my words often fall on stony ground and I am often seen as some renegade huckster spoiling the fun.[33]

As most folk are still holding their understanding at the physical or astral level, their concerns are physical and emotional. Even those of a strong spiritual bent stay focused on the astral plane euphoria of paradise as the goal of their strivings. Few of these wish to hear that heaven, as conventionally conceived, is an illusion catering to the desires of the emotional body.[34]

Thiis world is a grand illusion, put in your path to trick you – to keep you fascinated and imprisoned as a limited being. Yet to many people on earth what you've just seen is the dream of all dreams come true, the heaven of all heavens. And indeed, compared to life on the dense earth, this truly is paradise, where people spend millennia exploring the vast scope and vistas of heaven and its joys.[35]

Anything that it is possible to create is in existence, and a soul relishing the abundance of these universes can cover endless vistas of sublime landscapes, and worlds of such profusion and wonder, that it is easy to be trapped and seduced by them for millennia to come.These worlds cater for the fulfillment of all our dreams in their essence, which we were unable to fulfil on the lower levels, and in an environment which is blissfull in an endless variety of ways... Yet, although we might consider this

> to be the goal and fulfillment of all our dreams, an awakened person who enters this world will become aware that this is not the ultimate reality or resting place, if there is such a thing, and will quickly turn his or her attention to a higher level still.[36]
>
> From up here I could see countless belief systems as incredibly complex shapes. I saw that once immersed in any of those structures the perspective of the world changed for good. The centre of the thought felt like the centre of the universe itself... How easy it seemed for people to become seduced and ensnared by these grand designs. The sheer presence of them, how each thought provided refuge, belonging and identity... How many people, I thought, understand that they have the power to rise above and observe these thoughts for what they are: temporary resting places, no more than inventions, giving us the illusion that we are in control.[37]

REINCARNATION REVISITED

We saw in chapter 8 that, whereas the traditional idea of reincarnation involves one life *after* another, Supersoul Spirituality replaces this with the concept of simultaneous lives that are all happening at the same time – irrespective of how hard this is for us to fully understand with our human brains. I discuss the theoretical arguments relating to this model in *Supersoul* itself.[38] But my change of perspective was mainly prompted by two things. First, modern spiritual commentators constantly refer to the 'eternal now' of the afterlife, or as they would call it the *inter*life, yet they never seem to follow this through to its logical conclusion. Indeed I was guilty of this myself in the *Books of the Soul* series, but then decided enough was enough. Second, while researching *The Power of You* I came across the thoughts of some of our most celebrated, higher sources of channelled wisdom, such as Mary Ennis's 'Elias', Jane Roberts's 'Seth' and Neale Donald Walsch's 'God', who are each quoted here in turn.[39]

> You choose your focuses and project from essence simultaneously. Therefore, all of your focuses are being

> accomplished within the now. It is only within your perception that they appear to be past or future.
>
> What you understand of reincarnation, and of the time terms involved, is a very simplified tale indeed... Reincarnation, in its own way, is also a parable. It seems very difficult for you to understand that you live in many realities – and many centuries – at one time.
>
> You are living this life, your presently realised life, in your past, your present, your future, all at once!.. You are also living other lives – what you call 'past lives' – right now as well, although you experience them as having been in your 'past' (if you experience them at all), and that is just as well. It would be very difficult for you to play this wonderful game of life if you had full awareness of what is going on.

Moreover, while researching *this* book I was delighted to find that one of our most contemporary yet ordinary channelled sources, Erik Medhus, confirms this view:[40]

> Imagine that every incarnation on earth is represented by a book... All the books are stacked on top of each another. Humans have only enough conscious awareness to concentrate on one page in one book at a time. That's important because to have the human experience, you have to be in the now. You can't have your head scattered in all directions, diluting the purpose of the life you're living, but all your lives are happening at the same time.

Some modern OOB pioneers seem to support this idea too. Here, for example, is Ziewe talking about his experience of observing supposedly 'past' lives:[41]

> What is fascinating is that the past-life event is not an experience like a detached memory or picture, but is experienced in a here-and-now environment with the same reality as if it happened in 'real life'. This throws our whole concept of time and space into question.

In this context it's interesting to note that in all the channelled,

NDE and OOB material used to put this book together, there's virtually no *hard* evidence for the conventional idea of returning into another incarnation. Reincarnation is *discussed* as a theoretical concept by quite a few of our sources.[42] But in only three of these are circumstances *actually encountered* in which souls are supposedly choosing the circumstances of, and preparing for, another life.[43] How do we explain this? Is it, first, just an omission on the part of all our other sources? This seems unlikely for such a crucial issue. Or second, and with respect to channelled material in particular, is it just the case that by the time any departed spirit is making plans to come back they're too far into the afterlife process to still be communicating with earth? But then we've repeatedly encountered them being guided around other areas of the afterlife realms that aren't their own natural habit, so perhaps this explanation falls short. Third, then, can this apparent omission be explained by the fact that it's simply *not* how things really work, at least for most departed spirits?

Another important point is, as we've seen, that *all* of our channelled sources continue to identify with the personalities of the lives they've just left, at least while they remain in the astral planes. This tends to go against the modern-but-conventional reincarnation model that has had huge exposure in the last half century, which holds that departed souls expand into their higher self – and thereby gain an awareness of all their past lives – fairly soon after the life review. Admittedly, as we'll see in Part 5, when spirits progress to the higher realms some at least start to gain a broader awareness of their other life personalities – but this tends to happen only after a substantial intermission in the mid and upper astral.

The other ubiquitous aspect of modern reincarnation material is the idea of spirits operating in relatively small 'soul groups', usually under the direction of one spirit guide, who talk about their past lives together, learn from same and even plan their next ones. By contrast, as we've seen, our sources maintain that departed spirits tend to process and even atone for the less desirable aspects of their earthly lives very much as individuals – albeit with help from guides and so on – and either live predominantly alone or band together based on mutual attraction to certain beliefs or pastimes, sometimes in sizeable communities. All of this bears no comparison with what's being described in modern reincarnation material.

To illustrate the problem that faces us, the following message from Lawrence indicates that disputes over various theories of reincarnation exist *even* in the afterlife planes. Here he is talking about how the topic is discussed within the 'university' environment he was residing in at the time he channelled *Post-Mortem Journal*, which we'll again discuss more in Part 5:[44]

> There is a divided body of opinion on this, one of the most controversial subjects, and many variants of the theory of rebirth are expounded and argued among us... Do all those who leave this sphere go higher? Do they continue the upward journey, or is there a limit to growth, and what sets this limit? These are some of the questions which bring us up against the limitations of our knowledge, and may have to wait for further experience before they find answers.

From a more general perspective, both Franchezzo's guide and Benson indicate that all knowledge doesn't automatically become available just because we've passed on:[45]

> In the spirit world there are a great number of different schools of thought... Neither spirits nor mortals can know everything, and spirits can only give you the teachings which their own particular schools of thought and advanced teachers give as their explanations. Beyond this they cannot go, for beyond this they do not know themselves; there is no more absolute certainty in the spirit world than on earth, and those who assert that they have the true and only explanation of these great mysteries are giving you merely what they have been taught by more advanced spirits who, with all due deference to them, are no more entitled to speak absolutely than the advanced teachers of some other school.

> There are many, many things here which we do not understand – and it will take eons of time before we even have a faint gleam of understanding them.[46]

I would suggest that the most relevant question we can ask at this point is this: how far does the influence of space-time extend? We know it operates in the earth or incarnate plane we're inhabiting now. We also know that some sort of time and even space *can* be experienced, albeit rather differently, in the astral plane. So is it possible that the influence of space-time can still be sufficient in the astral to allow souls to become caught up in an illusion of *returning* to earth for what would then *appear* to be a *next* life? Monroe certainly follows this view, claiming that the 'inner rings' of the mid astral are dominated much more by the 'human time-space illusion' than by the 'nonphysical reality' that dominates the 'outer rings'.[47]

I too have come to the conclusion that the answer to this second question just may be 'yes'. If we can trap ourselves in the manifold illusions of the heaven worlds already discussed, it seems likely that we can also trap ourselves in the illusion of reincarnation – even if ultimately, from the true perspective of the higher realms, there's no time and everything's happening in the now. This is exactly the view adopted by Phinn's 'higher self', or in our terms supersoul:[48]

> When we monads send out our beloved explorers into the antipodes of consciousness we know that many of you will become so enmeshed in the depths of physicality, and the charge of excited desire that is the reincarnation cycle, not to mention the almost innumerable belief systems concocted by various individuals and groups trying to make some kind of sense of the hardship and suffering of the physical plane, that you will not only quickly lose track of home base and its inherent divinity, but also soon deny any trace of that quality in yourselves. That you can cycle through the physical and astral worlds chasing your tail, as the saying goes, is a recognised and inherent risk. In fact it was built into the design from the

> beginning. You are free to traverse the worlds of form for as long as your illusion sustains your desire to penetrate it.
>
> We are content to wait while you become caught in the attractive traps of honour, pride and achievement; of religious devotion and tribal loyalty. We are content because we have so much else to focus on, so many divine sparks ensouling forms of one type or another, that even a large group being 'lost' in the folds of illusion for centuries can easily be coped with. Lost in hell, lost on earth, lost in heaven, it's all the same to us. We're interested in how you cope, your strategies and how you develop them.

So can we agree with this suggestion that not only is repeatedly cycling through our earth system a possibility, but also it's no big problem if we do? After all we saw in chapter 7 that the ultimate purpose of all consciousness is simply to gain experience, so such recycling definitely adds to our supersoul's databanks. To answer this question I would suggest we need to ask another: is it the earth or the astral planes that provide the better quality of experience when it comes to consciousness expansion?

We partially addressed this question in the Preface but, to recap, modern reincarnation material holds that earth is one of the hardest 'proving grounds' around, and that the afterlife planes are too replete with love and balance to be able to provide any possibility of progression. Yet we've quite clearly seen that this is a nonsense. Indeed Panchadasi suggests that 'on the astral there is accomplished as much in the direction of improvement and progress as would be possible in only quite a number of earth lives'.[49] This includes life reviews, introspection, balancing and the development of emotional equilibrium, and the move towards a more universally loving, selfless attitude – and we now know that all this *doesn't* just happen automatically when we transition into the mid astral. What is more, of course, there are then the exponentially greater possibilities for expansion that await in the higher planes, as we'll see in Part 5.

To reinforce the argument, Jane Sherwood's EK makes a similar assertion to Panchadasi:[50] 'These planes of being are really to be thought of as the true home of the human race. The earth, in spite of its importance as a preliminary training for another great cycle of living, is a kind of exile. Here with us is the bulk of living experience both in numbers and time.' It seems, therefore, that in fact the challenges of the earth plane only scratch the surface of the almost limitless opportunities for experience, progression and expansion that await in higher, less restricted planes.

So are all those who *do* reincarnate merely 'blind repeaters' – that is, souls drawn back into earthly incarnation by their attachment to its karmic pains and pleasures, with no real direction and purpose? Or might they actually be planning their next lives too? Modern reincarnation material suggests that we ourselves plan each life in advance while in spirit form, and set the challenges we'll face – particularly those whose lessons we haven't yet properly learned – because by repeated incarnation into different types of lives we 'learn' and 'grow'. This is a hugely attractive idea, not least because it seems to explain so much of our apparent suffering – and reassures us that it isn't just random.

But if the whole traditional model is fundamentally wrong, as I now believe the evidence suggests, then those who champion it – as I myself used to under my schema of Rational Spirituality – are misleading people in three important ways. First, as we've just seen, it may well be that growth and expansion is achieved far more in the afterlife than in the earthly plane. Second, instead of getting people to take full responsibility for their lives, they're allowing them to act as victims by blaming their life plans for adverse circumstances they've actually *attracted*. Third, they're helping to condemn people to trapping themselves on the reincarnatory wheel by setting a whole new set of expectations as to what they'll experience in the afterlife.

Of course the basic idea of reincarnation has been around for millennia, but at least previously it was usually tied up with the notion of waking up from blind repetition so as to *escape* from its karmic bonds. Whereas the unfortunate turn that the new, life-planning model has taken is that it actively *encourages* people to indulge themselves in what may well prove to be the entirely misguided illusion of the desirability of repeated incarnation. Moreover, given the tens of thousands of people who've been attracted to this model in the last half century, it would be no great surprise if they have, by their collective expectations, managed to create special areas in which they *do* plan their next lives before they return. But as yet we have little experiential confirmation of this from OOB explorers, while most of our channelled sources were writing before this model became widespread.

To sum all this up, let's imagine the sort of instructions our supersoul might give us as it projects us into the earth plane:

> I want you to enjoy yourself in the game as much as you can. You will forget me as the real you for a while. So your aim is to remember who you really are as early as possible, which will either be in the earth plane or in one of the various planes of consciousness – or levels of the game – that you'll encounter after you pass on. But beware! The illusions of the game are extremely strong. If you become too addicted they'll suck you in and you'll keep thinking you have to return in order to grow. I am telling you now, that is *not* your prime purpose. I want you just to discover and enjoy your vast creative powers – and the best way to do that is by progressing back up through the various planes.

So becoming trapped in the reincarnation cycle can be literally compared to someone who has become hooked on a particular computer game that can potentially be played ad infinitum. They keep playing it again and again, each time looking to do whatever they need to do to *progress* to the next level, and it literally becomes their whole existence. Apart from grabbing a bit of food and sleep between sessions, they engage in and think of nothing else but the game. The world outside of it ceases to exist for them, except perhaps for an occasional intuition that what they're doing is none too healthy. This intuition will be ignored at first but gradually, as time wears on, it will become stronger and stronger – until it can no longer be overlooked. Then, finally, they'll turn the computer off and remember there's a whole other life out there, just waiting for them to enjoy it.

26

CONCLUSION

Just as in Part 3 we have seen a remarkable and impressive consistency in our various sources' reports of the mid astral planes, and of the type of existence we can look forward to there. The message again is that the more we prepare, the sooner we'll acclimatise and the more enjoyable the experience will be. So, apart from attempting to build up spiritual capital while in human form by kind and loving actions and attitudes, as discussed in chapter 20, is there anything else we can do to prepare ourselves?

VISITING THE ASTRAL DURING SLEEP

Journeying OOB to the astral while asleep seems to be something that many humans do, and it appears it prepares us for the afterlife in terms of developing our astral body and of being ready for astral conditions generally. Yet we know that not *all* humans do this, because we've seen there are some departed spirits whose astral body is extremely poorly developed when they arrive in the afterlife planes. Why is this? The answer provided by our sources is that humans who don't build up their spiritual natures on earth effectively just 'sleep through' any nocturnal opportunities for astral development. Having said that many of us will have woken up from a dream and *known* we were with people with whom we were acquainted, or in a place we recognised – even if we don't always remember the details unless we make a specific and immediate effort at recall. Moreover, while the people we meet can sometimes be departed friends or family, at other times we don't know them from our earthly lives at all.

Giving us their perspective on this issue as departed spirits here are Julia Ames, David Hatch, Robert Benson, Jane Sherwood's EK and Philip Gilbert:

> Sometimes the soul is so immersed in matter, it is so preoccupied with the affairs of the world, that even when sleep liberates the higher soul it sees nothing of us. Mostly, however, we can see... and communicate freely with the spirits of our living friends. But they seldom can communicate their impressions to the physical consciousness.[1]

> I have met a very interesting man... He is a lover who for ten years waited here for his love to come to him. They said on earth that he was dead, and they urged her to love another; but she could not forget him, for every night he met her soul in dreams, every night she came out to him here, and sometimes she could recall on waking all that he had said to her in sleep.[2]

> You must know that when the physical body sleeps, the spirit body temporarily withdraws from it, while still remaining connected to it by a magnetic cord. This cord is the veritable lifeline between the spirit body and the earth body. The spirit thus situated will either remain in the vicinity of the earth body, or it will gravitate to that sphere which its earthly life, so far, has entitled it to enter. The spirit body will thus spend part of the lifetime of the earthly body in spirit lands. And it is upon these visits that one meets relatives and friends who have passed on before, and it is similarly upon these visits that parents can meet their children, and thus watch their growth. There must, however, be a sufficient bond of attachment... or else this law will not come into operation.[3]

> You only crave for sleep so that your astral bodies may be set free for refreshment in our living air. They become exhausted by their interaction with the clumsy physical matter of your body, and so must be released regularly into what is really their native atmosphere.[4]

> People who are already advancing on earth find in sleep that they can get away from earth conditions and travel, so when they finally come over they soon drop into their new life.[5]

By contrast John reports that, as a spirit accompanied by his mother, he finds himself walking through a doorway in a wall that he recognises from his former earthly dreams:[6] 'The memories came flooding back. Yes, I had spent a third of my earth life in these surroundings! Here I had spent my truly waking moments whilst my earth body slept. Here I had found solace as a child, comfort as a young man, rest and peace as a soldier.' His mother tells him that he spent time with his guides and others in this environment while he was still incarnate, then adds: 'There are many places similar to this where almost all the people living on earth spend time.' Later he refers to going back to this 'point of recollection' himself while in spirit to in turn meet others who are still incarnate:[7] 'Many an old friend I met there, and thus I was able to keep abreast with all that was taking place upon earth.' Elsewhere he explains why this isn't a universal human phenomenon:[8]

> I should mention that not all earth people come to this world at night. Some remain very close to their bodies, so close in fact that they rarely leave them. Others do move a short distance but only upon the earth plane, while there are some who go only to the lower regions of this higher world. But those who are earnestly searching for the truth, who really love, and wish to rise spiritually above the conditions in which they live, come here regularly to the meeting places.

From an OOB perspective, modern pioneers such as William Buhlman, Waldo Vieira, Jurgen Ziewe and Robert Bruce all briefly mention that they encounter sleeping astral visitors on their journeys.[9] But some of their forerunners tend to provide further details. Charles Leadbeater, for example, disagrees with the majority of our channelled sources by claiming that most people *don't* use their opportunities for astral development during sleep:[10]

> In deep slumber the higher principles in their astral vehicle almost invariably withdraw from the body, and hover in its immediate neighbourhood, though in quite undeveloped persons they are practically almost as much asleep as the body is. In some cases, however, this astral vehicle is less lethargic, and floats dreamily about on the various astral currents, occasionally recognising other people in a similar condition, and meeting with experiences of all sorts, pleasant and unpleasant, the memory of which, hopelessly confused and often travestied into a grotesque caricature of what really happened, will cause the man to think next morning what a remarkable dream he has had. All cultured people have at the present time their astral senses very fairly developed so that, if they were sufficiently aroused to examine the realities which surround them during sleep, they would be able to observe them and learn much from them. But, in the vast majority of cases, they are not so aroused, and they spend most of their nights in a kind of brown study, pondering deeply over whatever thought may have been uppermost in their minds when they fell asleep. They have the astral faculties, but they scarcely use them.

Swami Panchadasi meanwhile concentrates on the activities of the committed 'occultist':[11]

> Many persons are able to travel in the astral body during ordinary sleep, but usually have no recollection of the same upon reawakening. The occultist on the other hand travels consciously and with a purpose, and always is wide-awake on such journeys. He is as much at home on the astral plane as on the physical one.

By contrast Peter Richelieu discusses premonitions received by sleeping astral visitors:[12]

> Whilst our physical bodies sleep, we function at the astral level in our astral bodies and there meet friends and relations who have died... In many ways it is a pity so few people remember what they do at night; if they did, they would be much less troubled about the state called death... I can now understand,

> though, why so many people have a feeling before bad news is received... It is because they have been told about it on the astral plane, and the following morning some slight remembrance of this has been brought back into the waking consciousness of the individual.

All of this raises the fascinating possibility of whether some of us are actually living a 'double life' on earth and in the astral. In chapter 24 we saw that Monroe Institute participants are encouraged to develop homes therein, but these aren't usually replicas of their earthly homes. Yet Frederick Sculthorp not only has a full astral replica of his home, but also of his shop:[13]

> It is peopled by those who have not long been in spirit... They have found their feet and are settled for the time being. My shop in spirit is not a replica of the one on earth as it is different and larger, but it contains the same sort of goods, such as books, stationery and greeting cards. At times there would be two or three young lady assistants and these I know as spirit acquaintances, but I did not know them on earth. No money is given for goods and one is glad to give a service.

More than this, though, he talks about regularly riding his motorbike and driving his car in spirit form – each the exact same model as he has in his earth life.[14] Indeed he provides pages of anecdotes about his 'other life'. Now, we saw in chapter 21 that these experiences clearly occur in an astral rather than a parallel-earth environment, not least because he regularly meets deceased family members during them. But he doesn't make it entirely clear whether he believes this to be a *full-on*, parallel, astral life, or if his astral counterpart is only operating when he's OOB.[15]

PRACTICAL ADVICE

Picking up from the foregoing, if we want to try and prepare as much as possible for the afterlife then there's a very obvious thing we can all do. Every night we should be setting the *intention* to have interesting and expansive experiences in the astral while asleep, and to be able to remember as much as possible of them when we awake. Intention is king here as in so many things – and it needs no elaborate rituals, just sincere desire. This leads us into the whole topic of 'lucid dreaming', in which the person 'wakes up' and is able to exercise some control over what happens. It seems likely that most of these experiences occur in the astral planes and, while some people dream lucidly more easily than others, many books have been written that provide recommended techniques.[16] This is, moreover, one way to work towards having conscious OOB experiences.

The other piece of practical advice is something that needs to be carried with us into afterlife awareness. It is, of course, that we should always be looking to progress, and thereby to expand our consciousness. This means not only avoiding the trap of getting caught in any sort of reincarnation cycle, but also making sure that the manifest charms of the myriad heaven worlds in the mid astral don't ensnare us for too long either. One of TE Lawrence's friends sums this up well:[17] 'Even paradise may not be enjoyed for too long lest it thwart one's proper growth.' Similarly Lawrence himself:[18] 'This notion of progress from plane to plane, as development justifies it, is common knowledge here.' Elsewhere he provides us with a wonderful message with which to close this part of the book:[19]

> If you can think of your most inspired moments – all too brief and infrequent in earthly experience – and imagine a life where this is the normal standard of living experience, you will have a faint idea of what the future holds for you. It is obvious that the capacity to know, feel and understand in this scale of intensity has to be attained by degrees and that, if it came before the cleansing process had at least been begun, it would be too keen an agony to bear.
>
> Even then our scale of intensity is weak compared to that of the higher planes. I suppose if you want to put it into pseudo-scientific terms you will explain it as world upon world, each of a higher system of vibration than its predecessor, but this really conveys very little. I want to put it in terms of actual living and

this is not easy. Perhaps it is a wasted effort since every one sooner or later will experience it for himself. But if this journal has a specific message it is an attempt to convey something of the quality of our living – its joy and beauty and fullness of life beyond any human comprehension.

PART FIVE

PLANES OF LEARNING, PROGRESSION & INTEGRATION

There is nothing more deadly than nirvana. At least your Christian concepts give you some twilight hopes of a stifling and boring paradise, where your individuality can at least express itself. But nirvana extends no such comfort. Instead it offers you the annihilation of your personality, in a bliss that destroys the integrity of your being. Run from such bliss!

Seth, 'The Nature of Personal Reality'

27

THE UPPER ASTRAL PLANES

In turning to these more refined planes, the key distinction I have attempted to make is between the relative stasis and earth-focus that generally characterises the mid astral, with the more progressive, expansive environment and activities that characterise the upper astral and beyond. To put it another way, time in the mid astral tends to be spent therapeutically recovering from earthly life, and in indulging in greater or lesser forms of recreational and belief-based illusions. Although there's an element of progression, broadly speaking this only returns a departed spirit to some form of equilibrium from which their consciousness can then truly start to expand. Having said that, it seems to me that in practice there's almost certainly no clear demarcation between the upper and mid astral planes, meaning departed spirits can be starting on the path of expansion while still enjoying some degree of recreation. After all, in any environment, 'all work and no play makes Jack a dull boy' as the saying goes.

Before we embark on this leg of the journey, we've already seen in Part 4 that trying to put various astral experiences and conditions into words that the human mind can understand is fraught with difficulty, because often they don't really have a human counterpart. This becomes increasingly the case as our sources rise up through the planes, and we can only admire their ingenuity as they take on what must sometimes seem an impossible and hugely frustrating task.

COMMUNICATING BY THOUGHT-FORM

One of the first things that stands out about descriptions of existence in the higher planes is that knowledge retention, reasoning and conceptual understanding all seem to be considerably expanded. For example, Robert Benson describes the new, unfailing nature of memory:[1]

> Of course, when we are in the spirit world our memories are persistently retentive. When we follow a course of study in any subject whatsoever, we shall find that we learn easily and quickly because we are freed from the limitations that the physical body imposes upon the mind. If we are acquiring knowledge we shall retain that knowledge without fail... Our minds have unlimited resources for intellectual expansion and improvement, however backward we may be when we come into the spirit world. And our intellectual progression will advance surely and steadily, according to our wish for it.

Meanwhile TE Lawrence indicates just how speeded up his reasoning has become, along with how all-encompassing and interconnected is his understanding of any new concept:[2]

> I wish I could convey something of the flame-like lucidity of our process of reasoning. The emotional grasp of an impression is followed by an immediate awareness of the essential being of a thing, and further thinking about it is a process of apprehending depth upon depth of meaning dwelling in the thing itself, and in its relations with its environment. I cannot tell you how slow, formal and dead your processes of reasoning appear to us. In a flash we have made the whole journey to a conclusion which it may take you hours of painful thought to reach, and which you will only cover in a superficial manner, since what escapes in your reasoning is the precious element of meaning – significance. This for us becomes heightened to a degree I cannot convey in words.

More generally, though, the transfer of information to expand consciousness in the higher planes seems to involve much more than the mere telepathy discussed in chapter 22. For example, George Vale Owen's mother Emma briefly makes reference to 'messages arriving in visible form and not in words'.[3] Similarly Philip Gilbert attends a conference where a spirit of light lectures the audience about humanity's possible future:[4] 'He did not speak in sound exactly... [but] in a series of vivid image pictures, formed in his aura, which floated over the audience, blending into our united auras, which seemed to spear-point themselves into a vast receiving station.' This seems to convey some sort of energetic process akin to the modern-day 'downloading' of information from one computer to another.

Indeed, coming right up-to-date, this is the very word that Erik Medhus uses:[5] 'It's not a conversation of words and sentences or a lecture. Instead the communication and education is sent on many levels: to my head, to my heart, to my entire energetic body. It's like an instant spirit-to-spirit download, and all the information gets transferred directly and completely.' Similarly Billy Cohen, discussing his communication with his guide:[6] 'We use telepathy to hear each other's thoughts. They aren't thoughts, really. They are much more wonderful than thoughts. These better-than-thoughts are like symphonies so gorgeous you cannot even imagine them.'

Turning to NDEs, it's not uncommon for these to involve a similar download of information. Betty Eadie's initial exchange with her Christ-guide seems to fall into this category:[7] 'His light now began to fill my mind, and my questions were answered even before I fully asked them. His light was knowledge. It had power to fill me with all truth... The answers were absolute and complete.' Similarly Eben Alexander describes being taught in 'the wordless, more than verbal way that all things are communicated in the worlds above this one', before adding: 'To experience thinking outside the brain is to enter a world of instantaneous connections that make ordinary thinking seem like some hopelessly sleepy and plodding event'.[8] The problem is that the subject can't always remember the information on their return because sometimes it covers advanced ideas their human brains simply can't take on board.

Perhaps the best example of all is Dannion Brinkley. After his life review in chapter 22 he's taken to a 'lecture hall' within a 'crystal city', where twelve beings of light direct 'boxes' at him one at a time, which the thirteenth finally reveals are all glimpses of future events on earth.[9] Not only does he retain the predictions downloaded to him via these boxes on his return to the earth plane, he also asserts that many of them subsequently came true.[10] In the meantime the beings of light also instruct him that he will need to create a series of 'therapy centres' for stress reduction, using sound and light techniques to create certain energy vibrations – which are probably similar to those described as being used to heal departed spirits in chapter 21. After his return to the earth plane he repeatedly revisits the crystal city while asleep and OOB to learn more about the technology he's to use. He also finds he has highly developed psychic powers – for example, just touching another person however briefly gives him instant, movie-like glimpses of key aspects of their life.[11]

More important for our current purposes is his general description of the knowledge-transfer process while in this learning environment: 'I had only to think a question to explore the essence of the answer. In a split second I understood how light works, the ways in which spirit is incorporated into the physical life, why it is possible for people to think and act in so many different ways. Ask and you shall perceive is the way I sum it up.'

Turning to our OOB pioneers, Frederick Sculthorp briefly remarks:[12] 'The effect upon me in these states is always the same. I seem to know more, or have greater access to knowledge.' Meanwhile Robert Monroe was clearly thinking of exactly this kind of instantaneous information download when, with his love of acronyms, he coined the term ROTE – which stands for 'related organised thought energy', and which he defines as:[13] 'A mental book or recording, complete with emotional and sensory patterns, transmitted from one mind to another.' Similarly Waldo Vieira:[14] 'We communicated through thought transmission without articulating any words. The consciousness, in this case, sends and receives complete ideas.'

HALLS OF LEARNING AND LIBRARIES

Moving now to various learning and educational experiences, these are often described as taking place in 'halls' or 'libraries'. For example, Franchezzo briefly mentions visiting a 'hall of lecture' where he listens to 'discourses delivered by advanced spirits from the higher spheres'.[15] Meanwhile two of Emily French and Edward Randall's communicants talk about the learning environment generally:[16]

> Our scientific researches and investigations are extended to all that pertains to the phenomena of universal truth; to all the wonders of the heavens and of the earth... The noble and sublime sciences of astronomy, chemistry and mathematics engage a considerable portion of our attention, and afford us an inexhaustible subject for study and reflection.
>
> It is a very active, pleasant life, and sometimes seems like a big university town or country, with busy students hurrying from lecture to lecture and class to class. All are congenial and light-hearted here.

Returning to Henry Lanchester's afterlife experiences, after his life review as reported in chapter 22 he goes to 'school' to learn more about his new, mid astral environment, before moving on to a college in what is more likely to be an upper astral 'university town'. Here he learns everything he can about the different planes, and how to communicate this information to incarnates still on earth – part of which involves finding out which people are most receptive.[17] Meanwhile a fourth entity who communicated via John Ward, 'JBP', describes various multi-library cities:[18]

> These libraries are on so vast a scale that they look almost like cities; there are many of them, of course, but each is divided

> into three sections. The first contains the forms of books which have ceased to exist. I mean by this, the actual volumes themselves... The second section is very different, for in it the books are not the forms of books made on earth but those created here. The best way in which I can describe them is to compare them with picture books. In short, they contain ideas in picture form, and can be read by us just as the thought-pictures of our friends can be understood by us... The third type are difficult to describe as books at all, for the picture idea has been carried out to its logical conclusion. The nearest thing to it on earth is the modern picture palace. Imagine a large room; at one end is a kind of stage, on which perform what at first sight appear to be real men and women. These are thought-forms, strongly visualised by the committee of scholars in charge of the room. Thus an episode in history will be enacted in all its detail before our eyes.

Similarly, if more briefly, David Hatch:[19] 'We entered a vast building like a library, and I caught my breath in wonder. It was not the architecture of the building which struck me, but the quantities of books and records. There must have been millions of them.' Meanwhile Vale Owen's mother Emma describes visiting a realm where 'many occupations are followed and studies pursued... and different branches of science are carried on'.[20] But as so often it's Benson who provides some of the most fascinating and eloquent descriptions of these learning environments. He begins with a brief, general review of a 'city of learning':[21]

> This city was devoted to the pursuit of learning, to the study and practice of the arts, and to the pleasures of all in this realm. It was exclusive to none, but free for all to enjoy with equal right. Here it was possible to carry on so many of those pleasant and fruitful occupations that had been commenced on the earth plane. Here, too, many souls could indulge in some agreeable diversion which had been denied them, for a variety of reasons, whilst they were incarnate.

He then moves on to a more detailed description of a 'hall of literature', where he's shown around by his guide Edwin:[22]

> It contained every work worthy of the name... Edwin led us into one spacious apartment which contained the histories of all the nations upon the earth plane. To anyone who has knowledge of earthly history, the volumes with which the shelves of this section of the great library were filled would prove illuminating. The reader would be able to gain, for the first time, the truth about the history of his country. Every word contained in these books was the literal truth. Concealment is impossible, because nothing but the truth can enter these realms... But I found that side-by-side with the statements of pure fact of every act by persons of historical note... was the blunt naked truth of each and every motive governing or underlying their numerous acts – the truth beyond disputation. Many such motives were elevated [but] many, many of them were bitterly base; many were misconstrued, many distorted...
>
> We passed through many other rooms where volumes upon every subject imaginable were at the disposal of all who wished to study them. And perhaps one of the most important subjects is that which has been called by some truly enlightened soul 'psychic science' – for science it is. I was astonished by the wealth of literature under this heading. Upon the shelves were books denying the existence of a spirit world... Many of the authors of them have since had the opportunity of looking again at their own works – but with very different feelings! They had become, in themselves, living witnesses against the contents of their own books.

This concept of the true underlying motives of all historical characters being exposed to full view is entirely consistent with the way the life review, and astral communication in general, works. Benson then moves on to a description of a 'hall of science':[23]

> Every field of scientific and engineering investigation, study, and discovery was covered, and here were to be seen so many of those men whose names have become household words and who, since passing into spirit, have continued their life's work with their fellow scientists with the full and immense resources of the spirit world at their command. Here they can solve those mysteries that baffled them when they were on earth. There is

> no longer any such thing as personal rivalry. Reputations have no more to be made, and the many material handicaps are abandoned for ever. It follows that where such a gathering of savants can exist, together with their unlimited resources, the results must be correspondingly great.

Elsewhere he provides an insight into how teachers in the various halls of learning are often making return visits from the higher realms that are their natural habitat:[24]

> Many of the people attached to the halls of learning have been there a great number of years as you reckon time. So devoted are they to their work that although they have progressed and virtually belong to a higher sphere, they prefer to remain where they are for some considerable period yet. They will retire from time to time to their own realm, and then return to take up their labours anew. The moment will eventually arrive when they will relinquish their position altogether to reside permanently in their own sphere, and then others equally capable will take their place.

By comparison Jane Sherwood's EK describes how groups of departed spirits come together in mutual interest and attraction in a more expansive environment than the mid astral:[25]

> Groups are formed more for the purposes of special interests and occupations than for national reasons, and thus we get aggregates of talent of a high level of attainment which cut across all artificial boundaries of nation and class. Here are brotherhoods of mutual interests having a rich and satisfying communal life... A social order emerges which brings satisfaction to all its members and enables each to arrive at full self-development.

Meanwhile to return to Lawrence's afterlife experiences, in chapter 23 we read about his sense that he must answer his inner 'call to action' rather than remain solitary. This is achieved when it occurs to him that he used to have a huge love of books and of the making of books in his earthly life, so he sets off to see if he can find astral activity of this nature.[26] This leads him to 'an ancient city where are seats of learning – not an exact replica of my own Oxford, but a university town of widely-spaced buildings of noble aspect'. Here he's drawn to meet Thomas, a man of similar interests:

> He is a quiet, studious soul but at the mention of book-making he was transformed. He led me away to his workshop and press and here are all the familiar tools of his art, only of better make and adapted to finer ends than any I have had the joy of handling before. We soon were deep in the technicalities of his craft and I have been welcomed as a learner and helper. Books are still needed, books are still being written and read and studied, but they are not being turned out in the senseless and shoddy profusion of earth. Such books as are being produced – fruits of wit, wisdom, love and beauty – are being handled with a care and skill of craftsmanship which delight me...
>
> In this cool, green-shaded workroom I am learning many new arts of engraving, printing and tooling and, in the pleasure of the hand and the exultation of seeing that the work is good, I am finding full satisfaction. My mind keeps pace with my hands in profitable thinking and I seem at last to have found a recipe for peace. I am also finding the fulfilment of worthy companionship. These men and women at the university are sometimes my peers but more often my superiors, and among us the pure springs of happy activity overflow in fun and sparkling humour. I begin to savour a fullness of life I have never attained before.

This sense of finding fulfilment he could never attain in his human life, and of actually fabricating books, seems to hark back to the earthly preoccupations of the mid astral. Yet it seems clear that the atmosphere in which he's operating is a progressive one. Here, for example, he describes meeting a new friend called Ingram who is studying metaphysics:[27]

> He is reading the higher philosophy which here takes the place of that studied on earth, for naturally the possession of added knowledge makes radical changes in the premises upon which knowledge is built. The mere fact of survival establishes a new

> basis of fact and negates all the materialistic hypotheses about which there is such endless and futile argument on earth. So a whole new edifice of knowledge has to be built not only in philosophy but also in science...
>
> So a lifetime of adventure of the mind is opened up for us with new horizons and inexhaustible possibilities. My new friend is absorbed in studies which include much that would be scorned as moonshine and metaphysics on earth, but which to us with our new terms of reference is inescapable reality. I am ruefully amused at the inhibitions of thought and imagination I brought with me from earth. Most of these I have had to shed. Having over-passed these limits I am no longer ready with scorn for speculative thought. Ingram's researches, therefore, fascinate me and I am beginning to share his interests.

Yet the following extract shows how Lawrence's learning and progression is often interspersed with more recreational interludes:[28]

> Since I found the university... my life has alternated between active work with Thomas on book production, occasional spells of more academic work and times when I have savoured the luxury of solitude in my cottage. This has made for me a well-balanced life, harmonising the main trends of my nature. There is no coercion here and no tyranny of time, so when one kind of life palls one can freely exchange it for another. There is a constant coming and going at the university and study, recreation and fellowship all play their parts in its life, but students frequently go off for spells of other kinds of experience and return when they are ready.

Meanwhile Frances Banks reports on a friend who is part of an astral group of doctors led by a 'radiant' former physician.[29] Elsewhere she too visits various 'halls of learning':

> I realised that I was in a university yet it was much more than that, for there were halls of learning, and a pervading atmosphere of thought which thrilled my soul and satisfied a deep yearning in me... Here there were many souls, groups of students, sometimes surrounding one who appeared to be a

> teacher, intent upon his discourse, or composed in deep meditation with him; sometimes in clusters eagerly discussing together; and sometimes a student alone and apart in contemplation.

She also describes how she has become a humble, new member of a group devoted to the study of mysticism, but mentions there are also groups specialising in 'science, human medicine and healing, evolutionary world patterns' and various other branches of study.[30] Eventually she ends up in a new home on a beautiful estate that she shares with the other members of her group.

In the same vein Arthur Ford describes what appears to be a relatively high-level 'temple of wisdom':[31]

> It has existed in its present form since the beginning of time... Here those souls who are in a proper state of advancement congregate each according to his own needs... The wisdom is bottomless and pours forth in the amount for which the soul thirsts at the moment... The temple of wisdom is not a place, of course, but a state of mind; for it is a consciousness of all the beauty of thought and awareness. We each no doubt see it in different lights... At the temple we are exposed to the greatest minds in the philosophic field... We go to the temple for instruction in the so-called secrets of the universe...
>
> Here in the temple of wisdom Socrates has sat, and Kant and Jung, and many of those so highly respected in the earth plane. Here they are also towering figures of greater or lesser degree. Some great minds in the temple were never recognised as such on earth, but grew through the simplicity of their beliefs into great masters who serve well in the temple here... This is an exciting world of growth and development; what a shabby thing it is for some souls to waste this God-given opportunity to feast our minds at the feet of such masters, who have lived on various planes but, because of their goodness, return... to help us grow.

Similarly, and much more recently, here is Medhus again showing the consistency of these reports across time:[32]

> Imagine a city of light that has these beautiful, ornate spires reaching to the sky. The most beautiful buildings on earth look really unimpressive in comparison. Heaven's buildings look almost crystalline... made of pure light. They're for specific activities like learning, listening to music, holding meetings, problem solving and a hell of a lot more. There are a lot of lecture halls where groups of spirits learn all sorts of things, like how to travel to different dimensions, how to manifest things, and how to become effective spirit guides, to name a few. We have libraries too, and they're amazing! They have books filled with so much wisdom it's unreal – books where I can pretty much learn about anything and everything in the universe... All knowledge can be found in these books, and all I have to do is merge with the energy of the book to get its information.

Turning to NDEs, one element of Eadie's experience is relevant here:[33]

> I was taken to another large room similar to a library. As I looked around it seemed to be a repository of knowledge, but I couldn't see any books. Then I noticed ideas coming into my mind... knowledge filling me on topics I had not thought about for some time – or in some cases not at all. Then I realised this was a library of the mind. By simply reflecting on a topic, as I had earlier in Christ's presence, all knowledge on that topic came to me.

Meanwhile George Ritchie is taken to an area where 'enormous buildings stand in a beautiful, sunny park'.[34] In some scientific experiments are being conducted, while another forms a huge library where 'rooms are lined floor to ceiling with documents on parchment, clay, leather, metal and paper', containing what he senses are 'all the important books of the universe'.

From an OOB perspective, Charles Leadbeater describes the freedom departed spirits have to study in whatever way they choose:[35]

> Realise the condition of the man when all necessity for this grinding toil is over... Then for the first time since earliest

> childhood that man is free to do precisely what he likes, and can devote his whole time to whatever may be his chosen occupation... If his fancy turns towards science or history, the libraries and the laboratories of the world are at his disposal, and his comprehension of processes in chemistry and biology would be far fuller than ever before, for now he could see the inner as well as the outer workings, and many of the causes as well as the effects. And... there is the wonderful additional delight that no fatigue is possible.

Swami Panchadasi is, in the meantime, brief:[36] 'On the highest sub-planes of the astral we find many regions inhabited by the philosophers, scientists, metaphysicians and higher theologians of the race... There are many schools of philosophy and metaphysics here.' As is Oliver Fox who, on by far the most interesting of his journeys, finds himself in a 'vast and lovely garden' where he 'joins a stream of people, robed in various colours, and enters a large lecture hall or temple'.[37] Unfortunately, though, the 'priest' or 'teacher' tells him he doesn't belong there, and that's enough to shock him back into his body. By contrast Caroline Larsen provides a more detailed description of visiting a 'hall of learning' with her anonymous guide:[38]

> As we descended... my eyes were almost blinded by the glory of the spectacle. From every direction thronged troops of spirits, apparently converging on a great building of amazing size, beauty and splendour. Each spirit seemed enveloped in a ball of flaming, white light... The scene was of marvellous beauty and indescribable brilliance. Almost at once my guide brought me to the lines of the moving procession and soon, with the rest, I entered the majestic hall toward which the spirits were thronging.
>
> It was an enormous auditorium, arranged in a semi-circle about a raised platform... The faces [of the assemblage] were vivid with intelligence and power, and glowing with sympathy, love and understanding. For these spirits had not only triumphed in self-mastery; they had attained wisdom and a knowledge of mysteries of which I could only faintly guess... A

> hush now fell on the congregation as five men in garments more shining than any I had yet seen ascended the platform and in turn began to speak.

Unfortunately she then adds: 'I could understand nothing, it exceeded my powers.' Sculthorp only briefly refers to 'museums and exhibitions', and a library containing 'beautifully bound books' that he senses contain 'spirit truth'.[39] Similarly brief is one of Rosalind McKnight's spirit friends, who refers to 'great halls of learning where all types of courses are offered'.[40] But Bruce Moen provides a more contemporary and detailed description of a visit to what the Monroe Institute calls the 'education centre':[41]

> Moments later I was standing in what looked like a huge library. Shelves of books lined the walls along both sides of the long, wide corridor where I was standing... They went up vertically at least twenty feet and then faded out into a kind of fog... The corridor extended in front of me as far as I could see. There had to be hundreds upon hundreds of thousands of books that I could just see from where I was standing.

Next, an assistant shows him how to work what he refers to as a 'holodesk', by placing a 'book' into a large slot in the side and selecting the viewing speed from the screen – the settings being 'savour, informational, relaxed or instant'. The contents then get played out as a '3D hologram'. He is also shown a 'holodeck', which is similar except the participant enters the story, but Moen doesn't try this out. Gordon Phinn's guide Henry is equally forthcoming:[42] 'Temples of wisdom are dotted around the spheres. There are many types of these structures, and each one is keyed to the level of enlightenment enjoyed by the local inhabitants. Architecturally they come in all shapes and forms, from very ancient to very modern. There are lectures, study groups, libraries and gardens for contemplation... Most people can't believe it when they first visit. For lifetime library users it's a dream come true. All of human history lies waiting for your lackadaisical perusal.'

To close this section, during one visit to a more 'space-age' setting Jurgen Ziewe encounters a 'vast information centre' that he perceives as being made up of huge numbers of ovoid structures:[43]

> Then, ahead, I saw a glow surrounding huge, organic, egg-shaped structures, growing out of the ground and resting on an ornate island inside a lagoon, like the nesting ground of a giant dragon. The island was covered with different clusters of spheres around a larger centre, hundreds of domes of different shapes, colours and designs, yet all belonging together, harmonising and complementing each other. This too was a city, a vast information centre. Each large dome, the smallest being at least hundreds of meters in height, formed a vestibule of knowledge and was frequented by swirling lights. Each part of the city was connected by enormous arched tunnels.
>
> I was amazed that I could see the inside and the outside simultaneously, as well as being able to connect instantly with the minds that populated this living structure, getting an intimate understanding of why they were here. Their commerce was knowledge, socialising, benefiting from each other's experience and presence, and merging consciousness, souls and minds... I discovered that each dome constituted a different point of interest which attracted like-minded people. The beauty of all this was the incredible diversity and complexity.

ARTISTIC ENDEAVOURS

We turn now to more artistic pursuits involving music, art and literature, although obviously there's a huge overlap with those described in the last section – and indeed with some of the reports covered in Part 4.

To start us off, Vale Owen's mother Emma describes visiting an area where there are many 'halls of music' adorned with towers:[44] 'Those who live there are engaged in the study of music and its combinations and effects, not only as to what you know as sound, but also in other connections.' She then elaborates by describing an actual concert:

> We were taken to an island in the midst of the lake and there, in a beautiful scene of trees and grass and flowers and terraces and arbours of trees and little nooks and seats of stone or wood, we heard the festival. First there came a chord, long and sustained, growing louder and louder, until it seemed to invade the whole landscape and waterscape and every leaf of every tree. It was the key given to the musicians on the various towers. It died into silence and all seemed very still. Then, gradually, we heard the orchestra. It came from many towers, but we could not tell any single contribution apart. It was perfect harmony, and the balance of tone was exquisite.
>
> Then the singers took up their part. It is of no use for me to try to describe this music of the heavenly spheres in earth language, but I may perhaps be able to give you some idea of the effect. Briefly, it made everything... not only more beautiful but lovely too... All our faces took on a more lovely hue and expression, the trees became deeper in colour, and the atmosphere gradually grew into a vapour of tints like a rainbow... The water reflected the rainbow tints, and our clothing also became intensified in colour.

Later she adds: 'Music enters into so many phases of our life here and, indeed, all seems music in these spheres of light – music and blended colour and beauty, all breathing love among all.' Similarly his guide Zabdiel talks about how light and music 'are often made to go hand-in-hand, blended in condition and effect'.[45] Meanwhile Ward describes visiting an art gallery with Lanchester during a trance vision:[46]

> 'Look at the pictures. These are ideas which were too exalted to be impressed upon any artist upon earth and are therefore here.' I then began to look at the pictures. I perceived that not only were they far more beautiful than anything I had ever seen on earth, but they differed in many ways difficult to describe. The colours were both more brilliant and yet more harmonious – further, from them issued a kind of light... There were all kinds of subjects – landscapes, portraits, dramatic pieces, etc. – but the most interesting and best works were

> those dealing with what, for lack of a better word, I will call the highest emotions. Thus there was one entitled 'The Divine Love'. It depicted a marvellous spirit form, strong, yet gentle, just, yet merciful. It seemed to be watching over a multitude of human beings... The truly marvellous thing about the whole picture was the expression on the face of the great spirit, and an atmosphere of 'divine love' which it is impossible to describe.

Elsewhere he makes a brief reference to visiting a 'school of music' in which 'magnificent symphonies' are being composed and played.[47] But again it's Benson who dominates this section with his supremely vivid reports. These commence with his report of a visit to a 'hall of painting' with his guide Edwin and friend Ruth, in which we find similarities with Ward's attempts to describe the difference between earthly and astral art.[48]

> The first hall that Edwin took us into was concerned with the art of painting. This hall was of very great size and contained a long gallery, on the walls of which were hanging every great masterpiece known to man. They were arranged in such a way that every step of earthly progress could be followed in proper order, beginning with the earliest times and so continuing down to the present day. Every style of painting was represented, gathered from all points of the earth... There were many groups listening to the words of able teachers, who were demonstrating the various phases in the story of art as exemplified upon the walls...
>
> A number of these pictures I recognised as I had seen their 'originals' in the earth's galleries. Ruth and I were astonished when Edwin told us that what we had seen in those galleries were not the originals at all! We were now seeing the originals for the first time. What we had seen was an earthly counterpart, which was perishable from the usual causes... But here we were viewing the direct results of the thoughts of the painter, created in the etheric before he actually transferred those thoughts to his earthly canvas. It could be plainly observed, in many cases, where the earthly picture fell short of

that which the painter had in his mind. He had endeavoured to reproduce his exact conception, but through physical limitations this exact conception had eluded him. In some instances it had been the pigments that had been at fault when, in the early times, the artist had been unable to procure or evolve the particular shade of colour he wanted. But though he lacked physically, his mind had known precisely what he wished to do...

Another great point of dissimilarity – and the most important – was the fact that here all these pictures were alive. It is impossible to convey any idea of this paramount difference. These spirit pictures must be seen here to understand it. I can only just suggest an idea... The subject stood forth almost as though it were a model... The colours glowed with life, even among the very early works before much progress had been made...

In other parts of this same building were rooms wherein students of art could learn all that there is to be learnt. The joy of these students is great in their freedom from their earthly restrictions and bodily limitations. Here instruction is easy, and the acquisition and application of knowledge equally facile to those who wish to learn. Gone are all the struggles of the student in the surmounting of earthly difficulties both of the mind and of the hands, and progress towards proficiency is consequently smooth and rapid... Is there any wonder that artists within this hall... were enjoying the golden hours of their spiritual reward?

Subsequently Benson moves on to a description of a 'hall of music':[49]

Most of what I saw in this hall of music was new to me, and a great deal of it very technical. I have since added appreciably to my small knowledge, because I found that the greater the knowledge of music the more it helped one to understand so many things of the life here, where music plays so important a part... Most individuals have some latent, innate, musical sense and, by encouraging it here, so much the greater can be their joy... The hall of music followed the same broad system as the

> other halls of the arts. The library contained books dealing with music, as well as the scores of vast quantities of music that had been written on earth by composers who had now passed into spirit, or by those who were still upon the earth... As before the library provided a complete history of music from the very earliest times... Many apartments were set aside for students who can learn of music in every branch, from theory to practice, under teachers whose names are known the earth world over...
>
> In music, it can be said that the spirit world starts where the earth world leaves off. There are laws of music here which have no application to the earth whatever... Earthly ears are not attuned to music that is essentially of the spirit realms... The many types of musical instrument so familiar on earth were to be seen in the college of music, where students could be taught to play upon them. And here again, where dexterity of the hands is so essential the task of gaining proficiency is never arduous or wearisome, and it is, moreover, so much more rapid than upon the earth. As students acquire a mastery over their instrument they can join one of the many orchestras that exist here, or they can limit their performance to their many friends...
>
> We were extremely interested in the many instruments that have no counterpart upon the earth plane. They are, for the most part, specially adapted to the forms of music that are exclusive to the spirit world, and they are for that reason very much more elaborate... It is natural that this building should be possessed of a concert hall. This was a very large hall capable of seating comfortably many thousands. It was circular in shape, with seats rising in an unbroken tier from the floor.

But perhaps most splendid of all is his description of attending a concert where the fusion of music and art – referred to briefly by Vale Owen's communicants above – finds glorious expression. I make no apologies for the length of the following excerpt:

> At the rear of the hall was the great centre of concert performances. It consisted of a vast amphitheatre like a great bowl sunk beneath the level of the ground, but it was so large

that its real depth was not readily apparent... As a concert was due to start very shortly, we seated ourselves on the grass at some considerable distance from the actual amphitheatre. I wondered whether we should be able to hear very much so far away, but our friend assured us that we should... We were in a delightful spot, with the trees and flowers and pleasant people all about us... The orchestra was composed of some two hundred musicians, who were playing upon instruments that are well known to earth, so that I was able to appreciate what I heard. As soon as the music began I could hear a remarkable difference from what I had been accustomed to hear on the earth plane. The actual sounds made by the various instruments were easily recognisable as of old, but the quality of tone was immeasurably purer, and the balance and blend were perfect...

We noticed that the instant the music commenced a bright light seemed to rise up from the direction of the orchestra until it floated in a flat surface level with the topmost seats, where it remained as an iridescent cover to the whole amphitheatre. As the music proceeded, this broad sheet of light grew in strength and density, forming... a firm foundation for what was to follow... Presently, at equal spaces round the circumference of the theatre, four towers of light shot up into the sky in long tapering pinnacles of luminosity. They remained poised for a moment and then slowly descended, becoming broader in girth as they did so, until they assumed the outward appearance of four circular towers, each surmounted with a dome, perfectly proportioned. In the meanwhile the central area of light had thickened still more, and was beginning to rise slowly in the shape of an immense dome covering the whole theatre. This continued to ascend steadily until it seemed to reach a very much greater height than the four towers, while the most delicate colours were diffused throughout the whole of the etheric structure...

The musical sounds sent up by the orchestra were creating, up above their heads, this immense musical thought-form, and the shape and perfection of this form rested entirely upon the purity of the musical sounds, the purity of the harmonies, and a

> freedom from any pronounced dissonance... The music was still being played, and in response to it the whole colouring of the dome changed, first to one shade, then to another, and many times to a delicate blend of a number of shades according to the variation in theme or movement of the music. It is difficult to give any adequate idea of the beauty of this wonderful musical structure... The music at last came to a grand finale, and so ended. The rainbow colours continued to interweave themselves.

If this doesn't set the heart racing at the glories we can expect when we make the transition to the upper astral, I don't know what will. In any case Benson then goes on to describe how this fusion of music and art is deliberately manipulated by expert composers:

> The expert musician can plan his compositions by his knowledge of what forms the various harmonic and melodic sounds will produce. He can, in effect, build magnificent edifices upon his manuscript of music, knowing full-well exactly what the result will be when the music is played or sung. By careful adjustment of his themes and his harmonies, the length of the work, and its various marks of expression, he can build a majestic form as grand as a Gothic cathedral. This is, in itself, a delightful part of the music art in spirit, and it is regarded as musical architecture. The student will not only study music acoustically, but he will learn to build it architecturally, and the latter is one of the most absorbing and fascinating studies... In the spirit world all music is colour, and all colour is music. The one is never existent without the other... And the perfect combination of both sight and sound is perfect harmony.

In chapter 23 Medhus briefly described experiences akin to what on earth we call synesthesia, where multiple senses are simultaneously engaged – for example, sounds are also seen as colours. This excerpt surely shows that those people who experience it are privy to an advanced glimpse of the wonders of the afterlife. In any case, Benson finally turns his attention to the plays that are put on in the upper astral:[50]

> Each theatre of this realm is familiar to us by the type of play that is presented in it. The plays themselves are frequently vastly different from those that are customary upon the earth plane... We can see many problem plays where social questions of the earth plane are dealt with, but unlike the earth plane our plays will provide a solution to the particular problem – a solution which the earth is too blind to adopt. We can go to see comedies where, I do assure you, the laughter is invariably much more hearty and voluminous than is ever to be heard in a theatre of the earth plane. In the spirit world we can afford to laugh at much that we once, when incarnate, treated with deadly seriousness and earnestness!
>
> We have witnessed grand historical pageants showing the greater moments of a nation, and we have seen, too, history as it really was, and not as it is often so fancifully written about in history books! But surely the most impressive and, at the same time, interesting experience is to be present at one of these pageants where the original participants themselves re-enact the events with which they were concerned, first as the events were popularly thought to have occurred, and then as they actually took place. These representations are among the most widely attended here... In such pageants the coarser, depraved and debased incidents are omitted entirely, because they would be distasteful to the audience and, indeed, to all in this realm. Nor are we shown scenes which are, in the main... nothing but battle and bloodshed and violence.

Benson is a hard act to follow sometimes, but Banks mentions 'halls of music' generally before describing rather more briefly how she attends a 'festival of light and music' that bears at least a little comparison with his concert:[51]

> These festivals are accompanied... with music on a grander scale that anything that is performed on earth... The notes form and are trilled as though by some unseen performers... There is a swelling of harmony until a particular chord or note is reached and held... The note, when at last reached and sounded in full, is held and vibrated at a pitch of intensity which sweeps every soul into harmony. Then light breaks

> through into the assembly. Light surrounds us, lifts us, touches us, awakens us... One is singing and yet not singing, with one voice... One is singing with the whole organism... It is sound, harmony and light in one.

More recently Medhus observes:[52] 'The music here doesn't come close to what I was used to in my human life... It tunes our energetic bodies; it tunes the soul and touches right to the core of it, like a vibrating tuning fork inside you.'

Similarly, from an NDE perspective and picking up from the last section, during the 'park' element of his experience Ritchie describes entering a building where 'music of a complexity I could not begin to follow was being composed and performed', including 'complicated rhythms using tones not on any scale that I knew'.[53]

Turning now to OOB material here are Leadbeater, Panchadasi and Larsen, all providing consistent reports of artistic astral endeavours:

> Suppose that a man's greatest delight is in music; upon the astral plane he has the opportunity of listening to all the grandest music that earth can produce, and is even able under these new conditions to hear far more in it than before, since here other and fuller harmonies than our dull ears can grasp are now within his reach. The person whose delight is in art, who loves beauty in form and colour, has all the loveliness of this higher world before him from which to choose.[54]

> We see the artist busily at work, turning out wonderful masterpieces; also musicians creating great compositions, of which they had vainly dreamt while in earth life.[55]

> I was guided to a high structure of artistic architecture whose entire top, arranged like a platform, seated a huge orchestra composed of all varieties of instruments, some familiar to me and others strange... The music began and immediately I was held entranced by its sweeping majesty, and by its overwhelming emotional appeal. I could not endure it, perhaps because I was still of earth. Completely overcome, I had to be led away.[56]

Finally, during one of his excursions Peter Richelieu witnesses great painters and musicians demonstrating their gifts and attempting to teach others at the same time.[57] He reports that he 'cannot describe the glorious colours', before being taken to look round a huge 'academy of the arts', which is where he meets his former love.

LOVE AND SERVICE

In Parts 3 and 4 we've already talked at length about the work of rescuers and guides, many of whom would otherwise have progressed to the upper astral and beyond. We have also seen that a key factor in the restoration of equilibrium for many departed spirits is to want to serve their fellows in whatever way they can. But, broadly speaking, in order for them to be able to progress to the upper astral they need to reach the point where their *every* action is motivated not by selfishness and ego but by altruism and love.

To confirm this point here are the brief observations of two of French and Randall's communicants and John and, from an OOB perspective, Emanuel Swedenborg, Larsen, Gladys Leonard and Sculthorp:

> It is the privilege and duty of everyone to develop the spirit by study and helping others.

> This is a life of service. Self must be eliminated.[58]

> This is the sum total of life: that thought and action be ruled by love.[59]

> They are all caught up in a love of their work and tasks out of a love of service – no one out of selfishness or a love of profit... We may gather the magnitude of heaven's pleasure simply from the fact that for everyone there it is delightful to share their pleasure and bliss with someone else; and since everyone in the heavens is like this, we can see how immense heaven's pleasure is.[60]

> Not only were they dwelling in complete harmony; the dream of the altruist had been realised! Each lived for the other, since in that pure sphere the interests of all were one... Each gloried in the greater merit of his fellow.[61]

> The watchword there is service.[62]

> The vibrations of such places have a very pleasant effect on the sensitive spirit body, and to be with others of that plane is better still as they emit a feeling of great friendship. This radiation of friendliness is very sincere and noticeable... This continuously emitted friendship towards others can be interpreted as unselfishness and consideration for others in all ways. This sounds simple but it can mean a great deal... There are no sects, dogmas or denominations with their earthly trimmings that have led to so much division and bloodshed throughout history. It is all very simple. These people are doing what a few spiritual teachers down the ages have taught, and which translated means: 'Love one another.' We can imagine the improvement there would be if we did this 'on earth as it is in heaven', because it has a wonderful effect there.[63]

Meanwhile Benson describes attending a ceremony at a temple where a spirit from a higher plane showers the audience with love:[64]

> Then, before our eyes, there appeared first a light... And in the centre there slowly took shape the form of our visitor... He carried with him to an unimaginable degree the three comprehensive and all-sufficing attributes of wisdom, knowledge and purity. His countenance shone with transcendental beauty; his hair was gold, while round his head was a lustrous diadem. His raiment was of the most gossamer-like quality, and it consisted of a pure, white robe bordered with a deep band of gold... His movements were majestic as he raised his arms and sent forth a blessing upon us all...
>
> It is not possible for me to convey to you one fraction of the exaltation of the spirit that I felt while in the presence, though distant, of this heavenly guest. But I do know that not for long could I have remained in that temple while he was there

> without undergoing the almost crushing consciousness that I was low, very, very low upon the scale of spiritual evolution and progression. And yet I knew that he was sending out to me, as to us all, thoughts of encouragement, of good hope, of kindness in the very highest degree, that made me feel that I must never, never despair of attaining to the highest spiritual realm, and that there was good and useful work ready for me to do in the service of man, and that in the doing thereof I would have the whole of the spiritual realms behind me – as they are behind every single soul who works in the service of man. With a final benediction upon us, this resplendent and truly regal being was gone from our sight.

INSPIRING HUMANS

Many great artists, writers, musicians, inventors and scientists have suggested that their work gains inspiration from other planes of consciousness, and here that view is confirmed by a number of our sources. Here are Franchezzo, two of French and Randall's communicants, Lanchester, Hatch, Vale Owen's mother Emma, Benson, Sherwood's EK, Banks' doctor friend mentioned above and Banks herself:

> Knowledge of electricity and kindred sciences has been given to men... All that is highest and purest and best comes from the inspiration of the spirit world.[65]

> We have schools for the development of the soul of man... To aid man in experimenting in chemistry and all other branches of science... We also instruct in political economy and laws governing humanity. We also point out conditions and means whereby to help the unprogressive and helpless portion of mankind.

> In the spirit world, as in your world, are numerous libraries. There men and women grow intellectually. Many books are composed and written in spirit spheres, and the authors sometimes endeavour to impress their words and wisdom upon the brain of some sensitive ones upon the earth sphere.[66]

Let me tell you that all inspiration comes from this side. The works of genius are really the inspirations of the spirits acting through that man who is really mediumistic... Art, literature, music, even mechanical inventions, are almost always inspired from this side... Men come over to us with some knowledge and a keen interest in various subjects, and in these more advanced surroundings they discover new laws, and in the light of this new knowledge inspire those who are following in their footsteps.[67]

[In a] world of patterns and paradigms... I saw forms of things which, so far as I know, have not existed on your planet... I saw wings that man could adjust to himself. I saw also new forms of flying machines. I saw model cities, and towers with strange wing-like projections on them... There are beautiful pictures here. Some of our artists try to impress their pictures upon the mental eyes of the artists of earth, and they often succeed in doing so.[68]

One house or college [of music]... was devoted to the study of the best methods of conveying musical inspiration to those who had a talent for composition on earth... From the colleges round the lake to the church or concert hall or opera house on earth there is a chain of trained workers who are constantly active in giving to earth some little gift of heavenly music.[69]

All the epoch-making discoveries have come from the spirit world... Our own spirit scientists can and do impress their earthly colleagues with the fruits of their investigation. In many cases where two men are working upon the same problem, the one who is in spirit will be far ahead of his confrere who is still on earth. A hint from the former is very often enough to set the latter upon the right track, and the result is a discovery for the benefit of humanity... Every one of them that is sent from the spirit world is for the advantage and spiritual progression of man... Many a spirit doctor has guided the hand of an earthly surgeon when he is performing an operation.[70]

Who shall say how much of the pure thought of the seeker after truth, be he saint, seer or scientist, originates in these

> higher spheres and is picked up and interpreted in human terms by men on earth? I think this may be why a new idea sometimes seems to spring to life in the minds of men in different places at the same time.[71]
>
> Research is being pursued actively and the seed-thoughts of these revolutionary ideas are now being projected into the minds of scientists and researchers in all nations – and which nation will get the breakthrough first is an interesting speculation for us.[72]
>
> Philosophers, scientists, researchers, priests, teachers... are parts of groups which influence and impress such movements on earth as psychic research, healing movements, religious cooperation, the advancement of science and all movements intended to bring light upon future worlds.[73]

Similar observations come from our OOB sources. For example, here are Panchadasi and Richelieu's sage:

> Many a work of art, musical composition, great piece of literature or great invention has been but a reproduction of an astral pattern.[74]
>
> Many groups of research students get together and exchange ideas... Their theories are in due time perfected and impregnated upon the minds and brain cells of doctors doing similar work in the physical world.[75]

Meanwhile Moen describes a 'hall of bright ideas' within the education centre we discussed above.[76] This is a 'hollow sphere around ten feet in diameter' that is connected to the 'grid of all possibilities'. Herein, as an experiment, he asks to see the design for 'the perfect surgical scalpel'. This is then created before his very eyes. For each property – such as hard versus soft, smooth versus rough, brittle versus malleable, number and size of teeth – he sees the 'perfect balance of polar opposites' being worked out until the optimum combination of all is reached, and his perfect scalpel is lying in his palm. The impression given is that this might then somehow be imprinted on the mind of someone on earth.

CONCLUSION

Yet again, just as in Parts 3 and 4, we find an impressive consistency in our sources' reports of these wondrous upper astral environments, which are characterised by learning, researching, information exchange, artistic endeavours, altruism and inspiration of the human race.

28

THE MENTAL PLANES

I have stuck with the conventional description of these planes as *mental* because it remains the best way to distinguish them from the astral. It would appear that they probably still involve some sort of perceived 'form', but nevertheless exhibit a more ethereal and fluid quality than the astral, operating as they do at a higher level of energy vibration. Of course, providing descriptions of these planes using human words and ideas now becomes more difficult again for our sources, but once more they make a valiant effort – and it will be even more important now to let them do the talking, so there will be little commentary from me. It is also the case that from now on the number of first-hand accounts of these higher realms starts to diminish because not all of our sources – whether departed spirits, NDE survivors or OOB pioneers – are able to operate therein. Nevertheless it seems likely that all departed spirits are destined to progress to these realms at some point.

THE SECOND DEATH

One event that does seem to clearly mark the progression from the upper astral to the mental planes is the shedding of the astral body. In these higher planes sprits use their mental body, which has an even finer composition. It appears that for many transitioning spirits this 'second death' again involves a period of sleep or unconsciousness. Let us begin with general descriptions from Franchezzo and one of Emily French and Edward Randall's communicants:

> The passing from the body of a lower sphere into that of a higher one is often, though not invariably, accomplished during a deep sleep.[1]
>
> When a spirit goes from one sphere to another, it is quite unlike death in earth life. He is warned that the change is near and has time to put his mind into a higher plane of thought, so that he will be prepared to meet the new life. He says farewell to all his friends. They join in a general thanksgiving and celebration, all congratulating and helping him on his way by strong uplifting thoughts. When the time comes he is put quietly to sleep, with the thought dominant in his mind that he is to make the change. When he awakes he is in his new home in the next higher sphere. He has disappeared from the old.[2]

By contrast TE Lawrence provides a wonderful eye-witness account of the progression towards and second death of Dr G, an associate who for some considerable time has been teaching at the 'university' in which we saw him residing in the last chapter:[3]

> He is continuing his usual work with his students and is always available to his friends, but we watch the progressive concentration of his life into a glowing interior brightness. It is as though the light and warmth that normally flow out from him to bless his friends is being withdrawn and collected within, so that this illumination burns through and is wasting away his outer lineaments. The end came suddenly. I called on him and was told that he was sleeping. We stood around and watched his still form and the light which waxed and waned there. In a breathtaking second the change came. The light gathered itself together and burnt itself to a keen thought of light so intense and inward that we gasped and turned aside. Then it had gone and only a wraith of our friend remained, which shrank away and disappeared as we watched.

Even better, Philip Gilbert describes the process first-hand – although as something he has to do several times because initially he's not fully ready, rather than as a one-off transition as described by Lawrence:[4]

> [In the higher planes] the form which you inhabit must be... very irradiated and responsive to the impressions of one's thought force. Such a form is acquired after a certain change which is well known here to all who study conditions, but 'second death' is a very clumsy name for it, for there is no resemblance whatever to the process of death as you know it...
>
> An inner withdrawal into a focus is the secret for all acquiring of transcendental knowledge... I practised it in regular rhythm over a long period. And then there was a time when I succeeded. There was a sensation as of a whirring, vibrating transmutation. It was as if I 'unpeeled myself', so difficult to put into words! I emerged into luminosity so intense that I ceased, on this occasion, further effort and just basked and blended with it. I was it – my form seemed to... absorb its very quintessence.
>
> I was aware this was more than those earlier swift tunings-in to the higher spheres, yet I was not clear how much more, or what was the nature of this new experience... Yet attempts were made to help me to find myself... For a while 'I too was love, I was pity' in a rich, absorbed fashion so that with my whole being I could exude benevolence. The feeling was so ardent, so overwhelming, that I felt like I was bursting for I was not advanced enough to take such emotions in my stride. I dithered and quivered, consciousness of this plane vanished and I was away...
>
> [Subsequently] I once more made the upward, emptying, inner action... There was a swirling and an updrawing suction as if my form was being dissolved around me, to leave only a void. It was almost pain as it is known on earth, so wringing was the sensation. I was 'unpeeling'. Beneath this overmantle was another. I began to glow so intensely that I could see the radiance emanating from my lower part. The whole still retained the general outline of a man.

Similarly Frances Banks describes the process as she feels it happening to her – albeit more gradually:[5]

> I am like a creature hibernating, and yet at the same time sloughing off a skin which I will no longer be needing. I feel sometimes like a snake gradually shedding its skin. These coils of lower density are slipping away from me. I am emerging from regrets of earth memories, from disillusions, from idealisations which become illusions, ephemeral and of no true worth. I am viewing each piece of skin which peels off from me in its right connection with the true self which it served to obscure. And more and more I become thankful for the reality which, God be praised, was there beneath the skin all the time. This is the self which is now becoming more and more outstanding, more revealed, more substantial. That self is substantial light. Perhaps that last sentence rings oddly to you.
>
> I am trying not to become obscure, but one's angle of vision alters on this plane of living. I realise that what is passing from me... is insubstantial, impermanent, decomposing as it drops from me into a dusty nothingness. What is left is essentially light, is reality, is permanent and is true. I call this my new body of light and that, indeed, is what it truly is. A body of light, not dense and material and dull and heavy as the physical body, not insubstantial, shadowy and unreal as the astral body... but brilliant, 'encelled' with light, ethereal in that there is no weight, no dragging down into matter, but enmeshed with colour and beauty into form and substance.

Meanwhile John describes one of his guides taking him to a place where a large crowd, which includes many of his friends, are apparently awaiting a special ceremony.[6] A 'shining being from a remote spiritual plane' comes among them, and John is told that various spirits are just about to experience their 'second passing'. Then much to his surprise it turns out he is one of them as the being approaches and tells him: 'Come. The road of many ways has led you home at last.' Unfortunately for us, however, he doesn't describe the experience itself.

From an OOB perspective, we saw in chapter 10 that some pioneers sometimes operate in their mental or 'second energy body' rather than their astral body, whether deliberately or otherwise. Here to provide general descriptions of the second death are Charles Leadbeater, Annie Besant, Peter Richelieu's sage and Albert Taylor:

> When... the soul reaches the limit of that [astral] plane, he dies to it in just the same way as he did to the physical plane. That is to say he casts off the body of that plane, and leaves it behind him while he passes on to higher and still fuller life. No pain or suffering of any kind precedes this second death but, just as with the first, there is usually a period of unconsciousness from which the man awakes gradually.[7]

> There comes a time when the bonds of the astral body are finally shaken off, while the soul sinks into brief unconsciousness of its surroundings, like the unconsciousness that follows the dropping off of the physical body, to be awakened by a sense of bliss, intense, immense, fathomless, undreamed of.[8]

> The man gradually falls asleep and awakes almost immediately in the mental world, having during that brief moment of sleep dropped his astral body forever. Friends meet him in the mental world in exactly the same way as friends met him when he passed from the physical to the astral world.[9]

> When the astral vehicle has been shed, a lighter, brighter, permanent, nonphysical body can be realised.[10]

GENERAL CONDITIONS

Let us now see what our sources have to say about the general conditions in the mental planes. John Ward's JBP recounts an interchange with an 'angelic being' about what happens beyond 'the wall' that separates the astral from the mental:[11] 'While refusing to give any details... they stated emphatically that the personal entity was not destroyed, though the form was affected.' Meanwhile Lawrence manages to communicate with Dr G after his transition, and the latter describes his difficulty in passing on information about his existence in the mental planes:[12]

> He had the same difficulty in conveying the differences to us as I have in making our conditions clear to an earth intelligence. In the transition from plane to plane alterations in the scope of consciousness produce baffling changes in the very framework of thought; categories of space and time are radically modified so that, to an unchanged consciousness more limited in its scope, these are almost incommunicable.

Gilbert too opens with the difficulty in describing this new environment:[13] 'The more I learn and merge into my true self, the more difficult it is to express what I see and do; the only absolute certainty is that I, the central I, is unchanged and somewhat as you knew me, only more so.' Elsewhere he describes how he can now create at will from 'universal mind', without having to make any reference back to the predominantly earth-style creations of the astral.[14] Then, picking up from the quote in the last section, he elaborates on the somewhat unsettling new level of spiritual power he now possesses:[15]

> These glowing emanations of my being came forth in spear-like rays. I seemed to be part of a vast scintillation of silver rays. My mental self became a point of creative though as I floated through these keenly piercing spears of light. There was, it seemed, a central point of focus from which these rays emerged, yet so active, so zigzag and inter-crossing were they that it was not easy to grasp, even with vision and perception combined, the root of this outsurging, and indeed, a certain awe withheld me, a wariness of what, in its impact upon me, seemed unleashed power in action. I am... learning the technique of adjusting to these new and strange conditions. I take it slowly, whatever it is, not trying to absorb everything at once. That is the secret here – to let yourself blend into conditions with a sort of active passivity which is not easy to acquire... In this sphere, even as one formulates a question one knows, for one taps universal mind.

Finally, after he has settled in, he provides a more general overview:[16]

> The mental world... is the functioning dynamo from which the world as you know it is motivated... It is the first clear-cut state of being which is grasped when one has succeeded in shedding earth conditions (including the astral world). To the questing spirit, it may appear at first that he has entered chaos, a blanket of darkness shot with coloured light. But this is only because he has, after his struggle to evolve out of the preoccupations of the astral, entered into a new phase, a reality so overwhelming that his new eyes cannot bear its wholeness... It is permeated with the direct rays of our source... God, if you like to call it that, but only as applied to our corner of eternity... In this realm of mind one creates a form at will, except for a certain core, an essence, vaguely human in shape, a 'glow' which is conscious. That is my basic 'me'...
>
> In the far reaches of mind, beyond human thought or experience, there are visions, sounds, conceptions so strange that there are no words to express them. I have seen colour rays emitting symphonic poems of sound... The art of becoming, or really entering the thought image, is one of the essential differences between my ways of functioning and yours... In this way one's inner self becomes full of true knowledge. At any time I can reel off the essential qualities of other objects, if I have been [blended with] them.

Continuing in the same vein, here are Arthur Ford and his control spirit, Lily:[17]

> [In] the higher planes... the level of consciousness is so much more rarefied that those on this [astral] plane cannot advance into them without great preparation... Those in the next higher state are more aware of us than we are of them. They progress to that state when their rough, earthbound edges are rounded off, and their mental and spiritual progression is such that they are ready for higher learning in the esoteric sense... To describe the difference in levels of consciousness is almost impossible to put into words... In this higher consciousness the soul of man is as alive and aware as ever it was in physical form, but is totally detached from the ties of physical form.

> When we are ready, by having completed our philosophic discussions and reassessed our errors of flesh, we feel a lightening of spirit and with little effort of thought are able to lift ourselves into a new consciousness... In the next phase where I spend most of my life I am transfigured, so to speak, wearing light rather than astral form... We here are able through antenna-like adjustments to attune ourselves to waves of sound and light that would electrocute or permanently deafen the physical man... As we attune to these higher frequencies, we find ourselves in a state most nearly described as fluid.

Meanwhile John describes how, after his transition, he moves back and forth between the mental and astral planes:[18]

> So began that journey which was to take me into a realm so far removed from yours that it is impossible to describe in earth's terms. No comparison exists between your world and life in the sphere I now call my home. I do not live there permanently, for I have come back to be among the many friends I first made here and to continue my work... When I feel the need to renew my spiritual energy, I can return home awhile to rest and meditate.

Turning to NDE reports, Eben Alexander is unusual in that he retains no sense of personal identity during his experience, allowing him to range more widely than usual through the higher planes without fear or longing clouding his emotions. In fact it appears that much of it may have taken place in the mental rather than astral planes, not least because of the following descriptions of how thought operates therein, which are some of the most vivid we possess. Although the distinction isn't always easy to make, they seem to take the thought-form communication discussed in the last chapter to another level again:[19]

> Thoughts entered me directly... they weren't vague, immaterial or abstract. These thoughts were solid and immediate – hotter than fire and wetter than water – and as I received them I was able to instantly and effortlessly understand concepts that

> would have taken me years to fully grasp in my earthly life… It will take me the rest of my life, and then some, to unpack what I learned up there. The knowledge given me was not 'taught'… Insights happened directly… Knowledge was stored without memorisation, instantly and for good. It didn't fade, like ordinary information does, and to this day I still possess all of it… That's not to say that I can get to this knowledge just like that… I have to process it through my limited physical body and brain. But it's there. I feel it, laid into my very being.

Elsewhere he again emphasises that this is a world of huge conceptual ideas:

> The physical side of the universe is as a speck of dust compared to the invisible and spiritual part… Up there, a question would arise in my mind and the answer would arise at the same time… It was almost as if… there was no such thing as a question without an accompanying answer. These answers were not simple 'yes' or 'no' fare, either. They were vast conceptual edifices, staggering structures of living thought, as intricate as cities. Ideas so vast they would have taken me lifetimes to find my way around if I had been confined to earthly thought.

From an OOB perspective, when Emanuel Swedenborg makes a brief reference to the inhabitants of the 'inmost heaven' it seems most likely that he's referring to the mental planes:[20]

> They are absorbed in the pleasures of wisdom. They see divine realities in particular objects. They actually do see the objects, but the corresponding divine realities flow directly into their minds and fill them with a sense of blessedness that affects all their sensory functions. As a result, everything they see seems to laugh and play and live.

Next we come to various general comments from the theosophists, Leadbeater and Besant:

> When a man leaves his physical body and opens his consciousness to astral life, his first sensation is of the intense

vividness and reality of that life, so that he thinks, 'Now for the first time I know what it is to live'. But when in turn he leaves that life for the higher one, he exactly repeats the same experience, for this life is in turn so much fuller and wider and more intense than the astral that once more no comparison is possible.[21]

The mental plane, as its name implies, is that which belongs to consciousness working as thought.... This world is the world of the real man... We have now to conceive of the intellectual consciousness as an entity, an individual, a being, the vibrations of whose life are thoughts, thoughts which are images, not words... Life on the mental plane is more active than on the astral, and form is more plastic. The spirit matter of that plane is more highly vitalised and finer than any grade of matter in the astral world... The matter is in constant, ceaseless motion, taking form under every thrill of life, and adapting itself without hesitation to every changing motion. 'Mind-stuff', as it has been called, makes astral spirit matter seem clumsy, heavy and lustreless...

In that region thought and action, will and deed are one and the same thing – spirit matter here becomes the obedient servant of life, adapting itself to every creative motion. These vibrations, which shape the matter of the plane into thought-forms, give rise also – from their swiftness and subtlety – to the most exquisite and constantly changing colours, waves of varying shades like the rainbow hues in mother-of-pearl, etherealised and brightened to an indescribable extent, sweeping over and through every form, so that each presents a harmony of rippling, living, luminous, delicate colours... Words can give no idea of the exquisite beauty and radiance shown in combinations of this subtle matter, instinct with life and motion.[22]

Swami Panchadasi, by contrast, is somewhat brief:[23] 'The joy, happiness and spiritual blessedness of these higher planes are beyond ordinary words.' As is Oliver Fox, who only hints at wondrous experiences:[24] 'I have gone further than many people along a certain path. I have talked with masters in another world. I have seen – though from afar – celestial beings, great shapes of dazzling flame, whose beauty filled the soul with anguished longing.'

Richelieu's sage, however, reverts to a more extensive description:[25]

> The mental world is a world of thought. Thoughts are the only realities; they are things just as much as chairs and tables are things only, in the same way that the mental body is composed of finer material than the physical, they too are composed of finer matter. It is quite impossible to do so but, if we could take any of our astral or physical matter into the world of thought, it would not exist for the people there... My greatest difficulty in explaining to you what conditions are like in the mental world is that there are no words which enable us to describe in detail conditions of consciousness which are entirely foreign to physical-plane understanding. At the mental level you do not see other people as individuals, nor as astral counterparts of physical forms, but as thought-forms of the individual concerned, and these thought-forms accord with the mental development of the individual.
>
> A man functioning at the mental level can be likened to a wireless set that both receives and transmits. The number of wavelengths which he can use... depends entirely upon the number of subjects with which such a man is familiar. He can receive in his set the thoughts of others providing he can tune into that particular wavelength – in other words if he has some knowledge of the subject of which the thought is composed – and he can carry on a conversation on that subject, because he himself can answer the thought-forms that he receives by transmission of his own thoughts, which would then be picked up by all other people having similar knowledge and interests... A person who... has made a study of one particular subject... would come in contact with other intellectuals who were masters of his subject.

Elsewhere Richelieu himself is taken on an OOB journey to the lowest level of the mental plane by his sage:[26]

> I am finding it almost impossible to describe in words what the mental world is like… We seemed to be suspended in space, but we were surrounded by all sorts of misty objects, which might or might not have been buildings, landscapes or people… All of them, even the forms which might have been men, seemed to be changing all the time. I did not actually see them with my eyes, but sensed them in a way which was quite different from anything I had experienced before. I could see the thought-forms that were floating behind me as well as I could see those which were in front of me.

One final source we haven't yet mentioned is the Cypriot mystic and healer Stylianos Atteshlis. His *Esoteric Teachings*, which first appeared in Greek in 1987 and was translated two years later, is arguably the best study of the use of OOB exploration in esoteric Christianity. His ideas were developed by 'direct study, observation, exercise and meditation'.[27] He doesn't have much of interest to say about the lower realms, but in respect of the mental he makes an interesting comparison:[28] 'If the [astral] world with its brilliant light, which is far beyond comparison with what we call light in the gross material world, is like a moonlit night, the [mental] world, by the same standards, would be like high noon in the Mediterranean.'

Let us now come more up-to-date, starting with Rosalind McKnight, who has a vivid experience of the mental planes accompanied by unseen guides:[29]

> My friends are putting something over my eyes to protect them because this light is so intense… I can feel it all through my energy body… I'm starting to descend into this strong light. I'm in a courtyard surrounded by walls that are pulsating energy. I can see some energy beings walking around… They are more or less human in form. But they are very tall and are pure energy, with shimmering colour. They seem to be pulsating, just as the rest of the atmosphere is… They are very beautiful beings of light.
>
> There is something taking place… They seem to be working on something. They are building an energy form. They're

> around a big ball... I can see funny bursts of light leaving their heads toward each other... It's as if they're communicating, but instead of hearing voices I'm seeing energy... I'm being told that the sounds I hear – what I thought was music – are the different levels of their thought energy... As these thoughts go back and forth they sound like music and appear as colour. It's beautiful to behold. They are having what we would call a conference.

Then a new being arrives as if from nowhere and creates an energy form right in front of them before handing it over – although McKnight admits that she has difficulty explaining what's going on because 'it's like noting I've ever seen before'. Apparently this act of creation causes much amusement amongst the beings, whose laughter appears to her as brilliant colours that are constantly changing. Meanwhile Gordon Phinn's guide Henry opens with a comparison between the astral and mental planes[30]

> On the astral there is plenty of 'time' to study and reflect... Here there is little or no such distinction. Souls absorb thought as flowers absorb sunlight. To think a thought is to enter into it wholly and completely, to understand its history, and revere its passage through many minds towards completion... Just as on earth, there are discussion groups to join, lectures to listen to, and studies to undertake. But here it can all be done without 'stepping outside'. Merely thinking deeply on any subject will deliver the thinker into an animated vortex of ever-multiplying ideas, as if she were interacting with many others... The surrounding landscapes are as varied and beautiful as those in the astral just visited, only more so. To shift from the upper astral to the lower mental is to be dazzled as much as the move from the physical to the astral. What I can say is, it just keeps getting better.

Turning finally to Jurgen Ziewe, as an artist he starts by discussing how sound and colour are even more inextricably and vividly linked:[31]

> Sound, colour and shape are synonymous, sound creates colour

> and pattern or shapes, and colour and shapes have a sound component. To any artist this is the home of true creativity, which has infinite power potential... Creativity in the next dimension utilises sensory tools that far surpass our own senses of sight, sound, smell and feeling... Consciousness is expanded greatly, promoting us to superhuman status. Every perception is more powerful, more evolved, and with new organs of perception we can enter new worlds so far removed from memories of our physical life that we may wonder at the grossness of the human creatures crawling on planet earth.

He then gives us an insight into the distinction between the astral and higher planes that seem to include the mental and beyond:[32]

> Out-of-body travellers may have had glimpses, while journeying in the higher astral planes, of the incredible powers coming to the fore when turning the strangest concepts and ideas into tangible realities to an almost unlimited extent. Compared to the magnificent cities and works of art on the astral dimensions, the creations of the most imaginative and talented Hollywood set designers will only ever appear second rate by comparison. Nevertheless, despite the huge potential for creativity, limitations still exist on the astral dimension. Despite all the marvellous achievements possible for us on the astrals, we are still handicapped by the chains of our personal egos, which prevents us from extending our viewpoint to multiple points of awareness in order to achieve real greatness.
>
> On the super dimensions we can see that creation is a tapestry of an infinite extent, continuously evolving, transforming... On the astral levels we were still set apart, burdened by our personal selves, with their need to stand out from the crowd and shine. Here we realise that we are an intimate and intrinsic part of a universal family and we shine simply by the presence of our inner light. The social role play of our egos – with their unfulfilled wishes and desires, personal and social identifications, and range of acting skills – is simply proof that we are still shielded from the reality of our innermost and true selves. But once we have shed the

limitations of these identifications we can embrace our greater, universal identity.

He goes on to provide the following more general overview of these higher planes, which sets us up nicely for the final chapter:[33]

> The higher a person ascends through the dimensions, the greater the power at their disposal. They also become more and more aware of an underlying intelligence, which permeates everything in the world around them. Everything is animated and has intrinsic intelligence and a serene presence. It now becomes clear why everything functions so beautifully, following the laws of attraction, imagination and creativity. The feeling is that this is a placid ocean of 'compassionate' intelligence, resting in a state of peace and awaiting human intent so it can make new forms and new creations.
>
> Something remarkable is happening to the people who dwell in these regions. Because there is an absence of separation, the overriding feeling is that of being home. Every feeling of being home or the desire to be home comes from this dimension. In the surrounding environment there is no such thing as inanimate matter. All matter on the higher dimensions is intensely alive and intelligent... When human intelligence is trying to mould the matter of this dimension creatively, it responds with eagerness and enthusiasm. Every act of creation is accompanied by incredible joy... There is little discrimination between the creator and the created as that which is created carries the 'soul' imprint of its creator. The identity of the creator is not restricted to a localised energy field, but can expand or contract by a simple effort of intent. The expansion of consciousness is multidimensional and transcends space and time.
>
> The inhabitants here and beyond this region have a symmetrical attractiveness and beauty, much more so than on the regions below. There appears to be a greater range of expression, subtly changing with fine nuances when they interact with one another, whilst maintaining their essential character and individuality. Interaction between people is very intimate and intense and extremely rewarding.

CONCLUSION

From some of these descriptions we might be forgiven for thinking that the transition to a purely mental existence is somewhat scary, because everything we ever thought we knew about perception and understanding seems to be turned on its head. Yet it's also clear that not only do we *not* make this second transition until we're fully ready, but also we can return to the lower realms at any time if we feel like it – to make contact with old friends who haven't transitioned yet, and so on.

Above all many of our sources emphasise that, if we thought the astral realms were magnificent, the mental are something else again. Which just goes to reaffirm that we really do have *so* much to look forward to after we leave our earthly existence.

29

THE HIGHEST PLANES

Needless to say providing descriptions of these highest planes using human words and ideas now becomes almost impossible for our sources, and it's where subjectivity and misinterpretation are most likely to creep in. To some extent the information and ideas presented here can really be little more than guesswork. But at least it's *educated* guesswork, based on arguably the most reliable testimony and evidence we've ever had available to us, and we must do the best we can with the descriptions provided. Jurgen Ziewe eloquently sums up the difficulty, while reassuring us of the ever-increasing glory that awaits:[1]

> When discussing these lofty dimensions, we have first to accept that they are experienced in a totally unfamiliar state of consciousness, expanded so greatly that there are no words to describe the state of mind... Though I may not be able to put everything into words, at the very least I can talk about effects. One thing is for sure, as we transcend from the lower to the higher dimensions, life becomes increasingly refined, harmonious, more euphoric and more glorious.

THE SUPERCONSCIOUS PLANES

If we cast our minds back to my conceptual model of the supersoul outlined in chapter 8, we can surmise that in the upper levels of the mental planes dealt with in the last chapter we might be starting to develop some sort of awareness of our parent consciousness, and of at least some of our – or its – 'other lives'. That is, the myriad other individual aspects of itself it has projected who are, have been or will be operating in various other human timeframes – although, remember, by now we'll be starting to have an understanding of how they can all be doing this concurrently in the eternal now. To illustrate this, Peter Richelieu's sage provides an excellent analogy to help explain the different time perspective operating in the higher planes:[2]

> Past, present and future are in reality one. Let me give you a physical plane example to illustrate this. Imagine for a moment a river that twists and turns every few hundred yards. A man stationed on the deck of a river steamer... can only see that stretch of river in which the steamer is sailing at the moment... Let us suppose that another man is taking the same route in a helicopter; he would see the whole course of the river in one long sweep... To this man the scenery that the steamer has passed is just as visible as the scenery which meets the eyes of the passengers at the present moment, or that such people will see in the near future. To him there is no past and no future; all is indeed the present.

Nevertheless it seems highly likely that it will only be when we reach the superconscious planes proper that, having remained primarily identified with our own earthly life personality up to this point, we'll begin the process of actually remerging or reblending with the far broader consciousness of our supersoul. Jurgen Ziewe was perhaps hinting at this in the last chapter when he described how we start to 'embrace our greater, universal identity'.

Many of the following descriptions seem to be dealing with these issues and, because it's almost impossible to know to what extent they involve the mental as opposed to the highest planes, I've brought them all together here. Note that in many of them our sources use phrases such as 'higher self', 'greater self', 'oversoul', 'group soul', 'monad' and similar, all of which represent, in our terms, the *supersoul*. As far as our channelled sources are concerned, any who had actually progressed to the highest planes would find it almost impossible to still be able to communicate with mediums on earth. But we can commence with several of Emily French and Edward Randall's communicants, who discuss what they've been *told* about these planes:[3]

> Progression is unlimited. It stretches away into the vast future. One may climb and soar, but never reach the end of all that can be done to make oneself a perfect being. I understand that there are seven spheres. I am in the fourth, but the last is without limit. Each plane is more ideally beautiful than the preceding; each, harder to tell about to earth's ears.
>
> In the last sphere each spirit keeps his individuality, but each has by then become so great and magnificent that he can mingle with other spirits in harmony, making one grand, wonderful whole.
>
> Here there is something much higher and better, a universal brotherhood and companionship, always growing closer and higher until complete blending is formed.
>
> We are told that the spirits in the sphere of exaltation do not lose their individuality... They have become so great and universal, we sometimes think they go beyond and must lose their personality, but we have no definite knowledge and it is generally accepted they do not. It is difficult to understand or appreciate what this last sphere is, the development is so beyond our comprehension.

Frederic Myers' identification of the planes in which various experiences are supposed to occur is somewhat confusing, and out of kilter with most of our other sources. However certain basic commonalities can be extracted, for example his general description of the highest planes:[4]

> There never has been and never will be an incarnate or discarnate being who has complete and certain knowledge of the realm of 'divine things'. For, even if he were capable of expressing the whole truth, yet he may not utter it for there is

> no language created by finite minds which can convey a clear and whole conception of God and universal life.

He also reveals that he shares in the experiences of his 'group soul' while still retaining his individual sense of identity:[5]

> It is not necessary for us to return to earth to gather into our granary this manifold variety of life and knowledge. We can reap, bind and bring much of it home by participating in the life of our group soul. Many belong to it and these may spread themselves in their journeys over past, present and future... Through our communal existence I perceive and feel the drama in the earthly journey of a Buddhist priest, of an American merchant, of an Italian painter, and I am, if I assimilate the life thus lived, spared the living of it in the flesh... You will recognise how greatly power of will, mind and perception can be increased through your entry into the larger self. You continue to preserve your identity and your fundamental individuality. But you develop immensely in character and in spiritual force. You gather the wisdom of the ages.

Elsewhere he adds that, even when we 'pass into the beyond and become one with God', individuality is retained:[6] 'This merging with... the great source of spirit does not imply annihilation. You still exist as an individual. You are as a wave in the sea; and you have at last entered into reality.' By comparison Jane Sherwood's EK describes how time becomes almost meaningless in the highest planes, before reinforcing the idea that even attaining 'nirvana' doesn't involve the extinction of individual identity:[7]

> The sense of duration and extent fails to operate at all when the highest spheres are reached. Consciousness is such that time and space become one and there is nothing that is not included in the eternal 'here' and 'now'... The highest planes of universal spiritual being are suggested by the Buddhist nirvana, often mistakenly regarded as loss of being, when it is really the most joyful and marvellous experience of the human soul at the peak of its development.

Meanwhile Philip Gilbert briefly describes how at one point he 'makes a big effort to merge, to blend all his aspects into one';[8] and Frances Banks talks about the idea of a group soul whose members can only make the final progression as a united and reintegrated team:[9]

> The group itself is made up of souls at all levels of consciousness, from the highest to the mediocre, but the spirit of the group only itself advances as the younger and less knowledgeable members make progress. It is a unified advance... When the group itself advances into the divine company, then there will be no 'stragglers'.

Elsewhere she describes the actual process of starting to reunite with hers:

> My joy was deep and strong when I realised that I had, indeed, found my own group even though I knew myself to be only on the outer fringe of their activities... Now your light can mingle with their brilliance and become one in intensity. Thought and aspiration grow into joy and ecstasy... This is but the initial stage of a journey into light, during which the surviving entity is gradually reunited with the whole soul... I also understand that, at higher levels of consciousness, group souls unite to form greater units.

Showing impressive consistency across time, Erik Medhus reports, albeit briefly, on how he can 'step into that energy where he has an awareness of all his lives'.[10] Meanwhile, after completing his initial healing and holographic life review as reported in chapter 22, Billy Cohen describes how he immediately 'becomes the universe', thereby appearing to bypass the astral and mental planes completely – and making his communication with his sister temporarily much harder on both sides:[11]

> I have spread out and expanded across the cosmos. I've got stars and moons and galaxies inside and around me... The thing about becoming the universe is – and I'm going to say this but the words aren't really going to do it justice – the more I let go of my so-called self, the better I feel. As I blend more and more

> into the universal energy I think, 'This is it, I'm going to lose myself.' But it feels so good I don't care, so I let go and blend. Then, lo and behold, I'm still myself, but more blissed out... My present bliss factor is four hundred million times the potency of the healing chamber I was in right after I died.

It is interesting that even this close-to-ultimate experience doesn't lead to the loss of a sense of self or of individual identity. In any case it's only *after* this that his vibration suddenly reduces and he finds himself in what appears to be a mental or even astral body, and meets his guide Joseph as also reported in chapter 22, all of which makes his communication with his sister easier again.[12] We can only surmise that higher beings may have manipulated his transition process to be unconventional and back-to-front so that he could provide us with a first-hand report of 'being the universe', although the effort he put into studying spiritual and esoteric topics during his earth life may have played a part too.

NDE reports of the highest planes are relatively rare, but Eben Alexander describes how it was impossible for him to unify completely with what he perceived to be 'all that is':[13]

> Just as my awareness was both individual yet at the same time completely unified with the universe, so also did the boundaries of what I experienced as my 'self' at times contract, and at other times expand to include all that exists throughout eternity... Even as my consciousness became identical with all and eternity, I sensed that I could not become entirely one with the creative, originating driver of all that is. At the heart of the most infinite oneness, there was still that duality.

Turning to an OOB perspective, here's Charles Leadbeater reporting at length on the 'Buddhic' plane, which falls within the superconscious level of our Astral Routemap model:[14]

> Our next step brings us into a region even less possible to be grasped by the lower mind; for when we follow the man into the intuitional world, developing the Buddhic consciousness, we are in the presence not only of an indefinite extension of various capacities, but also of an entire change of method.

From the causal body we looked out upon everything, understanding, seeing everything exactly as it is and appraising it at its true value, yet still maintaining a distinction between subject and object, still conscious that we looked upon that which we so thoroughly comprehended. But now a change has come; the comprehension is more perfect and not less, but it is from within instead of from without. We no longer look upon a person or upon an object, no matter with what degree of kindliness or of sympathy; we simply are that person or that object...

To enter that plane at all is to experience an enormous extension of consciousness, to realise himself as one with many others... Yet in all this strange advance there is no loss of the sense of individuality, even though there is an utter loss of the sense of separateness... A stage below this, while we were still in the higher mental plane, we learned to see things as they are, to get behind our preconceptions of them, and to reach the reality which lay behind what we had been able to see of them. Now we are able to see the reality which lay behind other people's divergent views of that same object; coming simultaneously up their lines as well as our own, we enter into that thing and we realise all its possibilities, because now it is ourselves, and its possibilities are possible also for us. Difficult to put into words; impossible fully to comprehend down here; and yet approaching and hinting at a truth which is more real than what we call reality in this world.

If we could instantly be transported to that level without passing slowly through the intermediate stages, most of what we found ourselves able to see would mean but little to us. To change abruptly even into the astral consciousness gives one so different an outlook that many familiar objects are entirely unrecognisable. Such a thing, for example, as a book or a water-bottle presents to us a certain appearance with which we are familiar; but if we suddenly find ourselves able to see that object from all sides at once, as well as from above and below, we shall perhaps realise that it presents an appearance so different that we should require a considerable amount of mental adjustment before we could name it with certainty. Add

> to that the further complication that the whole inside of the body is laid out before us as though every particle were separately placed upon a table, and we shall again see that additional difficulties are introduced. Add to them again yet another fact – that while we look upon all these particles as described, we are yet at the same time within each of those particles and are looking out through them, and we shall see that it becomes an absolute impossibility to trace any resemblance to the object which we knew in the physical world.

He then moves on to nirvana, and reinforces the comments made by Sherwood's EK earlier:[15]

> What can we say of the next stage of consciousness, that which has often been called nirvana? This noble word has been translated to mean annihilation, but nothing could be further from the truth than this, for it represents the most intense and vivid life of which we know anything.
>
> Perhaps it may not unfairly be described as annihilation of all that we on the physical plane know and think of as the man; for all his personality, all his lower qualities, have long ago utterly disappeared. Yet the essence is there; the true man is there; the divine spark, descended from the deity himself, is still there, though now it has grown into a flame – a flame that is becoming consciously part of that from which it came; for here all consciousness merges into him, even though it still retains all that was best in the feeling of individuality. The man still feels himself just as he does now, but full of a delight, a vigour, a capacity for which we have simply no words down here. He has in no way lost his personal memories. He is just as much himself as ever, only it is a wider self...
>
> In the intuitional world his consciousness had widened so as to take in that of many other people. Now it seems to include the entire spiritual world, and the man feels that he is on the way to realising the divine attribute of omnipresence; for he exists not only in all those others, but also at every point of the intervening space, so that he can focus himself wherever he will, thus realising exactly the well-known phrase that he is a

> circle whose centre is everywhere and circumference nowhere. He has transcended intellect as we know it, yet he knows and understands far more fully than ever before...
>
> It is hopeless to attempt to describe this life which transcends all life that we know, and yet is so utterly different from it as to seem almost a negation of it – a splendour of purposeful life as compared with a mere blind crawling along darkened ways. For this indeed is life and this is reality, as far as we can reach it at present; although we doubt not for a moment that beyond even this indescribable glory there extend yet greater glories, which surpass it even as it surpasses this catacomb life of earth.

It is perhaps unsurprising that his fellow theosophist Annie Besant makes similar observations. In particular she provides a wonderfully constructed analogy to demonstrate why any assertion that progression to a nirvanic state of consciousness involves the annihilation of the individual represents a woeful misinterpretation of the experience:[16]

> The nirvanic is the plane of the highest human aspect of the God within us... It is the plane of pure existence, of divine powers in their fullest manifestation – what lies beyond... is hidden in the unimaginable light of God. This nirvanic consciousness... is the consciousness attained by those... who are called Masters. They have solved in themselves the problem of uniting the essence of individuality with non-separateness and live, immortal intelligences, perfect in wisdom, in bliss, in power...
>
> The nirvanic consciousness is the antithesis of annihilation; it is existence raised to a vividness and intensity inconceivable to those who know only the life of the senses and the mind. As the farthing rushlight to the splendour of the sun at noon, so is earthbound to nirvanic consciousness, and to regard it as annihilation because the limits of the earthly consciousness have vanished is as though a man, knowing only the rushlight, should say that light could not exist without a wick immersed in tallow.

Meanwhile Yram reports that he 'travelled from dimension to dimension', not satisfied until he had attained 'that almost indescribable state when one is no more than a unity-multiplicity with the higher energy of nature'.[17] Elsewhere he bears out Leadbeater's assertion that references to 'circles and circumferences' are commonplace when discussing the state of consciousness of these higher realms:[18]

> The further one penetrates into the more subtle states of matter, the further does this lucidity increase, to attain its absolute fullness at that point where our own universe contacts the infinite, to which it gravitates. In this supreme state man has become a god, fecundating his portion of the universe with the conscious life, of which he has now become both the centre and the circumference.

He closes with a description of 'supermen' that would, if the word *men* was replaced by *souls*, be completely in line with my own definition:[19]

> We learn of the existence of supermen, whom our ancestors used to consider as gods. The extraordinary power of their auras, the perfection of the qualities one recognises in them, the perfect mechanism of the dimension where they are to be found, surpass in simplicity all that men could have imagined concerning the gods.

Similarly, at the end of her book Caroline Larsen provides an account of travelling beyond our solar system and on into the 'abyss of space' where, like Yram, she's overwhelmed by entities of incredible radiance:[20]

> Spirits of high superiority and authority such as I had never seen even in the fourth plane passed in every direction, singly and in larger or smaller groups. A white light of intense power emanated from each, and enveloped them in a flaming radiance, that varied in intensity in proportion to their spiritual power. All were garbed in glowing white. The combined brilliancy of the light thus produced flooded all space... The

> mere sight of these majestic spirits even from afar was enough to convince the beholder that they were the rulers and controllers of the whole universe, of matter and of spirit. The overpowering dominance of their personalities subdued my spirit so that, staring and stupefied, I trembled and shrank at their presence.
>
> Two in particular, a man and a woman spirit, burned with the light of two flaming suns dimming all others near them with the intense lustre of their white radiance... Dazzled, I cowered, raising my hand to my forehead in an involuntary tribute of humility and awe... They appeared to be gods rather than perfect spirits, yet I was informed that they had once dwelt in human form... By spiritual development they had risen to the highest power and, as my guide explained, they were now a part of that supreme power that rules and guides both the material and spirit universe... It was a glorious moment for me when I beheld these marvellous beings, and knew the happiness of their close presence.

Perhaps one of the most annoying of Robert Monroe's many acronyms is INSPECs, or the 'intelligent species' he repeatedly encounters on his travels. We would be hard put to invent a name less in keeping with the sort of entities Yram and Larsen are describing above – yet that is surely what they are:[21]

> I am in a bright white tunnel and moving rapidly. No, it is not a tunnel but a tube, a transparent, radiating tube. I am bathed in the radiation which courses through all of me, and the intensity and recognition of it envelop my consciousness and I laugh with great joy. Something has changed, because the last time they had to shield me from the random vibration of it. Now I can tolerate it easily...
>
> The tube seems to become larger as another joins it from one side, and another waveform melds into me and we become one. I recognise the other immediately, as it does me, and there is the great excitement of reunion, this other I and I. How could I have forgotten this! We move along together, happily exploring the adventures, experience and knowledge of the other. The tube widens again and another I joins us, and

> the process repeats itself. Our waveforms are remarkably identical and our patterns grow stronger as they move in phase. There are variegations in each which, when combined with another related anomaly, create a new and important modification of the total that we are.
>
> The tube expands again and I am no longer concerned with its walls as still another I enters the waveform flow... Steadily and surely, one I after another joins us. With each, we become more aware and remember more of the total. How many does not seem important. Our knowledge and ability is so great that we do not bother to contemplate it. It is not important. We are one.

Then, at last, the collective entity he's remerging with reveals who it really is:

> 'We know who we are, and one I laughs and we all laugh at the name this I [Monroe] has given us. We are an INSPEC, just one. There are many others around us.'

On another of his journeys Monroe asks to penetrate further still, and to be given an outside view of the very centre of creation, or at least of that centre that relates to the universe we know.[22]

> Even closed tightly the radiation was so strong that it was nearly unbearable. I felt as if sweat were pouring off me, I was melting, but it wasn't heat. And I began to heave with great racking sobs and I couldn't understand why. Then the radiation eased and I opened a little. There was a form between me and the radiation, shielding me, and I could perceive a corona effect all around the form from the radiation beyond. It reminded me deeply of religious paintings I had seen, only this was live and in something far different from pigmented colour.
>
> 'This is as close as you can tolerate. We are diverting most of the effective energy patterns, which are in themselves only the random residue, the leakage as you might call it, from the fundamental. Focus through us rather than the outer rim. It will help.'
>
> With great difficulty I narrowed and held onto the centre of the form. And I began to cool and calm down. Slowly my

> rational and observing self began to emerge again, dominating the overwhelming emotional surge that had enveloped me. It was as if I perceived through a darkly tinted window and I had to work continually to keep the emotion below the threshold level, the wondrous and brilliant joy, awe, reverence, melded into one yet with flashes of each sparking momentarily… all coursing through me as I responded to the radiation, unable to prevent it and barely keeping it under control. This would most emphatically be the ultimate heaven, the final home.

This latter sentence proves that here Monroe feels himself to be dealing with the highest possible level of awareness that still relates to our system. Meanwhile Stylianos Atteshlis briefly returns to the theme of retaining some sense of individuality:[23]

> Within superlight we are no longer in the worlds of separation and existence, but in the states of at-one-ment and beingness. We have entered into absolute beingness without, however, being totally absorbed by the highest godhead. We are within absolute beingness but can, all the same, distinguish between 'I am', 'you are' and being… We have earned this independence; the microcosm has entered the macrocosm.

One OOB pioneer we've not yet mentioned is Vee Van Dam, whose *Psychic Explorer* was published in 1989 and contains over twenty years of exploration. He has little of use to say about the lower and intermediate planes, but with reference to the highest he too briefly discusses the idea of 'group beings' who project parts of themselves into the lower planes then 'come home' again.[24] By contrast William Buhlman provides three fascinating and lengthy descriptions of meeting and even merging with higher aspects of himself:[25]

> As I stare the light becomes blinding. A part of me wants to turn away, but I don't. It feels as if the outer layers of myself are being burned away – my old concepts, beliefs, assumptions and conclusions are incinerated by the intensity of the light. I can take no more and scream out, 'What is this?' Instantly I'm drawn within the light. My mind is overwhelmed as I realise

that I have merged with a greater, more expansive part of myself. I suddenly understand that I am the engine of my life – I'm the creative force within me. I recognise that I have separated from myself. For several moments the light and I are one. I feel a deep peace and interconnectedness I have never known before. For the first time I realise that I can create whatever reality I choose – my creative power is beyond my comprehension. I now know that I have limited myself by the ideas and beliefs I have accepted, and I recognise the need to release all my limits, fears and expectations. A profound sense of empowerment sweeps through me as I scream inside, 'I will remember this!'

I'm drawn to what appears to be a column of pure white light. As I move closer to the light, the sheer power of its radiation is overpowering. I stop and try to adjust… I slowly move forward and touch the light. An intense surge of energy flows through my entire being. I'm suddenly immersed in an ocean of pure knowledge. I'm flooded with memories of all I've been, all I've done, all that I am… I lie still and review the experience with a feeling of awe. I absolutely know that the column of white light was really me – not just another part of me, but the pure me, the very essence of all I am. Is it possible that we are really that incredible? Now I feel separated and alone; yet, at the same time, I feel connected to something far greater than I've ever imagined.

My awareness is blinded by the intensity of the light. I begin to back away and shield myself from the crushing energy. The entity continues to communicate with my mind. 'I will adjust… Not many of your kind venture this far in… You are ready or you would not be here. All of us are where we should be. I was once as you and you shall be as I; we are all on a great journey together. Your perception of me is inaccurate. I am but a child compared to others who dwell within the universe. The possible evolution of consciousness is unlimited.'

Gordon Phinn provides a number of descriptions of the higher planes, some of them written from the apparent perspective of his 'higher self', but arguably the best is relatively brief:[26] 'A shining white sea of light with golden points twinkling like stars, and I know from previous visits that each point is a monad or higher self.' He then temporarily merges with his own, and experiences the earthly lives of various of its other projections. Similarly Ziewe reports at eloquent length on several experiences in 'sublime dimensions':[27]

> The atmosphere was much brighter still than before, more penetrating and yet very subtle, reaching into every atom of my being. I began to feel uncomfortable. It was like coming in from the cold into a warm room, still wearing a heavy coat.
>
> It became unbearable. Something had to give. I was no longer a cohesive entity. I was conscious that my body was being unrelentingly pulled apart atom by atom. The old molecules, which had made me what I thought of as myself, wanted to resist, seeking some snug shelter somewhere in a darker region no longer reachable. I felt like a condemned man, dying a nonphysical death. But in the end it was only my resistance which had to perish. Letting go of my attachment to my novel costume – my body – was in fact a great liberation. I was keen to take a look at the vast spectrum of these veils – an endless chain of lives, paraded in millions of images in front of my disembodied eyes.
>
> The process began to feel joyful once I understood not to cling on to the old, heavy matter of my body and the burden of the past. Whatever the forces were that ripped me apart, they did so not because they wanted to destroy me, but out of love, pure and unconditional. They wanted me to join them, become part of them, so I could enter their native realm. There was no turning back. It was as if I was pulled by invisible strings, all eager to call me home. This was accompanied by a sweet and beckoning sound, which evolved into a choir of enchanting sound, with voices so sweet that there was no way I could have resisted. I left behind all that I had valued so much, which was really little more than idle games played with childlike earnestness, and dreams indulged in and lifetimes struggling in search of happiness.

With my new pair of eyes I became accustomed to my new surroundings, as if I was coming into sunlight for the first time after being trapped in a dark dungeon for years. Before me a sea of pleasure opened in warm, sparkling waves and a disembodied soprano voice urged me to plunge my heart and soul into this open ocean... After the ecstatic storm of my transformation had passed, there was peace. It was like a gathering of my new critical faculties; a calibrating of my new instruments of perception. I soon forgot everything I had learned in the limited world of earth and began to prepare myself for a totally new cognitive experience. I was not in a place or in a time any longer, or in any form; instead I was everywhere simultaneously, except there wasn't a 'where' at all. There was just I.

I stood on the shores of a vast and glorious ocean... This ocean was just pure light in essence... and the waves came rolling in towards me as gigantic mountains of crashing light, overwhelming me completely... There was no fear because there was only light, and the waves that rolled towards me crashed through me, lifting me into an unknown ecstasy. There was no letting up: wave after wave rolled over me and, when I thought I could stand no more, a greater joy swallowed me up and carried me with it into lands of bliss...

When the tide ebbed away there was immense peace... All stress, all need and want had gone, everything I had strived for had found fulfilment. Whatever I wanted lay there before me in its absolute essence, in total stillness and emptiness combined... I had ceased to be. This was unformed, an unmanifested thrill. Until now I had been bathed in something which could be understood as the cradle or essence of love, but this was far beyond that. It was a super-dimension of choice-less love, which was as clear as crystal. All remotely human feelings had been stripped from it and replenished with utter purity. It was pure intelligence, pure consciousness. It was reality in essence...

Here, stripped of all that I called myself, I was at the heart of nature at its most powerful, most quintessential. I was omniscient, omnipresent and infinite. The instant a question

> was raised, my universal mind had it answered on a level unheard of, guided by a universal wisdom, purpose and plan... I knew I was only at the outer edges of creation, and that beyond waited dimensions too far beyond our human state of evolution.

One of the most common themes in these descriptions is that, however much our sources feel they're blending with a more expanded consciousness in these planes, they still retain a sense of individual identity even if not of separateness. This seems to completely validate the concept of the 'holographic soul' that I first postulated back in 2007, and subsequently amended to reflect the 'holographic *super*soul', defined as follows:[28]

> Soul consciousness is holographic. We are both individual aspects of our supersoul, and full holographic representations of it, all at the same time. However this does not mean that soul individuality is in itself an illusion. The principle of the hologram is that the part contains the whole, and yet is clearly distinguishable from it.
>
> The primary aim of all supersouls, in diversifying into all the many holographic aspects of themselves that operate in a multitude of realms throughout a multitude of universes, is to experience all that is and can be. So as individualised aspects of our supersoul we have been projected into this 'earth' reality to paint the best picture we can with the palette of 'birth givens' mixed for us by our supersoul.

THE METACONSCIOUS PLANES

We have already seen several of our sources reporting that beyond the superconscious planes lie others even more expanded and, advanced, but quite beyond even their elevated level of spirit understanding. Franchezzo, for example, reports on his guide's view of the highest planes of all:[29] 'How can any pretend to show you the ultimate end of that which has no end, or sound the great depths of an infinite thought which has no bottom?' Similarly Gilbert feels unable to comment on them properly:[30]

> As far as I know no conscious entity, however advanced... has ever returned into even the most advanced form of mind after a willed act of emerging into the final essence, so that we have no record to guide us. We know that some of the great ones have done so, but whether they have merged into some other aspects of form in the cosmos we do not know.

Yet other sources do attempt to provide some sort of commentary, and to understand their perspectives we can again usefully refer back to my supersoul model. We can speculate that the metaconscious planes are the final ones that bear any relation to our human system, universe, hologram or whatever we want to call it. Of course they almost certainly lie partly outside of it as well, which means we can have little concept of their nature. But we can surmise that at least some of their inhabitants will be fully reintegrated supersouls waiting to get involved in new creative ventures in other systems.

For example, George Vale Owen's mother Emma makes a brief reference to 'the creation of some new cosmos or system' in a realm 'high above this state in which we are at present'.[31] Meanwhile one section of Van Dam's book deals with channelled messages he describes as coming from 'beyond the beyond', in which we find the following:[32]

> You will carry on with your evolution and then eventually anchor yourself on the monadic level, in preparation for the greater leap into super-universes of which you will know next to nothing – except that they exist, and that they are there to be explored.

From an NDE perspective, Mellen-Thomas Benedict's is arguably the most expanded of all:[33]

> I found myself in a profound stillness, beyond all silence. I could see or perceive forever, beyond infinity. I was in the void. I was in pre-creation, before the big bang. I had crossed over the beginning of time / the first word / the first vibration. I was in the eye of creation. I felt as if I was touching the face of God. It was not a religious feeling. Simply, I was at one with absolute

> life and consciousness. When I say that I could see or perceive forever, I mean that I could experience all of creation generating itself. It was without beginning and without end. That's a mind-expanding thought, isn't it? Scientists perceive the big bang as a single event that created the universe. I saw during my life after death experience that the big bang is only one of an infinite number of big bangs creating universes endlessly and simultaneously. The only images that even come close in human terms would be those created by super computers using fractal geometry equations...
>
> It took me years after I returned from my near-death experience to assimilate any words at all for the void experience. I can tell you this now: the void is less than nothing, yet more than everything that is! The void is absolute zero; chaos forming all possibilities. It is absolute consciousness; much more than even universal intelligence... What mystics call the void is not a void. It is so full of energy, a different kind of energy that has created everything that we are... So creation is god exploring god's self through every way imaginable, in an ongoing, infinite exploration through every one of us... In this expanded state, I discovered that creation is about absolute pure consciousness, or god, coming into the experience of life as we know it.

Turning to OOB reports, Leadbeater describes how 'divine consciousness' creates different worlds to play in:[34]

> Let us try to imagine what the consciousness of the divine must be – the consciousness of the solar deity altogether outside any of the worlds or planes or levels which we ever conceived. We can only vaguely think of some sort of transcendent consciousness for which space no longer exists, to which everything (at least in the solar system) is simultaneously present, not only in its actual condition, but at every stage of its evolution from beginning to end. We must think of that divine consciousness as creating for its use these worlds of various types of matter, and then voluntarily veiling itself within that matter, and thereby greatly limiting itself. By taking upon itself a garment of the matter of even the highest of these worlds, it

> has clearly already imposed upon itself a certain limitation; and equally clearly each additional garment assumed, as it involves itself more and more deeply in matter, must increase the limitation... Of the condition of consciousness of the solar deity outside the planes of his system, we can form no true conception.

Bruce Moen meanwhile refers to supposedly meeting the 'planning intelligence' who created our entire 'earth-life system', who tells him about the various 'greater selves' found in the very highest planes:[35]

> When they leave home they leave my universe system and go... to other systems, which they create... The fixed pattern of evolution is toward satisfying a greater and greater curiosity for greater and greater awareness.

Then during another journey he's given a glimpse of the creative potential of what I would call his *reintegrated supersoul*, but which he refers to as his 'graduated disk':[36]

> As a graduated disk I could create any lifeforms, planets, suns or environments I chose to include in my creation. I could create an earth-like planet with carbon-based lifeforms, or any other I chose. I could include a physical-world lifetime cycle or modify it to a pure thought-form based existence, or anywhere in between. Whatever choices I made in the creation of my system would be my choices.

Finally Waldo Vieira describes a fascinating projection into the highest planes in which he encounters a 'free consciousness':[37]

> There were no human forms or faces, only centres of energy radiation constituting familiar consciousnesses, some of whom were noteworthy by their deeds... All of them had been converted into pure light. They had no names, nor were they identifiable by their forms, but I knew them and was united with them through common experiences. I was suddenly sure of being a participant in a formless gathering composed of bodiless points of mental focus... that was taking place in a

nirvanic atmosphere that was of an unimaginable level of mental elevation, unapproachable with earthly descriptions, and indefinable in known terms... It was clear that a higher consciousness would manifest itself through everyone present. This indeed occurred, gently and smoothly... It was a free consciousness. A lucid vortex of vibrant, energetic emanation; free from matter, form and space...

Are all free consciousnesses alike in their evolutionary multiple genius? They are at a stage of evolution that is inconceivable from our planetary point of reference, in conditions unappreciable by the human brain, with universal sentiments inaccessible to us with our perceptions, traditions and conditioning... A constant 'nirvanic orgasm' cast those consciousnesses present into the peace of this nebulous whirl. Each consciousness appeared to have the potential to proliferate a large portion of the universe, being the centre and the periphery, a part and the whole. A creator in action... Doubtless visions equal to this one have, throughout the millenniums, launched the foundations on which all religious beliefs were built.

CONCLUSION

Since this book would have been nothing without the illuminating experiences of our sources, it feels appropriate to conclude our trip through the multiple layers and predominantly boundless joys of the afterlife with some observations from three of them. Although they're relatively random, they're nevertheless entirely uplifting and somehow fitting. So, to play us out, here are Eben Alexander, Mellen-Thomas Benedict and William Buhlman:

> Love and compassion are far more than the abstractions many of us believe them to be. They are real. They are concrete. And they make up the very fabric of the spiritual realm. In order to return to that realm we must once again become like it, even while we are stuck in and plodding through this one.[38]

> From what I have seen I would be happy to be an atom in this universe. An atom. So to be the human part of god ... this is the

most fantastic blessing. It is a blessing beyond our wildest estimation of what blessing can be. For each and every one of us to be the human part of this experience is awesome and magnificent. Each and every one of us, no matter where we are, screwed up or not, is a blessing to the planet, right where we are.[39]

I am often asked what I will do when I take my final breath... I am not content to simply 'go to the light'. I am not content to accept past acquaintances and comfortable surroundings as my new reality. In fact, I am not content to settle for any form-based reality as my spiritual home. I absolutely know that there is so much more available beyond the realms of form. There exist magnificent dimensions of living light simply waiting for us; all we need do is awaken and accept their reality.[40]

APPENDIX
The Ten Principles of Supersoul Spirituality

This summary is taken from chapter 7 of *Supersoul*:

1. We are multidimensional, expeditionary soul probes sent out by a supersoul consciousness possessing a wisdom and power of divine proportions. Myriad supersouls are involved in the simulation game we call 'human life on earth', which is just one of myriad different realities soul probes are sent into.
2. After death we continue to identify with the personality of the life we just left, so this and the 'soul' are the same consciousness.
3. Although we're still engaged in the growth of consciousness, we don't develop in a linear fashion as we move from one reincarnatory life to another. Instead the lives of all soul probes projected by the supersoul are happening at the same time – even if they're operating in different human eras – and they interact as a complex matrix. By logic alone this means the 'interlife' is only an *after*life, and possibly a *pre*life too.
4. 'My' many lives means nothing unless we're genuinely adopting our supersoul level of consciousness, which involves appreciating that we're far more powerful and multi-faceted than we normally recognise. Any experiences we have of 'past' or 'future' lives are most likely those of other 'resonant souls' from our supersoul with whom we have an especially close connection – for example because of strongly shared traits or challenges, or because they act as contrasts.
5. Each of us is fundamentally responsible for creating our own

experience in each moment of now. We're not limited by 'past karma' from this life or a supposedly previous one unless we believe we are. Nor will other resonant souls tend to be able to exert a strongly disruptive influence over us unless we believe they can and choose to let them.

6. Our supersoul chooses our 'birth givens', and these vary considerably. They include our own sex, our main psychological and physical traits and propensities – in terms of both challenges and strengths – and the socio-economic position and geographical location of our parents. On that basis we're here to 'paint the best picture we can with the palette we've been given'. Other than that any pre-birth planning of events in our adult lives, or 'soul contracts' with others, are probably kept to a minimum to give us maximum free will to direct our experience. It's also unlikely that most of us have a preplanned 'life purpose', because again this would tend to detract from our free will to follow whatever purpose we desire – and to change that purpose, should we so choose, at any time.

7. Angels and guides may well be other aspects of our own supersoul, and they won't tend to interfere with our experience on the basis that they supposedly 'know best' and 'want to keep us on our path'. Usually therefore synchronicities will only represent the sophisticated underlying dynamics of how our *own* creation and attraction process crystallises into our experience of the physical.

8. Having said that, insights and guidance are always available if we *proactively* ask for them, or if we *attract* them to ourselves automatically by our conscious intentions and actions. Such guidance might come, for example, from wiser, non-incarnate aspects of our supersoul consciousness, or from other resonant souls who've overcome similar challenges. We can also provide guidance to them by overcoming our own challenges, if they're open to it.

9. On rare occasions we might make a new agreement with our supersoul, at a subconscious level, to take on a new challenge in our adult lives. But it's always best to take responsibility for any challenge by assuming you created or attracted it, or at least by knowing you control your reaction to it. Any tendency to ascribe challenges to 'past' karma, life plans or soul contracts can lead to an abrogation of responsibility for what we're creating in the now, and detract from our extensive power to turn any situation around.
10. Under a matrix model *everything* can be seen as altruistic, because everything that each soul experiences is designed to add to the databanks of the supersoul consciousness. Any particularly challenging circumstances or birth givens can best be seen in the context of 'taking one for the team', and each of us can be characterised as a 'lead representative of team supersoul gaining experience at the coalface of space-time on behalf of the collective'.

SOURCE REFERENCES

The use of excerpts from the books of Gordon Phinn and Jurgen Ziewe has been kindly granted by the authors. The remaining quotes come from books where either the author is no longer alive or they're covered by 'fair usage' rules.

Publication details for the books referenced below can be found in the bibliography. All website references were accurate at the time of publication.

PREFACE

1. Although we should appreciate that that there may be two main types of ghost. On the one hand 'imprints', which are energetic 'recordings' on the fabric of particular places that have witnessed high levels of trauma and emotion, and can be thought of as a tape on an endless loop that repeats certain behaviour. On the other genuine trapped 'spirits' that represent the genuine consciousness of the departed, who can act and react of their own volition.
2. Buhlman, *The Secret of the Soul*, chapter 7, pp. 118–19.

PART 1: CAN WE PROVE THE AFTERLIFE EXISTS?

1 THE SCIENTIFIC VIEW

1. *The Observer*, 25 Jan 1931.
2. Einstein, *The World as I See It*, p. 7.
3. Russell's background is described in *From Science to God*, chapter 1.
4. The term 'hard problem of consciousness' was coined by David Chalmers, professor of philosophy at the University of Arizona.
5. *From Science to God*, chapter 2, p. 26.
6. Ibid., chapter 3, p. 36. There follows an excellent description of how consciousness evolved through the different lifeforms.
7. This is a summary of ibid., chapter 4.
8. These topics are discussed in more depth in Lawton, *The Power of You*, chapters 3 and 4 and also in *Sh*t Doesn't Just Happen*, chapters 2 and 3.

2 MEDIUMSHIP EVIDENCE

1. A summary of the cross correspondences was prepared by Montague Keen in 1993 and can be found at www.montaguekeen.com/page46.html. See also www.victorzammit.com/book/4thedition/chapter16.html and philipcoppens.com/eagerdead.html.
2. Typical rebuttals can be found at en.wikipedia.org/wiki/Cross-Correspondences.
3. Leonard, *My Life in Two Worlds*, chapter 44, pp. 175–6.
4. Lodge, *Raymond or Life and Death*, Part 2, chapter 4. The photograph is included.
5. For the background see Cummins, *The Scripts of Cleophas*, Introduction, pp. 9–10.
6. Schwartz, *The Truth About Medium*, chapter 6.
7. Ibid., chapter 8.
8. For example see Delorme, Arnaud et al, 'Electrocortical activity associated with subjective communication with the deceased', *Frontiers in Psychology*, 20 November 2013. For the full paper see journal.frontiersin.org/article/10.3389/fpsyg.2013.00834.
9. For the background see www.leslieflint.com .
10. For the background see Heagerty, *The French Revelation*, Introduction and chapter I.
11. For various obituaries, tributes and independent references to the characters of both these individuals, including doctors' reports on French's deafness and ailments, see ibid., chapter 4 and Appendices.
12. Funk's own write-up of his tests is reproduced in ibid., chapter 3; see especially pp. 226–7.
13. Ibid., chapter 3, pp. 246–7.

3 REMOTE VIEWING EVIDENCE

1. For the background see, for example, en.wikipedia.org/wiki/Stargate_Project.
2. Mayer, *Extraordinary Knowing*, chapter 7, pp. 110–11.
3. Ibid., chapter 7, pp. 116–18.

4 NEAR-DEATH EXPERIENCE EVIDENCE

1. Lawton, *The Big Book of the Soul*, chapter 1, pp. 12–19. These cases were originally reported in Sabom, *Light and Death*, chapter 3, pp. 41–6 (Pam Reynolds); van Lommel et al, 'Near-Death Experience in Survivors of Cardiac Arrest: A Prospective Study in the Netherlands', *The Lancet* 358 (Dec 2001), pp. 2039–45 (false teeth); Berman, *The Journey Home*, chapter 2, pp. 31–7 and Atwater, *Beyond the Light*, chapter 5, p. 81 (George Rodonaia); and Clark, 'Clinical Interventions with Near-Death Experiencers' in Greyson and Flynn, *The Near-Death Experience*, pp. 242–55 (Maria).
2. Rawlings, *Beyond Death's Door*, chapter 1, pp. 21–2.
3. Ibid., chapter 5, pp. 71, 73 and 75.
4. Rivas and Smit, 'An NDE with Veridical Perception...', *Journal of Near-Death Studies* 31:3 (2013), pp. 179–86.
5. The AWARE study first reported results on 7 October 2014; details can be found at www.southampton.ac.uk/news/2014/10/07-worlds-largest-near-death-experiences-study.page.
6. Alexander, *Proof of Heaven*, chapter 6, p. 34.
7. Ibid., chapter 15, p. 82; chapter 28, pp. 129–35; chapter 31, pp. 143–4; chapter 33, pp. 150 and 153; and chapter 35, p. 169.

5 OUT-OF-BODY EXPERIENCE EVIDENCE

1. See, for example, Paul Twitchell, *Eckankar* (Illuminated Way Publishing, 1987), chapter 7.
2. See, for example, Black, *Ekstasy* (Bobbs-Merrill, 1975), chapter 3.
3. For the background see en.wikipedia.org/wiki/Emanuel_Swedenborg.
4. See, for example, Swedenborg, *Heaven and Hell*, chapter 36, pp. 176–7 (section 321) and chapter 53, p. 308 (section 514).
5. Although multiple versions of most of these anecdotes exist, some of the best details can be found in Cyriel Sigstedt's 1952 work *The Swedenborg Epic* (Kessinger, 2007), chapter 31.
6. Hardy, *Tess of the D'Urbervilles* (Wordsworth Editions, 1993), chapter 18, p. 106.
7. See Lawton, *Supersoul*, chapter 4, pp. 49–55.

8. For the background see Turvey, *The Beginnings of Seership*, Preface, pp. 32–6.
9. Ibid., Introduction, pp. 54–5.
10. Ibid., chapter 7, pp. 191–4.
11. His projection experiences are discussed in ibid., chapter 7; those involving house visits and so on can be found on pp. 196–9. The remainder of the chapter deals with his documented attempts to take control of mediums conducting séances in his local area – which, as he rightly points out, are more open to criticism by sceptics.
12. Morrell, *The Twenty-Fifth Man*, chapter 27, pp. 318–9.
13. Ibid., chapter 27, pp. 325–6 and chapter 28, pp. 332–3 and 340.
14. Ibid., chapter 28, pp. 334–5 and 342.
15. Muldoon and Carrington, *Projection of the Astral Body*, Introduction, pp. xxv and xxix.
16. These were *Manifestations du Fantôme des Vivants* by Hector Durville, and *Méthode de Dédoublement Personnel* by Charles Lancelin. For more on the latter see Lawton, *The Big Book of the Soul*, chapter 7, p. 218. Note that another French pioneer of hypnosis-based OOB experiences was Pierre Emile Cornillier; see Black, *Ekstasy*, chapter 4, p. 34.
17. Although the book is undated, piecing together various autobiographical elements provided by Fox reveals the date; see *Astral Projection*, chapter 2, p. 24, chapter 3, p. 32 and chapter 11, p. 154.
18. For a summary of his different types of experience see ibid., chapter 10, pp. 133–4 and 141–5.
19. Ibid., chapter 5, pp. 56–9.
20. Leonard, *My Life in Two Worlds*, chapter 20.
21. For the background see Sculthorp, *Excursions to the Spirit World*, chapter 1.
22. Tart, 'A Parapsychological Study of OBEs in a Selected Subject', *Journal of the American Society for Psychical Research* 62:1 (1968), pp. 3–27.
23. Monroe, *Journeys Out of the Body*, chapter 19, p. 243.

24. Ibid., chapter 3, pp. 46–58.
25. For the background see Campbell, *My Big T.O.E.*, Book 1, section 1; and in particular chapter 9, p. 79 (binaural beats) and chapters 13–14 (early OOB experiences).
26. They are condensed into ibid., Book 1, section 1, chapter 10, in particular pp. 84–6.
27. Vieira, *Projections of the Consciousness*, chapter 47, pp. 164–5.
28. See www.youtube.com/watch?v=Xug3tii0WaQ.
29. Minero, *Demystifying the Out-of-Body Experience*, chapter 1, p. 15. The original source is Meira, 'Assisted Lucid Projection', *Journal of Conscientiology* 8:31 (2006), p. 249.
30. These partnered explorations continue throughout the four volumes but see, for example, the multiple examples with his colleague and friend Rebecca in *Voyage Beyond Doubt*, Part 1. Further examples can be found in *Voyage to Curiosity's Father*, especially chapters 9–10 and 12–14, although others are recorded in later chapters.

6 CONCLUSION

No endnotes.

PART 2: A NEW TAKE ON THE SEVEN PLANES

7 THE BIG PICTURE

1. For a more detailed summary of his 'Big Theory of Everything' see Lawton, *Supersoul*, chapter 5.
2. For details of 'origin traditions' from all around the world, see Lawton, *The History of the Soul*, chapter 8.
3. Dack, *The Out-of-Body Experience*, chapters 8 and 10. The specific case is described in chapter 13, pp. 293–5.
4. Aardema, *Explorations in Consciousness*, chapter 4, pp. 109–15.
5. Campbell, *My Big T.O.E.*, Book 3, section 5, chapter 81, p. 693. For a summary of this idea of parallel theoretical timelines see Lawton, *Supersoul*, chapter 5, pp. 88–9.
6. Monroe, *Journeys Out of the Body*, chapter 6, pp. 94–100.

8 SUPERSOUL SPIRITUALITY

No endnotes.

9 WHAT DO WE MEAN BY 'PHYSICAL'?

No endnotes.

10 WHAT DO WE MEAN BY 'OUT-OF-BODY'?

1. See for example Buhlman, *The Secret of the Soul*, chapter 9, pp. 152–7; Ziewe, *Multidimensional Man*, Appendix, p. 216; and Ophiel, *Astral Projection*, section 1, p.8.
2. Ziewe reports: 'At first I was suspicious about the authenticity of this method. I later discovered that once the higher mind is tuned into the right frequency that it is possible to glean new information of the multi dimensional levels via deep trance. It is important though not to fall victim to the imagination and to adhere strictly to a "reality consciousness" which functions independently from our subjective self. We need to be fully tuned into the "present" without any attachment to our ego identity.' Taken from his paper *What is it Like to be Dead?* at www.multidimensionalman.com. Modern OOB pioneer Robert Bruce similarly reports that he uses deep meditation to visit higher planes; see *Astral Dynamics*, Part 6, chapter 27, pp. 309 and 311–12.

11 A STATE OF THE ART APPROACH

1. Sinnett, *Collected Fruits of Occult Teaching* (Kessinger, 1997), pp.175–6. My sincere thanks go to OOB pioneer Gordon Phinn for devoting considerable time to searching for this quote.
2. The Astral Routemap model at least partly reflects the views of a number of modern OOB pioneers. See for example the diagrams and explanations of the planes in Buhlman, *Adventures in the Afterlife*, Glossary, pp. 260–3 and in Ziewe, *Multidimensional Man*, Appendix, p. 216.
3. In terms of our sources these include, for example, Franchezzo (see Farnese, *A Wanderer in the Spirit Lands*, chapter 6, p. 34), Philip (see Gilbert, *Philip in the Spheres*, Part 1, chapter 2, p. 24 and chapter 3, p. 31) and Ziewe, *Multidimensional Man*, Part 2, p. 94.

4. Based loosely on a simplified version of Bladon's standard theosophical terms; see Weschcke and Slate, *Astral Projection* (Llewellyn, 2012), chapter 1, pp. 20–1.

12 THE ASTRAL ROUTEMAP MODEL

No endnotes.

13 PRELUDE TO REMAINING PARTS

1. Ames via Stead, *After Death*, Part 1, chapter 2, p. 25.
2. Franchezzo via Farnese, *A Wanderer in the Spirit Lands*, chapter 27, p. 134.
3. Benson via Borgia, *Life in the World Unseen*, Part 1, chapter 2, p. 10.
4. Myers via Cummins, *The Road to Immortality*, chapter 3, p. 13.
5. Swedenborg, *Heaven and Hell*, chapter 47, pp. 260–1 (section 455) and chapter 48, p. 264 (section 461).
6. Besant, *Ancient Wisdom*, chapter 3, p. 92.
7. Richelieu, *A Soul's Journey*, chapter 2, p. 19.
8. Taylor, *Soul Traveller*, chapter 8, p. 90.
9. Atteshlis, *The Esoteric Teachings,* chapter 4, p. 53.
10. Ames via Stead, *After Death*, Part 2, chapter 2, p. 65 and chapter 4, p. 102.
11. Ford via Montgomery, *A World Beyond*, chapter 5, p. 50.
12. Swedenborg, *Heaven and Hell*, chapter 42, p. 232 (section 405).

PART 3: PLANES OF CONFUSION, DELUSION & OBSESSION

14 THE NEAR-EARTH PLANE

1. Heagerty, *The French Revelation*, chapter 2, p. 95.
2. For the background see Geoff Cutler's website new-birth.net, and ibid., Preface and Part 1, chapter 1.
3. Ibid., Part 1, chapter 8, p. 42.
4. Ibid., Part 1, chapter 8, p. 42.
5. Gilbert, *Philip in the Spheres*, Part 1, chapter 2, p. 13.
6. The only exception to this is when he's asked about the fate of

specific famous people in Montgomery, *A World Beyond*, chapter 9.

7. Ibid., chapter 4, p. 36.
8. For the background see Ritchie, *Return from Tomorrow*, chapter 2, pp. 23–6 and chapter 5, p. 58.
9. Ibid., chapter 5, p. 59.
10. Ibid., chapter 5, pp. 66–9.
11. Leadbeater, *Life After Death*, chapter 2, p. 15.
12. Besant, *Ancient Wisdom*, chapter 3, pp. 106–7.
13. Larsen, *My Travels in the Spirit World*, chapter 3, pp. 25–32.
14. Ibid., chapter 3, pp. 33–4, 38–9, 42–5 and 50–4.
15. Ibid., chapter 4, pp. 67–8.
16. Monroe, *Far Journeys*, chapter 11, p. 153.
17. Phinn, *Eternal Life*, Preface, p. vi. Somewhat unusually the messages were seeded to him by images or 'thought-forms' rather than in words or via automatic writing; more on the process of thought transfer can be found in ibid., p. 200.
18. Phinn, *More Adventures in Eternity*, p. 222.
19. Gilbert, *Philip in the Spheres*, Part 1, chapter 2, pp. 13–16.
20. Ibid., Part 1, chapter 2, pp. 19–20.
21. Farnese, *A Wanderer in the Spirit Lands*, chapter 33, p. 166.
22. Heagerty, *The French Revelation*, chapter 2, pp. 57, 60 and 108.
23. John, *Road of Many Ways*, chapter 15, p. 114.
24. Ibid., chapter 7, p. 44.
25. Leadbeater, *The Astral Plane*, chapter 3, pp. 38–9.
26. Besant, *Ancient Wisdom*, chapter 3, pp. 108–9 and 117.
27. McKnight, *Soul Journeys,* chapter 10, p. 152.
28. Vieira, *Projections of the Consciousness*, chapter 45, p. 158.

15 THOSE WHO DON'T BELIEVE IN AN AFTERLIFE

1. For the background see Sherwood, *The Country Beyond*, chapters 1 and 2; and *Post-Mortem Journal*, Introduction.
2. The writing sample from Sherwood is reproduced in *The Country*

Beyond, chapter 2, p. 43, while that from Lawrence himself is a copy of a letter he wrote to George Brough, the manufacturer of the motorcycles he loved, reproduced at www.morebikes.co.uk/37210. Lawrence himself describes the process of initial contact from his perspective, and his surprise to see Sherwood's automatic writing coming out as 'a facsimile of his own', in *Post-Mortem Journal*, chapter 4, p. 15.

3. Sculthorp, *Excursions to the Spirit World*, chapter 3, p. 42.
4. Sherwood, *Post-Mortem Journal*, chapter 1, pp. 5–6.
5. Ibid., chapter 1, pp. 6–7.
6. See, for example, Heagerty, *The French Revelation*, chapter 2, pp. 110–11 and 114–16.
7. Ibid., chapter 2, pp. 48–9.
8. For the background see Ward, *Gone West*, Introduction.
9. For example one such experience is prefaced with the following typical OOB preliminary: 'I found myself floating over my body, and then began to whirl away into space. I seemed to pass through the ceiling into the open air, but yet was able to look right into my bedroom.' See ibid., Part 1, chapter 32, p. 72.
10. Ibid., Part 1, chapter 18, p. 41.
11. Ibid., Part 1, chapter 26, p. 41.
12. Ibid., Part 3, chapters 1–2, pp. 164–7 and chapter 3, p. 169.
13. Gilbert, *Philip in the Spheres*, Part 1, chapter 2, p. 18.
14. Ibid., Part 1, chapter 5, p. 55.
15. Montgomery, *A World Beyond*, chapter 4, p. 35.
16. Swedenborg, *Heaven and Hell*, chapter 47, p. 260 (section 456).
17. Ibid., chapter 46, p. 257 (section 452).
18. Leadbeater, *The Astral Plane*, chapter 3, pp. 49–51.

16 THE LOWER ASTRAL GENERALLY

No endnotes.

17 INDIVIDUAL HELLS

1. Heagerty, *The French Revelation*, chapter 2, pp. 42, 105–6, 111–12

and 117–18.

2. Ibid., chapter 2, pp. 74, 120 and 176.
3. Ward, *Gone West*, Part 3, chapter 3, p. 168.
4. Ibid., Part 3, chapter 4, pp. 171–2.
5. Borgia, *Life in the World Unseen*, Part 1, chapter 8, pp. 43–4.
6. Cummins, *The Road to Immortality*, chapter 3, p. 16.
7. Sherwood, *The Country Beyond*, chapter 4, p. 69.
8. Montgomery, *A World Beyond*, chapter 6, pp. 57–8.
9. John, *Road of Many Ways*, chapter 10, pp. 64–6.
10. Sandys, *The Awakening Letters*, p. 185.
11. For the background see Greaves, *Testimony of Light*, Biographical Introduction and Part 1, pp. 22–5.
12. Ibid., Part 1, pp. 97–8.
13. Extracted from Benedict's own account reproduced at www.near-death.com/experiences/exceptional/mellen-thomas-benedict.html.
14. Larsen, *My Travels in the Spirit World*, chapter 3, pp. 45–8.
15. Leonard, *My Life in Two Worlds*, chapter 23, pp. 76–7.
16. Ibid., chapter 23, p. 80.
17. Sculthorp, *Excursions to the Spirit World*, chapter 3, p. 38.
18. McKnight, *Cosmic Journeys*, chapter 22, pp. 270–1.
19. Phinn, *More Adventures in Eternity*, p. 63.
20. Phinn, *Eternal Life*, pp. 103–7.
21. Ibid., pp. 112–14.
22. Ziewe, *Multidimensional Man*, Part 2, pp. 97–9.
23. Extracted from Ziewe's paper *Life After Death 1 – General Phenomena* at www.multidimensionalman.com.
24. Ziewe, *Multidimensional Man*, Part 2, pp. 95 and 104–5.
25. Ibid., Part 2, pp. 95–6.

18 THE DEPTHS OF HELL

1. This initial material is a summary of Farnese, *A Wanderer in the Spirit Lands*, chapters 1–3.

2. Ibid., chapter 6, pp. 33–6 and chapter 9, pp. 42–3.
3. What follows is a summary of ibid., chapter 19.
4. What follows is a summary of ibid., chapter 20.
5. What follows is a summary of ibid., chapter 21.
6. Ibid., chapter 23, pp. 165–6.
7. Ward, *Gone West*, Part 1, chapter 2, p. 7.
8. Ibid., Part 2, chapter 2.
9. Ibid., Part 2, chapters 7–11.
10. Ibid., Part 2, chapters 15–18.
11. For the background see Vale Owen, *The Life Beyond the Veil*, Editor's Preface and General/Biographical Notes, pp. xi–xlix.
12. As an example see ibid., Book 1, chapter 2, pp. 44–6.
13. Ibid., Book 3, chapters 27–9.
14. Ibid., Book 3, chapters 30–1.
15. Ibid., Book 3, chapters 32–3.
16. Borgia, *Life in the World Unseen*, Part 1, chapter 9, p. 46.
17. Ibid., Part 2, chapter 6, pp. 73–5.
18. For the background see mainly Barker, *Letters from a Living Dead Man*, Introduction, pp. 8–11.
19. Ibid., Letter 23, p. 64.
20. Ibid., Letter 18, p. 47.
21. Ibid., Letter 36, pp. 108–9.
22. Ritchie, *Return from Tomorrow*, chapter 5, pp. 70–2.
23. Ibid., chapter 5, pp. 74–7.
24. Summarised from Berman, *The Journey Home*, chapter 5, pp. 84–91. Storm himself describes his experience in full in his 2005 book *My Descent into Death*.
25. Alexander, *Proof of Heaven*, chapter 5, pp. 29 and 31–2.
26. Ibid., chapter 7, p. 38.
27. For the background see Rawlings, *Beyond Death's Door*, Introduction.
28. Ibid., chapter 7, p. 117.

29. Ibid., chapter 1, pp. 17–21.
30. Ibid., chapter 5, pp. 65–6.
31. Ibid., chapter 7, especially pp. 103–6, 108–10, 113 and 118.
32. Ibid., chapter 7, pp. 106–7 and 111–12.
33. Greyson and Bush, 'Distressing Near-Death Experiences', *Psychiatry* 55 (1992), pp. 95–8.
34. Ibid., pp. 98–106.
35. Swedenborg, *Heaven and Hell*, chapter 61, p. 356 (section 586); for the number of hells see chapter 61, p. 358 (section 588).
36. Ibid., chapter 49, p. 282 (section 480).
37. See, for example, ibid., chapter 46, p. 450 (section 257), chapter 57, p. 332 (section 547) and chapter 58, p. 335 (section 552).
38. Ibid., chapter 58, pp. 335–7 (sections 552–3).
39. Ibid., chapter 59, p. 348 (section 571).
40. Ibid., chapter 61, pp. 356–7 (sections 585–6).
41. Ibid., chapter 59, p. 349 (section 574).
42. Besant, *Ancient Wisdom*, chapter 3, pp. 101–6.
43. Leadbeater, *The Astral Plane*, chapter 3, p. 45.
44. Leadbeater, *Life After Death*, chapter 3, pp. 23–4.
45. For the background see en.wikipedia.org/wiki/William_Walker_Atkinson. Also for his limited comments on the mechanisms of OOB travel see Panchadasi, *The Astral World*, chapter 2 and chapter 4.
46. For further discussion see Lawton, *The Power of You*, Preface, pp. 2–3. The phrase was first used by Helena Blavatsky in *Isis Unveiled* in 1877, but was brought to prominence by various New Thought pioneers in the late nineteenth and early twentieth centuries – decades before its resurrection in the late twentieth century.
47. Panchadasi, *The Astral World*, chapter 7, pp. 53–6.
48. Yram, *Practical Astral Projection*, Part 1, chapter 2, p. 23.
49. Ibid., Part 1, chapter 8, pp. 100–1.
50. Ibid., Part 1, chapter 17, pp. 141–2.
51. Larsen, *My Travels in the Spirit World*, chapter 4, pp. 66–9.

52. Ibid., chapter 4, p. 64.
53. Ibid., chapter 4, pp. 71–2.
54. Sculthorp, *Excursions to the Spirit World*, chapter 2, pp. 20–1.
55. Ibid., chapter 2, pp. 25–7.
56. Ibid., chapter 2, p. 29.
57. Ibid., chapter 3, p. 44.
58. Monroe, *Journeys Out of the Body*, chapter 8, pp. 120–1.
59. Monroe, *Far Journeys*, chapter 7, pp. 88–9.
60. Dack, *The Out-of-Body Experience*, chapter 9, p. 190.
61. Moen, *Voyage Beyond Doubt*, chapter 10.
62. Phinn, *Eternal Life*, p. 152.
63. Ibid., p. 103.
64. Ibid., pp. 63–4.
65. Ziewe, *Multidimensional Man*, Part 2, pp. 96–7.
66. Ibid., Part 2, p. 94.

19 MORE ON RESCUE AND RETRIEVAL

1. Sandys, *The Awakening Letters II*, pp. 15–21.
2. Sandys, *The Awakening Letters*, pp. 127–9.
3. Heagerty, *The French Revelation*, chapter 2, pp. 102–3, 109 and 121–33.
4. Leonard, *My Life in Two Worlds*, chapter 23, p. 78.
5. John, *Road of Many Ways*, chapters 3 and 4.
6. Larsen, *My Travels in the Spirit World*, chapter 4, pp. 61–3.
7. Monroe, *Ultimate Journey*, chapter 9, pp. 117–24 and chapter 10.
8. Moen, *Voyage Beyond Doubt*, chapter 11, pp. 93–7 and chapter 14, pp. 111–17. Further examples can be found in *Voyages into the Unknown*, chapter 4, pp. 96–104 and 126–9 and chapter 5, pp. 141–9 and 155–60.
9. Ziewe, *Multidimensional Man*, Part 2, p. 95.
10. Ward, *Gone West*, Introduction, p. v.
11. Sherwood, *Post-Mortem Journal*, chapter 8, pp. 31–2.

12. Greaves, *Testimony of Light*, Part 1, pp. 98–102.
13. Gilbert, *Philip in the Spheres*, Part 1, chapter 3, pp. 30–1 and 35.
14. Ritchie, *Return from Tomorrow*, chapter 5, pp. 77–9.
15. Phinn, *More Adventures in Eternity*, p. 239.
16. Borgia, *Life in the World Unseen*, Part 1, chapter 9, p. 46.
17. Gilbert, *Philip in the Spheres*, Part 1, chapter 2, p. 25.
18. Monroe, *Far Journeys*, Epilogue, p. 240.
19. Vieira, *Projections of the Consciousness*, chapter 15, pp. 62–3.
20. See, for example, Gilbert, *Philip in the Spheres*, Part 1, chapter 6, pp. 70–1 and Part 2, chapter 4, pp. 184–6.
21. McKnight, *Cosmic Journeys*, chapter 20, p. 247.
22. Vieira, *Projections of the Consciousness*, chapter 18, pp. 70–1.
23. Leadbeater, *Life After Death*, chapter 9.
24. Monroe, *Far Journeys*, Epilogue, p. 240.

20 CONCLUSION

1. Leonard, *My Life in Two Worlds*, chapter 23, p. 79.
2. Farnese, *A Wanderer in the Spirit Lands*, chapter 26, p. 128.
3. Ibid., chapter 26, p. 127.
4. For a more detailed discussion of this sometimes controversial view see Lawton, *Sh*t Doesn't Just Happen*, pp. 47–50.
5. Sherwood, *The Country Beyond*, chapter 4, p. 59.
6. Gilbert, *Philip in the Spheres*, Introduction, p. xxiii.
7. Bruce, *Astral Dynamics*, 'A Few last Words', p. 342.
8. Farnese, *A Wanderer in the Spirit Lands*, chapter 27, p. 71.
9. Gilbert, *Philip in the Spheres*, Part 1, chapter 2, pp. 20 and 25.
10. This is the heading for chapter 49 in Swedenborg's *Heaven and Hell*.
11. Besant, *Ancient Wisdom*, chapter 3, p. 92.
12. Heagerty, *The French Revelation*, chapter 4, pp. 255–6.
13. Ward, *Gone West*, Part 1, chapter 18, p. 41.
14. Leonard, *My Life in Two Worlds*, chapter 23, p. 78.

15. Greaves, *Testimony of Light*, Part 1, p. 61.
16. Panchadasi, *The Astral World*, chapter 7, p. 57.
17. Heagerty, *The French Revelation*, chapter 2, pp. 90–1.
18. Ibid., chapter 2, pp. 19 and 52.
19. Montgomery, *A World Beyond*, chapter 10, p. 120.
20. Ritchie, *Return from Tomorrow*, chapter 1, p. 20.
21. Yram, *Practical Astral Projection*, Part 2, chapter 5, p. 192.

PART 4: PLANES OF TRANSITION, RECREATION & ILLUSION

21 ASSISTANCE, HEALING AND ACCLIMATISATION

1. For explicit confirmation see, for example, Greaves, *Testimony of Light*, Part 1, p. 53 or Phinn, *Eternal Life*, pp. 152 and 208–9.
2. Ward, *Gone West*, Part 1, chapter 15, p. 37.
3. Barker, *Letters from a Living Dead Man*, Letter 33, p. 97.
4. See, for example, ibid., Letter 20, p. 52; Letter 15, p. 37; and Letter 12, p. 32.
5. Ibid., Letter 11, p. 28.
6. Vale Owen, *The Life Beyond the Veil*, Book 1, chapter 1, p. 19.
7. Ibid., Book 1, chapter 3, pp. 69–72 and chapter 5, pp. 97–103.
8. Gilbert, *Philip in the Spheres*, Part 1, chapter 5, pp. 52–3.
9. John, *Road of Many Ways*, chapter 1.
10. Ibid., chapter 2.
11. Ibid., chapter 7, p. 43.
12. Sandys, *The Awakening Letters*, pp. 47–9.
13. Ibid., pp. 20–1.
14. Richelieu, *A Soul's Journey*, chapter 4, pp. 55–8.
15. Ibid., chapter 9, pp. 155–6.
16. Monroe, *Ultimate Journey*, chapter 13, p. 180.
17. Monroe, *Journeys Out of the Body*, chapter 5, pp. 80–1.
18. Phinn, *Eternal Life*, pp. 3–5 and 12.
19. Ibid., pp. 96–9.

20. Ibid., pp. 187–90.
21. Ziewe, *Multidimensional Man*, Part 2, p. 100.
22. See, for example, Eadie, *Embraced by the Light*, p. 83. Also in Sherwood, *The Country Beyond*, chapter 4, p. 61, EK reports: 'Much of the apparent suffering of a death-bed is not consciously felt by the sufferer. His real life is already half retired from the mortal body and neither experiences nor records its pangs.'
23. Moen, *Voyages into the Unknown*, chapter 6, pp. 184–7.
24. Heagerty, *The French Revelation*, chapter 2, pp. 56–7.
25. Ward, *Gone West*, Part 1, chapter 36, p. 83.
26. Borgia, *Life in the World Unseen*, Part 2, chapter 3, p. 62.
27. John, *Road of Many Ways*, chapter 8, pp. 48–51.
28. Ibid., chapter 14, pp. 101–4.
29. Ibid., chapter 14, pp. 104–7.
30. Sandys, *The Awakening Letters II*, pp. 24–5.
31. Sandys, *The Awakening Letters*, pp. 52–4.
32. Sandys, *The Awakening Letters II*, pp. 70–1.
33. Moen, *Voyage Beyond Doubt*, chapter 5, pp. 46–57.
34. Moen, *Voyages Into the Unknown*, chapter 1.
35. Phinn, *Eternal Life*, pp. 125–8.
36. Ibid., p. 143.
37. Phinn, *More Adventures in Eternity*, pp. 78–9 and 83–4.
38. Ibid., pp. 236–7.
39. Besant, *Ancient Wisdom*, chapter 3, p. 97.
40. See, for example, Heagerty, *The French Revelation*, chapter 2, p. 119.
41. Moen, *Voyage Beyond Doubt*, chapter 16.
42. Sherwood, *Post-Mortem Journal*, chapter 2, pp. 8–11.
43. Farnese, *A Wanderer in the Spirit Lands*, chapter 4, pp. 23–6.
44. Ibid., chapter 13, p. 55.
45. Heagerty, *The French Revelation*, chapter 2, p. 36.
46. Ward, *Gone West*, Part 1, chapter 19, p. 46.

47. Ibid., Part 1, chapter 28, p. 66.
48. See, for example, Vale Owen, *The Life Beyond the Veil*, Book 1, chapter 2, pp. 40–1 and chapter 5, p. 116.
49. Ibid., Book 1, chapter 4, p. 82.
50. Ibid., Book 3, chapter 3, pp. 311–12 and chapter 11, pp. 349–50.
51. Borgia, *Life in the World Unseen*, Part 1, chapter 4, pp. 19–21.
52. Sherwood, *The Country Beyond*, chapter 5, pp. 84–5.
53. Ibid., chapter 8, pp. 128–9.
54. Ibid., chapter 7, pp. 106–7.
55. Gilbert, *Philip in the Spheres*, Part 1, chapter 7, p. 73 and chapter 8, p. 81.
56. Greaves, *Testimony of Light*, Part 1, pp. 27–32.
57. Ibid., Part 1, pp. 86–7.
58. Ibid., Part 1, pp. 35–6.
59. Ibid., Part 1, pp. 50–1.
60. Ibid., Part 1, p. 58.
61. Ibid., Part 1, pp. 88–96.
62. John, *Road of Many Ways*, chapter 8, p. 48.
63. Sandys, *The Awakening Letters*, pp. 15–17, 23–5 and 32–3.
64. Sculthorp, *Excursions to the Spirit World*, chapter 1, pp. 10–11.
65. Ibid., chapter 3, p. 50.
66. Ibid., chapter 5, p. 68 and chapter 3, p. 39.
67. Moen, *Voyages into the Afterlife*, chapter 6, pp. 57–9.
68. Phinn, *Eternal Life*, pp. 14–17.
69. Ibid., pp. 11–12.
70. Phinn, *More Adventures in Eternity*, pp. 163–73.
71. Vieira, *Projections of the Consciousness*, chapter 43, p. 153.
72. Ibid., pp. 195–6.
73. Ziewe, *Vistas of Infinity*, pp. 120–2.
74. Bruce, *Astral Dynamics*, Part 5, chapter 22, pp. 264 and 268.
75. Sculthorp, *Excursions to the Spirit World*, chapter 3, pp. 36–7.

76. Ibid., chapter 3.
77. Richelieu, *A Soul's Journey*, chapter 6, p. 76.
78. Sculthorp, *Excursions to the Spirit World*, chapter 3, p. 43.
79. Panchadasi, *The Astral World*, chapter 3, p. 24.
80. Phinn, *Eternal Life*, pp. 146–7.
81. Vale Owen, *The Life Beyond the Veil*, Book 1, chapter 4, p. 83.
82. Larsen, *My Travels in the Spirit World*, chapter 4, pp. 59–61.
83. Ziewe, *Multidimensional Man*, Part 2, pp. 127–8.
84. John, *Road of Many Ways*, chapter 12, pp. 83–4.
85. Sandys, *The Awakening Letters*, p. 112.
86. Yram, *Practical Astral Projection*, Part 1, chapter 17, pp. 139–41.
87. Sculthorp, *Excursions to the Spirit World*, chapter 2, pp. 21–3.
88. Ibid., chapter 3, p. 45.
89. Phinn, *Eternal Life*, p. 153.
90. Ziewe, *Multidimensional Man*, Part 2, pp. 117–120.
91. Ibid., Part 2, pp. 122–4.
92. Ibid., Part 2, pp. 128–33.
93. Ibid., Part 2, p. 114.
94. Ziewe, *Vistas of Infinity*, p. 105.
95. Bruce, *Astral Dynamics*, Part 6, chapter 28, p. 313.
96. Buhlman, *The Secret of the Soul*, chapter 8, pp. 137–8.
97. Ziewe, *Multidimensional Man*, Part 2, pp. 160–1.

22 SMOOTH TRANSITIONS AND LIFE REVIEWS

1. Vale Owen, *The Life Beyond the Veil*, Book 1, chapter 2, p. 41.
2. Sherwood, *Post-Mortem Journal*, chapter 4, p. 15.
3. Sherwood, *The Country Beyond*, chapter 8, pp. 128–9.
4. Gilbert, *Philip in the Spheres*, Part 1, chapter 2, p. 24.
5. Montgomery, *A World Beyond*, chapter 1, p. 11.
6. Swedenborg, *Heaven and Hell*, chapter 51, p. 293 (section 491).
7. Larsen, *My Travels in the Spirit World*, chapter 4, p. 61.

8. Monroe, *Ultimate Journey*, chapter 18, pp. 253–4.
9. Moen, *Voyages Into the Unknown*, Epilogue, pp. 220–1.
10. Ibid., chapter 6, p. 59.
11. For the background see Stead, *After Death*, Preface, Introduction and Biography.
12. See, for example, ibid., Part 2, chapter 3, p. 88 and chapter 4, p. 105.
13. See, for example, ibid., Part 2, chapter 2, p. 70, chapter 3, p. 79, chapter 4, pp. 94–5, chapter 5, p. 116, chapter 6, p. 114 and chapter 7, p. 142.
14. Ibid., Part 1, chapter 1, pp. 19–21.
15. Ibid., Part 2, chapter 2, p. 65.
16. Heagerty, *The French Revelation*, chapter 2, p. 49.
17. Ibid., chapter 2, pp. 39–40.
18. Ward, *Gone West*, Part 1, chapter 6, p. 15.
19. Ibid., Part 1, chapter 9, p. 22.
20. Borgia, *Life in the World Unseen*, Part 1, chapter 2, pp. 7–8.
21. Ibid., Part 2, chapter 7, p. 77 and Part 1, chapter 3, p. 13.
22. Sherwood, *The Country Beyond*, chapter 4, p. 61.
23. John, *Road of Many Ways*, chapter 5.
24. Sandys, *The Awakening Letters*, pp. 83–5.
25. Ibid., pp. 99–103.
26. Sandys, *The Awakening Letters II*, p. 60.
27. Medhus, *My Life After Death*, Foreword, p. xv.
28. Ibid., chapter 25, p. 157.
29. Ibid., Afterword, p. 194.
30. Ibid., chapter 1.
31. Ibid., chapter 2.
32. Ibid., chapter 3.
33. Ibid., chapter 4.
34. Ibid., chapter 16, p. 114.
35. Ibid., chapter 4, pp. 49–50.

36. The proofs and signs are spread throughout the book; her reluctance is expressed in Kagan, *The Afterlife of Billy Fingers*, chapter 16, p. 96.
37. Ibid., chapter 24, pp. 137–8 and chapter 30, pp. 168–9.
38. Ibid., chapter 1, p. 12.
39. Swedenborg, *Heaven and Hell*, chapter 46, p. 255 (section 449).
40. The entirety of Part 2 of ibid. is an account of this intermediate world.
41. Ibid., chapter 46, pp. 256–7 (section 450).
42. Fenwick, *The Truth in the Light*, chapter 1, p. 10.
43. Brinkley, *Saved by the Light*, chapter 1, p. 6 and chapter 2, pp. 7–8.
44. McKnight, *Cosmic Journeys*, chapter 15, pp. 166–7.
45. Heagerty, *The French Revelation*, chapter 2, pp. 44–5.
46. For satanic references see, for example, Eadie, *Embraced by the Light*, pp. 89 and 108.
47. Ibid., pp. 40–2.
48. Ritchie, *Return from Tomorrow*, chapter 5, pp. 57–8.
49. Phinn, *More Adventures in Eternity*, pp. 54–9.
50. Taylor, *Soul Traveller*, chapter 8, p. 93.
51. Stead, *After Death*, Part 2, chapter 1, p. 53.
52. Farnese, *A Wanderer in the Spirit Lands*, chapter 11, p. 49.
53. Ward, *Gone West*, Part 1, chapter 16, p. 39.
54. Sherwood, *Post-Mortem Journal*, chapter 1, p. 7.
55. Kagan, *The Afterlife of Billy Fingers*, chapter 15, pp. 89–90.
56. Ibid., chapter 20, p. 117.
57. Larsen, *My Travels in the Spirit World*, chapter 4, p. 72.
58. Borgia, *Life in the World Unseen*, Part 2, chapter 14, pp. 100–1.
59. Various sources support this view; see, for example, Besant, *Ancient Wisdom*, chapter 3, p. 94; and Myers in Cummins, *The Road to Immortality*, chapter 3, p. 16.
60. Farnese, *A Wanderer in the Spirit Lands*, chapter 27, pp. 134–6 and 140.
61. Heagerty, *The French Revelation*, chapter 2, p. 38.

62. Ibid., p. 48.
63. Ward, *Gone West*, Part 1, chapter 6, p. 16.
64. Borgia, *Life in the World Unseen*, Part 2, chapter 9, pp. 82–3.
65. Sherwood, *The Country Beyond*, chapter 9, pp. 135–8.
66. Sherwood, *Post-Mortem Journal*, chapter 3, pp. 13–14.
67. Ibid., chapter 7, p. 27.
68. Cummins, *The Road to Immortality*, chapter 3, p. 16.
69. Greaves, *Testimony of Light*, Part 1, pp. 33–7.
70. Ibid., Part 1, pp. 58–60.
71. Medhus, *My Life After Death*, chapter 4, pp. 49–50 and chapter 5.
72. Ibid., chapter 9.
73. Kagan, *The Afterlife of Billy Fingers*, chapter 1, p. 13 and chapter 3, p. 27.
74. Ibid., chapter 4, p. 32.
75. Ibid., chapter 6, pp. 42–4.
76. Ibid., chapter 7, p. 49.
77. Eadie, *Embraced by the Light*, pp. 112–14.
78. Brinkley, *Saved by the Light*, chapter 2, pp. 9, 14 and 19–20 and chapter 4, p. 25.
79. Ibid., chapter 13, pp. 144–6.
80. Ibid., chapter 14, pp. 157–8.
81. Swedenborg, *Heaven and Hell*, chapter 47, pp. 266–8 (sections 462b–463).
82. Ziewe, *Vistas of Infinity*, pp. 25–36.

23 THE MID ASTRAL GENERALLY

1. Stead, *After Death*, Part 2, chapter 1, p. 58, chapter 2, p. 64 and chapter 4, p. 102.
2. Heagerty, *The French Revelation*, chapter 2, p. 36.
3. Ibid., chapter 2, p. 49.
4. Barker, *Letters from a Living Dead Man*, Letter 11, p. 30.
5. Sherwood, *The Country Beyond*, chapter 4, p. 63.

6. Cummins, *Beyond Human Personality*, chapter 3, p. 20.
7. Greaves, *Testimony of Light*, Part 1, pp. 29–30.
8. John, *Road of Many Ways*, chapter 9, p. 56.
9. Ibid., chapter 5, p. 35.
10. Medhus, *My Life After Death*, chapter 1, p. 10.
11. Ritchie, *Return from Tomorrow*, chapter 1, p. 20.
12. Swedenborg, *Heaven and Hell*, chapter 48, p. 265 (section 462a).
13. Sculthorp, *Excursions to the Spirit World*, chapter 4, p. 54.
14. Ziewe, *Multidimensional Man*, Part 2, p. 162.
15. Greaves, *Testimony of Light*, Part 1, p. 84.
16. See Gilbert, *Philip in the Spheres*, Part 1, chapter 3, p. 26 and John, *Road of Many Ways*, chapter 8, p. 45.
17. Swedenborg, *Heaven and Hell*, chapter 18, p. 88 (section 162).
18. See Ward, *Gone West*, Part 1, chapter 1, p. 2 and chapter 11, p. 28; and Borgia, *Life in the World Unseen*, Part 2, chapter 34, p. 66.
19. Sherwood, *Post-Mortem Journal*, chapter 7, p. 29.
20. Sherwood, *The Country Beyond*, chapter 4, p. 71and chapter 6, pp. 94–5.
21. Vale Owen, *The Life Beyond the Veil*, Book 1, chapter 6, p. 141.
22. Montgomery, *A World Beyond*, chapter 1, p. 10.
23. Medhus, *My Life After Death*, chapter 15, p. 109.
24. Alexander, *Proof of Heaven*, chapter 31, p. 143.
25. Stead, *After Death*, Part 2, chapter 1, p. 57.
26. Farnese, *A Wanderer in the Spirit Lands*, chapter 10, p. 47.
27. Heagerty, *The French Revelation*, chapter 2, p. 36.
28. Barker, *Letters from a Living Dead Man*, Letter 16, p. 40.
29. Vale Owen, *The Life Beyond the Veil*, Book 1, chapter 2, p. 37.
30. John, *Road of Many Ways*, chapter 17, p. 135.
31. Medhus, *My Life After Death*, chapter 13, p. 101.
32. Borgia, *Life in the World Unseen*, Part 1, chapter 4, p. 22.
33. Sherwood, *The Country Beyond*, chapter 6, p. 100.

34. Alexander, *Proof of Heaven*, chapter 12, p. 70.
35. See, for example, Taylor, *Soul Traveller*, chapter 8, p. 91 and Bruce, *Astral Dynamics*, Part 5, chapter 22, p. 267.
36. Moen, *Voyages Into the Afterlife*, chapter 7, p. 85.
37. Swedenborg, *Heaven and Hell*, chapter 22, p. 100 (section 192).
38. Greaves, *Testimony of Light*, Part 1, p. 75.
39. Ward, *Gone West*, Part 1, chapter 1, p. 3.
40. Barker, *Letters from a Living Dead Man*, Letter 11, p. 29.
41. Borgia, *Life in the World Unseen*, Part 1, chapter 4, pp. 23–4.
42. Greaves, *Testimony of Light*, Part 2, p. 132.
43. Medhus, *My Life After Death*, chapter 4, p. 49.
44. Sherwood, *Post-Mortem Journal*, chapter 4, p. 17.
45. Medhus, *My Life After Death*, chapter 8, pp. 69–70.
46. Borgia, *Life in the World Unseen*, Part 1, chapter 4, p. 23.
47. John, *Road of Many Ways*, chapter 17, p. 135.
48. Cummins, *Beyond Human Personality*, chapter 3, p. 20.
49. Swedenborg, *Heaven and Hell*, chapter 51, p. 294 (section 494).
50. McKnight, *Soul Journeys,* chapter 11, p. 172.
51. Sherwood, *Post-Mortem Journal*, chapter 5, p. 19.
52. Bruce, *Astral Dynamics*, Part 6, chapter 27, p. 310.
53. Sculthorp, *Excursions to the Spirit World*, chapter 5, p. 66.
54. Ziewe, *Vistas of Infinity*, p. 128.
55. Stead, *After Death*, Part 1, chapter 2, pp. 25–7 and Part 2, chapter 4, p. 95.
56. Farnese, *A Wanderer in the Spirit Lands*, chapter 4, p. 23.
57. Vale Owen, *The Life Beyond the Veil*, Book 1, chapter 2, p. 48 and chapter 5, p. 103.
58. Borgia, *Life in the World Unseen*, Part 2, chapter 12, pp. 94–5.
59. Sherwood, *Post-Mortem Journal*, chapter 4, p. 18.
60. Ibid., chapter 2, p. 9.
61. Greaves, *Testimony of Light*, Part 1, p. 61.

62. John, *Road of Many Ways*, chapter 10, pp. 69–70.
63. Swedenborg, *Heaven and Hell*, chapter 6, p. 26 (section 48).
64. Richelieu, *A Soul's Journey*, chapter 7, p. 118.
65. Stead, *After Death*, Part 2, chapter 1, p. 48.
66. Heagerty, *The French Revelation*, chapter 2, pp. 29, 35–6 and 98.
67. Ward, *Gone West*, Part 1, chapter 10, p. 24.
68. Barker, *Letters from a Living Dead Man*, Letter 15, p. 38.
69. Vale Owen, *The Life Beyond the Veil*, Book 1, chapter 2, p. 48.
70. Cummins, *Beyond Human Personality*, chapter 3, p. 20.
71. Gilbert, *Philip in the Spheres*, Part 1, chapter 3, p. 29.
72. Greaves, *Testimony of Light*, Part 1, pp. 75–6 and 87.
73. Montgomery, *A World Beyond*, chapter 3, pp. 24 and 28. The chapter is entitled 'Thoughts are Things'.
74. Medhus, *My Life After Death*, chapter 12, p. 93.
75. Alexander, *Proof of Heaven*, chapter 20, pp. 102–3.
76. Leadbeater, *Life After Death*, p. 18.
77. Panchadasi, *The Astral World*, chapter 8, p. 60.
78. Yram, *Practical Astral Projection*, Part 1, chapter 17, p. 141.
79. Taylor, *Soul Traveller*, chapter 8, p. 91.
80. Ziewe, *Multidimensional Man*, p. 146 and *Vistas of Infinity*, p. 127.
81. Greaves, *Testimony of Light*, Part 1, p. 75.
82. Eadie, *Embraced by the Light*, pp. 43–71, especially p. 58.
83. Buhlman, *Adventures Beyond the Body*, Part 1, chapter 2, p. 67.
84. Taylor, *Soul Traveller*, chapter 8, p. 91.
85. McKnight, *Soul Journeys*, chapter 11, p. 173.
86. Especially *The Power of You*, *Sh*t Doesn't Just Happen!!* and *The God Who Sometimes Screwed Up*.
87. Vale Owen, *The Life Beyond the Veil*, Book 1, chapter 2, p. 38.
88. Ibid., Book 3, chapter 11, pp. 346–8.
89. Gilbert, *Philip in the Spheres*, Part 1, chapter 5, pp. 50–1 and chapter 7, p. 74.

90. Medhus, *My Life After Death*, chapter 12, p. 96.
91. Leadbeater, *The Astral Plane*, p. 33 and *Inner Life II*, p. 15.
92. Monroe, *Ultimate Journey*, Glossary, p. 272 and Part 1, chapter 11, p. 149.
93. Phinn, *Eternal Life*, pp. 101–2, 59–60 and 152–3.
94. Extracted from Ziewe's paper *Life After Death 5 – The Intermediate Dimensions* at www.multidimensionalman.com.
95. Buhlman, *Adventures Beyond the Body*, Part 1, chapter 2, p. 67.
96. Ziewe, *Multidimensional Man*, Part 2, p. 113.
97. Gilbert, *Philip in the Spheres*, Part 1, chapter 5, p. 50.
98. Sculthorp, *Excursions to the Spirit World*, chapter 2, p. 21.
99. Extracted from Ziewe's paper *Life After Death 5 – The Intermediate Dimensions* at www.multidimensionalman.com.
100. Heagerty, *The French Revelation*, chapter 2, p. 83.
101. Ward, *Gone West*, Part 1, chapter 10, p. 24 and chapter 21, p. 51.
102. Barker, *Letters from a Living Dead Man*, Letter 28, p. 78.
103. Vale Owen, *The Life Beyond the Veil*, Book 1, chapter 4, pp. 82 and 84.
104. Borgia, *Life in the World Unseen*, Part 2, chapter 2, p. 59.
105. Sherwood, *Post-Mortem Journal*, chapter 9, p. 35.
106. Cummins, *The Road to Immortality*, chapter 3, p. 14.
107. Gilbert, *Philip in the Spheres*, Part 1, chapter 6, p. 70.
108. Swedenborg, *Heaven and Hell*, chapter 48, p. 264 (section 461).
109. Leadbeater, *Life After Death*, p. 14.
110. Panchadasi, *The Astral World*, chapter 8, pp. 60–1.
111. Sculthorp, *Excursions to the Spirit World*, chapter 1, p. 9 and chapter 4 p. 54.
112. Extracted from Ziewe's paper *Life After Death 3 – The Lowest Dimensions* at www.multidimensionalman.com.
113. Bruce, *Astral Dynamics*, Part 6, chapter 27, p. 310.
114. Stead, *After Death*, Part 1, chapter 1, p. 23 and Part 2, chapter 2, p. 63.

115. Farnese, *A Wanderer in the Spirit Lands*, chapter 13, p. 56 and chapter 16, p. 64.
116. Barker, *Letters from a Living Dead Man*, Letter 16, p. 41.
117. Vale Owen, *The Life Beyond the Veil*, Book 1, chapter 1, p. 19.
118. Borgia, *Life in the World Unseen*, Part 2, chapter 9, p. 83.
119. Sherwood, *Post-Mortem Journal*, chapter 5, p. 21.
120. Greaves, *Testimony of Light*, Part 1, p. 107 and Part 2, p. 136.
121. John, *Road of Many Ways*, chapter 9, p. 55.
122. Swedenborg, *Heaven and Hell*, chapter 42, p. 236 (section 414).
123. Sculthorp, *Excursions to the Spirit World*, chapter 3, pp. 38 and 41, and chapter 4, p. 59.
124. Bruce, *Astral Dynamics*, Part 6, chapter 27, p. 310.
125. Sherwood, *Post-Mortem Journal*, chapter 9, p. 36.
126. Stead, *After Death*, Part 1, chapter 1, p. 23 and Part 2, chapter 2, p. 71.
127. Ward, *Gone West*, Part 1, chapter 11, p. 28.
128. Barker, *Letters from a Living Dead Man*, Letter 27, p. 75.
129. Borgia, *Life in the World Unseen*, Part 1, chapter 3, pp. 17 and 13–14.
130. Sherwood, *The Country Beyond*, chapter 4, p. 76.
131. Sherwood, *Post-Mortem Journal*, chapter 4, p. 16 and chapter 9, p. 35.
132. John, *Road of Many Ways*, chapter 9, p. 56.
133. Farnese, *A Wanderer in the Spirit Lands*, chapter 13, p. 57.
134. Borgia, *Life in the World Unseen*, Part 1, chapter 3, pp. 14–15.
135. Richelieu, *A Soul's Journey*, chapter 7, p. 97.
136. McKnight, *Soul Journeys*, chapter 12, pp. 179–80.
137. Medhus, *My Life After Death*, chapter 8, p. 67.
138. Farnese, *A Wanderer in the Spirit Lands*, chapter 32, p. 159.
139. Heagerty, *The French Revelation*, chapter 2, pp. 7 and 62.
140. Vale Owen, *The Life Beyond the Veil*, Book 1, chapter 1, p. 5 and chapter 4, p. 74.
141. Borgia, *Life in the World Unseen*, Part 1, chapter 2, p. 9 and chapter

3, p. 16, and Part 2, chapter 2, p. 60 and chapter 7, p. 76.

142. Sherwood, *The Country Beyond*, chapter 4, pp. 64–5.

143. Sherwood, *Post-Mortem Journal*, chapter 9, p. 35 and chapter 10, p. 38.

144. Greaves, *Testimony of Light*, Part 1, p. 35.

145. Montgomery, *A World Beyond*, chapter 5, p. 47.

146. John, *Road of Many Ways*, chapter 16, p. 117.

147. Medhus, *My Life After Death*, chapter 11, pp. 89–91.

148. Sandys, *The Awakening Letters*, p. 186.

149. Medhus, *My Life After Death*, chapter 8, pp. 68 and 70.

150. Eadie, *Embraced by the Light*, pp. 74 and 78–80.

151. Larsen, *My Travels in the Spirit World*, chapter 6, pp. 85–6.

152. Richelieu, *A Soul's Journey*, chapter 9, p. 157.

153. Sculthorp, *Excursions to the Spirit World*, chapter 4, p. 56.

154. McKnight, *Soul Journeys,* chapter 12, p. 181.

155. Ziewe, *Multidimensional Man*, Part 2, p. 164.

156. Bruce, *Astral Dynamics*, Part 6, chapter 27, p. 309.

157. Vale Owen, *The Life Beyond the Veil*, Book 2, chapter 4, pp. 202–4 and Book 1, chapter 5, p. 114.

158. Swedenborg, *Heaven and Hell*, chapter 51, p. 294 (section 494).

159. Sherwood, *Post-Mortem Journal*, chapter 8, p. 32.

160. Sherwood, *The Country Beyond*, chapter 9, pp. 140–1.

161. Sherwood, *Post-Mortem Journal*, chapter 8, p. 32.

162. Sherwood, *The Country Beyond*, chapter 4, p. 71.

163. Cummins, *Beyond Human Personality*, chapter 3, p. 17.

164. Ward, *Gone West*, Part 1, chapter 25, p. 58.

165. Sherwood, *Post-Mortem Journal*, chapter 2, p. 9.

166. Sandys, *The Awakening Letters*, p. 125.

167. Medhus, *My Life After Death*, chapter 18, pp. 120–1.

168. Yram, *Practical Astral Projection*, Part 2, chapter 7, p. 207.

169. Phinn, *Eternal Life*, p. 171.

170. Heagerty, *The French Revelation*, chapter 2, pp. 92, 134, 137–8 and 141.
171. Barker, *Letters from a Living Dead Man*, Letter 11, p. 28.
172. Vale Owen, *The Life Beyond the Veil*, Book 1, chapter 2, pp. 42–3.
173. Borgia, *Life in the World Unseen*, Part 2, chapter 10, pp. 85–7.
174. Greaves, *Testimony of Light*, Part 1, p. 62.
175. Swedenborg, *Heaven and Hell*, chapter 37, pp. 182–9 (sections 329–30, 332, 337, 340 and 345).
176. Larsen, *My Travels in the Spirit World*, chapter 7, pp. 88–9.
177. Sculthorp, *Excursions to the Spirit World*, chapter 3, p. 47.
178. McKnight, *Soul Journeys,* chapter 10, pp. 158–9.

24 HEAVENLY LIFE

1. Ward, *Gone West*, Part 1, chapter 2, p. 6.
2. Heagerty, *The French Revelation*, chapter 2, p. 205.
3. Swedenborg, *Heaven and Hell*, chapter 6, pp. 24–5 (sections 44–6).
4. Sculthorp, *Excursions to the Spirit World*, chapter 4 pp. 54–5.
5. McKnight, *Cosmic Journeys*, chapter 19, p. 232.
6. Ziewe, *Multidimensional Man*, Part 2, p. 137.
7. Farnese, *A Wanderer in the Spirit Lands*, chapter 11, pp. 50–1.
8. Vale Owen, *The Life Beyond the Veil*, Book 1, chapter 2, p. 37.
9. Borgia, *Life in the World Unseen*, Part 2, chapter 5, p. 71.
10. Sherwood, *Post-Mortem Journal*, chapter 4, pp. 17–18.
11. Farnese, *A Wanderer in the Spirit Lands*, chapter 33, p. 165.
12. Heagerty, *The French Revelation*, chapter 2, pp. 94–5.
13. Greaves, *Testimony of Light*, Part 1, p. 66.
14. Borgia, *Life in the World Unseen*, Part 2, chapter 12, p. 92.
15. Farnese, *A Wanderer in the Spirit Lands*, chapter 13, p. 55, chapter 27, p. 133, chapter 28, p. 142 and chapter 32, pp. 159–62.
16. Borgia, *Life in the World Unseen*, Part 2, chapter 8, p. 81.
17. Sherwood, *Post-Mortem Journal*, chapter 4, p. 16 and chapter 5, pp. 19–20.

18. John, *Road of Many Ways*, chapter 11, pp. 79–81.
19. Ibid., chapter 13, pp. 96–100.
20. Medhus, *My Life After Death*, chapter 12, pp. 93–5.
21. For examples see ibid., chapters 24 and 26.
22. John, *Road of Many Ways*, chapter 16, p. 118.
23. Sculthorp, *Excursions to the Spirit World*, chapter 3, p. 37.
24. Moen, *Voyages into the Afterlife*, chapter 6, pp. 54–5.
25. Farnese, *A Wanderer in the Spirit Lands*, chapter 32, p. 159 and chapter 33, p. 165.
26. Heagerty, *The French Revelation*, chapter 2, p. 38.
27. Vale Owen, *The Life Beyond the Veil*, Book 1, chapter 4, p. 74.
28. Borgia, *Life in the World Unseen*, Part 1, chapter 3, p. 14.
29. Sherwood, *The Country Beyond*, chapter 4, p. 70.
30. John, *Road of Many Ways*, chapter 9, p. 53.
31. Rawlings, *Beyond Death's Door*, chapter 6, pp. 94–5 and 97–9, and chapter 7, p. 120.
32. Alexander, *Proof of Heaven*, chapter 7, pp. 38–41.
33. Swedenborg, *Heaven and Hell*, chapter 21, pp. 97–8 (sections 184–5).
34. Panchadasi, *The Astral World*, chapter 7, p. 58.
35. Fox, *Astral Projection*, chapter 7, pp. 79–81.
36. Leonard, *My Life in Two Worlds*, chapter 22, p. 74.
37. Richelieu, *A Soul's Journey*, chapter 7, pp. 109–12.
38. Phinn, *Eternal Life*, p. 73.
39. Bruce, *Astral Dynamics*, Part 5, chapter 22, p. 265.
40. Ziewe, *Multidimensional Man*, Part 2, p. 151.
41. Heagerty, *The French Revelation*, chapter 2, p. 95.
42. Ward, *Gone West*, Part 1, chapter 2, p. 6.
43. Borgia, *Life in the World Unseen*, Part 1, chapter 10, p. 50.
44. Ibid., Part 2, chapter 8, pp. 80–1.
45. Gilbert, *Philip in the Spheres*, Part 1, chapter 2, pp. 21–2 and chapter

3, p. 29.

46. Medhus, *My Life After Death*, chapter 12, p. 96, chapter 18, pp. 119–20 and chapter 22, p. 137.
47. Richelieu, *A Soul's Journey*, chapter 2, p. 23 and chapter 4, p. 51.
48. Ibid., chapter 7, pp. 89–90.
49. Sculthorp, *Excursions to the Spirit World*, chapter 3, p. 40.
50. Ibid., chapter 3, pp. 32–3.
51. Ibid., chapter 2, p. 31.
52. Ibid., chapter 5, pp. 68–9.
53. McKnight, *Soul Journeys,* chapter 11, p. 170.
54. Phinn, *Eternal Life*, pp. 151 and 165.
55. Ziewe, *Multidimensional Man*, Part 2, pp. 138, 155 and 162–3.
56. Extracted from Ziewe's paper *Life After Death 5 – The Intermediate Dimensions* at www.multidimensionalman.com.
57. As an example see Ward, *Gone West*, Part 1, chapters 24–5.
58. Ibid., Part 2, chapter 11, pp. 89–91.
59. Stead, *After Death*, Part 2, chapter 1, p. 51.
60. Borgia, *Life in the World Unseen*, Part 2, chapter 9, p. 84.

25 ILLUSION

1. Heagerty, *The French Revelation*, chapter 2, p. 144.
2. This theme is expanded in Lawton, *What Jesus Was Really Saying*.
3. Ward, *Gone West*, Intro, p. iv.
4. Barker, *Letters from a Living Dead Man*, Letter 17, p. 44.
5. John, *Road of Many Ways*, chapter 10, p. 64.
6. Sherwood, *Post-Mortem Journal*, chapter 9, p. 37.
7. Borgia, *Life in the World Unseen*, Part 1, chapter 2, p. 10.
8. Ibid., Part 1, chapter 4, p. 19.
9. Ibid., Part 1, chapter 3, pp. 17–18.
10. Ibid., Part 1, chapter 8, p. 41.
11. Ibid., Part 2, chapter 1, pp. 55–6.

12. Extracted from Benedict's own account reproduced at www.near-death.com/experiences/exceptional/mellen-thomas-benedict.html.
13. Besant, *Ancient Wisdom*, chapter 3, pp. 110–11.
14. Panchadasi, *The Astral World*, chapter 9, p. 69.
15. Richelieu, *A Soul's Journey*, chapter 7, p. 89.
16. McKnight, *Soul Journeys,* chapter 12, p. 180.
17. Phinn, *Eternal Life*, pp. 61–2.
18. Ibid., p. 155.
19. Moen, *Voyage to Curiosity's Father*, chapter 20, pp. 172–86.
20. Ritchie, *Return from Tomorrow*, chapter 6, pp. 84–5.
21. Barker, *Letters from a Living Dead Man*, Letter 16, p. 41 and Letter 17, p. 46.
22. Cummins, *The Road to Immortality*, chapter 3, pp. 9 and 18.
23. Greaves, *Testimony of Light*, Part 1, pp. 64 and 118.
24. Montgomery, *A World Beyond*, chapter 3, p. 29.
25. Kagan, *The Afterlife of Billy Fingers*, chapter 18, pp. 104–6.
26. Besant, *Ancient Wisdom*, chapter 3, p. 112.
27. Yram, *Practical Astral Projection*, Part 1, chapter 17, p. 137.
28. Larsen, *My Travels in the Spirit World*, chapter 4, pp. 76–8.
29. Richelieu, *A Soul's Journey*, chapter 7, p. 90.
30. Sculthorp, *Excursions to the Spirit World*, chapter 3, p. 32.
31. Ibid., chapter 3, pp. 48–9.
32. Moen, *Voyages into the Unknown*, Epilogue, p. 221.
33. Phinn, *Eternal Life*, pp. 131 and 166–7.
34. Phinn, *More Adventures in Eternity*, p. 234.
35. Ziewe, *Multidimensional Man*, Part 3, p. 204.
36. Ibid., Part 2, p. 169.
37. Ibid., Part 3, p. 199.
38. Lawton, *Supersoul*, chapters 6 and 7.
39. The quotes are taken from Elias, communication dated 28 Jun 97; Roberts, *Seth Speaks*, chapter 22; and Walsch, *Conversations with*

God II, chapter 5. For further details and quotes see Lawton, *The Power of You*, chapter 2, pp. 41–4.

40. Medhus, *My Life After Death*, chapter 21, p. 133.
41. Ziewe, *Multidimensional Man*, Part 1, p. 55.
42. The channelled sources in which the traditional concept of reincarnation is *discussed* are mainly those by Barker, Cummins, Sherwood, Gilbert, Greaves, 'John', Montgomery and Sandys; the OOB sources include mainly Besant and Leadbeater, the similarly Eastern-influenced Panchadasi and Richelieu, Monroe and his protégée Moen, Twitchell, Van Dam, Phinn and Vieira.
43. The first of these is Hatch, who describes a young friend called Lionel choosing and visiting his parents in advance of his rebirth (see Barker, *Letters from a Living Dead Man*, Letter 34, pp. 100–4); he also refers to himself and other spirits making decisions about their return into incarnation (see, for example, Letter 21, pp. 56–7 and Letter 26, p. 72). The second is Eadie, who is taken to a 'place where many spirits prepared for life on earth' (see *Embraced by the Light*, p. 89). The third is Phinn, who describes visiting a 'garden of return' (see *More Adventures in Eternity*, pp. 176–99). I happen to know that the latter has plenty of conscious knowledge of 'interlife' material from authors such as Michael Newton and even my own earlier work. As for Eadie, despite the strongly Christian flavour of her book, the many chapters that deal with her exchange of information with various guides reads somewhat like a modern but conventional handbook of reincarnation containing all the standard aspects – not just of next-life planning, but also of life review with a 'council of elders' (*Embraced by the Light*, pp. 108–9), soul groups, growth by incarnation on the earth plane, and so on. Hatch's is a harder case to analyse, his material being much earlier, but he had written a number of esoteric books in his earth life and admits to knowledge of, for example, theosophy.
44. Sherwood, *Post-Mortem Journal*, chapter 6, p. 22.
45. Farnese, *A Wanderer in the Spirit Lands*, chapter 15, p. 62.
46. Borgia, *Life in the World Unseen*, Part 1, chapter 4, p. 19.
47. Monroe, *Far Journeys*, Epilogue, p. 241.
48. Taken from the draft manuscript of Phinn's third book, *You Are*

History.

49. Panchadasi, *The Astral World*, chapter 8, p. 66.
50. Sherwood, *The Country Beyond*, chapter 4, p. 68. This despite the fact that he places his comments in the context of a conventional view of reincarnation.

26 CONCLUSION

1. Stead, *After Death*, Part 2, chapter 2, pp. 67–8.
2. Barker, *Letters from a Living Dead Man*, Letter 19, p. 48.
3. Borgia, *Life in the World Unseen*, Part 2, chapter 10, pp. 87–8.
4. Sherwood, *The Country Beyond*, chapter 4, p. 76.
5. Gilbert, *Philip in the Spheres*, Part 1, chapter 8, pp. 80–1.
6. John, *Road of Many Ways*, chapter 9, pp. 57–60.
7. Ibid., chapter 12, p. 83.
8. Ibid., chapter 17, p. 138.
9. See Buhlman, *The Secret of the Soul*, chapter 8, p. 135; Vieira, *Projections of the Consciousness*, chapter 51, p. 186; Ziewe, *Multidimensional Man*, Part 2, p. 135; and Bruce, *Astral Dynamics*, Part 6, chapter 28, p. 313.
10. Leadbeater, *The Astral Plane*, pp. 24–5.
11. Panchadasi, *The Astral World*, chapter 2, p. 18.
12. Richelieu, *A Soul's Journey*, chapter 2, p. 20 and chapter 4, p. 57.
13. Sculthorp, *Excursions to the Sprit World*, chapter 3, p. 37.
14. Ibid., chapter 3, p. 44.
15. Ziewe seems to have similar experiences where, as on earth, he's an artist who has his astral work exhibited; see *Vistas of Infinity*, pp. 122 and 169.
16. See, for example, Londoner Charlie Morley's various books and workshops.
17. Sherwood, *Post-Mortem Journal*, chapter 6, p. 23.
18. Ibid., chapter 9, p. 37.
19. Ibid., chapter 10, p. 38.

PART 5: PLANES OF LEARNING, PROGRESSION & INTEGRATION

27 THE UPPER ASTRAL PLANES

1. Borgia, *Life in the World Unseen*, Part 2, chapter 9, p. 83.
2. Sherwood, *Post-Mortem Journal*, chapter 10, p. 38.
3. Vale Owen, *The Life Beyond the Veil*, Book 1, chapter 4, p. 79.
4. Gilbert, *Philip in the Spheres*, Part 1, chapter 5, p. 61.
5. Medhus, *My Life After Death*, chapter 22, p. 138.
6. Kagan, *The Afterlife of Billy Fingers*, chapter 23, p. 132.
7. Eadie, *Embraced by the Light*, p. 43.
8. Alexander, *Proof of Heaven*, chapter 12, p. 70 and chapter 15, p. 85.
9. Brinkley, *Saved by the Light*, chapter 4, p. 26 and chapter 5.
10. These predictions included, for example, war in the Middle East in the 1990s, and the collapse of the Soviet Union. Later he would write down 117 events that he witnessed, which started to come true from 1978 onwards. He claims that, in 18 years, 95 of them came true.
11. Ibid., chapter 11, pp. 117–19.
12. Sculthorp, *Excursions to the Sprit World*, chapter 4, p. 53.
13. Monroe, *Ultimate Journey*, Glossary, p. 275.
14. Vieira, *Projections of the Consciousness*, chapter 43, p. 153.
15. Farnese, *A Wanderer in the Spirit Lands*, chapter 34, p. 174.
16. Heagerty, *The French Revelation*, chapter 2, pp. 68 and 80.
17. Ward, *Gone West*, Part 1, chapter 12, pp. 30–1 and chapter 13, p.34.
18. Ibid., Introduction, pp. iv–v.
19. Barker, *Letters from a Living Dead Man*, Letter 14, p. 35.
20. Vale Owen, *The Life Beyond the Veil*, Book 1, chapter 4, pp. 77–8.
21. Borgia, *Life in the World Unseen*, Part 1, chapter 5, p. 25.
22. Ibid., Part 1, chapter 5, p. 25.
23. Ibid., Part 1, chapter 8, p. 40.
24. Ibid., Part 2, chapter 13, p. 97.
25. Sherwood, *The Country Beyond*, chapter 4, p. 70.

26. Sherwood, *Post-Mortem Journal*, chapter 5, pp. 20–1. It is interesting to note that Benson provides a detailed description of the astral printing process in Borgia, *Life in the World Unseen*, Part 1, chapter 5, p. 28.
27. Ibid., chapter 6, p. 22.
28. Ibid., chapter 8, p. 31.
29. Greaves, *Testimony of Light*, Part 1, pp. 48–9 and 72–3.
30. Ibid., Part 2, pp. 133 and 143.
31. Montgomery, *A World Beyond*, chapter 5, pp. 46–7 and 51–3.
32. Medhus, *My Life After Death*, chapter 13, pp. 99–100.
33. Eadie, *Embraced by the Light*, p. 76.
34. Ritchie, *Return from Tomorrow*, chapter 6, pp. 80–3.
35. Leadbeater, *Life After Death*, pp. 25–6.
36. Panchadasi, *The Astral World*, chapter 9, p. 72.
37. Fox, *Astral Projection*, chapter 10, p. 148.
38. Larsen, *My Travels in the Spirit World*, chapter 8, pp. 97–101.
39. Sculthorp, *Excursions to the Sprit World*, chapter 3, p. 40.
40. McKnight, *Soul Journeys*, chapter 11, p. 171.
41. Moen, *Voyages into the Afterlife*, chapter 7, pp. 74–8 and 82.
42. Phinn, *Eternal Life*, pp. 118 and 164.
43. Extracted from Ziewe's paper *The Super Dimensions 4 – Consensus Realities* at www.multidimensionalman.com.
44. Vale Owen, *The Life Beyond the Veil*, Book 1, chapter 2, pp. 28–31.
45. Ibid., Book 2, chapter 4, p. 224.
46. Ward, *Gone West*, Part 1, chapter 24, p. 56.
47. Ibid., chapter 25, p. 58.
48. Borgia, *Life in the World Unseen*, Part 1, chapter 5, pp. 25–6.
49. Ibid., Part 1, chapter 7, pp. 35–8.
50. Ibid., Part 2, chapter 8, p. 80.
51. Greaves, *Testimony of Light*, Part 1, pp. 49 and 110–11.
52. Medhus, *My Life After Death*, chapter 13, p. 102.

53. Ritchie, *Return from Tomorrow*, chapter 6, p. 82.
54. Leadbeater, *Life After Death*, pp. 25–6.
55. Panchadasi, *The Astral World*, chapter 8, pp. 64–5.
56. Larsen, *My Travels in the Spirit World*, chapter 7, p. 93.
57. Richelieu, *A Soul's Journey*, chapter 7, pp. 91–4 and 96–8. Generally his journeying often seems to reflect his love of music.
58. Heagerty, *The French Revelation*, chapter 2, pp. 43 and 60.
59. John, *Road of Many Ways*, chapter 16, p. 130.
60. Swedenborg, *Heaven and Hell*, chapter 41, p. 225 (section 393) and chapter 42, p. 228 (section 399).
61. Larsen, *My Travels in the Spirit World*, chapter 6, pp. 86–7.
62. Leonard, *My Life in Two Worlds*, chapter 22, p.75.
63. Sculthorp, *Excursions to the Sprit World*, chapter 4, p. 53.
64. Borgia, *Life in the World Unseen*, Part 1, chapter 10, pp. 52–3.
65. Farnese, *A Wanderer in the Spirit Lands*, chapter 30, p. 149 and chapter 33, p. 166.
66. Heagerty, *The French Revelation*, chapter 2, p. 75.
67. Ward, *Gone West*, Part 1, chapter 23, p. 54.
68. Barker, *Letters from a Living Dead Man*, Letter 12, p. 31 and Letter 16, p. 42.
69. Vale Owen, *The Life Beyond the Veil*, Book 1, chapter 2, pp. 28–9.
70. Borgia, *Life in the World Unseen*, Part 1, chapter 8, p. 40 and Part 2, chapter 11, p. 91.
71. Sherwood, *The Country Beyond*, chapter 7, p. 118.
72. Greaves, *Testimony of Light*, Part 1, p. 70.
73. Ibid., Part 1, p. 116.
74. Panchadasi, *The Astral World*, chapter 8, p. 65.
75. Richelieu, *A Soul's Journey*, chapter 8, p. 128.
76. Moen, *Voyages into the Afterlife*, chapter 7, pp. 79–80.

28 THE MENTAL PLANES

1. Farnese, *A Wanderer in the Spirit Lands*, chapter 12, pp. 52–3.

2. Heagerty, *The French Revelation*, chapter 2, pp. 79–80.
3. Sherwood, *Post-Mortem Journal*, chapter 6, p. 24.
4. Gilbert, *Philip in the Spheres*, Part 3, chapter 3, pp. 284–7.
5. Greaves, *Testimony of Light*, Part 1, p. 124.
6. John, *Road of Many Ways*, chapter 19, pp.147–50.
7. Leadbeater, *Life After Death*, chapter 4, p. 37.
8. Besant, *Ancient Wisdom*, chapter 3, p. 114.
9. Richelieu, *A Soul's Journey*, chapter 8, p. 133.
10. Taylor, *Soul Traveller*, chapter 8, p. 88.
11. Ward, *Gone West*, Introduction, p. vi.
12. Sherwood, *Post-Mortem Journal*, chapter 7, p. 26.
13. Gilbert, *Philip in the Spheres*, Part 2, chapter 1, p. 93.
14. Ibid., Part 2, chapter 4, pp. 178–9.
15. Ibid., Part 3, chapter 3, p. 288.
16. Ibid., Part 3, chapter 4, pp. 294–6 and 301–2.
17. Montgomery, *A World Beyond*, chapter 14, pp. 149–55.
18. John, *Road of Many Ways*, chapter 19, p.150.
19. Alexander, *Proof of Heaven*, chapter 14, pp. 77–8, chapter 9, pp. 46 and 49, and chapter 15, pp. 82–3.
20. Swedenborg, *Heaven and Hell*, chapter 50, p. 291 (section 489).
21. Leadbeater, *Life After Death*, chapter 4, pp. 38–9.
22. Besant, *Ancient Wisdom*, chapter 4, pp. 118, 120 and 123–4.
23. Panchadasi, *The Astral World*, chapter 9, p. 76.
24. Fox, *Astral Projection*, chapter 11, p. 157.
25. Richelieu, *A Soul's Journey*, chapter 10, pp. 172–3.
26. Ibid., chapter 10, pp. 178–9.
27. Atteshlis, *The Esoteric Teachings*, front cover flap. For his definition of 'exosomatosis', the Greek for OOB, see the Glossary, p.191.
28. Ibid, chapter 9, p. 102.
29. McKnight, *Cosmic Journeys*, chapter 17, pp. 200–1.
30. Phinn, *Eternal Life*, pp. 172–4.

31. Ziewe, *Multidimensional Man*, Part 2, pp. 168–9.
32. Extracted from Ziewe's paper *The Super Dimensions 2 – Main Characteristics* at www.multidimensionalman.com.
33. Ziewe, *Multidimensional Man*, Part 2, pp. 167–8.

29 THE HIGHEST PLANES

1. Ziewe, *Multidimensional Man*, Part 2, p. 170.
2. Richelieu, *A Soul's Journey*, chapter 11, p. 186.
3. Heagerty, *The French Revelation*, chapter 2, pp. 28, 71–2 and 80–1.
4. Cummins, *Beyond Human Personality*, chapter 3, p. 9.
5. Ibid., chapter 4, p. 42.
6. Cummins, *The Road to Immortality*, chapter 9, p. 39.
7. Sherwood, *The Country Beyond*, chapter 6, pp. 94–5 and chapter 16, p. 231.
8. Gilbert, *Philip in the Spheres*, Part 3, chapter 3, p. 291.
9. Greaves, *Testimony of Light*, Part 1, pp. 119 and 137–9.
10. Medhus, *My Life After Death*, chapter 21, p. 133.
11. Kagan, *The Afterlife of Billy Fingers*, chapter 12, pp. 75–6 and chapter 14, pp. 83–4.
12. Ibid., chapter 15, pp. 88–9.
13. Alexander, *Proof of Heaven*, chapter 33, pp. 160–1.
14. Leadbeater, *The Monad*, chapter 2, pp. 51–2 and 55–7.
15. Ibid., chapter 2, pp. 58–60.
16. Besant, *Ancient Wisdom*, chapter 6, pp. 184–6.
17. Yram, *Practical Astral Projection*, Part 1, chapter 2, p. 23.
18. Ibid., Part 1, chapter 11, pp. 84–5.
19. Ibid., Part 2, chapter 1, p. 163.
20. Larsen, *My Travels in the Spirit World*, chapter 9, pp. 103–6.
21. Monroe, *Far Journeys*, chapter 9, pp. 120–2.
22. Ibid., chapter 13, pp. 178–9.
23. Atteshlis, *The Esoteric Teachings*, chapter 10, pp. 109–10.
24. Van Dam, *The Psychic Explorer*, section 4, pp. 109–10.

25. Buhlman, *Adventures Beyond the Body*, chapter 2, pp. 47, 55–7 and 60–1.
26. Phinn, *More Adventures in Eternity*, pp. 294–5.
27. Ziewe, *Multidimensional Man*, Part 3, pp. 196–7 and 206–8.
28. For the original definition see Lawton, *The Wisdom of the Soul*, chapter 2, p. 58. The amended version can be found in *Supersoul*, chapter 8, pp. 160–1. For a full explanation see www.ianlawton.com/holsoul.html.
29. Farnese, *A Wanderer in the Spirit Lands*, chapter 15, p. 63.
30. Gilbert, *Philip in the Spheres*, Part 3, chapter 4, p. 300.
31. Vale Owen, *The Life Beyond the Veil*, Book 1, chapter 3, p. 64.
32. Van Dam, *The Psychic Explorer*, section 13, p. 301.
33. Extracted from Benedict's own account reproduced at www.near-death.com/experiences/exceptional/mellen-thomas-benedict.html.
34. Leadbeater, *The Monad*, chapter 1, pp. 1–2 and 5.
35. Moen, *Voyage to Curiosity's Father*, chapter 29, pp. 247–8.
36. Ibid., chapter 22, p. 198.
37. Vieira, *Projections of the Consciousness*, chapter 60, pp. 213–15.
38. Alexander, *Proof of Heaven*, chapter 15, p. 85.
39. Extracted from Benedict's own account reproduced at www.near-death.com/experiences/exceptional/mellen-thomas-benedict.html.
40. Buhlman, *The Secret of the Soul*, chapter 8, p. 144.

BIBLIOGRAPHY

This bibliography is limited to the books specifically referenced in this work. The details given below are for the imprint or edition consulted, although the original date of publication quoted in the main text may have been earlier.

SCIENCE, MEDIUMSHIP AND REMOTE VIEWING

Campbell, Thomas, *My Big T.O.E.*, Lightning Strike, 2007.

Einstein, Albert, *The World as I See It*, Citadel Press, 2006 (first published 1934).

Mayer, Elizabeth, *Extraordinary Knowing*, Bantam, 2008.

Roy, Archie, *The Eager Dead*, Book Guild Publishing, 2008.

Russell, Peter, *From Science to God*, New World Library, 2005.

Schwartz, Gary, *The Truth About Medium*, Hampton Roads, 2005.

CHANNELLED MATERIAL

Barker, Elsa, *Letters from a Living Dead Man*, White Crow, 2009 (first published 1913).

Barker, Elsa, *War Letters from the Living Dead Man*, White Crow, 2010 (first published 1915).

Barker, Elsa, *Last Letters from the Living Dead Man*, White Crow, 2010 (first published 1919).

Borgia, Anthony, *Life in the World Unseen*, Two Worlds Publishing, 1997 (first published 1954).

Borgia, Anthony, *More About Life in the World Unseen*, Square Circles Publishing, 2013 (first published 1956).

Borgia, Anthony, *Here and Hereafter*, Square Circles Publishing, 2013 (first published 1959).

Cummins, Geraldine, *The Scripts of Cleophas*, The Psychic Book Club, 1928.

Cummins, Geraldine, *The Road to Immortality*, White Crow Books, 2012 (first published 1932).

Cummins, Geraldine, *Beyond Human Personality*, White Crow Books, 2013 (first published 1935).

Dowding, Hugh, *Lychgate*, White Crow, 2014 (first published 1945).

Franchezzo (channelled by A Farnese), *A Wanderer in the Spirit Lands*, 2007, Wilder Publications (first published 1896).

Gilbert, Alice, *Philip in Two Worlds*, Psychic Book Club, 1949.

Gilbert, Alice, *Philip in the Spheres*, The Aquarian Press, 1952.

Greaves, Helen, *Testimony of Light*, Rider, 2005 (first published 1969).

Heagerty, N Riley, *The French Revelation*, White Crow Books, 2015.

'John', *Road of Many Ways*, Bennu Books, 1975.

'John', *Pilgrims on the Road*, Unknown, 1976.

Kagan, Annie, *The Afterlife of Billy Fingers*, Coronet, 2014.

Lodge, Sir Oliver, *Raymond or Life and Death*, Methuen & Co, 1916.

Medhus, Elisa, *My Son and the Afterlife*, Atria Books, 2013.

Medhus, Erik and Elisa, *My Life After Death*, Atria Books, 2015.

Montgomery, Ruth, *A World Beyond*, Fawcett, 1972.

Sandys, Cynthia, *The Awakening Letters*, Neville Spearman, 1978.

Sandys, Cynthia, *The Awakening Letters: Volume Two*, C.W. Daniel, 1986.

Sherwood, Jane, *The Country Beyond*, C.W. Daniel, 1991 (first published in 1944).

Sherwood, Jane, *Post-Mortem Journal: Communications from TE Lawrence*, Divine Truth, 1964.

Stead, William, *After Death: Letters from Julia*, CreateSpace, 2012 (first published 1905).

Vale Owen, George, *The Life Beyond the Veil*, Square Circles Publishing, 2013 (first published in four volumes in 1920-1).

Ward, John, *Gone West: Three Narratives of After Death Experiences*, Rider & Son, 1920.

NEAR-DEATH EXPERIENCES

Alexander, Eben, *Proof of Heaven*, Piatkus, 2012.

Berman, Phillip, *The Journey Home*, Pocket Books, 1998.

Brinkley, Dannion and Perry, Paul, *Saved by the Light*, Piatkus, 2011 (first published 1994).

Eadie, Betty, *Embraced by the Light*, Thorsons, 2003 (first published 1992).

Fenwick, Peter and Elizabeth, *The Truth in the Light*, Berkley, 1997.

Greyson, Bruce and Flynn, Charles P (eds.), *The Near-Death Experience*, Charles C Thomas, 1984.

Rawlings, Maurice, *Beyond Death's Door*, Sheldon Press, 1979.

Ritchie, George, *Return from Tomorrow*, Chosen Books, 2007 (first published 1978).

Storm, Howard, *My Descent Into Death*, Clairview Books, 2008.

OUT-OF-BODY EXPERIENCES

Aardema, Frederick, *Explorations in Consciousness*, Mount Royal Publishing, 2012.

Atteshlis, Stylianos, *The Esoteric Teachings*, The Stoa Series, 1992.

Besant, Annie, *Ancient Wisdom: An Outline of Theosophical Teachings*, Kessinger Publishing, 1998 (first published 1898).

Bruce, Robert, *Astral Dynamics*, Hampton Roads, 2009.

Buhlman, William, *Adventures Beyond the Body*, HarperOne, 1996.

Buhlman, William, *The Secret of the Soul*, HarperOne, 2001.

Buhlman, William, *Adventures in the Afterlife*, Osprey Press, 2013.

Dack, Graham, *The Out-of-Body Experience*, OOBEX Publishing, 1999.

Fox, Oliver (Hugh Callaway), *Astral Projection*, Citadel Press, 1962 (first published 1938).

Larsen, Caroline, *My Travels in the Spirit World*, Tuttle, 1927.

Leadbeater, Charles, *The Astral Plane*, Theosophical Publishing House, 1895.

Leadbeater, Charles, *The Inner Life* (2 volumes), Aziloth Books, 2011 (first published 1911).

Leadbeater, Charles, *Life After Death*, Theosophical Publishing House, 1912.

Leadbeater, Charles, *The Monad and Other Essays*, Theosophical Publishing House, 1929 (first published 1920).

Leonard, Gladys, *My Life in Two Worlds*, Cassell & Co, 1931.

McKnight, Rosalind, *Cosmic Journeys*, Hampton Roads, 1999.

McKnight, Rosalind, *Soul Journeys*, Hampton Roads, 2005.

Minero, Luis, *Demystifying the Out-of-Body Experience*, Llewellyn, 2012.

Moen, Bruce, *Voyages into the Unknown*, Hampton Roads, 1997.

Moen, Bruce, *Voyage Beyond Doubt*, Hampton Roads, 1998.

Moen, Bruce, *Voyages into the Afterlife*, Hampton Roads, 1999.

Moen, Bruce, *Voyage to Curiosity's Father*, Hampton Roads, 2001

Monroe, Robert, *Journeys Out of the Body*, Broadway Books, 2001 (first published 1971).

Monroe, Robert, *Far Journeys*, Doubleday, 1985.

Monroe, Robert, *Ultimate Journey*, Broadway Books, 2000 (first published 1994).

Morrell, Ed, *The Twenty-Fifth Man*, New Era Publishing, 1924.

Muldoon, Sylvan and Carrington, Hereward, *Projection of the Astral Body*, Rider, 1929.

Muldoon, Sylvan and Carrington, Hereward, *The Phenomena of Astral Projection*, Rider, 1951.

Panchadasi, Swami (William Walker Atkinson), *The Astral World*, The Book Tree, 2000 (first published 1915).

Phinn, Gordon, *Eternal Life and How to Enjoy It*, Hampton Roads, 2004.

Phinn, Gordon, *More Adventures in Eternity*, O Books, 2008.

Richelieu, Peter, *A Soul's Journey*, Thorsons, 1996 (first published 1953).

Sculthorp, Frederick, *Excursions to the Spirit World*, Greater World Association, 1969 (first published 1961).

Swedenborg, Emanuel (trans. George F. Dole), *Heaven and Hell*, Swedenborg Foundation, 2002 (first published 1758).

Taylor, Albert, *Soul Traveller*, New American Library, 2000.

Turvey, Vincent, *The Beginnings of Seership*, University Books, 1969 (first published 1909).

Van Dam, Vee, *The Psychic Explorer*, Skoob Books, 1989.

Vieira, Waldo, *Projections of the Consciousness*, International Academy of Consciousness, 2007.

'Yram' (Marcel Forhan), *Practical Astral Projection*, Samuel Weiser, 1974 (first published as *Le Médecin de l'Âme* in 1925).

Ziewe, Jurgen, *Multidimensional Man*, lulu.com, 2008.

Ziewe, Jurgen, *Vistas of Infinity*, lulu.com, 2016.

INDEX

THE SUPERSOUL SERIES

all published by Rational Spirituality Press *www.rspress.org*
see also *www.ianlawton.com*

RESEARCH BOOKS

[Volume 1] SUPERSOUL (2013) is the main reference book for Supersoul Spirituality, containing out-of-body and channelled evidence that each and every one of us is a holographic reflection of a supersoul that has power way beyond our wildest imaginings.

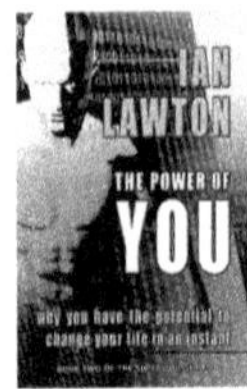

[Volume 2] THE POWER OF YOU (2014) compares modern channelled wisdom from a variety of well-known sources, all emphasising that each of us is consciously or unconsciously creating every aspect of our own reality, and that this is what the current consciousness shift is all about.

[Volume 3] AFTERLIFE (2019) is a state-of-the-art, clear, reliable guide to the afterlife based on the underlying consistencies in traditional channelled material and modern out-of-body research.

SIMPLE BOOKS

SH*T DOESN'T JUST HAPPEN!! (2016) introduces Supersoul Spirituality by explaining how and why we ourselves create or attract everything we experience in our adult lives... so that we are never victims of chance, God's will, our karma or our life plans.

WHAT JESUS WAS REALLY SAYING (2016) is a fundamental reinterpretation of the Christian message that uses excerpts from the Gospels to propose that, through his supposed miracles, Jesus was trying to show us that each of us is a creator god of the highest order and can manipulate the illusion we call reality at will.

THE GOD WHO SOMETIMES SCREWED UP (2018) charts the author's progression from motorcycle and car racer, to pyramid explorer and researcher of ancient civilisations, to spiritual philosopher... with analysis and examples of how he has created or manifested all the various aspects of his life, both good and bad.

DEATH SHOULD BE FUN!! (2019) is a light-hearted look at the afterlife, concentrating on the unlimited possibilities we have to create wondrous new experiences in the higher planes of consciousness... as long as we have a map of the territory, and we're aware that we're in control and that the sky's the limit.

IAN LAWTON was born in 1959. Formerly an accountant, sales exec, business and IT consultant and avid bike and car racer, in his mid-thirties he changed tack completely to become a writer-researcher specialising in ancient history and, more recently, spiritual philosophy. His first two books, *Giza: The Truth* and *Genesis Unveiled*, sold over 30,000 copies worldwide.

In his *Books of the Soul Series* he originated the ideas of Rational Spirituality and of the holographic soul. But since 2013 he has been developing the more radical worldview of Supersoul Spirituality in the *Supersoul Series*. A short film clip discussing the latter can be found at *www.ianlawton.com* and on YouTube.

Lightning Source UK Ltd.
Milton Keynes UK
UKHW020510241019
352206UK00012B/874/P